Lecture Notes
in Business Information Processing   **480**

LNBIP reports state-of-the-art results in areas related to business information systems and industrial application software development – timely, at a high level, and in both printed and electronic form.

The type of material published includes

- Proceedings (published in time for the respective event)
- Postproceedings (consisting of thoroughly revised and/or extended final papers)
- Other edited monographs (such as, for example, project reports or invited volumes)
- Tutorials (coherently integrated collections of lectures given at advanced courses, seminars, schools, etc.)
- Award-winning or exceptional theses

LNBIP is abstracted/indexed in DBLP, EI and Scopus. LNBIP volumes are also submitted for the inclusion in ISI Proceedings.

Yiliu Tu · Maomao Chi
Editors

E-Business

Digital Empowerment for an Intelligent Future

22nd Wuhan International Conference, WHICEB 2023
Wuhan, China, May 26–28, 2023
Proceedings, Part I

 Springer

Editors
Yiliu Tu (iD)
University of Calgary
Calgary, AB, Canada

Maomao Chi (iD)
China University of Geosciences
Wuhan, China

ISSN 1865-1348 ISSN 1865-1356 (electronic)
Lecture Notes in Business Information Processing
ISBN 978-3-031-32298-3 ISBN 978-3-031-32299-0 (eBook)
https://doi.org/10.1007/978-3-031-32299-0

This Springer imprint is published by the registered company Springer Nature Switzerland AG
The registered company address is: Gewerbestrasse 11, 6330 Cham, Switzerland

Preface

The annual Wuhan International Conference on E-Business (WHICEB) is an AIS affiliated conference. The 22nd Wuhan International Conference on E-Business (WHICEB 2023) was held at Wuhan from May 26 to 28, 2023. WHICEB promotes intellectual research and facilitates academic and corporate networking in e-business and related fields. The intent is to encourage academic research and business development through exchanging ideas about e-business, global and corporate financial issues, and the necessity for continuous innovation. The conference aims at presenting innovative research findings, solutions and approaches to make the Internet a productive and efficient vehicle for global commerce. Whether running an e-business or transforming a business into an e-business, we constantly encounter challenges ranging from technological to behavioral issues, from marketing to data analysis issues, and from effectiveness to security issues. In recent years all over the world initiatives have been started for the next step of development, i.e., Industry 4.0 or the fourth industrial revolution. After consumer-oriented mass production we focus nowadays on personalized products and services, which demands cyber physical systems, cloud computing and big data. There are integration issues for management of technology, management of supply chains, management of human resources and management of knowledge and intelligence that are being resolved in an e-business environment. Organizations, regardless of their locations and sizes, should consider having a strategic decentralized planning effort that includes e-business as a pillar for sustainable competitive advantage.

The proceedings of the 22nd WHICEB document the breadth and depth of research from different aspects of business and from different disciplines that have major implications for e-business. There are fifteen tracks in the proceedings and the proceedings will be listed in the appropriate indexes. The selected best papers from the proceedings will be recommended to international academic journals including but not limited to the following: Electronic Commerce Research and Applications, Electronic Commerce Research, and International Journal of Networking and Virtual Organizations (Compendex).

The research papers in the proceedings went through a double-blind peer review process. Papers were accepted based upon a clear research methodology and contributions to the knowledge of e-business including but not limited to case study, experiment, simulation or survey. The efforts made by our track chairs in reviewing submissions are really appreciated, for they ensured the quality of the proceedings. On behalf of the conference organization, I thank them for their professional diligence. They are: Xiaobo (Bob) Xu, Weiyong Zhang and Fei Ma, *Digital Empowerment and Social Impact*; Yaobin Lu, Ling Zhao and Jiang Wu, *Artificial Intelligence & IoT (AIoT) Enabled Business Innovation*; Guoyin Jiang, Xiaodong Feng and Wenping Liu, *Computing and Complexity in Digital Platforms*; Dongxiao Gu, Jia Li, Ying Yang, Zhixiong Zhang, Fenghong Liu, Yiming Zhao, Shuping Zhao and Xiaoyu Wang, *Data Analytics and Data Governance in Behavioral and Social Science Studies*; Cong Cao, Xiuyan Shao, Jun Yan and Wen-Lung Shiau, *Digital Economy*; Zhongyun (Phil) Zhou, Yongqiang Sun and Xiao-Ling Jin, *Digital Enablement and Digital Governance*; Yi Wang, Yuan Sun, Si Shi and Jindi Fu, *Digital Technologies and New Ways of Working*; Xiaoling Li, Lu Wang and Qing Huang, *E-business Strategy & Digital Marketing*; Shaobo Wei, Xiayu Chen, Jinmei Yin and Hua Liu, *Emerging Technologies and Social Commerce*; Nannan Xi, Hongxiu Li, Juan Chen and Juho Hamari, *Engaging Technologies*; Zhaohua Deng, Tailai Wu and Jia Li, *Healthcare Service and IT Management*; Haichao Zheng, Yuxiang Zhao, Bin Zhu, Bo Xu and Kai Li, *Human-Machine/Robot Interaction in the Era of AI*; Hefu Liu, Zhao Cai and Meng Chen, *Information Systems and Operations Management*; Zhao Du, Fang Wang, Shan Wang and Ruoxin Zhou, *Information Technology in Education*; Chunmei Gan, Yong Liu and Ming Yi, *User Behavior in Information Systems*.

This year, the proceedings consists of two volumes. The papers which are included in the proceedings have gone through at least three double-blind reviews by the members of the Editorial Board of the Proceedings. We would like to thank all of them for their invaluable contribution, support and efforts.

Yiliu Tu

Maomao Chi

Organization

Conference Hosts

The Center for International Cooperation in E-Business, China University of
  Geosciences, Wuhan, China
School of Economics and Management, China University of Geosciences, Wuhan,
  China
Baden-Wuerttemberg Cooperative State University Heidenheim, Heidenheim,
  Germany
College of Business, Alfred University, Alfred, New York, USA

Organizers

The Center for International Cooperation in E-Business, China University of
  Geosciences, Wuhan, China
School of Economics and Management, China University of Geosciences, Wuhan,
  China

Conference Co-chairs

Jing Zhao   China University of Geosciences, China
Juergen Seitz   Baden-Wuerttemberg Cooperative State
                           University Heidenheim, Germany
Doug Vogel   Harbin Institute of Technology, China

Conference Honorary Chair

Wilfred V. Huang (Deceased)   Alfred University, USA

Publication Chairs and Proceedings Editors

Yiliu (Paul) Tu   University of Calgary, Canada
Maomao Chi   China University of Geosciences, China

Program Committee

Chairs

Weiguo (Patrick) Fan	University of Iowa, USA
Zhen Zhu	China University of Geosciences, China

Members

Yukun Bao	Huazhong University of Science & Technology, China
Zhao Cai	University of Nottingham Ningbo China, China
Cong Cao	Zhejiang University of Technology, China
Meng Chen	Soochow University, China
Xiayu Chen	Hefei University of Technology, China
Xusen Cheng	Renmin University of China, China
Maomao Chi	China University of Geosciences, China
Zhaohua Deng	Huazhong University of Science & Technology, China
John Qi Dong	University of Dublin, Ireland
Rong Du	Xidian University, China
Qiang Gong	Zhongnan University of Economics and Law, China
Dongxiao Gu	Hefei University of Technology, China
Tailai Wu	Huazhong University of Science and Technology, China
Juho Hamari	Tampere University, Finland
Zhongyi Hu	Wuhan University, China
Yi Jiang	China University of Geosciences, China
Yuanchun Jiang	Hefei University of Technology, China
Xiaoling Jin	Shanghai University, China
Hongxiu Li	Tampere University, Finland
Jia Li	East China University of Science and Technology, China
Mengxiang Li	Hong Kong Baptist University, China
Xiaoling Li	Chongqing University, China
Hefu Liu	University of Science and Technology of China, China
Yaobin Lu	Huazhong University of Science & Technology, China
Jian Mou	Pusan National University, Korea
Rohit Nishant	University of Laval, Canada

Xiaoliang Shen	Wuhan University, China
Si Shi	Southwestern University of Finance and Economics, China
Yongqiang Sun	Wuhan University, China
Yuan Sun	Zhejiang Gongshang University, China
Yiliu (Paul) Tu	University of Calgary, Canada
Kanliang Wang	Renmin University, China
Shan Wang	University of Saskatchewan, Canada
Lu Wang	Zhongnan University of Economics and Law, China
Yi Wang	Southwestern University of Finance and Economics, China
J. Christopher Westland	University of Illinois at Chicago, USA
Qiang Wei	Tsinghua University, China
Shaobo Wei	University of Science and Technology of China, China
Hong Wu	Huazhong University of Science & Technology, China
Jiang Wu	Wuhan University, China
Tailai Wu	Huazhong University of Science & Technology, China
Nannan Xi	Tampere University, Finland
Huosong Xia	Wuhan Textile University, China
Jinghua Xiao	Sun Yat-sen University, China
Wenlong Xiao	Zhejiang University of Technology, China
Xiaobo (Bob) Xu	Xi'an Jiaotong-Liverpool University, China
Jun Yan	University of Wollongong, Australia
Xiangbin Yan	University of Science and Technology Beijing, China
Junjie Zhou	Shantou University, China
Zhongyun Zhou	Tongji University, China
Ling Zhao	Huazhong University of Science & Technology, China
Weiyong Zhang	Old Dominion University, USA

Session Chairs

Kanliang Wang	Renmin University, China
Jinghua Xiao	Sun Yat-sen University, China
Rong Du	Xidian University, China
Yi Jiang	China University of Geosciences, China

Organization Committee

Chair

Shuwang Yang   China University of Geosciences, China

Members

Yao Zhang   China University of Geosciences, China
Fei Wang   China University of Geosciences, China
Jing Wang   China University of Geosciences, China
Xiaochuan Wang   China University of Geosciences, China
Luxi Lin   China University of Geosciences, China
Qian Zhao   China University of Geosciences, China
Rui Guo   China University of Geosciences, China
Jianzhong Xiao   China University of Geosciences, China
Guangmin Wang   China University of Geosciences, China
Jundong Hou   China University of Geosciences, China
Sheng Cheng   China University of Geosciences, China

Secretary General

Yao Zhang   China University of Geosciences, China

International Advisory Board

Chairs

Joey George   Iowa State University, USA
Robert Kauffman   Copenhagen Business School, Denmark
J. Christopher Westland   University of Illinois at Chicago, USA

Pacific Asian

Patrick Chau   University of Hong Kong, China
Guoqing Chen   Tsinghua University, China
Wei Kwok Kee   City University of Hong Kong, China
Ting-Peng Liang   National Sun Yat-sen University, Taiwan
Feicheng Ma   Wuhan University, China

Jiye Mao	Renmin University, China
Michael D. Myers	University of Auckland, New Zealand
Bernard Tan	National University of Singapore, Singapore
Kanliang Wang	Renmin University, China
Nilmini Wickramasinghe	Swinburne University of Technology, Australia
Kang Xie	Sun Yat-sen University, China
Qiang Ye	Harbin Institute of Technology, China
J. Leon Zhao	City University of Hong Kong, China

North American

Bob Carasik	Wells Fargo Bank, USA
Weiguo Fan	Virginia Tech, USA
Joey George	Iowa State University, USA
Zhangxi Lin	Texas Tech University, USA
Ning Nan	University of British Columbia, Canada
Paul A. Pavlou	Temple University, USA
Arun Rai	Georgia State University, USA
Richard Watson	University of Georgia, USA
Christopher Yang	Drexel University, USA
Han Zhang	Georgia Institute of Technology, USA
Zhongju Zhang	Arizona State University, USA

European

David Avison	ESSEC, France
Niels Bjorn-Andersen	Copenhagen Business School, Denmark
Marco De Marco	Università Cattolica, Italy
Reima Suomi	Turku School of Economics, Finland
Yao-Hua Tan	Vrije University Amsterdam, The Netherlands
Hans-Dieter Zimmermann	Eastern Switzerland University of Applied Sciences, Switzerland

Editorial Board of the Proceedings

Editors

Yiliu (Paul) Tu	University of Calgary, Canada
Maomao Chi	China University of Geosciences, China

Digital Empowerment and Social Impact

Xiaobo (Bob) Xu	Xi'an Jiaotong-Liverpool University, China
Weiyong Zhang	Old Dominion University, USA
Fei Ma	Chang'an University, China

Artificial Intelligence and IoT (AIoT) Enabled Business Innovation

Yaobin Lu	Huazhong University of Science & Technology, China
Ling Zhao	Huazhong University of Science & Technology, China
Jiang Wu	Wuhan University

Computing and Complexity in Digital Platforms

Guoyin Jiang	University of Electronic Science and Technology of China, China
Xiaodong Feng	Sun Yat-sen University, China
Wenping Liu	Hubei University of Economics, China

Data Analytics and Data Governance in Behavioral and Social Science Studies

Dongxiao Gu	Hefei University of Technology, China
Jia Li	East China University of Science and Technology, China
Ying Yang	Hefei University of Technology, China
Zhixiong Zhang	China Academy of Sciences, China
Fenghong Liu	China Academy of Sciences, China
Yiming Zhao	Wuhan University, China
Shuping Zhao	Hefei University of Technology, China
Xiaoyu Wang	First Affiliated Hospital of Anhui University of Chinese Medicine, China

Digital Economy

Cong Cao	Zhejiang University of Technology, China
Xiuyan Shao	Southeast University, China
Jun Yan	University of Wollongong, Australia
Wen-Lung Shiau	Zhejiang University of Technology, China

Digital Enablement and Digital Governance

Zhongyun (Phil) Zhou	Tongji University, China
Yongqiang Sun	Wuhan University, China
Xiao-Ling Jin	Shanghai University, China

Digital Technologies and New Ways of Working

Yi Wang	Southwestern University of Finance and Economics, China
Yuan Sun	Zhejiang Gongshang University, China
Si Shi	Southwestern University of Finance and Economics, China
Jindi Fu	Hangzhou Dianzi University, China

E-Business Strategy and Digital Marketing

Xiaoling Li	Chongqing University, China
Lu Wang	Zhongnan University of Economics and Law, China
Qing Huang	Chongqing Technology and Business University, China

Emerging Technologies and Social Commerce

Shaobo Wei	Hefei University of Technology, China
Xiayu Chen	Hefei University of Technology, China
Jinmei Yin	Nanjing University of Aeronautics and Astronautics, China
Hua Liu	Anhui University, China

Engaging Technologies

Nannan Xi	Tampere University, Finland
Hongxiu Li	Tampere University, Finland
Juan Chen	Anhui University of Finance and Economics, China
Juho Hamari	Tampere University, Finland

Healthcare Service and IT Management

Zhaohua Deng	Huazhong University of Sci. & Tech., China
Tailai Wu	Huazhong University of Sci. & Tech., China
Jia Li	East China University of Science and Technology, China

Human-Machine/Robot Interaction in the Era of AI

Haichao Zheng	Southwestern University of Finance and Economics, China
Yuxiang Zhao	Nanjing University of Science and Technology, China
Bin Zhu	Oregon State University, USA
Bo Xu	Fudan University, China
Kai Li	Nankai University, China

Information Systems and Operations Management

Hefu Liu	University of Science and Technology of China, China
Zhao Cai	University of Nottingham Ningbo China, China
Meng Chen	Soochow University, China

Information Technology in Education

Zhao Du	Beijing Sport University, China
Fang Wang	Wilfrid Laurier University, Canada
Shan Wang	University of Saskatchewan, Canada
Ruoxin Zhou	University of International Business and Economics, China

User Behavior in Information Systems

Chunmei Gan	Sun Yat-sen University, China
Yong Liu	Aalto University, Finland
Ming Yi	Central China Normal University, China

Best Paper Award and Journal Publication Committee

Chairs

Yiliu (Paul) Tu	University of Calgary, Canada
Maomao Chi	China University of Geosciences, China

Members

Alain Chong	University of Nottingham Ningbo China, China
Chris Yang	Drexel University, USA
J. Christopher Westland	University of Illinois at Chicago, USA
Doug Vogel	Harbin Institute of Technology, China
Patrick Chau	University of Nottingham Ningbo China, China
Jun Wei	University of West Florida, USA
John Qi Dong	University of Groningen, The Netherlands
Weiguo (Patrick) Fan	University of Iowa, USA
Wen-Lung Shiau	Zhejiang University of Technology, China

Sponsors

Association for Information Systems (AIS)
China Association for Information Systems (CNAIS)
China Information Economics Society
University of Calgary, Canada
Swinburne University of Technology, Australia
University of North Dakota, USA
New Jersey Institute of Technology, USA
University of Turku, Finland
Harbin Institute of Technology, China
Huazhong University of Science & Technology, China
Wuhan University, China
Wuhan University of Technology, China
Zhongnan University of Economics and Law, China
Huazhong Normal University, China
Wuhan Textile University, China
Digital Economy Research Centre, UNNC-SUS Tech, China

Sponsoring Journals

Electronic Commerce Research (SSCI index)
Electronic Commerce Research and Applications (SSCI index)
Electronic Markets-The International Journal on Networked Business (SSCI index)
Internet Research (SSCI index)
Journal of Organizational and End User Computing (SCI & SSCI index)
Journal of Information & Knowledge Management (Compendex & Scopus index)
International Journal of Networking and Virtual Organizations (Compendex & Scopus
    index)
Journal of Systems and Information Technology (Compendex & Scopus index)

Contents – Part I

Contents – Part II

Bibliometric Analysis on the Research Hotspots of Recommender Systems

Jiangping Wan(✉), Siting Lin(✉), and Jing Zhang

School of Business Administration, South China University of Technology, Guangzhou 510640, China
csjpwan@scut.edu.cn, 202220131906@mail.scut.edu.cn

Abstract. Research on the hot topics and future development trends of recommender system is of great significance for improving the accuracy of recommendation results and saving users' time. A total of 867 SCI and SSCI literatures related to recommender system were selected from the Web of Science database from 2013 to July 2022. The visual knowledge graph analysis tool CiteSpace was used to analyze the temporal and spatial distribution characteristics, knowledge basis, research hotspots and frontiers of personalized recommendation technology research from five dimensions: literature growth trend, regional distribution, literature co-citation relationship, keyword co-occurrence and emergence. The participation of Chinese and American researchers are much higher than that of other countries and the exchange and cooperation between countries need to be strengthened. The research focuses on the application of algorithm in recommender system, improvement of collaborative filtering algorithm, model construction, social network and neural network. The research frontiers include feature extraction of users and projects, machine learning and attention mechanism.

Keywords: Recommender System · Personalized · Implicit Need · User Profiling · Algorithm · Knowledge Graph · Bibliometric

1 Introduction

The problem of information overload in human society is becoming more and more serious. As one of the effective ways to solve the problem of information overload, recommender systems have become a hot research direction, but the academic community has not reached a consensus on its definition. Paul Resnick et al. [1]. First gave the definition of recommender system. They believed that without sufficient personal experience, we always tend to rely on the recommendation of others to make choices. The existence of recommender systems helps and enhance this natural social process, and its value is to establish a good matching relationship between the recommendation project and the user. Yehuda Koren et al. [2] pointed out that for e-retailers and content providers, the key to improve user satisfaction and loyalty is to match consumers with the most appropriate products. The recommender system can analyze the user's interest pattern in the product and provide personalized recommendation in line with the user's preference.

© The Author(s), under exclusive license to Springer Nature Switzerland AG 2023
Y. Tu and M. Chi (Eds.): WHICEB 2023, LNBIP 480, pp. 1–13, 2023.
https://doi.org/10.1007/978-3-031-32299-0_1

Good recommender systems can add another dimension of user experience. SunMingxuan et al. [3] believe that personalized recommendation is an important research topic currently being carried out in the field of machine learning and data mining. Hongyan Liu et al. [4] believe that recommender system is essentially a simulation of user behavior. It presents the processing results to users through analysis and processing of feature data information, requirements that meet users' preferences. Yu Meng et al. [5] believe that the core of recommendation technology is to generate a list of items that users are interested in through the analysis of users' historical behaviors, interest preferences, demographic characteristics and other information, and present the top items in the list to users. The above views revolve around the prediction of users' interest preference, that is, the mining of users' specific needs [6].

The essence of recommendation algorithm is to associate users with items in a certain way. For example, social recommendation, content-based filtering, collaborative filtering and so on. In short, the basic task of the recommender system is to contact users and items to solve the problem of information overload [8].

Social recommendation obtains social behavior data through social networks, social search, social media, social bookmarking, social news, social knowledge sharing, social games, blogs, wikis, recommendation systems, question-and-answer communities, query logs, tags, etc., and makes use of computer technology, such as machine learning, data mining, natural language processing and other research to dig out collective wisdom.

Content-based filtering makes recommendations by comparing similarities or correlations between items. The approach ignores the user's purchase behavior and only considers the similarity between the goods.

Collaborative filtering has become one of the most used approaches to provide personalized services for users. The key of this approach is to find similar users or items using user-item rating matrix so that the system can illustrated recommendations for users. The approach is usually based on similarity algorithms, such as cosine, Pearson correlation coefficient etc. It is not much effective, especially in the cold user conditions.

The above views revolve around the prediction of users' interest preference, that is, the mining of users' specific needs [6]. There are explicit and implicit user needs [7]. Explicit needs can be expressed explicitly in some way (such as keywords, natural language description, etc.), and such needs can be met by search engine technology [8]. However, most of the time, users' needs are difficult to be accurately expressed.

Academia and industry have put forward many technical methods to construct user profile. One is explicit user feature extraction or simple processing, which is easy to understand. The other is the implied representation and learning of user characteristics, which is easy for subsequent quantitative calculation [24]. For example, the profiles can associate users with appropriate products. A movie profile includes its characteristics, the participating actors, and so forth. User profiles include demographic information or answers provided on a suitable questionnaire [7].

This paper gives the definition of recommender system as follows: it explores and understands the implicit needs of users from user behavior data through user profiling, model and algorithm, and provides personalized recommendation service: that is, contact users and items to solve the problem of information overload. In order to illustrate the rationality and universality of this definition, the recommended technologies in different application scenarios are described (Table 1). Although there are many application scenarios of recommender systems, its connotation can be summarized as understanding and meeting users' implicit needs from user behaviors.

Table 1. Recommender systems in different application scenarios

Application scenario	User behavior	User's invisible demand
Product recommendation	User's purchase behavior record, purchase evaluation, click, collection, etc	The products users want to buy
News recommendation	News click, browse, etc	Hot news users want to read
Short video recommendation	Users' watching, liking, forwarding and other behaviors	Short videos that users currently want to watch and conform to mainstream values
Job recommendation	Posts and companies delivered by users and other basic information	Job positions that match user skills and are fair to sensitive attributes such as gender

For example, the matrix factorization models can consider additional information such as implicit feedback, temporal effects, and confidence levels, and has illustrated that are superior to classic nearest-neighbor techniques for producing product recommendations in Netflix Prize competition [7].

CiteSpace, a visual analysis tool, can display the research hotspot, frontier and development trend of a certain discipline in a certain period through the bibliometric research of a specific discipline field, and clearly show the overall picture of a certain discipline field [11].

The organization of this paper is as follows: Sect. 2 data sources and research methods, Sect. 3 literature statistical analysis, Sect. 4 research hotspots and frontier analysis, Sect. 5 discussion and inspiration, and Sect. 6 conclusions.

2 Data Sources and Research Methods

2.1 Data Sources

The literature data used in this paper comes from the core collection of the Web of Science database, and the literatures of SCI and SSCI are retrieved. Select the search formula "TI = (Personalized OR Algorithm*) AND Recommendation*" to search, the time range is from 2013 to 2022, and the time of document data export is July 26, 2022. A total of 1126 documents were retrieved, and then manual reports, book reviews and other literatures with little relevance were screened out, and duplicate literatures were deleted, and finally 867 literature data were obtained.

2.2 Research Methods

This paper uses CiteSpace software for bibliometric analysis to visualize the scientific knowledge structure, regularity and distribution of documents, mainly from the following four dimensions: (1) Statistical analysis of documents, the annual number of published documents in the field of personalized recommendation, country; (2) Co-citation analysis of documents: visualize the connection between research topics among documents, and identify important hot documents, which represent the knowledge base under the research topic; (3) Keyword cluster analysis: On the basis of the keyword co-occurrence network, the network of core keyword co-occurrence is aggregated into categories[12], and the research hotspots in the field of personalized recommendation are analyzed; (4) Focus on the keywords, analyze the research frontier changes and development trends in the field of personalized recommendation (Fig. 1).

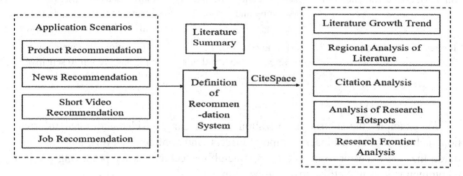

Fig. 1. Research model

3 Statistical Analysis of Literature

3.1 Analysis of Literature Growth Trend

The annual publication volume can reflect the historical development track of a certain field, and is used to measure the changes in the attention and popularity of the field [13]. The specific value and month-on-month growth rate of the annual publication volume in the personalized recommendation field from 2013 to 2022 is illustrated in Table 2. Since the retrieval time is July 26, 2022, the number of papers in 2022 is not complete. We use the function to fit the curve of the annual number of published papers, and select the exponential function model with the greatest degree of fit to obtain the results in Fig. 2.

It can be seen that the number of published papers from 2013 to 2015 decreased to a certain extent, but the decline was not large, and the number of published papers in the past three years has been at a low level combining Table 2 and Fig. 1. Since 2015, the number of published articles has shown an upward trend, and the increase has become larger and larger. Until 2020, the number of published articles has decreased compared with 2019, which may be the impact of the epidemic. In 2021, the number of published articles will show an upward trend again. In general, the number of publications in the field of personalized recommendation has increased exponentially in the past decade, indicating that this field has received more and more attention from the academic community and has become a current research hotspot [1]; from the perspective of future trends, this field The number of published papers and research results will increase, and related research will be more in-depth.

Table 2. The number of annual published literature

Year	2013	2014	2015	2016	2017	2018	2019	2020	2021	2022
Published literature	40	37	35	45	62	95	140	121	174	118
Chain growth rate	–	−0.075	−0.054	0.286	0.378	0.532	0.474	−0.136	0.138	–

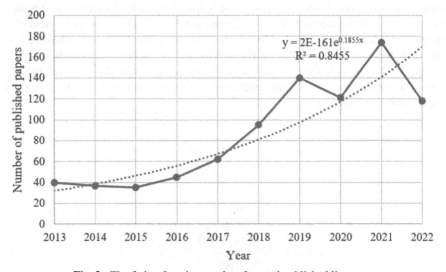

Fig. 2. The fitting function results of annual published literature

3.2 Regional Analysis of Literature

Several major countries and their cooperative research relationships in personalized recommendation research are illustrated in Fig. 3. The larger the node is, the more documents the country publishes, and the connection between the nodes indicates that there is a cooperative relationship between the two nodes. The literature proportion and centrality of the top 10 countries by the number of published papers are illustrated in Table 3. Centrality is an important structural indicator that can be used to measure the strength of cooperative research between a country and other countries. The greater the centrality, the closer the country is to cooperate with other countries.

In the field of personalized recommendation, the country with the largest number of publications is China, accounting for 74.7% of all documents, and it is the core country in this field. Followed by the United States, India, Australia, etc., but compared with China, the second-ranked United States publishes less than 1/6 of China's, and there are obvious faults, which also shows that China is in a leading position in the field of personalized recommendation. In the index of centrality, China is also much higher than other countries, which also means that the research cooperation between China and other countries is very close. Followed by the United Kingdom, India, and the United States, the centralities of these countries are all greater than 0.1, and these countries also play a role as a bridge in the research. Most of the remaining countries have published less than 10 papers, and the centrality of the intermediary is close to 0, indicating that in the remaining countries, the research on personalized recommendation is still in their infancy, and there are few external exchanges, and the research in this field has not attracted enough focus on.

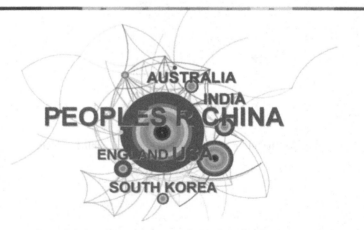

Fig. 3. Major countries and their collaborative research relationships for personalized recommendation research

Table 3. Top 10 countries by publication volume

Country	Records	Percentage(%)	Centrality
China	648	74.7	0.77
USA	100	11.5	0.14
India	41	4.7	0.16
Australia	35	4.0	0.07
South Korea	32	3.7	0.01
England	29	3.3	0.20
Canada	18	2.1	0.03
Saudi Arabia	17	2.0	0.05
Japan	15	1.7	0.06
Singapore	11	1.3	0.03

4   Research Hotspots and Frontier Analysis

4.1   Citation Analysis

Co-citation analysis of documents is a research method to measure the degree of relationship between documents. If two documents are cited by the same one or more documents at the same time, the two documents have a citation relationship. We can understand the current knowledge base in the field of personalized recommendation through reading the highly cited literature, the top 6 most cited papers is illustrated in Table 4.

Among them, He et al. proposed a general framework of deep neural network based on collaborative filtering by combining matrix factorization technology [14]. Zhang Shuai et al. made a more comprehensive summary and induction of recommender system technology based on deep learning [15]. Lu, Linyuan et al. summarized the new technology of recommender system, and introduced the macroscopic behavior of recommender system from the physical level [16]. Liu, Haifeng et al. proposed an innovative similarity calculation method by capturing the contextual information of user comments and considering the global preference of user behaviour [17]. Zhou, Tao et al. considered the two indicators of diversity and accuracy at the same time, and combined the heat-spreading (HeatS) algorithm and probabilistic spreading (ProbS) algorithm in a linearly weighted way, and proposed a hybrid recommendation algorithm [18]. Cui et al. proposed a recommendation model with an improved K-means with cuckoo search (CSK-means) considering the changes of user interests over time [19]. The current knowledge base in the field of personalized recommendation is mainly the research of neural network, collaborative filtering algorithm and hybrid recommendation algorithm. The influence of factors on the recommendation results cannot be ignored.

Among them, He et al. proposed a general framework of deep neural network based on collaborative filtering by combining matrix factorization technology [14]. Zhang Shuai et al. made a more comprehensive summary and induction of recommender system technology based on deep learning [15]. Lu, Linyuan et al. summarized the new

Table 4. Top 6 most cited papers

Cited Frequency	Centrality	First author (year)	Literature title
50	0.28	He, Xiangnan (2017)	Neural Collaborative Filtering
27	0.07	Zhang Shuai (2019)	Deep Learning based Recommender System: A Survey and New Perspectives
20	0.25	Lu, Linyaun (2012)	Recommender Systems
17	0.05	Liu,Haifeng (2014)	A new user similarity model to improve the accuracy of collaborative filtering
16	0.10	Zhou,Tao (2010)	Solving the apparent diversity-accuracy dilemma of recommender systems
13	0.01	Cui Zhihua (2020)	Personalized Recommendation System Based on Collaborative Filtering for IoT Scenarios

technology of recommender system, and introduced the macroscopic behavior of recommender system from the physical level [16]. Liu, Haifeng et al. proposed an innovative similarity calculation method by capturing the contextual information of user comments and considering the global preference of user behaviour [17]. Zhou, Tao et al. considered the two indicators of diversity and accuracy at the same time, and combined the heat-spreading (HeatS) algorithm and probabilistic spreading (ProbS) algorithm in a linearly weighted way, and proposed a hybrid recommendation algorithm [18]. Cui et al. proposed a recommendation model with an improved K-means with cuckoo search (CSK-means) considering the changes of user interests over time [19]. The current knowledge base in the field of personalized recommendation is mainly the research of neural network, collaborative filtering algorithm and hybrid recommendation algorithm. The influence of factors on the recommendation results cannot be ignored.

4.2 Analysis of Research Hotspots

Keywords are highly refined and summarized literature content, and keyword frequency analysis can effectively identify research hotspots in the field of personalized recommendation. Using CiteSpace software for keyword analysis, the keyword co-occurrence map in is obtained (Fig. 4) after merging nodes with the same semantics and deleting nodes with little relevance to the research. Keywords have co-occurred before. The keywords with high frequency and high centrality is illustrated in Table 5.

Keywords with high frequency and high centrality usually represent the research focus and hotspot in this field [13]. Through the observation and analysis of tabular data, it is concluded that the current research hotspots in the field of personalized recommendation are in the following: the construction of recommendation systems, the research of collaborative filtering, the construction of models, social networks, and neural networks.

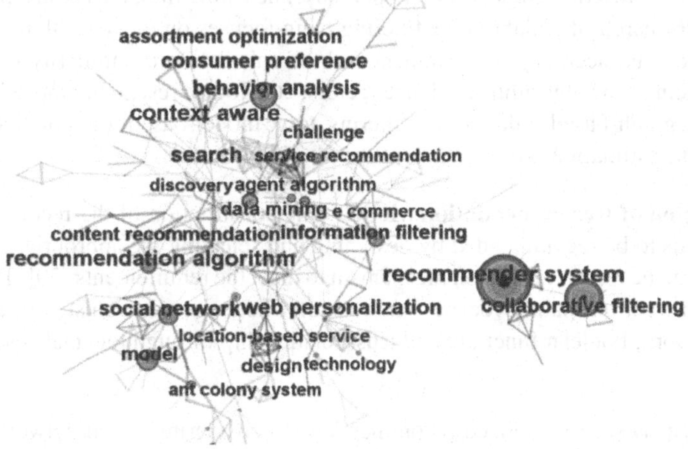

Fig. 4. Keyword co-occurrence graph

Table 5. Keywords with high frequency and high centrality

Keywords	Frequency	Centrality	Related Words
Recommender System	355	0.29	collaborative filtering, context-aware computing, implicit social network, clustering, federated learning
Collaborative Filtering	176	0.11	interest evolution model, balance factor anytime algorithm, similarity measure, knowledge graph, baseline estimation
Model	62	0.11	cluster method, trust relationship, model, consumer heterogeneity, boolean function, social network
Social Network	55	0.19	interest influence, graph database, graph, boundary work, adaptive recommendation, trust relationship
Neural Network	35	0.11	deep learning, behavior analysis, rating prediction, cloud computing

Construction of Recommendation System. The words that are related to recommender systems in the co-occurrence graph include collaborative filtering, hybrid algorithms, context-aware computing, clustering, implicit social networks, federated learning, information retrieval, information filtering, etc. Recommendation algorithms that are represented by filtering and context-aware technology are still the key research contents.

Research on Collaborative Filtering. The vocabulary which is related to collaborative filtering is interested in evolutionary model, balance factor, time algorithm, similarity calculation, knowledge graph, topic model, baseline estimation, bias adjustment, accuracy, etc. Research of collaborative filtering main focuses on the algorithm in terms of optimization and accuracy improvement and the calculation of similarity is improved by introducing time algorithms, balance factors, etc. Today, researchers widely concern knowledge graph-based collaborative filtering, topic model-based collaborative filtering, and baseline estimation-based collaborative filtering.

Construction of Recommendation Model. The construction of the recommendation model needs to be recommended by designing and selecting the appropriate algorithm according to the recommendation mechanism to meet the requirements [20]. The current model construction mainly focuses on consumer heterogeneity, clustering algorithm, social network, boolean function, and trust relationship through the analysis of related keywords.

Social Networks. Personalized recommendation considering social network is also a current research hotspot. In recommendation based on social network, it is often necessary to consider the trust relationship between friends and the influence of interest in social network, so these two are the research focus in social network. At present, most scholars use the graph model for research.

Neural Network. With the development of big data and cloud computing technology, the application of neural network in the field of personalized recommendation has been a hot research topic in recent years, focusing on rating prediction, deep learning, and user behavior analysis etc.

4.3 Research Frontier Analysis

Different from research hotspots, research fronts refer to topics with strong development potential and academic research value in the subject area [11]. Keyword emergence means that the word frequency of a keyword surges in a certain period of time and suddenly becomes a hotspot in academia. This paper intends to summarize the research trends in the field of personalized recommendation through the analysis of emerging keywords in different periods, and to explore future research directions with potential and scientific research value. The parameter γ takes the value of 1.0, the minimum emergence time is 1 year, and the emergent keywords are obtained (Table 6).

It can be seen from Table 6 that in the early days, due to the development of information technology such as the Internet, big data, and cloud computing, personalized recommendation in cloud computing environment and personalized recommendation of network services became the research hotspot at that time. By 2017, the focus in the field of personalized recommendation has become recommendation based on association rules. Matrix factorization technology has been proved to have good performance in the case of sparse data as early as in the Netflix competition held in 2006 [12], and in 2019–2020, it has attracted the attention of scholars in the field of recommendation again. During this period, the main focus of decomposition technology is to improve the matrix decomposition model by combining more contextual information. In the past three years, three emerging keywords are feature extraction, machine learning, and attention mechanism, indicating that these three topics are currently relatively active and may become research hotspots in the future.

Table 6. Burst Keywords

Keywords	Year	Strength	Begin	End	2013--2022
cloud computing	2013	2.63	2014	2017	
web personalization	2013	2.71	2015	2016	
association rule	2013	3.31	2017	2019	
matrix factorization	2013	3.34	2019	2020	
feature extraction	2013	2.47	2020	2022	
machine learning	2013	2.43	2020	2022	
attention mechanism	2013	3.17	2021	2022	

5 Discussion and Inspiration

Today, there is a gap between academic research and the implementation of industry [7]. In our understanding, it is necessary to strengthen the interaction between academic research and industry practice.

It should be standardized that the data preprocessing methods, common recommendation tasks, evaluation indicators and evaluation methods of recommendation scenarios of the recommender system through cooperation, and also be created the score ranking of common recommendation tasks on the open data set.

Regularly publish newer, larger, higher quality industrial data sets. It should encourage industry to regularly publish anonymous data sets for new application requirements that are more complex, have more user needs, have more product characteristics, and have a richer knowledge graph, and find ways to do so.

User profiling includes simple attribute features (such as age, gender, etc.) and complex pattern features (such as network implied representation, etc.), which can be applied to a wide range of social media application systems to improve user experience and system services. The recommender system meets the user's personalized information needs (e.g. implicit needs) with the user profiling which has played a very important role in the business of many commercial companies, and the application scenarios are very rich.

6 Conclusions

This paper introduces the development status of recommender systems in detail, including cloud computing, web personalization, association rule, matrix factorization, feature extraction, machine learning, and attention mechanism six phases, and predicts the future development directions to bring inspiration for researchers and practitioners.

References

1. Resnick, P., Varian, H.R.: Recommender systems. Commun. ACM **40**(3), 56–58 (1997)
2. Koren, Y., et al.: Matrix factorization techniques for recommender systems. Computer **42**(8), 30–37 (2009)
3. Sun, M., et al.: Estimating probabilities in recommendation systems. J. Roy. Stat. Soc. Ser. c-Appl. Stat. **61**(3), 471–492 (2012)
4. Liu, H., et al.: Combining user preferences and user opinions for accurate recommendation. Electron. Commer. Res. Appl. **12**(1), 14–23 (2013)
5. Yu, M., He, W., Zhou, X., et al.: Review of recommendation system. Comput. Appl. **42**(6), 1898–1913 (2022). (in Chinese)
6. Qi, H., Zhang, M., et al.: Interpretation of 2021 MIT technology review's Top 10 breakthrough technologies. China Sci. Found. **35**(3), 402–418 (2021). (in Chinese)
7. He, X., et al.: Scientific connotation and development suggestions of recommendation system. Commun. China Comput. Feder. **18**(8), 50–54 (2022). (in Chinese)
8. Xiang, L.: Recommender System Practice, 1st edn. People's Posts and Telecommunications Press, Beijing (2014). (in Chinese)
9. Chen, H., Wang, Z.: A survey of personalized recommendation algorithms. Enterp. Sci. Technol. Dev. **35**(2), 56–57 (2019). (in Chinese)
10. Shi, Y.: A survey of personalized recommendation algorithms. Intell. Comput. Appl. **10**(8), 110–112 (2020). (in Chinese)
11. Chen, Y., Chen, C., Liu, Z., et al.: The methodology function of CiteSpace mapping knowledge domains. Sci. Sci. Res. **33**(2), 242–253 (2015). (in Chinese)
12. Wang, L., Li, S.: Analysis of hotspot and frontier of domestic "internet plus traditional industries" based on cite space. Inf. Sci. **35**(2), 150–156 (2017). (in Chinese)
13. Zheng, J., Yang, X., Li, X.: Visualization analysis of recommendation system based on CiteSpace. Sci. Technol. Eng. **21**(34), 14634–14643 (2021). (in Chinese)
14. He, X., et al.: Neural collaborative filtering. In: 2017 Proceedings of the 26th Inter-national Conference on World Wide Web (www 2017), pp. 173–182. ACM, Beijing (2017)
15. Zhang, S., et al.: Deep learning based recommender system: a survey and new perspectives. ACM Comput. Surv. **52**(1), 1–38 (2019)
16. Lu, L., et al.: Recommender systems. Phys. Rep.-Rev. Sect. Phys. Lett. **519**(1), 1–49 (2012)
17. Liu, H., et al.: A new user similarity model to improve the accuracy of collaborative filtering. Knowl.-Based Syst. **56**, 156–166 (2014)
18. Zhou, T., et al.: Solving the apparent diversity-accuracy dilemma of recommender systems. Proc. Natl. Acad. Sci. United States Am. **107**(10), 4511–4515 (2010)
19. Cui, Z., et al.: Personalized recommendation system based on collaborative filtering for IoT scenarios. IEEE Trans. Serv. Comput. **13**(4), 685–695 (2020)
20. Song, Y., Sun, Y.: Research hotspots, trends and implications of recommendation algorithms for digital learning resources in China. J. Yunan Normal Univ. (Nat. Sci. Ed.) **42**(3), 60–66 (2022). (in Chinese)
21. Luo, L., et al.: Personalized recommendation by matrix co-factorization with tags and time information. Expert Syst. Appl. **119**, 311–321 (2019)
22. Cui, W., Xu, L., Du, C., et al.: Privacy-preserving matrix factorization algorithm in recommender system. Comput. Appl. Softw. **38**(5), 316–322 (2021). (in Chinese)

23. Liu, H., Li, K., He, X., et al.: User portrait diversified label recommendation for information cocoons. Library **41**(3), 83–89 (2022). (in Chinese)
24. Zhao, X., Ding, X.: Analysis on the construction and application of user portrait in recommender system. Commun. China Comput. Feder. **13**(11), 47–54 (2017). (in Chinese)
25. Li, T.: Research on Video Recommendation Method Based on Prospect Theory. Henan University of Economics and Law (2020). (in Chinese)

Research on Knowledge Sharing Efficiency Evaluation of Open Innovation Community: A Case of Xiaomi Community

Jian Tian[✉] and Xuefeng Gao

School of Economics and Management, Jiangsu University of Science and Technology,
Zhenjiang 212100, China
tianjian@just.edu.cn

Abstract. Under the platform economy, more and more enterprises attract users to participate in innovation by means of Open Innovation Communities (OIC) and improve organizational performance through knowledge sharing. How to evaluate the efficiency of knowledge sharing scientifically is of great significance. In this paper, a total of 61 "circles" datum of the Xiaomi community were acquired as examples and divided into categories, and they were evaluated the knowledge sharing efficiency using the three-stage DEA model. The results showed that environmental factors and random interference had a strong impact on the efficiency of knowledge sharing in the community of enterprises. The comprehensive technical efficiency of 91.67% of the "circles" decreased significantly after adjustment, mainly due to low scale efficiency. The number of users featured posts, the number of fans, employee participation and the percentage of authenticated users had a positive impact on the efficiency of knowledge sharing in the community, and the number of user posts and community size had a negative impact on the efficiency of the community knowledge sharing. Finally, it discussed countermeasures and suggestions to improve the efficiency of knowledge sharing in the enterprise-hosted community from three aspects: community scale, community incentive system, and personalized service.

Keywords: Open innovation community (OIC) · Knowledge sharing efficiency · Three-stage DEA model · Xiaomi community

1 Introduction

With the rapid development of the Internet and Web 2.0 technology level, virtual communities with online social functions have become an innovative platform for communication and knowledge sharing among members of all parties [1]. Open Innovation Community (OIC) is a virtual community for users to implement innovation activities, and an Internet platform for resource circulation, user participation in innovation and knowledge sharing [2]. From the viewpoint of the founding body, OIC can be divided into two types: the company's self-built type and the knowledge discussion type created by a third party. Domestic and international companies are increasingly starting to

Y. Tu and M. Chi (Eds.): WHICEB 2023, LNBIP 480, pp. 14–26, 2023.
https://doi.org/10.1007/978-3-031-32299-0_2

establish OIC, such as My Starbucks Idea, Niketalk, Haier Open Partnership Ecosystem, Xiaomi Community, Club of HUAWEI, and so on. OIC is an important environment for all participants to carry out knowledge sharing, and the effect of user knowledge sharing largely represents its development and construction level [3]. However, as the scale of the community continues to expand, the "knowledge trend" in the community is mainly dominated by the government, and the breadth of knowledge sharing in the community is not enough. Moreover, the community faces problems such as low user activity and low enthusiasm for knowledge sharing due to a flood of users who have been "diving" for a long time after entering the community. Therefore, community managers need to understand users' needs and study what factors influence users' knowledge sharing to develop targeted promotion strategies, mobilize community users' enthusiasm to participate in knowledge sharing, and promote enterprises to broaden the path of innovative knowledge acquisition, and promote knowledge sharing for enterprises' innovative activities.

2 Literature Review

There are impacts on behavior, mechanism and efficiency evaluation of knowledge sharing in OICs that have generated considerable recent research interest.

2.1 Research on Influencing Factors of User's Behavior Knowledge Sharing in OIC

Nambisa et al. showed that the degree of user self-presentation, available social learning opportunities, corporate recognition, and recognition of users with creative sharing experience have a significant positive effect on users' sustained creative sharing behavior [4]. A study by Zhou found that factors such as innovation self-efficacy, outcome expectation, and social identity have significant positive effects on the knowledge sharing behavior of users of OICs [5]. Ying et al. explored the positive impact of the satisfaction of three psychological needs-autonomy, relatedness, and competence-on user's knowledge sharing behavior through the mediating role of psychological ownership [6]. Scholars have studied the effects of personal, environmental, and psychological factors on OIC knowledge sharing, but most studies have focused on the single-factor level and have not explored the interplay between multiple factors.

2.2 Research on Knowledge Sharing Mechanism of OIC

Rajabion et al. classified the knowledge sharing mechanisms in OICs into three categories: social mechanisms, incentive mechanisms, and medical mechanisms [7]. Wang et al. explored the mechanism of virtual community rewards on explicit and tacit knowledge sharing in virtual communities using intrinsic motivation as a potential mediator and showed that virtual community rewards have significant effects on both explicit and tacit knowledge sharing, highlighting the role of hedonic and self-efficacy in mediating the relationship between rewards and tacit knowledge sharing [8]. Li et al. proposed an incentive mechanism for the knowledge sharing behavior of leading users in OICs based on evolutionary games and pointed out that incentives are beneficial to promote knowledge sharing [9]. Regarding the research on the knowledge sharing mechanism of open innovation communities, scholars have mostly focused on the governance mechanism and incentive mechanism, and the exploration of the knowledge sharing mechanism of OIC is yet to be enriched.

2.3 Research on Efficiency Evaluation of Knowledge Sharing in OIC

Lee et al. used the DEA-Malmquist index method to analyze the changes in knowledge sharing efficiency in communities at the organizational, sectoral, and community levels [10]. Zhang used fuzzy hierarchical analysis for OIC knowledge sharing performance evaluation [11]. Yuan. et al. used the SBM model to measure knowledge sharing efficiency in an online health community and used the Tobit model to analyze whether environmental factors (e.g., user factors, community factors) interfered with the knowledge sharing efficiency of the community [12]. The research methods mostly adopt traditional DEA methods, fuzzy hierarchical analysis, and SBM models to measure the knowledge sharing efficiency, without eliminating the interference of environmental factors and random errors in the efficiency.

Xiaomi Community is an official platform developed by Xiaomi to facilitate user communication, consultation, help, complaints and proposals, and it is also a typical representative of an enterprise OIC s with mature operation and high user activity in China. Xiaomi developed the MIUI system with 1/3 of the ideas coming from fans and 80% of the modifications coming from the Xiaomi community. Hence, the paper introduces a scheme that firstly a total of 12 types of "circles" with high activity in the Xiaomi community are selected as the research objects, secondly adopts a three-stage DEA model to measure the knowledge sharing efficiency of the enterprise self-built OICs. Then, eliminating the influence of environmental factors and random errors on the knowledge sharing efficiency of the enterprise self-built OICs reflects the actual value of the knowledge exchange efficiency of the enterprise self-built OICs more realistically. Finally, it proposes suggestions to promote the knowledge sharing efficiency of the OIC, furthermore, to provide reference and reference for the enterprise to build an OIC.

3   Variables Selection and Data Sources

3.1   Input and Output Variables Selection

Ren believes that knowledge sharing is achieved through the interactive communication of community members, and the posting behavior of users is one of the manifestations [15]. Therefore, the input variables selected in this paper mainly considered three dimensions of personnel, knowledge source and time input in knowledge sharing input, and number of users, number of posts, and discussion time were selected.

The number of views measures the breadth of knowledge dissemination in knowledge sharing output. The number of comments is an inaccessible part of knowledge sharing activities in the community, and its number reflects the breadth of knowledge sharing among users. The number of replies refers to the communication among responders, reflecting the deepening of knowledge sharing levels in the OIC and the depth of knowledge sharing among users [16]. Therefore, the number of views, comments and replies from the time of posting to the statistical time were selected as the knowledge sharing output indicators. Based on the principles of systematization, availability and operability of data, this paper constructed the evaluation index of knowledge sharing efficiency of OIC. As shown in Table 1.

Table 1. Input and output evaluation indicators

Indicator type	Indicator name	Indicator meaning
Input indicators	Users $X1$	The human input in knowledge sharing
	Posts X_2	Knowledge source input in knowledge sharing
	Discussion Time X_3	The time investment in knowledge sharing
Output indicators	Views Y_1	The breadth of knowledge dissemination
	Comments Y_2	The breadth of knowledge sharing among users
	Replies Y_3	The depth of knowledge sharing among users

3.2 Environmental Variables Selection

According to the research of Simar et al., environmental variables need to select factors that affect DMU efficiency but DMU is uncontrollable [17]. Zhao et al. pointed out that users are the fundamental factors that determine the quality and quantity of knowledge sharing [18]. Xie et al. concluded that the community environment has a significant positive effect on knowledge sharing [19]. In this paper, considering the characteristics of OICs and data availability, the internal influencing factors of knowledge sharing efficiency of enterprise OICs were classified into two types of factors: one was user

Table 2. Description of environment variables

Indicator dimension	Indicator name	Indicator meaning
User factors	User Posts E_1	Total number of user posts
	User featured posts E_2	The number of user's featured posts
	Fans E_3	Number of user fans
Community factors	Community scale E_4	The ratio of community participants to posts
	Employee participation E_5	The proportion of official employee posts to posts
	The proportion of authenticated users E_6	The proportion of personal tags among community posting users

factors that included the number of user posts, the number of users featured posts and the number of fans, another was community factors that included community scale, employee participation and the percentage of authenticate users. As shown in Table 2.

3.3 Data Sources and Processing

According to the activities of the Xiaomi community, the first 61 "circles" were selected, and divided into 12 categories due to the discussion content, including: "Mobile Phone", "Tablet PC", "MIUI System", "MIUI Application", "APP Circle", "Computer", "Wearable Device", "Daily Life", "MI Fans Circle", "Game", "TV" and "Smart life". Then, writing Python codes, it obtained data items that included user information, post information, and discussion information of the "Featured" section in the 12 categories of "circles" in the Xiaomi Community from 2020 to 2021.

Because the Xiaomi community was revamped and updated in October 2019, the earliest data available in the community was October 2019. Hence this paper screened out more than 800,000 pieces of data crawled and retained the data from 2020–2021. In this paper, 12 types of "circles" in the Xiaomi community were analyzed, therefore $n = 12$. As the research needs, the window width was chosen as 2 ($d = 2$). Therefore, there was 1 window in this paper, and the number of decision units was $n \times d$, or 24 decision units. The content of the community comments and replies was screened and found that there was the behavior of "bump", therefore invalid content in the comments and replies was eliminated. The correlation analysis of input and output variables of knowledge sharing in the "Featured" section of Xiaomi community's 12 "circles" was shown in Table 3, which showed that all variables were significant at the 1% significance level. In addition, it passed the correlation test, which was satisfied the "homogeneity" hypothesis of the model [20].

Table 3. Correlation analysis of input-output variables

Variables	X_1	X_2	X_3	Y_1	Y_2	Y_3
X_1	1					
X_2	0.812***	1				
X_3	0.824***	0.847***	1			
Y_1	0.927***	0.703***	0.758***	1		
Y_2	0.971***	0.747***	0.685***	0.906***	1	
Y_3	0.956***	0.800***	0.883***	0.970***	0.896***	1

Note: *** indicates significance at a 1% level of significance

4 Empirical Analysis

4.1 Analysis of Efficiency of Knowledge Sharing in OIC Based on Initial Data

MaxDea 8 software was used to calculate the initial value of knowledge sharing efficiency of the enterprise OIC and obtain the comprehensive technical efficiency (TE), pure technical efficiency (PTE), and scale efficiency (SE) of knowledge sharing in the Xiaomi community from 2020 to 2021. As shown in Table 4, η represents the efficiency of the mean annual.

The overall knowledge sharing efficiency of the enterprise OIC was not high. When the influence of environmental variables and random errors were not eliminated, the comprehensive technical efficiency of the Xiaomi community was 0.873 and 0.741 respectively, which was not effective for DMU. Only "MIUI System" was always DMU effective, whereas the comprehensive efficiency and the output level of "APP Circle", "Game" and "Smart Life" were low. During 2020- 2021, the comprehensive technical efficiency, pure technical efficiency, and scale efficiency of knowledge sharing in the Xiaomi community all showed a downward trend. Only the efficiency of "Daily Life" was improved to DEA effective, indicating that the community's utilization of input factors was still insufficient, and the scale structure of the community still had space for optimization. Meanwhile, the pure technical efficiency of the Xiaomi community was lower than the scale efficiency. Only 50% of the "circles" in the community had pure technical efficiency higher than the average level, and 66.67% of the "circles" had scale efficiency higher than the average level. It can be concluded that the lack of pure technical efficiency mainly affected the comprehensive efficiency of the enterprise OIC. It shows that there are still problems in the internal management technology of the enterprise OIC, which restrict the comprehensive efficiency of community knowledge sharing and need to be improved and adjusted according to the specific situation.

Table 4. DEA Knowledge Sharing Efficiency of 12 Types of "Circles" in Xiaomi Community

Circles	The year 2020			The year 2021			η
	TE	PTE	SE	TE	PTE	SE	
Mobile Phone	1.000	1.000	1.000	0.736	0.736	1.000	0.868
Tablet PC	1.000	1.000	1.000	0.704	0.729	0.966	0.852
MIUI System	1.000	1.000	1.000	1.000	1.000	1.000	1.000
MIUI Application	0.835	0.840	0.994	0.663	0.672	0.987	0.749
APP Circle	0.769	0.781	0.985	0.553	0.972	0.569	0.661
Computer	0.787	0.959	0.821	0.708	0.852	0.831	0.748
Wearable Device	1.000	1.000	1.000	0.773	0.895	0.864	0.887
Daily Life	0.933	0.933	0.999	1.000	1.000	1.000	0.966
MI Fans Circle	1.000	1.000	1.000	0.802	0.810	0.991	0.901
Game	0.799	0.871	0.917	0.559	0.872	0.641	0.679
TV	0.653	0.845	0.772	0.791	1.000	0.791	0.722
Smart Life	0.698	0.757	0.922	0.600	0.659	0.911	0.649
Xiaomi Community	0.873	0.916	0.951	0.741	0.850	0.879	0.807

Referring to Liu's definition of the critical point [20], the PTE and SE mean values (0.883 and 0.915) of the enterprise OIC knowledge sharing are set as the critical point, and the PTE and SE that constitute the efficiency of community knowledge sharing are divided. The overall knowledge sharing efficiency of the OIC can be divided into three types (as shown in Fig. 1). The first category is "high-high". Hence, "MI Fans Circle", "Daily Life", "MIUI System" and "Wearable Device" had higher knowledge sharing efficiency and less space for improvement and needed to improve PTE and SE slightly. The second category is "high-low", it has two types. One is a "PTE high, SE low" type of "circle" that included "Computer", and "TV", another is an "SE high, PTE low" type of "circle" that included "Mobile Phone", "Tablet PC", "MIUI System" and "Smart Life", and more "circles" in the community needed to improve PTE. The third category is "low-low" that PTE and SE are lower than the critical point, which "Game" and "APP Circle" were owned in it and needed to improve both PTE and SE.

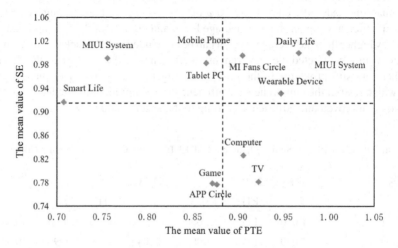

Fig. 1. Stage I: the classification by the mean value of PTE and SE in OIC

4.2   The Influences of Environmental Factors on Efficiency

Frontier 4.1 software was used to perform SFA regression on the input slack variables of decision making units and various environmental factors. As can be seen from Table 5, most of the regression coefficients of environmental variables (89%) had passed the significance test of 1% and 10%, and passed the mixed chi-square (LR) unilateral test at the significance level of 1%. It indicated that the SFA model was reasonable, and the selected six environmental variables were desirable, and each environmental variable had an impact on the input slack variables of the OIC. What is more, under the 1% significance level, the γ values of the three input slack variables tended to 1, which indicates that MI plays a dominant role in the knowledge sharing efficiency of OICs.

In the SFA regression model, if the coefficient value is positive, it shows that the increase of environmental variables will cause the increase of the slack variables, and if

Table 5. Regression results of the SFA model

Categories	Number of users slack variable	Number of posts slack variable	Lasting time slack variable
C	315.32^{***}	32.78^{***}	26893.71^{***}
E_1	11.96^{***}	-0.04	1116.59^{***}
$E2$	-33.30^{***}	0.84^{***}	-5976.32^{***}
$E3$	-0.01^{***}	0.00	-0.73^{***}
E_4	13.93^{***}	-0.17^{*}	763.55^{***}
E_5	-3589.88^{***}	-50.04^{***}	-320903.29^{***}
E_6	-3383.72^{***}	-54.68^{***}	-382816.40^{***}
σ^2	10137236^{***}	4373.35^{***}	136648640000^{***}
Γ	0.99999999^{***}	0.99999999^{***}	0.99999999^{***}
Log likelihood	-212.86	-118.38	-327.72
LR test	9.83^{***}	14.84^{***}	7.97^{***}

Note: *, * *, * * * indicate significance at 10%, 5%, 1% levels, respectively

the coefficient value is negative, it indicates that the increase of environmental variables will reduce the slack variables. The specific analysis is as follows:

User factors. The number of user posts had a significant positive impact on the number of user slack variables and the discussion time slack variable. The number of user featured posts had a significant negative impact on the number of user slack variable and discussion time slack variable, and had a significant positive impact on the number of posts slack variable. The number of fans had a significant negative impact on the number of user slack variables and the discussion time slack variable. The results show that the more user posts, the less community user and discussion time, and the more user featured posts, the more community user and discussion time, however it is not conducive to the increase of community posts. In other words, blindly pursuing a large number of user posts, although it greatly increases the input of knowledge sources, users obtaining useful information from a large number of posts is very difficult, and community knowledge sharing efficiency is not high. On the other hand, the user featured posts set up by the community are high-quality content. Therefore, Users can accurately obtain useful information, and the creators of featured posts are more capable of solving users' problems, which is conducive to enhancing knowledge exchange among users and promoting the improvement of comprehensive technical efficiency of knowledge sharing in the enterprise OIC.

Community factors. The community size had a significant positive impact on the number of user slack variable and discussion time slack variable, and had a significant negative impact on the number of posts slack variable. The employee participation and the percentage of authenticated users had a significant negative impact on the slack variable of the three input variables. This shows that blindly expanding the scale of the community will cause a waste of personnel input and time input. Although the number of posts in the community has increased, it is not conducive to the high-quality development of the community. The employee participation and the percentage of authenticated users were proportional to the efficiency of knowledge sharing in the OIC, and the absolute value of these two environmental factors was much higher than other variables, indicating that the more employees participated in the OIC and the more high-quality users have a significant effect on the improvement of community knowledge sharing efficiency. Hence, compared with blindly expanding the size of the community, efficient and reasonable management and attracting more high-quality users can promote the sharing of knowledge in the OIC, moreover enhancing the efficiency of knowledge sharing in the community.

4.3 Analysis of Efficiency of Knowledge Sharing in OIC Based on Adjusted Data

By eliminating the influence of environmental variables and random errors, adjusting the original data, and using MaxDea 8 software to recalculate, the knowledge sharing efficiency of the third-stage enterprise OIC is obtained. As shown in Table 6, η represents the efficiency of the mean annual.

Table 6. Stage III DEA: Knowledge Sharing Efficiency of 12 Types of "Circles" in Xiaomi Community

Circles	The year 2020			The year 2021			η
	TE	PTE	SE	TE	PTE	SE	
Mobile Phone	1.000	1.000	1.000	0.773	0.794	0.974	0.886
Tablet PC	0.087	0.856	0.102	0.566	0.846	0.670	0.327
MIUI System	1.000	1.000	1.000	1.000	1.000	1.000	1.000
MIUI Application	0.749	0.892	0.839	0.473	0.919	0.515	0.611
APP Circle	0.354	0.769	0.460	0.296	0.820	0.361	0.325
Computer	0.107	1.000	0.107	0.406	0.849	0.478	0.257
Wearable Device	0.977	1.000	0.977	0.650	1.000	0.650	0.813
Daily Life	0.525	0.696	0.754	0.086	1.000	0.086	0.305
MI Fans Circle	1.000	1.000	1.000	0.741	0.823	0.900	0.870
Game	0.518	1.000	0.518	0.250	1.000	0.250	0.384
TV	0.070	0.857	0.081	0.257	0.861	0.299	0.163
Smart Life	0.141	0.628	0.224	0.376	0.854	0.440	0.259
Xiaomi Community	0.544	0.892	0.589	0.489	0.897	0.552	0.517

Comparing Tables 4 and 6, it can be seen that the knowledge sharing efficiency of the adjusted enterprise OIC was significantly lower than that of the first-stage. In other words, after eliminating the influence of environmental factors and random interference, the average value of comprehensive technical efficiency and scale efficiency of knowledge sharing in the Xiaomi community was significantly lower than that before adjustment, and the average value of pure technical efficiency was slightly higher than that before adjustment (0.011), which indicates that the external environment has a strong influence on the comprehensive technical efficiency of knowledge sharing in Xiaomi community, and if the influence of environmental factors is not eliminated, the comprehensive technical efficiency of Xiaomi community will be overestimated. In addition, the low scale efficiency was the main reason for the low comprehensive technical efficiency in the third stage of the Xiaomi community. By moderately expanding the scale of community development, reducing resource waste and improving the level of organization and management, the knowledge sharing efficiency of the enterprise OIC consequently has 48.30% rising space.

Specifically, after input adjustment, only the "MIUI System" was in the production frontier, indicating that its knowledge sharing was indeed efficient after removing the impact of environmental and random factors. As the most discussed and concerned "circles" in the Xiaomi community, "MIUI System" was indeed at the leading level in technology and management. In terms of pure technical efficiency, including one pure technical effective "circle", 66.67% of the "circles" had higher PTE after the adjustment than before the adjustment, indicating that the previous inefficiency was mainly affected by the environmental or random disturbance, and the external environment was an unfavorable factor for the internal management ability of the community. In terms of scale efficiency, 91.67% of the "circles" SE after adjustment was lower than that before adjustment, indicating that a favorable environment and active management strategy were conducive to scale increase, whereas the community itself should improve management level to adapt to environmental development.

Adjusted region division based on efficiency critical point. With reference to the previous classification, (0.894, 0.570) was the critical value after adjustment (see Fig. 2). Analyzing Tables 4, 6, and Fig. 2, it can be seen that the change range of SE in all "circles" was higher than that of PTE, indicating that environmental factors mainly affected the scale efficiency of knowledge sharing in the enterprise OIC.

With the first category of "high-high", after adjustment, "Mobile Phone" and "MIUI Application" were changed from "high-low" to "high-high", which indicated that environmental factors and random errors mainly affected its PTE, therefore improving technical efficiency and management level was likely to achieve DEA effectively. With the second category of "high-low", "Game" changed from "low-low" to "high-low", and the pure technology was effective, indicating that the internal resource allocation of the "circles" was reasonable, however the scale efficiency needed to be improved. With the third category of "low-low", 41.67% of the "circles" pure technical efficiency and scale efficiency was lower than the community average, which had a lot of space for growth and needed to manage and scale.

4.4 Further Discussion

Based on the empirical research results of knowledge sharing efficiency of enterprise OICs, to improve the knowledge sharing efficiency of enterprise OICs and help enterprises make full use of knowledge resources:

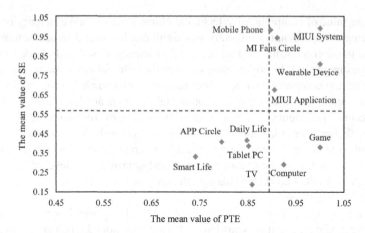

Fig. 2. Stage III: the classification by the mean value of PTE and SE in OIC

For lack of scale efficiency, low efficiency of knowledge sharing. Firstly, enterprise OICs should pay attention to community scale construction and improve the overall allocation of community resources. Secondly, it should establish a sound community management system, create a unique community culture, and enhance the user's sense of belonging and identity. Finally, it should pay attention to the high-quality presentation of knowledge sources, should screen high-quality posting content and strictly prohibit "bump" behavior, and promote effective knowledge sharing in enterprise OICs.

Based on the influence of environmental factors on the efficiency of knowledge sharing in the enterprise OIC, the results show that the quality of community members and the participation of employees have a promoting effect on the efficiency of knowledge sharing. It is necessary to explore high-quality original creators, and improve community incentive policies and internal incentive systems. What is more, the main concern of enterprises should not be to disseminate marketing information, but should focus on building community value.

The enterprise OIC should pay attention to the personalized recommendation algorithm, carry out accurate knowledge push, and meet the knowledge needs of different users. When the push content of the enterprise OIC is consistent with the user's knowledge sharing willingness, it is easier to arouse the resonance between the user and the community, and further, stimulate the user's knowledge sharing behavior.

5 Conclusion and Prospect

This paper used the three-stage DEA model to measure the knowledge sharing efficiency of the Xiaomi community during 2020–2021, and draws the following conclusions:

After eliminating the influence of environmental factors and random errors, 91.67% of the "circles" had a significant decrease in overall technical efficiency and scale efficiency and a slight increase in pure technical efficiency. For the enterprise OIC, the external environment has a strong influence on the efficiency of community knowledge sharing, resulting in a false high comprehensive technical efficiency before adjustment and a low scale efficiency, which is the main reason for the low comprehensive technical efficiency in the third-stage of the enterprise OIC.

The knowledge sharing efficiency of enterprise OICs is greatly influenced by environmental factors. The number of user posts was negatively correlated with personnel input and time input, and only increasing knowledge source input was not conducive to improving knowledge sharing efficiency. The number of user featured posts and fans was positively correlated with personnel input and time input, and high-quality knowledge exchange and user authority can promote the improvement of the enterprise OIC knowledge sharing efficiency. Community size was negatively correlated with personnel input and time input, which affected the improvement of knowledge sharing efficiency. However, employee participation and the percentage of authenticated users had positive effects on the knowledge sharing efficiency of the enterprise OIC.

Enterprise OICs can be divided into three categories. For "high-high" OICs, knowledge sharing within the community is ideal, and the maximum output can be achieved with the given input. For "high-low" OICs, the scale of the community should be adjusted and resource allocation should be rationalized, or community knowledge management and institutional changes should be emphasized to enhance the efficiency of knowledge sharing. For "low-low" OICs, they should start from both management level and scale expansion, increase personnel and resource investment, and improve overall technical efficiency.

Due to the revision of the Xiaomi community and the degree of data openness, the volume of data used in the study is relatively small and the environmental variables are not perfect. In the subsequent study, to expect to get more perfect knowledge sharing research results of enterprise OICs, it can add different communities for comparison, and improve the way of collecting data to obtain more data volume and other environmental variables that affect efficiency.

Acknowledgement. This research was supported by the National Social Science Foundation of China under Grant 17BGL028.

References

1. Felin, T., Zenger, T.R.: Closed or open innovation? problem solving and the governance choice. Res. Policy **43**(5), 914–925 (2014)
2. Debaere, S., Coussement, K., De Ruyck, T.: Multi-label classification of member participation in online innovation communities. Eur. J. Oper. Res. **270**(2), 761–774 (2018)
3. Zhang, H., Ren, L., Liu, W., Zhou, H.: Study on user knowledge collaborative innovation based on super-network——example of open innovation community "Pollen Club." J. China Soc. Sci. Tech. Inf. **04**, 402–413 (2021). (in Chinese)
4. Nambisan, S., Wright, M., Feldman, M.: The digital transformation of innovation and entrepreneurship: progress, challenges and key themes. Res. Policy **48**(8), 103773 (2019)
5. Yang, L., Wang, Z., Hou, G.: Research on influence factors of knowledge sharing behavior of online user innovation communities. New Century Library (02), 55–59+86 (2020). (in Chinese)
6. Jiang, Y., Liao, J., Chen, J., Hu, Y., Du, P.: Motivation for users' knowledge-sharing behavior in virtual brand communities: a psychological ownership perspective. Asia Pac. J. Mark. Logist. **34**(10), 2165–2183 (2022)

7. Rajabion, L., Nazari, N., Bandarchi, M., Farashiani, A., Haddad, S.: Knowledge sharing mechanisms in virtual communities: a review of the current literature and recommendations for future research. Hum. Syst. Manag. **38**(4), 365–384 (2019)
8. Wang, N., Yin, J., Ma, Z., Liao, M.: The influence mechanism of rewards on knowledge sharing behaviors in virtual communities. J. Knowl. Manag. **26**(3), 485–505 (2021)
9. Li, C., Huang, H., Zhang, F.: Knowledge sharing behavior incentive mechanism for lead users based on evolutionary game. J. Comput. Appl. **41**(6), 1785–1791 (2021). (in Chinese)
10. Lee, S., Hong, J.: Analyzing the change in knowledge sharing efficiency of knowledge networks: a case study. Inf. Technol. Manage. **20**(1), 41–53 (2018). https://doi.org/10.1007/s10799-018-0292-5
11. Zhang, K.: Research on Knowledge Sharing in Open Innovation Community. Jilin University, Jilin, China, Doctor (2017). (in Chinese)
12. Yuan, Y., Zhang, Y., Ma, R., Wang, Y., He, P., Yu, Q.: Knowledge exchange efficiency of online health community based on SBM-TOBIT model. Inf. Sci. **05**, 106–114 (2021). (in Chinese)
13. Charnes, A., Cooper, W.W., Rhodes, E.: Measuring the efficiency of decision making units. Eur. J. Oper. Res. **2**(6), 429–444 (1978)
14. Charnes, A., Cooper, W.W.: Preface to topics in data envelopment analysis. Ann. Oper. Res. **2**(1), 59–94 (1984)
15. Ren, L.: Influencing factors and development approaches of knowledge sharing in online open innovation community. Inf. Sci. **09**, 48–53 (2019). (in Chinese)
16. Yang, R., Huang, S., Wang, Y.: Research on evaluation efficiency of knowledge exchange in online healthy community based on three-stage DEA model. Inf. Stud. Theory Appl. **10**, 122–129 (2020). (in Chinese)
17. Simar, L., Wilson, P.W.: Estimation and inference in two-stage, semi-parametric models of production processes. J. Econ. **136**(1), 31–64 (2007)
18. Zhao, K., Stylianou, A.C., Zheng, Y.: Predicting users' continuance intention in virtual communities: the dual intention-formation processes. Decis. Support Syst. **55**(4), 903–910 (2013)
19. Xie, R., Zhang, W.: An empirical study on the impact of platform environmental factors on knowledge sharing in virtual communities. Technol. Soc. **71**, 102094 (2022)
20. Liu, W.: Technological innovation efficiency of high-tech industries considering environmental factor in China—Comparison of two periods from 2000–2007 and from 2008–2014. Sci. Res. Manag. **11**, 18–25 (2016). (in Chinese)

Stock Price Overvaluation and Digital Transformation Investment of Listed SMEs: Impact Analysis and Path Testing

Weiwei Gan, Wenbin Qu[✉], and Dian Su

School of Economics and Management, China University of Geosciences (Wuhan), Wuhan, Hubei, China
2582355265@qq.com

Abstract. Based on the investment perspective, this paper takes the data of listed companies on China's SME Board from 2013 to 2019 as a research sample, and conducts an impact analysis and path test on the relationship between stock price overvaluation and investment in digital transformation of listed SMEs. Overall, the results of this paper support the equity financing channel hypothesis that overvaluation of stock prices promotes the capital investment of digital transformation of listed SMEs, but does not support the rational catering channel hypothesis. The research conclusions of this paper provide reference ideas for promoting the digital transformation investment of listed SMEs in China.

Keywords: Stock Price Overvaluation · Digital transformation investments · Equity financing · Rational pandering

1 Introduction

As China's economic construction enters a new journey, the development of enterprises is facing many challenges such as slowing market demand and rising comprehensive factor costs, how to achieve "cost reduction, efficiency improvement and quality improvement" has become the key for enterprises in various industries to seek survival and development, and digital transformation is considered to be the only way to achieve this vision. According to the World Economic Forum's white paper "The Impact of the Fourth Industrial Revolution on Supply Chains", digital transformation has reduced costs and increased revenue by 17.6% and revenue by 22.6% for manufacturing companies, 34.2% for logistics services and 33.6% for revenue, and 7.8% and 33.3% for retail, respectively. Today, with the rapid development of China's digital economy, the concept of digital development is deeply rooted in the hearts of the people, and more and more enterprises have or are undergoing digital transformation.

However, the current situation of digital transformation of enterprises in China is not optimistic. According to data released by authoritative organizations such as Accenture, only 16% of the leading enterprises with remarkable digital transformation results in Chinese enterprises in 2021, although more small and medium-sized enterprises are also engaged in digital transformation and invest resources in intelligent operation and construction, but their transformation effect is still far behind that of leading enterprises. In this regard, many scholars believe that resource endowments and technical barriers are the main reasons for the significant difference in the results of digital transformation of enterprises. Liu et al. (2021) pointed out that, the digital transformation of Chinese enterprises mainly faces problems such as "not turning" due to weak transformation capabilities, "unwilling to turn" due to high transformation costs, and "dare not turn" due to long transformation cycles [1]. Especially for small and medium-sized enterprises with poor resource endowment and technical strength, promoting digital management and transformation requires a lot of capital investment and precipitation costs, and how to choose a scientific digital transformation path according to the characteristics of the industry, scale volume, technological advantages and other characteristics, and formulate a reasonable investment plan, is a practical problem that must be considered to promote digital transformation. Accenture (2021) also pointed out in its report that the systematic nature of digital transformation makes digital transformation investment have the characteristics of long cycle and slow results, while SME managers are mostly eager to see results, unwilling to bear the losses caused by the cost-benefit imbalance during the transformation, and often adopt a small repair strategy to deploy digitalization. As a result, the digital transformation effect is increasingly different from that of leading companies.

In recent years, with the continuous development and growth of domestic and foreign capital markets, the impact of capital market stock price changes on the investment of enterprises in the real economy has become a new focus of academic research on enterprise investment issues. Scholars at home and abroad generally believe that overvaluation of stock prices plays a significant positive role in promoting investment in the real economy of enterprises and expanding the scale of enterprise investment. Inspired by the soaring stock prices of the US technology industry in the 90s of last century, Internet technology companies have expanded their investment scale and triggered the revolution of the information technology industry, Lu et al. (2017) studied the impact of stock pricing in China's capital market on industrial structure adjustment, and found that overvaluation of stock prices will trigger an increase in the amount of capital input of enterprises, produce capital change effects, and thus trigger industrial expansion and upgrading [2]. Various studies have shown that the stock price of the capital market has a non-negligible impact on the investment development of enterprises. However, no scholars at home and abroad have conducted in-depth discussions on the relationship between stock price overestimation and enterprise digital transformation investment, especially for listed small and medium-sized enterprises whose stock prices have always been overvalued in China, what impact will stock price overestimation have on their digital transformation investment, and through what channels? At present, there is a lack of research in these areas. Therefore, this paper combines equity financing and rational pandering channel theory, and conducts an in-depth study of the influence relationship between stock price overvaluation and the digital transformation investment of listed SMEs in China, so as to provide reference and suggestions for promoting the digital transformation investment of listed SMEs.

2 Literature Review

2.1 Stock Price Overvaluation and Corporate Investment

According to past research, overvaluation of stock prices is usually caused by imperfect market mechanisms and irrational investors, and. Such as scholars Miller (1977), Meng and Huang (2018) based on research on European and Chinese capital markets, respectively, found evidence that short selling mechanisms affect the pricing efficiency of stock markets by reflecting investor sentiment [3, 4]; Further, Dong et al. (2020) analyzed the behavior of investors in European, American and domestic capital markets based on the assumption of limited investor cognition and limited decision-making, and found that the real capital market is full of a large number of irrational people, limited by various cognitive biases, these investors cannot make consistent and unbiased estimates of the market in a rational person's way, and cannot fully integrate all public information into the stock price in a timely manner, causing the stock price to deviate from its intrinsic value. Under the influence of restricted market arbitrage, it is difficult for stock market prices to quickly fall back to the real level, resulting in the phenomenon that stock prices deviate from their intrinsic value for a long time [5].

As the bridge connecting the real economy and the capital market, the impact of stock overvaluation on corporate investment is self-evident. Especially in recent years, the overvaluation of stock prices to stimulate the investment vitality of the real economy and promote the transformation and upgrading of the industrial structure has become a hot topic in financial research. In terms of investment, Baker and Wurgler (2002) found that stock fluctuations in the capital market affect companies' investment and financing decisions, and that listed companies generally have the behavior of choosing market timing, managers choose to issue new shares to raise funds when the stock price is overvalued, and buy back shares when the stock price is undervalued [6]. Based on this choice of market timing, Baker et al. (2003) put forward the view of equity financing channels, arguing that the cost of equity capital of a company is affected by market valuation, and the mispricing of stocks indirectly affects the company's investment through external financing cost factors [7]. Bakke and Whited (2010), Campello and Graham (2013) also obtained empirical evidence in their research that high financing constraint companies issue shares to raise funds for investment when stock prices are overvalued, and that low financing constraint companies' investment expenditures are not affected by irrational stock price movements, providing empirical support for equity financing channels [8, 9]. Compared with the view of equity financing channels, rational catering channels break through the framework constraints of enterprises needing to raise financing before investing, believing that even if enterprises do not have a thirst for funds, their investment decisions will still respond to investor sentiment. For example, Polk and Sapienza (2009) studied managers' pandering investment behavior from the perspective of external governance pressure, arguing that if managers do not make relevant investment decisions according to the expectations of short-sighted investors, investors will bring governance crises to companies through irrational behaviors such as shortening the holding period and frequently selling stocks in the short term [10]. Dong et al. (2020) also empirically tested the difference in the degree of market catering to the market by the investment decisions of different projects based on empirical evidence in the US capital market, and believed that because the uncertainty of R&D and innovation expenditure is greater, external investors will not be able to accurately judge the future growth of enterprises, so compared with fixed asset investment, the characteristics of enterprises using R&D expenditure to cater to investor sentiment are more significant [5].

2.2 Digital Transformation Investment of Enterprises

Enterprise digital transformation refers to the process of enterprises using digital technology to digitize all the physical information of various elements and processes of enterprises, promote the optimization of the allocation of human, technology, capital and other element resources, and promote the transformation of business processes and production methods. Previous studies have mostly discussed the impact of digital transformation on enterprise development from the perspective of enterprise transformation, such as the motivation, mechanism, path and effect of transformation. In fact, for enterprises undergoing digital transformation, one of the most urgent practical problems to solve is digital transformation investment. Promoting digital transformation requires a large amount of capital investment and precipitation costs, and managers must choose a scientific digital transformation path according to the characteristics of the industry, scale and technical advantages, and formulate reasonable investment plans. In terms of investment form, the research of early scholars on enterprise digital transformation investment mostly focuses on the deployment and upgrading of IT facilities, for example, some scholars used hardware investment and software investment to build enterprise digital investment indicators respectively, exploring the impact of enterprise digital transformation on improving manufacturing productivity. With the rise of the wave of cross-border integration between the real economy and the Internet virtual economy, enterprises started paying more attention to forming their own "soft power" by accumulating intangible assets in the process of digital transformation, and management information systems, manufacturing execution systems and cloud service platforms (IaaS, PaaS and SaaS) are becoming the main investment means for enterprises to implement digital transformation. Considering that the digital transformation process may include comprehensive investment in human, material, financial, intellectual and other aspects of enterprises, Zhang et al. (2021) used the characteristics of accounting treatment of intangible assets to propose the proportion of intangible assets related to digital transformation in the annual reports of listed enterprises to measure the level of digital investment of enterprises, and empirically examined the impact of digital transformation on audit pricing [11]. Some other scholars were inspired by the big data mining method of finance texts, and proposed to build a keyword dictionary driven and applied to the digital transformation of enterprises, and portrayed the degree of transformation from the perspective of word frequency statistics involving the digital transformation of enterprises in the annual reports of listed enterprises. They believed that the annual report of a listed company reflects the company's summary of the previous year's operation, and the more frequently a certain type of keyword appeared in the annual report, the more attention and resources the company usually invested in this regard.

3   Research Hypotheses

3.1   Overestimation of Share Price and Digital Transformation Capital Investment of Listed SMEs - Equity Financing Channels

Generally speaking, any large-scale investment activity of enterprises cannot be separated from the support of financing, and the successful realization of digital transformation depends to a large extent on whether enterprises can obtain sufficient funds through external financing. According to the view of equity financing channels, overvalued stock prices ease financing constraints by reducing the cost of corporate equity financing, thereby promoting corporate investment.

In the context of China's imperfect capital market mechanism and irrational investors, corporate stock prices are often overvalued, and because of the full understanding of enterprise business information, managers can often assess the true value of stocks more accurately than investors, so when the stock price is overvalued by the market, rational managers can make full use of the stock price information difference with investors to make financing decisions that are conducive to the investment needs of enterprises. In addition, from the perspective of the preference of enterprise financing methods, the digital transformation of enterprises has the characteristics of long investment cycle and slow results, and enterprises are bound to bear the operational risks caused by the imbalance of cost and income in the process of transformation, and the risk sharing mechanism of equity financing can more effectively help enterprises obtain sustainable financial support when short-term returns of technology research and development decline, so the connection between equity financing and enterprise digital transformation investment will be closer. Therefore, this paper proposes:

Hypothesis 1: The overvaluation of stock price has a positive effect on the digital transformation capital investment of SMEs through equity financing channels.

3.2   Overestimation of Share Price and Digital Transformation Capital Investment of Listed SMEs - Rational Catering Channel

Compared with equity financing channels, rational catering channels break through the framework constraints that enterprises need to raise financing before investing, and believe that even if there is no thirst for funds, managers of companies with overvalued stock prices will still make investments that cater to market expectations in order to balance external governance pressure. Previous studies have shown that stock price overvaluation is mostly caused by the irrational behavior of market investors, and this stock price overvaluation state is difficult to maintain stability, once investors are dissatisfied with the decline of the company's stock price, their chasing and killing behavior will bring many adverse effects to corporate governance, so when the stock price is overvalued, managers have an incentive to make investments that cater to market expectations in order to maintain or push up short-term stock prices. From a macro perspective, China's capital market still has problems such as imperfect information mechanism and strong speculative atmosphere, and investor sentiment is easily misled by market wind direction and imagination. In this case, external market investors can only judge the value of the enterprise and its development by observing the company's behavior, including investment. When managers realize this and stimulate investor optimism by exhibiting investment behaviors that are approved by investors, the company's stock price rises and vice versa. For example, in order to meet the needs of China's high-quality economic development, the government has issued a number of policies and regulations in recent years to encourage enterprises to carry out digital transformation, and many small and medium-sized investors in the capital market are also more willing to invest in such enterprises because of their positive expectations for digital transformation enterprises, which just provides an opportunity for managers to use digital transformation investment to cater to investor sentiment and inflate the company's stock price. Therefore, this paper proposes:

Hypothesis 2: The overvaluation of stock price has a positive effect on the digital transformation capital investment of SMEs through rational catering channels.

4   Research Design

4.1   Variable Selection

Interpreted variable. The explanatory variable of this paper is the degree of digital transformation investment of listed SMEs (*Digital*). Looking at the existing literature, the mainstream methods for quantifying enterprise digitalization indicators in academia at present include digital technology asset measurement method and big data text analysis method, that is, to measure the degree of enterprise digitalization from the two perspectives of the book value of digital technology related assets in the enterprise's financial report in the current year and word frequency statistics involving enterprise digitalization transformation. Whereas enterprises are accustomed to using investment projects such as management information system, manufacturing execution system and cloud service platform (IaaS, PaaS and SaaS) as the way to promote digital transformation, this paper starts from the perspective of digital technology asset measurement, and draws on the research experience of Zhang et al. (2021) and Chen et al. (2022), The proportion of the part of intangible assets related to digital transformation in the total intangible assets disclosed in the notes to the financial reports of listed enterprises at the end of the year is taken as the basis for measuring the capital investment indicators of enterprises in digital transformation [11, 12]. Specifically, when the detailed item of intangible assets includes keywords related to digital economy and technology such as "software", "network", "client", "management system", "intelligent platform", and related patents, the detailed item is marked as "enterprise digital transformation input". In order to ensure the accuracy of the screening, this paper also manually reviews the screened detailed items.

Explain variable. The explanatory variable of this paper is the overvaluation of stock prices (*Overv*). Drawing on the research of Rao and Yue (2012), Xu (2017), Liu and Xu(2019), we use the ratio of intrinsic value per share to market price (V/P) to measure the degree of overvaluation of stock prices of listed companies [13–15].

Specifically, in the V/P method, the intrinsic value per share of listed companies is calculated by the company's residual income model (RIM) in the next three years.

$$V_t = b_t + \frac{f(1)_t - r \times b_t}{(1 + r)} + \frac{f(2)_t - r \times b(1)_t}{(1 + r)^2} + \frac{f(3)_t - r \times b(2)_t}{(1 + r)^2 \times r} \tag{1}$$

where V_t is the intrinsic value per share, $f(x)_t (x = 1, 2, 3)$ is the company's earnings forecast by analysts, b_t is the carrying value of equity per share, and r is the company's cost of capital. Considering that different capital costs have little impact on the estimation of internal value, the capital cost is fixed at 5% by reference to the research of Liu and Xu (2019) [15]. In addition, considering the optimism, lagging and sample selection bias of analysts in China when forecasting company earnings, this paper uses the research of Hou et al. (2012) and Rao and Yue (2012) for reference to forecast analysts' earnings $f(x)_t$ is replaced by the earnings forecast estimated by the company's fundamental information [13, 16]. The specific prediction model is as follows:

$$Earnings_{i,t+j} = \alpha_0 + \alpha_1 Asset_{i,t} + \alpha_2 Dividend_{i,t} + \alpha_3 DD_{i,t} + \alpha_4 Earnings_{i,t} + \alpha_5 NegEn_{i,t} + \alpha_6 Accrual_{i,t} + \varepsilon_1 \tag{2}$$

Among them, $Earnings_{i,t+j}(j = 1, 2, 3)$ is the earnings per share of company i in the next j years, measured by dividing operating profit by total equity; $Asset_{i,t}$ and $Dividend_{i,t}$ represents total assets per share and cash dividends per share respectively; $DD_{i,t}$ is a dummy variable, representing whether to pay cash dividends; $Earnings_{i,t}$ Represents earnings per share for the year; $NegEn_{i,t}$ is a dummy variable, representing whether the company is losing money; $Accrual_{i,t}$ is an accrual per share, measured by the difference between operating profit and net cash flow from operating activities.

Compare the calculated intrinsic value V with the closing price P of the stock at the end of April of the next year to get V/P. As this paper only considers the situation of overvaluation of stock prices, only data samples with $V/P < 1$ are selected for research in subsequent studies. Considering that V/P is a reverse indicator, in order to correctly understand the empirical results, we construct the variable $Overv = |1 - V/P|$ to measure the degree of overvaluation of stock prices. The value range of $Overv$ is $(0, 1)$, and the larger the value is, the more serious the overvaluation of the listed company's share price is.

Intermediary variable. Drawing on the research of Baker (2003), Wang et al. (2018), this paper selects the ratio of the cash raised by the company's stock issuance in the current year to the total assets of the company at the beginning of the year as the proxy for equity financing channel strength ($Equity$) to test the equity financing channel [10, 12]; And combined with Polk, Sapienza (2009) and Zhu (2013)'s view that the more short-sighted investors are, the more likely they are to cause catering behavior of managers, this paper selects the annual average turnover rate of corporate stocks to measure the degree of investors' short-sightedness, which is used to test rational catering channels [11, 17].

Control variables. Referring to the existing literature on stock price overvaluation and digital transformation, set the following control variables: asset-liability ratio (Lev), individual stock return (Ret), enterprise size ($Size$), company growth ($Growth$), enterprise age (Age), dual power ($Dual$), number of analysts ($Coverage$). The specific calculation method is consistent with the above study and will not be repeated here. For the interpretation and measurement of the above variables, see Table 1.

Table 1. Variable definitions

Variable	Definition
Digital	The proportion of intangible assets related to digital transformation in the Company's annual report to the total intangible assets
Overv	$Overv = |1 - V/P|$.
Equity	Cash raised by issuing shares/total assets at the beginning of the year
Short	Measured by the average annual turnover rate of the company's stocks
Lev	The ratio of total liabilities to total assets at the end of the period
Ret	Annual stock yield
Size	The natural logarithm of the Company's total assets at the end of the year
Growth	The growth rate of the company's sales for the year
Age	The number of years since the establishment of the company
Share	Equity ratio of the largest shareholder
Coverage	The number of analysts (teams) who follow the company
Year	Control year fixed effect
Industry	Control industry fixed effects

4.2 Model Design

This paper studies the relationship between overvaluation of stock prices and the digital transformation investment of listed SMEs, and examines the influence of equity financing channels and rational catering channels. Therefore, referring to the research of Wen and Ye (2014) [18], this paper has designed four models to test the impact mechanism of stock price overvaluation on the digital transformation investment of listed SMEs: Model (3) only controls the year and industry fixed effects, and examines the impact of stock price overestimation on the digital transformation capital investment of listed SMEs; Model (4) adds the complete set of control variables for further testing; Model (5) replaces the original explanatory variable (Digital) with an intermediary variable (Path) on the basis of model (4) to test the impact of stock price overvaluation on equity financing and investor short-sightedness. Model (6) introduces channel variables (Path) on the basis of model (4) to test the path effect of equity financing and rational catering channels on the relationship between overvaluation of stock prices and digital transformation investment of listed SMEs. In order to reduce the endogenous impact of corporate investment and financing behavior in the equity financing channel on the current stock price volatility, this paper deals with the over valuation of independent variable stock price and channel variable (Path) for a period of delay, to reflect the authenticity and rationality of the experiment.

$$Digital_t = \beta_0 + \beta_1 \, over \, v_{t-1} + Year + Industry + \varepsilon_t \tag{3}$$

$$Digital_t = \beta_2 + \beta_3 Over \, v_{t-1} + \beta_4 Contrals_t + \varepsilon_t \tag{4}$$

$$Path_{t-1} = \beta_5 + \beta_6 Overv_{t-1} + \beta_7 Contrals_t + \varepsilon_t \tag{5}$$

$$Digital_t = \beta_8 + \beta_9 Overv_{t-1} + \beta_{10} Path_{t-1} + \beta_{11} Contrals_t + \varepsilon_t \tag{6}$$

In the model, *Contrals* represents the collection of all control variables, and *Path* is replaced by *Equity* and *Short*.

4.3 Sample Selection and Data Sources

This paper uses the data of listed companies on China's SME Board and GEM from 2013 to 2019 as a sample to study the relationship between overvaluation of stock prices and the digital transformation investment of listed SMEs. The data is mainly derived from CSMAR database, enterprise annual reports, Sina Finance Network, etc., among which the digital transformation capital investment index is measured by the proportion of intangible assets related to digital transformation in the annual reports of listed enterprises with reference to the research of Zhang et al. (2021) and Chen et al. (2022). The process of collating the research data as follows: exclude the serious lack of data and ST and *ST and listed companies in the financial and insurance industry, and exclude the sample of undervalued stock prices. A total of 7129 sets of year-company sample observations were obtained. In order to exclude the interference of some extreme values on the experimental results, the relevant continuous variables were also shrunk by 1% and 99%.

5 Empirical Analysis and Testing

5.1 Regression Results and Analysis

In this paper, regression tests are carried out on the relevant variables according to the regression model designed above, and the regression results are shown in Table 3. Column (1) shows the regression coefficient results of the digital transformation capital investment variable (*Digital*) and the stock price overvalued variable (*Overv*) when only controlling for the industry and year fixed effect; After adding the complete set of control variables, the regression coefficient result of the overvalued variable (*Overv*) in column (2) is 0.037, which is significant at the confidence level of 1%, indicating that the overvaluation of stock price plays a significant positive role in promoting the capital investment of digital transformation of listed SMEs. In order to further examine the mechanism path of the impact of overvaluation of stock prices on SMEs' digital transformation investment, based on the mediation effect testing method proposed by Wen and Ye (2014) [18], and combined with the research of predecessors, this paper selects two proxy variables, equity financing and investor short-sightedness, respectively, to test equity financing channels and rational catering channels.

According to the results of columns (2), (3) and (4) in Table 2, after adding equity financing variable (*Equity*) to the model, the coefficients of stock price overestimation (*Overv*) and equity financing (*Equity*) are significantly positive, indicating that the impact of stock price overvaluation on promoting the digital transformation investment of SMEs

Table 2. Regression results

	(1)	(2)	(3)	(4)	(5)	(6)
	$LnDigital_{t+1}$	$LnDigital_{t+1}$	Equity	$LnDigital_{t+1}$	Short	$LnDigital_{t+1}$
Overv	0.054^{***}	0.037^{***}	0.153^{***}	0.034^{***}	1.207^{***}	0.038^{***}
	(0.009)	(0.011)	(0.007)	(0.011)	(0.096)	(0.011)
Equity				0.071^{***}		
				(0.023)		
Short						0.021
						(0.017)
Controls	No	Yes	Yes	Yes	Yes	Yes
N	7129	7129	7129	7129	7129	7129
r2	0.301	0.311	0.519	0.311	0.375	0.311

$^{*}p < 0.1$, $^{**}p < 0.05$, $^{***}p < 0.01$, Standard errors in parentheses

has a partial intermediary effect on equity financing channels, that is, equity financing channels are established, hypothesis1 is certified.

According to the results of columns (2), (5) and (6) in Table 3, after adding the investor short-sighted variable (*Short*) to the model, the coefficient of stock price overvaluation is still significantly positive, but the coefficient of the short-sighted variable of investors is not significant. In order to confirm the existence of rational pandering channels, this paper did 1000 Bootstrap sampling tests with reversion of relevant variables. The test results are shown in Table 3, and the confidence interval for indirect effects includes 0, indicating that there is no intermediary effect, and the overvaluation of stock prices does not affect the digital transformation investment of SMEs through rational catering channels, and hypothesis 2 is not valid. This is similar to the conclusion reached by Xiao and Qu (2012) in their study on the impact of stock price overvaluation on firms' R&D investment [19]. This shows that the uncertainty, risk, and lagging returns of digital transformation may have been investors' enthusiasm for buying stocks to a certain extent, so the effect of managers catering to the needs of short-sighted investors and achieving the purpose of maintaining or pushing up short-term stock prices is not significant.

Table 3. Bootstrap sampling inspection results

	Observed coefficient		Bias	Bootstrap		
				std. err.	[95% conf .interval]	
_bs_1 : r(ind_eff)	−0.0002	0.0002	0.0020	−0.0045	0.0045	(P)
				−0.0096	0.0016	(BC)
_bs_2 : r(dir_eff)	0.0036	0.0081	0.0175	−0.0040	0.0624	(P)
				−0.0044	0.0540	(BC)

P: Percentile, BC: Bias-corrected

5.2 Robustness Test

In order to verify the reliability of the empirical conclusions, this paper draws on the research of other scholars, and uses text analysis to re-measure the capital investment of SMEs in digital transformation for robustness analysis, and the variable acquisition method in this paper is the same as that of Wu Fei et al. (2021), specific procedures are omitted here. The regression result show that the impact of overvaluation on the digital transformation investment of SMEs is still positive, and equity financing channels are established. The rational pandering channel still failed the 1,000 Bootstrap sampling tests with replay, which is consistent with the above results.

Due to space limitations, this article does not show the robustness test results and is retained for future reference.

6 Conclusion

Based on the investment perspective, this paper takes the data of listed companies on China's SME board and GEM from 2013 to 2019 as the research sample, and conducts impact analysis and path test on the relationship between overvaluation of stock prices and digital transformation input of listed SMEs. Overall, the results of this paper support the equity financing channel hypothesis that overvaluation of stock prices promotes the capital investment of digital transformation of listed SMEs, but does not support the rational catering channel hypothesis.

The research conclusions of this paper have strong practical and theoretical significance. On the one hand, based on real data samples, this paper analyzes the impact analysis and path test on the relationship between stock price overvaluation and digital transformation capital investment of listed SMEs from the empirical level, verifies the existence of equity financing channels, and enriches the theoretical research on the fields related to stock price overvaluation and digital transformation of SMEs. On the other hand, currently listed SMEs in China are generally facing the problem of insufficient investment in the process of digital transformation, and the research conclusion of this paper shows that overvaluation of stock prices can reduce the cost of equity financing of enterprises and actively create investment opportunities for digital transformation of enterprises. From this point of view, the research conclusions of this paper provide reference ideas for promoting the digital transformation investment of listed small and medium-sized enterprises in China.

References

1. Liu, S., Yan, J., Zhang, S., Lin, H.: Can the digital transformation of enterprise management improve the efficiency of input and output. Manag. World 37(05), 170–190+13 (2021)
2. Lu, R., Jing, H., Cui, X.: Econ. Res. J. 52(11), 104-118 (2017)
3. Miller, E.M.: Risk, uncertainty, and divergence of opinion. J. Financ. 32(4), 1151–1168 (1977)
4. Meng, Q., Huang, Q.: Does the short selling mechanism reduce the overvaluation of the stock price? J. Manag. Sci. 21(04), 43–66 (2018)
5. Dong, M., David, H., Hong, T.S.: Misvaluation and corporate inventiveness. J. Finan. Quant. Anal. 56(8) (2020)

6. Baker, M., Wurgler, J.: Market timing and capital structure. J. Finan. **57**(1) (2002)
7. Baker, M., Stein, J.C., Wurgler, J.: When does the market matter? stock prices and the investment of equity-dependent firms. Q. J. Econ. **118**(3) (2003)
8. Bakke, T.-E., Whited, T.M.: Which firms follow the market? an analysis of corporate investment decisions. Rev. Finan. Stud. **23**(5) (2010)
9. Campello, M., Graham, J.R.: Do stock prices influence corporate decisions? evidence from the technology bubble. J. Finan. Econ. **107**(1) (2013)
10. Polk, C., Sapienza, P.: The stock market and corporate investment: a test of catering theory. Rev. Financ. Stud. **22**, 187–217 (2009)
11. Zhang, Y., Li, X., Xing, M.: Enterprise digital transformation and audit pricing. Audit Res. **03**, 62–71 (2021)
12. Chen, Z., Jiang, K., Yin, M.: Can digital transformation alleviate the "expensive financing" of enterprises. Econ. Dyn. **08**, 79–97 (2022)
13. Rao, P., Yue, H.: Residual income model and future return of stocks. Account. Res. (09), 52–58+97 (2012)
14. Xu, S.: Do equity incentives reinforce management's motivation to cater to them? evidence from R&D investment by listed companies. Econ. Manag. **39**(06), 178–193 (2017)
15. Li, J., Xu, L.: Capital market mispricing, financing constraints and corporate financing mode selection. J. Financ. Res. **12**, 113–129 (2015)
16. Hou, K., Dijk, M., Zhang, Y.: The implied cost of capital: a new approach. J. Account. Econ. **53**(3), 504–526 (2012)
17. Zhu, Z.: Investor sentiment and investment decisions of listed companies: a study based on catering channels. J. Bus. Econ. Manag. (06), 60–67+85 (2013)
18. Wen, Z., Ye, B.: Mediation effect analysis: method and model development. Adv. Psychol. Sci. **22**(05), 731–745 (2014)
19. Xiao, H., Qu, X.: R&D investment pandering behavior: rational catering channels and equity financing channels? based on empirical evidence of Chinese listed companies. Account. Res. (02), 42–49+96 (2012)

A Tripartite View on Performance Matrices of Live Commerce

Ruihao Li[1], Qian Wang[1], Xinlin Yao[2(⊠)], Xixi Li[1], and Xiangbin Yan[1]

[1] School of Economics and Management, University of Science and Technology Beijing, Beijing, China
[2] Business School, Nankai University, Tianjin, China
xinlinyao@nankai.edu.cn

Abstract. Live commerce is a novel form of social commerce in which streamers engage following fans through real-time interactions and deliver vivid presentation of products. We propose a tripartite view of the core elements in the live commerce context, including streamers as sellers, following fans as consumers, and streaming videos of product demonstration, that potentially affect live commerce performance matrices in terms of sales volume, sales efficiency, and fan growth number. We analyzed an archival data of 373 livestreaming shopping shows with 34925 products collected during Double 11 Day of 2020 on Taobao Live, one of the largest live commerce platforms in China. The empirical analysis reveals that: (1) *streamers'* social capital positively affected sales volume and sales efficiency, but negatively impacted fan growth number; (2) *following fans'* engagement promoted sales volume, sales efficiency, and fan growth number; (3) *products'* live demonstration increased sales volume, decreased sales efficiency, but did not affect fan growth number. Our research offers nuanced understandings of how the three elements of streamers, fans, and product streaming videos affect performance matrices of live commerce.

Keywords: Live Commerce · Streamers' Social Capital · Following Fans' Engagement · Products' live Demonstration · Product Sales Volume · Product Sales Efficiency · Fan Growth Number

1 Research Motivation

Live commerce is a rapidly growing phenomenon that integrates live streaming technology and e-commerce. Platforms such as Taobao Live, TikTok, and Kuaishou have garnered immense popularity in China, with approximately 841 million people shopping online as of June 2022, of which 469 million engage in live commerce, accounting for over half of the total online shoppers [1]. Furthermore, the market value of live commerce in China has skyrocketed from RMB ¥120 billion in 2018 to RMB ¥2.27 trillion in 2021, with a projected value of RMB ¥4.9 trillion by 2023 [2]. However, live commerce is facing practical challenges as stakeholders focus on different performances matrices. Streamers, for instance, may run their businesses in various ways, including soliciting donations, subscriptions, and product sales from their followers [4]. Nonetheless, they may give less consideration to the sales per unit time which could lead to suboptimal sales performance. Consumers, on the other hand, may concentrate on interactions with streamers and other consumers by prioritizing the number of followers over product quality, potentially leading to irrational shopping behavior [5]. Furthermore, live platforms struggle to balance the interests of streamers and consumers, given the extreme skewness of streamer popularity distribution, which implies that viewers may watch unpopular but interesting live shows alongside popular ones [4]. To address these challenges, a comprehensive perspective is required to observe the different performance matrices in live commerce. Therefore, this research aims to adopt a tripartite view to examine the influence of streamers, consumers, and products on performance matrices in live commerce. By exploring how these three factors interact, we aim to develop a deeper understanding of the dynamics of live commerce and identify ways to balance the interests of all stakeholders for a healthy and sustainable live commerce ecosystem.

While live commerce has generated much interest from managers and scholars, research on the topic remains in its preliminary stages [3]. Extant research on live commerce has primarily focused on investigating the impacts of one or two perspectives, such as streamers, consumers, and products, on purchases or sales. For instance, Chen et al. and Kang et al. examined the impact of streamers' interactivity on purchase intention and consumers' engagement behaviors [6, 7], While Bründl et al. and Yu et al. examined the effect of viewers' engagement and behaviors on gift paying and subscriptions [8, 9]. Additionally, Lu and Chen investigated the impact of the similarity between streamers and consumers on purchase intention [10] whereas Gao et al. and Chen et al. focused on the influence of streamers' and products' factors on consumers' purchase intention [11, 12]. Despite these previous contributions, there is a dearth of literature that simultaneously considers the interplay between the three critical roles of streamers, consumers, and products in live commerce. Therefore, the aim of this study is to provide a more comprehensive understanding of the interplay between streamers, consumers, and products and their impact on performance metrics in live commerce.

To summarize, the objective of this research is to provide a comprehensive understanding of the fundamental components of live commerce, including streamers as sellers, following fans as consumers, and streaming videos of product demonstrations, and to investigate their impact on performance metrics in live commerce, such as sales volume, sales efficiency, and fan growth number. Our study explores the mechanism by which streamer, following fan, and product factors influence performance metrics in live commerce and offer practical recommendations for streamers, platforms, and other stakeholders involved in live commerce. To achieve this goal, we collaborated with an electronic commerce company to collect data and conducted an empirical analysis to test our proposed model.

2   A Tripartite View on Performance Matrices in Live Commerce

The advent of web 2.0 technology and the outbreak of the COVID-19 pandemic have dramatically transformed the traditional shopping patterns of people, leading to the emergence of a new trend in e-commerce, known as live commerce [13]. Live commerce is a novel form of social commerce that leverages live streaming technology to facilitate social interaction between sellers and buyers [14, 15]. Compared to conventional e-commerce, live commerce exhibits several unique features that make it stand out. For example, live streaming technology enables streamers to showcase the appearance and features of a product in a comprehensive manner, providing consumers with abundant product information and demonstrations in video format [10]. Moreover, consumers can engage in real-time interaction with streamers by sending bullet messages and obtaining targeted responses without leaving the product page [16]. These features not only satisfy users' demands for product information but also enhance the chance of transaction success during the live session [17]. As a result, live commerce has gained immense popularity among consumers and has become a rapidly expanding sector in the e-commerce industry. The success of live commerce can be attributed to its ability to offer an immersive and interactive shopping experience, which not only enhances consumers' confidence in making purchase decisions but also creates a sense of community among buyers and sellers. Furthermore, live commerce enables sellers to develop a loyal fan base, who can provide valuable feedback and recommendations to improve the product and the shopping experience. Overall, the emergence of live commerce has transformed the e-commerce landscape, offering a new way for consumers to shop and interact with sellers. As such, there is a growing need to understand the underlying mechanisms and factors that contribute to the success of live commerce.

In our research, we develop a framework that consists of three performance matrices to evaluate the effectiveness of live commerce, namely sales volume, sales efficiency, and fan growth number. *Sales volume* is a crucial indicator the performance of a live session. Given the massive user traffic, live commerce has the potential to generate high purchasing power, and its sales effect surpasses that of other sales patterns. However, the sales volume can significantly vary among different streamers, and even the same streamer's sales volume of different products can fluctuate widely. Scholars have denoted significant attention to this point and explored various influencing factors. For example, Bharadwaj et al. identified that the streamer's facial emotions have negative effects on sales [18]. Luo et al. examined the impact of streamers' linguistic persuasive styles on sales [19]. Additionally, Luo, Chen, and Zhou uncovered the influence of live streaming room factors on sales [20]. *Sales efficiency* represents the ratio of product sales to the number of potential consumers reached during a live session. Previous researches have demonstrated that e-commerce can improve sales efficiency [21]. Moreover, the sales efficiency of a product can affect manufacturers' selection of sales patterns [22, 23]. However, it is unclear whether live commerce can enhance sales efficiency and what the underlying factors are. *Fan growth number* reflects the degree of audience attraction to streamers' products demonstration and interactions with their audiences [24]. It signifies the transformation of consumers from being interested in the content to becoming fans of the streamers. Fan growth number is a critical indicators of the streamers' overall performance, but few studies have focused on this variable. Therefore, we regard the three elements of live commerce performance matrices as the dependent variable of our study.

In our research, we present a tripartite view of the core elements in the context of live commerce. These elements include streamers as sellers, following fans as consumers, and streaming videos of product demonstrations. We investigate how these elements influence the performance matrices in live commerce (see Fig. 1). We specifically focus on the influence of streamers' social capital, consumer engagement, and product demonstration on sales volume, sales efficiency, and fan growth number. *Streamers'* social capital is a significant variable that is rooted in the structure of social relationship network between streamers and their followers [25]. It reflects the status and identity that streamers occupy in their social network [26]. In the context of live commerce, streamers play a crucial role in connecting consumers with products. As such, their social capital can influence the audience's perception of the product, thereby affecting their purchase decision [27]. Consumer engagement is another important factor in live commerce. It refers to the level of interaction and connection that consumers have with a seller's products or activities [16]. In live commerce, consumers engage with the streamer through live chat and by using "like" function to express their feelings. They can also ask questions about product information and receive useful answers to help them make better choices [28]. While previous research has examined the antecedents of consumer engagement, such as trust [29], perceived value [16], and bonds, [30] few studies have investigated its consequences. In our research, we consider consumer engagement as an important antecedent and examine its effect on the performance matrices. We measure *following fans'* engagement by analyzing the number of "like"s and bullet messages [31]. In addition, numerous studies have focused on the impact of product attributes on consumers' purchase intention. For instance, some researchers have investigated the effect of product quality and brand on purchase intention [12], while others have examined the influence of product physical and value similarities [10]; and Gao et al. focused on how product information completeness, accuracy, and currency affected purchase intention [11]. In the context of live commerce, consumers mainly obtain product information through products' demonstration. The richness and accuracy of the information can be reflected by the length of product demonstration. Therefore, in our research, we investigate the

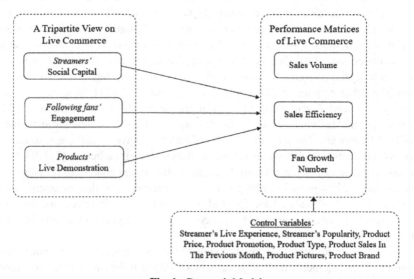

Fig. 1. Research Model

effect of *product's* live demonstration on performance matrices such as sales volume, sales efficiency, and fan growth number.

3 Data and Variables

The present study utilizes data collected from Taobao Live in order to investigate our research model. Taobao, the largest online shopping platform in China, boasts a monthly active mobile shopping user base of nearly 1.1 billion as of July 2022. Of these users, Taobao accounts for approximately 80%, with an active user count of 875 million [32]. Since 2016, Taobao has been a key player in the live commerce market, with its Gross Merchandise Volume (GMV) reaching RMB ¥720 billion by the close of 2021, and its transaction volume is continuing to grow [33]. Moreover, Taobao is responsible for the inception of "Double Eleven", the world's largest shopping festival, in 2009. During the two-week shopping extravaganza that took place until November 11, 2021, Taobao generated RMB ¥513.3 billion in transactions [34]. These factors make Taobao Live a valuable data source for our research.

To gather the necessary data for our analysis, we collaborated with an electronic commerce company and obtained 48431 product sales records from 386 Taobao streamers' live shows that took place on November 11, 2020. The data collected provided comprehensive information on streamers, consumers, and products, including details such as streamers' fan counts, the volume of bullet messages and "likes", product titles, and time. To ensure the validity of our data, we carefully scrutinized the records and deleted data related to products that had been removed from Taobao during the analysis period. We also excluded records with abnormal information regarding coupons and links to lottery winners. Furthermore, we eliminated records for products with demonstration video lengths that were either too short or too long. As a result, we retained 34925 valid observations for 373 Taobao streamers' live shows in our analysis. These steps were taken to ensure that our data was both accurate and reliable for our research purposes.

First, the live commerce performance matrices of interest in our study included sales volume, sales efficiency, and fan growth number. Sales volume is defined as the number of products sold during a live session, while fan growth number refers to the change in the number of streamers' followers before and after the live session. We also measured the sales efficiency of each product, which represents the product's sales volume per minute. To calculate the sales efficiency, we divided the sales volume of a product sold during the live session by the length of the live session.

Second, three key independent variables are *streamers'* social capital, *following fans'* engagement, and *products'* live demonstration. As previously mentioned, social capital refers to an individual's or group's social relationship network and the benefits generated by utilizing the network [35]. In the context of live commerce, streamers have their own social network of followers, which enables them to leverage the power of their followers to promote their live content and increase product sales. Therefore, we used the number of followers to measure *streamers'* social capital. Taobao Live provides real-time chat and "like" functions for consumers, allowing them engage with streamers during their live broadcast by sending bullet messages and giving "like". Consequently, we measured the *following fans'* engagement by dividing the number of bullet messages and "like"s by the number of products broadcasted during the live session. Our collected data contained information on the start time of a product's demonstration and the next product's demonstration, allowing us to calculate the video length (in minutes) of a particular product demonstrated in a live session to measure *products'* live demonstration.

Finally, to ensure the robustness and accuracy of our analysis, we included several control variables related to streamers and products. These control variables included streamers' live experience, streamers' popularity, product price, product promotion, product type, product sales in the previous month, product pictures, and product brand. Our data collection and measurement techniques were carefully chosen to ensure the validity and reliability of our findings, making our study a valuable contribution to the field of live commerce research.

Table 1 displays the descriptive statistics of our sample. It is worth noting that the continuous variables, except for promotion, are highly skewed, which suggests that a log transformation may be necessary in our regression analysis. However, the minimum value of fan growth number is negative and cannot be transformed logarithmically. Therefore, we standardized fan growth number and other continuous variables after the logarithm to address this issue.

Table 1. Descriptive Statistics

Variable	Mean	Std	Min	Max
Sales	547.590	4573.177	0	266400
Efficiency	780.131	15561.117	0	1982748.092
FanNum	−30112.980	532527.493	− 7707000	6984000
Capital	5834451.052	7961203.582	0	42736000
Engage	1432.113	12616.512	0	325315.661
Demo	3.795	8.684	0.103	199.967
Exp	723.210	421.627	0	2484
Pop	0.130	0.332	0	1
Price	1693.408	12757.779	0.010	999999
Prom	0.382	0.267	0	0.999
Type	0.800	0.400	0	1
Priorsales	86216.624	554334.784	0	20316300
Pic	5.510	0.754	1	11
Brand	0.160	0.371	0	1

Note: Sales: sales volume; Efficiency: sales efficiency; FanNum: fan growth number; Capital: *streamers'* social capital; Engage: *following fans'* engagement; Demo: products' live demonstration; Exp: streamers' live experience; Pop: streamers' popularity; Price: product price; Prom: product promotion; Type: product type; Priorsales: product sales in the previous month; Pic: product pictures; Brand: product brand

4 Regression Model and Results

We used Stata 17.0 software to test our conceptual model. Since that our research model had three dependent variables, we built three models separately (model 1 for sales volume, model 2 for sales efficiency, and model 3 for fan growth number). Our modeling formulas were described as follows:

$$\log(\text{Sales}) = \beta_0 + \beta_1\log(\text{capital}) + \beta_2\log(\text{Engage}) + \beta_3\log(\text{Demo}) + \beta_4\log(\text{Exp})$$
$$+ \beta_5\text{Pop} + \beta_6\log(\text{Price}) + \beta_7\text{Brom} + \beta_8\text{Type} + \beta_9\log(\text{Priorsales}) + \beta_{10}\log(\text{Pic}) + \beta_{11}\text{Brand} + \varepsilon \quad (1)$$

$$\log(\text{Efficiency}) = \beta_0 + \beta_1\log(\text{capital}) + \beta_2\log(\text{Engage}) + \beta_3\log(\text{Demo}) + \beta_4\log(\text{Exp})$$
$$+ \beta_5\text{Pop} + \beta_6\log(\text{Price}) + \beta_7\text{Brom} + \beta_8\text{Type} + \beta_9\log(\text{Priorsales}) + \beta_{10}\log(\text{Pic}) + \beta_{11}\text{Brand} + \varepsilon \quad (2)$$

$$\text{FanNum} = \beta_0 + \beta_1\log(\text{capital}) + \beta_2\log(\text{Engage}) + \beta_3\log(\text{Demo}) + \beta_4\log(\text{Exp})$$
$$+ \beta_5\text{Pop} + \beta_6\log(\text{Price}) + \beta_7\text{Brom} + \beta_8\text{Type} + \beta_9\log(\text{Priorsales}) + \beta_{10}\log(\text{Pic}) + \beta_{11}\text{Brand} + \varepsilon \quad (3)$$

In the above three equations, sales (sales volume), sales efficiency (Efficiency), and fan growth number (FanNum) are dependent variables. *Streamers'* social capital (Capital), *following fans'* engagement (Engagement), and *products'* live demonstration (Demo) are key independent variables reflecting a tripartite view of the core elements in the live commerce context (sellers, consumers, and products). As for control variables, streamers' live streaming experience (Exp) and streamers' popularity (Pop) are seller-related control variables. Product price (Price), product promotion (Prom), product type (Type), product sales in the previous month (Priorsales), product pictures (Pic), and product brand (Brand) are product-related control variables.

Table 2 shows the model regression results. Model 1 examines the effects of *streamers'* social capital, *following fans'* engagement, and *products'* live demonstration on sales volume. Model 2 examines their influence on sales efficiency, and model 3 tests their impact on fan growth number. In each model, we first built a baseline model which contained only control variables. Then we added our three key independent variables to pinpoint their effect on the dependent variable. All three models show some interesting results. In Model 1, *streamers'* social capital ($\beta_1 = 0.055^*$, $p < 0.1$), *following fans'* engagement ($\beta_2 = 0.170^{***}$, $p < 0.01$), and *products'* live demonstration ($\beta_3 = 0.048^{***}$, $p < 0.01$) were all positively related to sales volume. In Model 2, *streamers'* social capital ($\beta_1 = 0.058^*$, $p < 0.1$) and *following fans'* engagement ($\beta_2 = 0.172^{***}$, $p < 0.01$) also had positive effects on sales efficiency, whereas *products'* live demonstration ($\beta_3 = -0.173^{***}$, $p < 0.01$) had a negative impact on sales efficiency. In Model 3, we found that *streamers'* social capital ($\beta_1 = -0.547^{**}$, $p < 0.05$) had a negative effect on fan growth number whereas *following fans'* engagement ($\beta_2 = 0.098^{**}$, $p < 0.05$) had a positive influence on it. *Products'* live demonstration ($\beta_3 = -0.028$, $p > 0.1$) had no significant influence on fan growth number.

Table 2. Regression Results

Variable	Model 1 (DV: Sales)		Model 2 (DV: Efficiency)		Model 3 (DV: FanNum)	
	(a)	(b)	(a)	(b)	(a)	(b)
Capital		0.055*(0.056)		0.058*(0.050)		− 0.547**(0.024)
Engage		0.170***(0.000)		0.172***(0.000)		0.098**(0.040)
Demo		0.048***(0.001)		− 0.173***(0.000)		− 0.028 (0.632)
Exp	− 0.008 (0.618)	− 0.013 (0.364)	− 0.044**(0.019)	− 0.035 (0.057)	− 0.094 (0.184)	− 0.037 (0.609)
Pop	0.226**(0.012)	0.005 (0.957)	0.305***(0.000)	0.006 (0.944)	0.140*(0.065)	0.983*(0.011)
Price	− 0.070***(0.000)	− 0.077***(0.000)	− 0.089***(0.000)	− 0.085***(0.000)	− 0.021 (0.644)	0.052 (0.127)
Prom	0.059***(0.001)	0.054***(0.000)	0.070***(0.001)	0.056***(0.003)	− 0.014 (0.819)	− 0.031 (0.613)
Type	0.145***(0.001)	0.146***(0.000)	0.100**(0.021)	0.106***(0.008)	− 0.162*(0.078)	− 0.018 (0.864)
Priorsales	0.611***(0.000)	0.589***(0.000)	0.559***(0.000)	0.578***(0.000)	0.018(0.552)	0.045(0.130)
Pic	0.014(0.179)	0.027***(0.004)	0.018*(0.088)	0.020***(0.046)	0.033(0.257)	0.025(0.378)
Brand	0.069(0.181)	0.016(0.675)	0.028(0.627)	0.0110.799)	0.022(0.866)	0.021(0.863)
R^2	45.00%	48.00%	41.19%	45.07%	4.94%	22.58%

Note: Sales: sales volume; Efficiency: sales efficiency; FanNum: fan growth number; Capital: *streamers'* social capital; Engage: *following fans'* engagement; Demo: *products'* live demonstration; Exp: streamers' live experience; Pop: streamers' popularity; Price: product price; Prom: product promotion; Type: product type; Priorsales: product sales in the previous month; Pic: product picture; Brand: product brand. p-values in parentheses, *** p < 0.01; ** p < 0.05; * p < 0.1

5 Discussions

Our research provides valuable insights into the performance matrices of live commerce by presenting a comprehensive tripartite view of the key elements that influence these metrics. To empirically examine the impact of streamers' social capital, consumer engagement, and product demonstration on sales volume, sales efficiency, and fan growth number, we analyzed a large dataset of 34,925 product sales records. Our findings indicate that *streamers'* social capital has a positive impact on both sales volume and sales efficiency. However, it negatively affects fan growth number. On the other hand, *following fans'* engagement plays a crucial role in promoting sales volume, sales efficiency, and fan growth number. This highlights the importance of fostering engagement between streamers and their followers in the live commerce context. Furthermore, our analysis reveals that *products'* live demonstration has a significant impact on sales volume but not on fan growth number. Specifically, product demonstration increases sales volume but decreases sales efficiency. This implies that while product demonstration can generate more sales, it may also prolong the purchasing process and reduce efficiency.

Our research contributes to the existing literature in several ways. Firstly, while prior literature have focused on exploring the perspectives of either streamers, consumers, and products [6, 8, 10, 11]. Our study offers a more comprehensive research model that considers all three elements in the live commerce context. This enables us to provide a more holistic view of the factors that influence the performance of live commerce platforms. Secondly, previous research has mainly focused on identifying the antecedents of sales or purchases [12, 18], neglecting the importance of sales efficiency or fan growth number. In contrast, our study examines the impact of streamers' social capital, consumer engagement, and product demonstration on all three performance matrices, providing a more nuanced understanding of the factors that contribute to the success of live commerce platforms. Thirdly, our study sheds new light on the relationship between streamers' social capital and fan growth number. Contrary to the widely held belief that a higher social capital leads to more followers, we find that *streamers'* social capital has a negative impact on fan growth number. This suggests that there may not be a Matthew effect in the live commerce context, challenging conventional wisdom in this area. Despite these contributions, our study is not without limitation. For instance, we only examine the linear relationship between variables, which may not capture the complexity of the interactions between streamers, consumers, and products. Further study can explore the non-linear relationships and attempt to identify the boundaries of moderate effects, such as the impact of different streamer or product types on the performance matrices. Overall, our research provides valuable insights into the factors that drive the performance of live commerce platforms and highlights areas for further investigation.

Our study yields practical implications for both streamers and platforms. First, our findings suggest that *streamers'* social capital has a negative impact on fan growth number, indicating that maintaining followers' attention becomes increasingly challenging as a streamer's follower count grows. Therefore, live platforms need not be concerned that highly popular streamers will disrupt the live commerce ecosystem, but should focus on enhancing consumers' viewing experience. Second, we find that *following fans'* engagement is positively associated with sales volume, sales efficiency, and fan growth number, while *products'* demonstration has a positive effect on sales volume but negatively impacts sales efficiency. To address this issue, streamers must not only manage the duration of product demonstrations, but also strive to enhance the efficiency of their sales pitch during demonstrations. Furthermore, they should frequently interact with consumers during live commerce sessions by asking questions and responding to bullet messages, which could also enhance the level of engagement and satisfaction of their following fans.

Acknowledgement. This research was supported by the National Natural Science Foundation of China under Grant 72002103, 72025101.

References

1. China Internet Network Information Center: The 50th Statistical Report on Internet Development in China. http://www.cnnic.net.cn/n4/2022/0914/c88-10226.html. Accessed 27 Dec 2022
2. Ma, Y.: Market value of live commerce in China 2018–2023. https://www.statista.com/statistics/1127635/china-market-size-of-live-commerce/. Accessed 27 Dec 2022
3. Zhang, M., Liu, Y., Wang, Y., Zhao, L.: How to retain customers: understanding the role of trust in live streaming commerce with a socio-technical perspective. Comput. Hum. Behav. **127**, 107052 (2022)
4. Zhao, K., Hu, Y., Hong, Y., et al.: Understanding characteristics of popular streamers on live streaming platforms: evidence from Twitch.tv. J. Assoc. Inf. Syst. **22**(4), 1076–1098 (2021)
5. Zhou, J.L., Zhou, J., Ding, Y., et al.: The magic of danmaku: a social interaction perspective of gift sending on live streaming platforms. Electron. Commer. Res. Appl. **34**, 100815 (2019)
6. Chen, H., Zhang, S., Shao, B., Gao, W., Xu, Y.: How do interpersonal interaction factors affect buyers' purchase intention in live stream shopping? the mediating effects of swift Guanxi. Internet Res. **32**(1), 335–361 (2022)
7. Kang, K., Lu, J., Guo, L., Li, W.: The dynamic effect of interactivity on customer engagement behavior through tie strength: evidence from live streaming commerce platforms. Int. J. Inf. Manage. **56**, 102251 (2021)
8. Bründl, S., Matt, C., Hess, T., Engert, S.: How synchronous participation affects the willingness to subscribe to social live streaming services: the role of co-interactive behavior on Twitch. Euro. J. Inf. Syst. 1–18 (2022)
9. Yu, E., Jung, C., Kim, H., Jung, J.: Impact of viewer engagement on gift-giving in live video streaming. Telematics Inform. **35**(5), 1450–1460 (2018)
10. Lu, B., Chen, Z.: Live streaming commerce and consumers' purchase intention: an uncertainty reduction perspective. Inf. Manag. **58**, 103509 (2021)
11. Gao, X., Xu, X.Y., Tayyab, S.M.U., Li, Q.: How the live streaming commerce viewers process the persuasive message: an ELM perspective and the moderating effect of mindfulness. Electron. Commer. Res. Appl. **49**, 101087 (2021)
12. Chen, C.D., Zhao, Q., Wang, J.L.: How livestreaming increases product sales: role of trust transfer and elaboration likelihood model. Behav. Inf. Technol. **41**(3), 558–573 (2020)
13. Chen, B., Wang, L., Rasool, H., Wang, J.: Research on the impact of marketing strategy on consumers' impulsive purchase behavior in livestreaming e-commerce. Front. Psychol. **13**, 905531 (2022)
14. Cai, J., Wohn, D.Y., Mittal, A., Sureshbabu, D.: Utilitarian and hedonic motivations for live streaming shopping. In: Proceedings of the 2018 ACM International Conference on Interactive Experiences for TV and Online Video, pp. 81–88 (2018)

15. Sun, Y., Shao, X., Li, X., Guo, Y., Nie, K.: How live streaming influences purchase intentions in social commerce: an IT affordance perspective. Electron. Commer. Res. Appl. **37**, 100886 (2019)
16. Wongkitrungrueng, A., Assarut, N.: The role of live streaming in building consumer trust and engagement with social commerce sellers. J. Bus. Res. **117**, 543–556 (2020)
17. Chen, H., Chen, H.T., Tian, X.: The dual-process model of product information and habit in influencing consumers' purchase intention: the role of live streaming features. Electron. Commer. Res. Appl. **53**, 101150 (2022)
18. Bharadwaj, N., Ballings, M., Naik, P.A., et al.: A new livestream retail analytics framework to assess the sales impact of emotional displays. J. Mark. **86**(1), 27–47 (2021)
19. Luo, H., Cheng, S., Zhou, W., Yu, S., Lin, X.: A study on the impact of linguistic persuasive styles on the sales volume of live streaming products in social e-commerce environment. Mathematics **9**, 1576 (2021)
20. Luo, H., Cheng, S., Zhou, W.: The factors influencing sales in online celebrities'live streaming. In: International Conference on Information Communication and Software Engineering, pp. 233–237 (2021)
21. Hasanah, H., Tirtana, R.A.: Advantage e-commerce technology in ornamental plant business. IOP Conf. Ser. Mater. Sci. Eng. **662**, 032045 (2019)
22. Yan, Y., Zhao, R., Xing, T.: Strategic introduction of the marketplace channel under dual upstream disadvantages in sales efficiency and demand information. Eur. J. Oper. Res. **273**, 968–982 (2019)
23. Xia, J., Niu, W.: A perspective on supplier encroachment in the era of e-commerce. Electron. Commer. Res. Appl. **40**, 100924 (2020)
24. Hou, W., Di, X., Li, J., et al.: Research on the behaviour and law of quantity growth of followers based on WeChat official account. Behav. Inf. Technol. **41**(8), 1724–1739 (2021)
25. Huang, Q., Chen, X., Ou, C.X., et al.: Understanding buyers' loyalty to a C2C platform: the roles of social capital, satisfaction and perceived effectiveness of e-commerce institutional mechanisms. Inf. Syst. J. **27**, 91–119 (2017)
26. Xu, P., Cui, B., Lyu, B.: Influence of streamer's social capital on purchase intention in live streaming e-commerce. Front. Psychol. **12**, 748172 (2022)
27. Hou, F., Guan, Z., Li, B.C., et al.: Factors influencing people's continuous watching intention and consumption intention in live streaming: evidence from China. Int. Res. **30**(1), 141–163 (2020)
28. Xue, J., Liang, X., Xie, T., Wang, H.: See now, act now: How to interact with customers to enhance social commerce engagement? Inf. Manag. **57**, 103324 (2020)
29. Guo, L., Hu, X., Lu, J., Ma, L.: Effects of customer trust on engagement in live streaming commerce: mediating role of swift Guanxi. Int. Res. **31**(5), 1718–1744 (2021)
30. Hu, M., Chaudhry, S.S.: Enhancing consumer engagement in e-commerce live streaming via relational bonds. Int. Res. **30**(3), 1019–1041 (2020)
31. Gruss, R., Kim, E., Abrahams, A.: Engaging restaurant customers on Facebook: the power of belongingness appeals on social media. J. Hospitality Tourism Res. **44**(2), 201–228 (2019)
32. Thomala, L.L.: Monthly active users of Taobao app in China 2022. https://www.statista.com/statistics/1327377/china-taobao-monthly-active-users/. Accessed 19 Dec 2022
33. Ma, Y.: Breakdown of GMV of leading live commerce platforms in China 2021, by platforms. https://www.statista.com/statistics/1339406/china-market-share-of-leading-live-commerce-platforms/. Accessed 19 Dec 2022
34. Ma, Y.: Alibaba's Singles' Day GMV 2011-202. https://www.statista.com/statistics/364543/alibaba-singles-day-1111-gmv/. Accessed 19 Dec 2022
35. Chen, X., Huang, Q., Davison, R.M.: The role of website quality and social capital in building buyers' loyalty. Int. J. Inf. Manag. **37**, 1563–1574 (2017)

Synergizes HeXie Management Framework with Program Management Approach for Industry 4.0 Transformation

Xin Wang[✉]

SICC Co., Ltd., Jinan 250118, P.R. China
Sewall.wang@gmail.com

Abstract. This dissertation explores the methodology for building intelligent manufacturing factories in medium and small-sized enterprises. Synergising HeXie management theory with a program management approach increases the industry 4.0 project success rate. Eventually, help those SMEs to achieve their strategic goals as a practical contribution. Also, the article optimises HeXie management theory from a conception to an applicable implementation model for Industry 4.0 projects.

Since Germany proposed the concept of Industry 4.0, there has been research in academia and industry to explore the technology of Industry 4.0 and the improved competitiveness of enterprises. Some articles explain that SMEs will have more challenges in transitioning to Industry 4.0 than large ones. The HXMT management theory generated for the CCAU (complexity, change, ambiguity, and uncertainty) environment could be suitable for integrating the oriental and occidental wisdom through coupling various project and program management methods. This article will use a Chinese semiconductor company's business case to validate the HXMT theme's effectiveness. Project management skills are a critical sub-factor of HeXie coupling to affect project management success significantly. Moreover, sustainability is a vital He-principal factor which impacts project success.

This article is an exploratory dissertation validating that the HeXie management model improves the success rate of Industry 4.0 projects by integrating technology elements and non-technology enablers, especially in Chinese SMEs.

Keywords: Industry 4.0 · Program management · Project management · HeXie Management · HXMT · Smart Manufacturing · Chinese SME

1 Introduction

1.1 Research Background

The demand for building SMART manufacturing capability by small-medium-sized manufacturing enterprises is still increasing in the post-COV-19 era (Lin, T. C. & Wang, K. J. 2021). The enterprises aim to improve their competitiveness and flexibility with

Y. Tu and M. Chi (Eds.): WHICEB 2023, LNBIP 480, pp. 50–61, 2023.
https://doi.org/10.1007/978-3-031-32299-0_5

Industry 4.0 technologies (Erasmus, J. et al. 2020). However, the guideline for managing an intelligent factory program is not fully explored. There are suggestions that the executing team have to perform effective project management following the PMBOK or Agile methodology (Frederico, G. F. 2021; Bożena Gajdzik, G. K. et al. 2022; Spałek 2017; Gentner, S. 2016). There is no unified definition of Smart manufacturing or Industry 4.0. (Apilioğullari, L. 2022; Shi, Z. et al. 2020). Academia describes it as creating innovative products most efficiently and faster through the cyber-physical system (CPS). It could combine information technology (IT) and operation technology (OT) through these hierarchical layers of the ISA-95 Model (Apilioğullar, L. 2022). The ISA95 model forms the backbone of Industry 4.0. Some researchers state that implementing Industry 4.0 projects in SMEs has more challenges and barriers than big enterprises (Kim, H. 2022). And Mosser, J. (2022) provides a GRMI4.0 guide to help design the smart factory. Several papers have studied various maturity models to characterize the intelligent factory (Lin, T. C. 2021). The practitioner claims that the intelligent factory project success rate is low since hard and soft skills are mandatory in the programme. A diverse skill set brings complexity; new Industry 4.0 technology causes change, these multi-dimension maturity models generate ambiguity, and external risk brings uncertainty. (Xi Y.M. et al. 2012) created HeXie Management Theory by integrating oriental and occidental wisdom, which establishes a clear vision and mission to direct the development of organisations and contributes to organising an integrated management system through the HeXie theme and HeXie coupling, especially in the CCAU environment. This article explores deploying HeXie management theory in executing Industry 4.0 projects as guidance. The HXMT model does not only close the GAP of lacking the guideline for managing an intelligent manufactory factory program, but it also inspires industry and academia to think about the pathway to the next learning cycle: Industry 5.0, which emphasises more on the human-centred paradigm (Zizic, M. C. 2022).

1.2 Research Significance

There is a Chinese small-medium-sized (SME) enterprise focusing on the product development, production and sales of third-generation semiconductor (SIC) wafer substrates. We name it S-company in the subsequent paragraphs. The paper's data is collected and validated from real smart factory projects in the S-company. To enhance its competitiveness, S-company has set a strategic goal to upgrade its manufacturing system to become an intelligent factory which meets Industry 4.0 in 3 to 4 years. These SMEs do not have solid financial capability and IT technical expertise. The journey of smart factories is a complex program that includes traditional IT (information technology), OT (automation technology), DT (data technology) even coupling with organisational culture changes. Meanwhile, the tendency of Sino-US technology decoupling is unavoidable. Furthermore, the COVID-19 epidemic increases project uncertainty. The author wishes to explore an intelligent factory program implementation model combining industrial practices with theory and verify the HXMT model by real project cases in the S-company. Figure 1 shows this article's targeted study area.

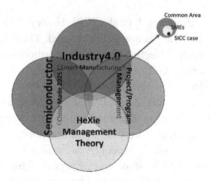

Fig. 1. The common area of Industry4.0, Program Management and HeXie management

2 Literature Review

2.1 Literature Review Method

This research is conducted in four steps: literature review, model formation, investigation of real project cases, and model validation. The literature review aims to collect articles on intelligent factories, Industry 4.0, project management, and HeXie management. Some Industry 5.0 literature is also cited as references.

2.2 Industry 4.0 and Project Management

Frederico, G. F. (2021) combines SCM 4.0 concepts and the ten knowledge areas mentioned in the Project Management Body of Knowledge framework (PMBOK). Jung, W.K. et al. (2020) describes an appropriate Smart Factory for SMEs. They claim it is challenging for small and medium-sized companies (SMEs) to build an appropriate smart factory' due to their financial and technical limitations. Erasmus J. et al. (2020) demonstrate that HORSE Project makes these advanced manufacturing technologies more accessible to European SMEs. It does not mention the project management methods of these actual cases. Li, S. et al. (2019) investigate different barriers organisations face in using big data analytics in an intelligent factory context. It proposes three barriers as a framework: Organisation-wide barriers (OB), Technical and data barriers (TDB) and People Barriers (PB). Successful project management of Industry 4.0 must overcome such OB, TDB and PB. Mosser, J. et al. (2022) provides a guide: GRMI4.0 for representing and modelling Industry 4.0 operation processes. It demonstrates the practical company developing a map model using a real case in the construction industry. Academia believes that project management's importance in Industry 4.0 is more significant than before. Gajdzik, B. & Kopeć, G. (2022) develop program management assumptions in Industry 4.0. It emphasises that executing projects in Industry 4.0 are performed under high volatility and uncertainty in the environment. Therefore, using Agile at the different stages of project management has a high possibility of success. Gentner, S. (2016) cites the number of the Standish Group Massachusetts, which shows that over 80% of projects fail. It states that manufacturing information systems and intelligent factory projects are full of traps for the unwary. It claims that applying Agile project management can overcome these challenges. Tortorella, G. L. & Fetterman, D. (2017) propose integrating LEAN approaches and Industry 4.0 technologies to improve operational and project performance. Vrchota J. et al. (2020) determine the crucial success factors in program management by Czech manufacturing enterprises' managers. The paper claims the essential enablers in project management are PM Experience and Leadership. Yin, Y. & Qin, S.F. (2019) looks at optimising the collaborative design by a performance evaluation method in executing the program of Smart Factory.

2.3 Industry 4.0 and HXMT Framework

Many enterprises and academic researchers use the ISA-95 model to describe the 5-layer technical architecture of an intelligent factory (Apiliogullar, L. 2022). The five levels and sub-projects mentioned in S-Company's industry 4.0 roadmap include hardware and software systems. The terminologies of intelligent manufacturing-related systems in the ISA-95 architecture diagram are explained as Fig. 2 shown: Level 0: Field. Level 1: PLC, Level 2: SCADA, Level 3: MES, Level 4: ERP.

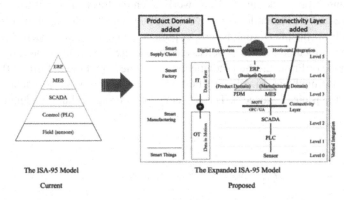

Fig. 2. Apilioğulları, L. (2022) upgrades ISA-95 model with more Industry 4.0 technology

Industry 4.0 must be not the end of the intelligent manufacturing journey. Pioneers are already exploring pathways to evolve to the industry 5.0 model in Fig. 3. Three key enablers moving to Industry 5.0 are introduced as people, organisation and technology by Zizic, M. C. et al. (2022), refers to Fig. 3. Besides technology, people and organisation factors return to the centre of the framework.

Performing industry 4.0 projects has to overcome four challenges: the complexity of the various technologies mentioned in the ISA-95 model, the rapid change of the external environment and internal end-user needs of dynamic business, ambiguity brought by organisational barriers and people barriers (Li, S. et al. 2019), and the uncertainty of the smart factory project success rate. It is a CCAU environment. The HeXie Management theory framework contains several vital elements, as shown in Fig. 4. Its effectiveness must be valuable for academic contributions and practical benefits of enterprises. Firstly, these environmental and Strategic (S) factors should consider as an input factor, which contains (L) Leadership, (O) Organization, and (E) Environment. The second aspect is

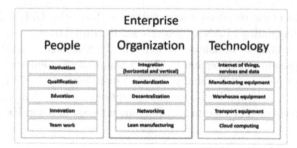

Fig. 3. Zizic, M. C. et al. (2022) forecast Industry 5.0 with three critical paradigms

the Xie Principle, a control mechanism for realising the industry 4.0 goal. It is designed as a 5-level based on ISA-95, for instance, ERP and MES. The third aspect is that the He Principle, an evolutionary mechanism, emphasises Chinese culture's integration. It highlights the importance of human-centred systems. Industry 4.0 is not to replace humans but to improve human life. This early Industry 5.0 exploration emphasises putting people and organisations back into the framework. Then the fourth aspect is to integrate the Xie Principle and He Principle with HeXie coupling. This article recommends combining Xie and He principles through a proper project management approach. The specific HeXie coupling method can be defined as the knowledge domain mentioned by PMBOK or the guidance of Prince2. The fundamental guideline is that the industry 4.0 PMs can flexibly choose methods. Finally, (P) Performance reflects the project management's success and the project's success. The two concepts are similar but not identical.

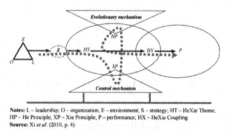

Notes: L – leadership; O – organization; E – environment; S – strategy; HT – HeXie Theme;
HP – He Principle; XP – Xie Principle; P – performance; HX – HeXie Coupling
Source: Xi *et al.* (2010, p. 4)

Fig. 4. The theoretical framework of HeXie management theory. Xi. Y.M. et al. (2012)

3 Methodology

3.1 Project Case Background

From 2021 to 2023, several projects are being implemented in S-company. A qualitative survey was designed for exploring the HeXie management theory's contributions to project success. These engaged projects include S-company's CPS network, data centre, ERP and MES projects. All of them aligned to ISA-95 model are considered in Table 1 list.

Table 1. S-company Smart Manufacturing Projects List.

Smart factory projects (A)	Smart factory projects (B)
CPS project	EAP/SCADA implementation
Data centre construction	WMS implementation
ERP upgradation	BI/Reporting development
MES implementation	AGV impementation
OA implementation	Automatical FG Warehouse

3.2 Proposed Model

The modified HXMT integrates technology and human-centricity culture, coupling with project management skills to deliver better results. It proposes a modified model for Industry 4.0 projects in Fig. 5. The triangle of the Xie Principle fills with ISA-95's 5 levels. The triangle of the He Principle introduces three elements: Human-centric, Resilient and Sustainable, emphasising People and Organisation importance. HeXie Coupling becomes a toolbox of PMBOK, Agile, Lean, DevOps, etc.

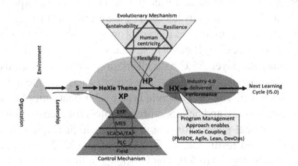

Fig. 5. The modified HXMT Model for Industry 4.0 projects.

Manufacturing industry is constantly evolving. The tendency is similar to the history of industrialisation, a spiral-shaped evolution model with the scientific and technological revolution. The Taiji figure is introduced to help practitioners understand synergise Xie with the He Principle. The simplified model reflects a dynamic evolutionary process. On the Xie-Principle side, the black background emphasises more scientific management and control, aims to achieve project management success. it replaces the workforce with solutions of industry 4.0. On the other side, with white background, He-Principle emphasises people-centred, sustainability and resilience. It focuses on putting people at the centre of focus. The two contradictory sides need to be synergised with appropriate project management and dynamic evolution. This is the purpose of introducing HeXie coupling as the 'S' red boundary of Fig. 6.

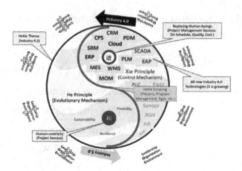

Fig. 6. Simplified HXMT Model for managing Industry 4.0 projects

3.3 Design Questionnaires

To validate the modified HeXie management model for effectively guide the Industry 4.0 project results, questionnaires survey is involved two outputs and four input variables in Fig. 7. Output A measures project management success and output B is an indicator of project success. The difference between project management and project success is challenging to define, Abylova, V., & Salykova, L. (2019). Project success emphasises achieving the project's objectives and creating value for the enterprise. Meanwhile, project management success is usually justified by the traditional project triangle: budget, time and quality. The Xie principle is a control mechanism based on control system optimisation and rational design. It has five levels, which are the ERP layer, the MES layer, the data acquisition layer, PLC as well as supporting data acquisition, and the machine in the field or logistics equipment. The overall Xie-principle index is calculated as the mean from C1 to C5. The He Principle is an evolutionary mechanism influencing organisational culture, values, and beliefs. Three enablers for industry 5.0 are considered when designing the critical factors for describing the He principle. These are human-centric, sustainability, and resilience. Zizic, M. C. et al. (2022) claim that these three drivers are pushing Industry 4.0 to 5.0. The HeXie Coupling guides the organisation to achieve its goals through the interaction of the Xie principle and He Principle. Project management takes the coupling role in synergising the He and Xie principles while conducting I4.0 projects. Four factors are selected to verify whether the PM performs

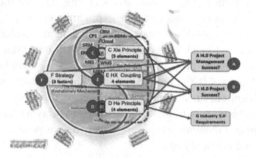

Fig. 7. Simplified HXMT Model for managing Industry 4.0 projects.

effectively during the project's progress. The strategy factor covers three elements of HeXie theory, which are leadership, organisation, and environment. All elements are extracted and quantised through the questionnaire.

4   Data Collection and Analysis

4.1   Data Samples

The invited respondents include the core members of S-company's intelligent factory project teams, which contain roles such as Project Manager, IT engineers, business unit users, outsourced software vendors, and other stakeholders. The PMs and IT engineers accounted for 89% of the responses. The top three primary responses are MES Implementation Project, EAP Data Collection Project, and the BI & Report development project. There are three steps being planned for data analysis. These are verifying variables A and B's correlation to verify project management success impact on project success indicator, validating correlation between C, D, E, F and output A project management success, and identifying correlation between C, D, E, F and output B project success indicators.

4.2   Project Management Success Analysis

In Fig. 8, a linear fitting model is adopted from the correlation analysis between the project success and project management success indicators. The horizontal axis is the project management success, and the vertical axis is the project success. The overall success possibility of successful project management projects is relatively high according to the linear fit line.

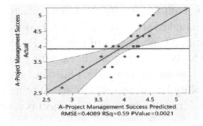

Fig. 8. Actual project management success index by Predicted PM success rate

The aim is to identify any correlation between output(A) Project management success indicator and HXMT variants: (C) Xie-principal factors, (D) He-principal factors, (E) HeXie coupling and (F) Strategy. According to the preliminary effect summary of Table 2, the (F) Strategy ranks as the top one, and the P-Value is 0.096, which is above the threshold of 0.05. Further verification is needed. Table 3 shows that the top sub-elements are (E2) knowing project management skills. The P-value reaches 0.059, which is close to the threshold of 0.05. It implies that project management skill is the dominant sub-factor affecting the success of smart factory project management. The (F) strategic is the secondary effect.

Table 2. Effect summary of HeXie management factors to project management success

Source	LogWorth		PValue
F-Strategy Factors	1.017		0.09612
D-He Principle Elements	0.625		0.23730
C-Xie Principle Elements	0.289		0.51368
E-HeXie Coupling Elements	0.065		0.86122

Table 3. Effect summary of HXMT sub-factors effect on project management success (Top5)

Source	LogWorth		PValue
E2: PM skills	1.226		0.05938
F3: Environment	0.752		0.17681
C2. MES readiness	0.726		0.18789
C1. ERP readiness	0.613		0.24394
C3. SCADA-EAP readiness	0.604		0.24864

4.3 Project Success Analysis

The second question that needs to be answered is which factors significantly impact (B) the project's success? It contains (B) project success indicator correlations with (D) He-principal factors, (F) Strategy factors, (C) Xie-principal factors, and (E) HeXie coupling factors. A fitting model is built to identify the primary factor. (D) The He-principal factor's P-value is 0.00237, ranked at the top in Table 4. Furthermore, using the project's success to fit the model with all sub-factors of (D). The P-value of (D2) sustainability reaches 0.00485 in Table 5. By comparing the linear fitting curves of project success's leverage residuals to (D1) human-centricity, (D2) Sustainability and (D3) Resilience. It shows that (D2) Sustainability has an apparent effect on project success. It proves that considering sustainability during the Industry 4.0 project is essential.

Table 4. Effect summary of HeXie management framework factors to project success

Source	LogWorth		PValue
D-He Principle Factors	2.624		0.00237
F-Strategy Factors	0.992		0.10190
C-Xie Principle Factors	0.484		0.32784
E-HeXie Coupling Factors	0.193		0.64192

Table 5. Effect summary of (D) He-principal sub-factors to project success.

Source	LogWorth		PValue
D2. sustainability	2.314		0.00485
D1. human-centricity	0.429		0.37204
D3. resilience	0.387		0.40975

5 Discussion

5.1 Top Success Factors

Based on the data analysis in Chapter 4, industry 4.0 project management success (A) positively correlates with (E2) project management skills. Moreover, (D) He-principle is the dominant enabler of I4.0 project success (B). Furthermore, (D2) Sustainability is vital to (D) sub-factors. The observation captured from the above discussion is consistent with observations in S-company Industry 4.0 project practices. When the project manager is skillful in project management, they control the project's scope, align tasks with the schedule plan, watch the quality closely, and reduce costs, achieving project management success. The project's success lies in whether the project creates value for the business operation and enterprises. So considering the sustainability of re-using resources to maximize the project outcome. The data analysis and practical observations are corroborated.

5.2 Project Case Discussion

When starting building CPS networks in S-company, the project time window is narrow. There are only two and a half months for construction. The project management team defines a clear plan and promptly monitors the project's progress. Since several working groups perform projects in parallel, the deployment of the MES and EAP system depends on the networks' readiness, and the network's project priority is optimized to align with the MES&EAP release schedule. It ensures that MES can be ready for production on time. Eventually, the networks project was delivered on time, on quality, and at cost. PM skills did play a critical role in project management success.

Another example is an ERP implementation project. In the early selection stage, the project team maintained the original ERP solution under the premise of maintaining the continuity of accounting but only revised the version to implement new master data naming rules, add consolidated reports module, cost module, interacts with MES system, and OA interfaces. In the implementation process, the experience of vendor engineers is limited, the project manpower is insufficient, and there are also defects in the master data collation process which consumes time to fix, resulting in project delays that are failures from a project management perspective. However, the project reuses the original system to minimize the impact of changing habits of end users, and it is also connected with MES eventually. Although several modules have not been accomplished on schedule, the oveall ERP function supports the business operation normally, which successfully supports the launch of MES. From the perspective of the project, it is successful due to system sustainability.

6 Conclusions and Limitations

6.1 Conclusions

It is deploying HeXie management theory in SMEs during digital transformation to help increase project & project management success. It improves the industry 4.0 project success by synergizing Xie-principal and He-principal enablers. Training project managers with professional PM skills is critical to increasing project management success. It belongs to the HeXie coupling factor, which integrates Xie and He principles. Such synergy could help Chinese SMEs realize the SMART manufacturing projects guided by Industry 4.0. To improve project success, He-principle will be recommended since the SMART manufacturing system needs to be sustainable and put people at the center of the whole system.

6.2 Limitations

The data in this article is collected from the real business case of the S-company smart factory program. Therefore, observations are influenced by the S-company's culture, leadership style, and specific corporate context, as well as some observations that would be impacted by social culture in China. Therefore, the sample size of the conclusions needs to be extended in future research.

References

Abylova, V., Salykova, L.: Critical success factors in project management: a comprehensive review. PM World J. VIII(V)

Apiliogullar, L.: Digital transformation in project-based manufacturing: developing the ISA-95 model for vertical integration. Int. J. Prod. Econ. **245** (2022). https://doi.org/10.1016/j.ijpe.2022.108413

Gajdzik, B., Kopeć, G.: General assumptions for project management in industry 4.0. (2022). https://doi.org/10.29119/1641-3466.2022.157.8

Erasmus, J., Vanderfeesten, I., Traganos, K., Keulen, R., Grefen, P.: The HORSE project: the application of business process management for flexibility in smart manufacturing. Appl. Sci. **10**(12) (2020). https://doi.org/10.3390/app10124145

Frederico, G.F.: Project management for supply chains 4.0: a conceptual framework proposal based on PMBOK methodology. Oper. Manag. Res. **14**(3–4), 434–450 (2021). https://doi.org/10.1007/s12063-021-00204-0

Gentner, S.: Industry 4.0: reality, future or just science fiction? how to convince today's management to invest in tomorrow's future! Successful strategies for Industry 4.0 and manufacturing IT. Chimia (Aarau) **70**, 628–633 (2016). https://doi.org/10.2533/chimia.2016.628

Jung, W.-K., et al.: Appropriate smart factory for SMEs: concept, application and perspective. Int. J. Precis. Eng. Manuf. **22**(1), 201–215 (2020). https://doi.org/10.1007/s12541-020-00445-2

Kim, H.: Performance from building smart factories of small- and medium-sized enterprises: the moderating effects of product complexity and company size. Int. J. Oper. Prod. Manag. **42**, 1497–1520 (2022). https://doi.org/10.1108/ijopm-10-2021-0654

Li, S., Peng, G.C., Xing, F.: Barriers of embedding big data solutions in smart factories: insights from SAP consultants. Ind. Manag. Data Syst. **119**, 1147–1164 (2019). https://doi.org/10.1108/imds-11-2018-0532

Lin, T.C., Wand, K.J.: Project-based maturity assessment model for smart transformation in Taiwanese enterprises. PLoS ONE **16**, e0254522 (2021). https://doi.org/10.1371/journal.pone.0254522

Mosser, J., Pellerin, R., Bourgault, M., Danjou, C., Perrier, N.: GRMI4.0: a guide for representing and modelling Industry 4.0 business processes. Bus. Process. Manag. J. **28**, 1047–1070 (2022). https://doi.org/10.1108/bpmj-12-2021-0758

Shi, Z., Xie, Y., Xue, W., Chen, Y., Fu, L., Xu, X.: Smart factory in Industry 4.0. Syst. Res. Behav. Sci. **37**, 607–617 (2020). https://doi.org/10.1002/sres.2704

Tortorella, G.L., Fetterman, D.: Implementation of industry 4.0 and LEAN production in Brazilian manufacturing companies. Int. J. Prod. Res. **56**, 2975–2987 (2017). https://doi.org/10.1080/00207543.2017.1391420

Vrchota, J., Řehoř, P., Maříková, M., Pech, M.: Critical success factors of the project management in relation to Industry 4.0 for sustainability of projects. Sustainability **13**(1) (2020). https://doi.org/10.3390/su13010281

Yin, Y., Qin, S.F.: An intelligent performance measurement approach for collaborative design in Industry 4.0. Adv. Mech. Eng. **11** (2019). https://doi.org/10.1177/1687814018822570

Xi, Y.M., Zhang, X.J., Ge, J.: Replying to management challenges: integrating oriental and occidental wisdom by HeXie management theory. Chin. Manag. Stud. **6**, 395–412 (2012). https://doi.org/10.1108/17506141211259104

Zizic, M.C., Mladineo, M., Gjeldum, N., Celent, L.: From Industry 4.0 towards Industry 5.0: a review and analysis of paradigm shift for the people, organisation and technology. Energies **15**(14) (2022). https://doi.org/10.3390/en15145221

Big Data-Based Recommendation Algorithm in E-commerce Personalized Marketing

Shujun Li[(⊠)], Li Li, Yiwen Cui, and Xueyan Wu

School of Economics and Management, Wuhan Railway Vocational College of Technology,
Wuhan 430205, China
sherrylee616@qq.com

Abstract. E-commerce recommendation algorithm is the core of the entire recommendation system, which plays a very important role in e-commerce personalized marketing. Its recommendation accuracy and efficiency directly affect the overall performance of the recommendation system. E-commerce recommendation algorithm based on data mining technology, in-depth analysis of various user data especially user access data, get each user's hobbies, interests and specific buying behavior characteristics. This paper analyzes the related technologies and algorithms of e-commerce recommendation system, and proposes the architecture of e-commerce recommendation system based on user behavior data. In order to meet the requirements of recommendation accuracy and real-time performance, the recommendation module designed in this paper is mainly composed of three modules: content-based recommendation module, collaborative filtering algorithm-based recommendation module and user behavior-based recommendation module, and the functions and technologies of each part are specifically analyzed. Finally, a personalized marketing scenario is created to evaluate the effect of the recommendation system.

Keywords: Data Mining · Personalized Recommendation Algorithm · Collaborative Filtering

1 Introduction

In the process of e-commerce personalized marketing, the recommendation system provides customers with product information and suggestions, helps users decide what products to buy, and simulates sales personnel to help customers complete the purchase process. Personalized recommendation is to recommend the information and goods that users are interested in according to their interest and purchase behavior. The e-commerce recommendation algorithm based on data mining technology deeply analyzes various user data, especially user access data, through data mining technology, and obtains their hobbies, interests and specific purchase behavior characteristics [1]. It generally includes the learning stage and the application stage. In the learning stage, the data mining system analyzes the data and establishes the corresponding recommendation model to explain the user's behavior patterns, also known as the pattern mining stage; In the application

© The Author(s), under exclusive license to Springer Nature Switzerland AG 2023
Y. Tu and M. Chi (Eds.): WHICEB 2023, LNBIP 480, pp. 62–71, 2023.
https://doi.org/10.1007/978-3-031-32299-0_6

phase, the recommendation algorithm provides users with real-time recommendation services according to the established recommendation model and user behavior, also known as the recommendation generation phase.

2 Common Recommendation Algorithms in E-commerce Personalized Marketing

2.1 Content Based Recommendation Algorithm

It is often used to integrate these behaviors according to the user's behavior history information to calculate the user's preferences, and then recommend the most similar content based on the user's preferences. The advantage of this method is that it does not need to consider other user characteristics, but its disadvantage is that the content available for analysis is limited. The biggest feature is excessive characterization, which may lead to the lack of innovation in the recommended content. Content based recommendation generally includes three processes:

Step 1: Content representation: extract some features for each item to represent the item;

Step 2: Feature learning: using the feature data of an item that a user likes or dislikes in the past to summarize the user's preferences;

Step 3: Generate a recommendation list, and recommend a group of items with the greatest relevance to the user by comparing the user profile obtained in the previous step with the characteristics of candidate items [2]. If we use a classification model in feature learning, we can simply return many items predicted by the model that are most likely to be of interest to the user as recommendations.

Taking the ant colony clustering algorithm as an example, its main architecture is as follows:

(1) Offline part: mainly use the ant colony clustering algorithm to prepare data, conduct data preprocessing, and get the recommendation pool. First, the user's access records are cleaned and identified offline, and the recommendation pool is obtained by clustering analysis according to the user's access paths to different commodities.

(2) Online part: mainly use the engine for recommendation. The recommendation system consists of three modules, namely user agent module, recommendation content generation module and recommendation generation module. As shown in Fig. 1.

2.2 Collaborative Filtering Recommendation Algorithm

The recommendation algorithm based on collaborative filtering is mainly used for prediction and recommendation. The algorithm finds user preferences by mining users' historical behavior data, divides users into groups based on different preferences, and recommends products with similar tastes. Collaborative filtering is to compare some behaviors and attributes of some users with those of other users, classify users with high similarity, and then the recommendation system can recommend a product to similar

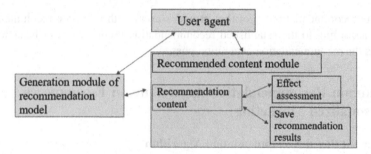

Fig. 1. Online architecture based on ant colony clustering algorithm

users. The accuracy of this recommendation system is significantly improved. However, each product must be purchased by many users before it can be recommended to other nearest neighbors [3]. In this way, some newly added products are difficult to be recommended. This problem is also known as the "cold start" problem of collaborative filtering. The recommended collaborative filtering algorithm is shown in Fig. 2.

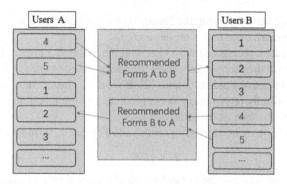

Fig. 2. Collaborative filtering algorithm recommendation

Collaborative filtering recommendation algorithms are divided into two categories, namely user based collaborative filtering algorithm and commodity based collaborative filtering algorithm. It performs well when the scoring matrix information is dense, and can capture some complex information, which often leads to unexpected surprises in practical applications, but it is not suitable for serious recommendation tasks such as public fund recommendation.

2.3 Recommendation Algorithm Based on Association Rules

Association rule-based recommendation algorithm can be divided into offline association rule recommendation model building stage and online association rule recommendation model application stage. In the offline phase, various association rule mining algorithms are used to establish association rule recommendation models; in the online stage, users are provided with real-time recommendation services according to the established association rule recommendation model and their purchase behavior. The offline establishment of association rule recommendation model can ensure the real-time performance of the algorithm. This algorithm uses data mining technology to obtain rules from a large number of past transaction data, which can be the association rules between goods purchased at the same time, or the sequence model of goods purchased in chronological order [4]. This algorithm is simple in calculation, but it is difficult to recommend commodities without association rules or sequence models.

3   Personalized Recommendation System for E-commerce Products Based on Data Mining

3.1   Overall Framework Design

The database in the server stores a large number of users' web page access path information and search keyword information data, which reflect users' search intention. Our mining and analysis of these data will greatly improve the efficiency of users' search for goods, thus improving users' satisfaction with e-commerce marketing, and thus promoting product sales. According to the analysis of compatibility and other issues, the functions of the recommendation system based on data mining include:

(1) Have a mechanism to promote new products.
(2) Analyze customer behavior sequence.
(3) Intelligently analyze the customer's keyword database and search path.
(4) Analyze customer behavior sequence. That is, analyze the products that customers may like within the specified time and organize them into a recommendation form.
(5) A recommended log can be saved regularly.
(6) Effectively analyze users' characteristics.

The above functional requirements analysis shows that the recommendation system based on data mining needs to avoid affecting the original online engine as much as possible, which requires minimizing the coupling between the recommendation system and the original online engine [5]. The framework of the recommendation system is shown in Fig. 3.

3.2   Design of Recommendation Modules

Content-Based Recommendation Module. Content-based recommendations are based on the similarity between projects. This kind of recommendation first needs to analyze the content of the items that customers have scored, generate a customer information archive, then list the items similar to the new archive from these existing items, sort the selected items (according to the rating), and combine the customer feedback information to recommend. Content based recommendation system is based on the comprehensive consideration of product information, customer information and users' interest in products, so as to obtain a list of recommended products after filtering by the recommendation system and thus personally recommend products to users. Figure 4 shows the content-based recommendation module.

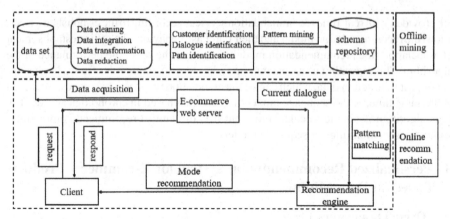

Fig. 3. Architecture of e-commerce personalized recommendation system

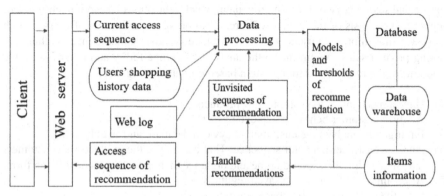

Fig. 4. Content-based recommendation module

Recommendation Module of Collaborative Filtering. (1) Main steps:

1) Obtain customer information. This part mainly obtains the customer's interest rating of the project.
2) Analyze the interest similarity between different customers. This part is to analyze the similarity of interests between customers to find the nearest neighbor.
3) From the nearest neighbor generated in step (2), find the items that users may like, and recommend them to new users according to their ratings. The structure of collaborative filtering personalized recommendation system is shown in Fig. 5.

The recommendation system needs to select users, find potential buyers, discover their potential purchase value, make them target users, and find similar content that users are interested in, so as to find the nearest neighbor and focus on recommending similar products to these users.

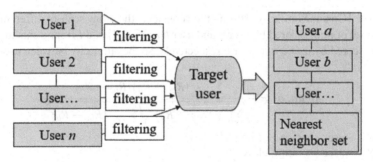

Fig. 5. Structure of collaborative filtering

(2) User-based collaborative filtering recommendation algorithm

User based collaborative filtering recommendation is to generate a Top-N recommendation list for target users based on the interests of neighbor users. It is based on the theoretical assumption that users who like similar items may have the same or similar preferences. User-based collaborative filtering recommendation uses statistical techniques to search for several nearest neighbors of the target user, and then predicts the target user's rating on the unsealed items according to the rating of the nearest neighbor, and selects the first few items with the highest prediction rating as the recommendation results to feed back to the user [6]. The rating of the user-based collaborative filtering recommendation algorithm is to generate the final recommendation result through the nearest neighbor's rating. The current user's rating on the unrated item is approximated by the weighted average of the nearest neighbor's rating on the item. User-based collaborative filtering recommendation algorithm can be divided into the following three stages:

The first stage: data representation. The user rating data can be represented by an $m * n$-order matrix R (m, n). Row m represents m users, column n represents n items, and element R in row i and column j represents the user i's rating on item j.

The second stage: nearest neighbor query. The nearest neighbor query is to search for several users whose scoring behavior is similar to that of the current user. The similarity between user a and user b is recorded as sim (a, b). The main methods to measure the similarity between users are:

1) Cosine similarity: the user's rating is regarded as a vector in the n-dimensional item space. If the user does not score the item, the user's rating for the item sets to 0. The similarity between users is measured by the cosine angle between vectors. Let the ratings of user a and user b on the n-dimensional term space be expressed as vectors $\vec{a}$ and $\vec{b}$ respectively, then the similarity sim (a, b) between user a and user b is as follows:

$$\sin(a, b) = \cos\left(\vec{a}, \vec{b}\right) = \frac{\vec{a}\,\vec{b}}{\left|\vec{a}\right| * \left|\vec{b}\right|}$$

2) Adjusted Cosine Similarity: This method considers the rating scale of different users. If the set of items scored by user a and user b as I I_{ab}, I_a and I_b represents the set of items scored by user a and user b respectively, so the similarity between user a and user b is:

$$sim(a, b) = \frac{\sum_{c\epsilon I_{ab}}(R_{ac} - \overline{R}_a)(R_{bc} - \overline{R}_b)}{\sqrt{\sum_{c\epsilon I_a}(R_{ac} - \overline{R}_a)^2}\sqrt{\sum_{c\epsilon I_b}(R_{bc} - \overline{R}_b)^2}}$$

R_{ac}—user a's rating of item c
R_{bc}—user b's rating of item c
$\overline{R}_a$—Average rating of user a
$\overline{R}_b$—average rating of user b

3) Correlation: the set of items scored by user a and user b as I_{ab}, then the similarity between user a and user b measured by Pearson correlation coefficient method is:

$$sim(a, b) = corr_{ab} = \frac{\sum_{c\epsilon I_{ab}}(R_{ac} - \overline{R}_a)(R_{bc} - \overline{R}_b)}{\sqrt{\sum_{c\epsilon I_{ab}}(R_{bc} - \overline{R}_b)^2}\sqrt{\sum_{c\epsilon I_{ab}}(R_{bc} - \overline{R}_b)^2}}$$

R_{ac}—user a's rating of item c
R_{bc}—user b's rating of item c
$\overline{R}_a$—Average rating of user a
$\overline{R}_b$—average rating of user b

The goal of nearest neighbor query is to find the user set $C = \{C_1, C_2...C_K\}$, in the entire user space for each user u, so that $u \notin C$, and the similarity $sim(u, C_1)$ between C_1 and u is the highest, the similarity $sim(u, C_2)$ to C_2 and u takes the second place, and so on.

The third stage: recommendation generation. According to the rating information of the current user's nearest neighbor on the item, the current user's rating on the unrated item is predicted to generate the top-N item recommendation [7].

Set the nearest neighbor set of user u as NN_u, then user u will give item i a prediction rating of $P_{u,i}$, which can be got from NN_u rating of user u. The calculation method is as follows.

$$P_{u,i} = \overline{R}_U + \frac{\sum_{n\epsilon NN_a}(R_{n,i} - \overline{R}_n)*sim(u, n)}{\sum_{n\epsilon NN_a}(|sum(u, n)|)}$$

The system uses the above method to predict the user's rating on all the items that have not been scored, and then selects the top N items with the highest predicted rating as the recommendation results to feed back to the current user.

Recommendation Module Based on User Behavior. The recommendation module based on user behavior is mainly divided into three parts in terms of architecture:

(1) Offline sorting.
(2) Data and index section.
(3) The online collection and analysis section.

The relevant functions of each part are described as Fig. 6.

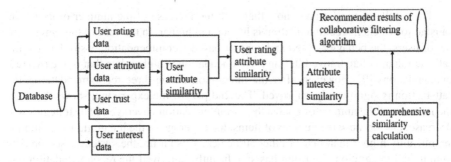

Fig. 6. Architecture of user behavior data-based recommendation

4 Effect and Evaluation

In order to verify the recommendation effect of this system, a small clothing sales website is selected as the experimental environment to observe the effect of different number of users. By comparing the coverage of content-based, collaborative filtering, user behavior-based recommendation and the recommendation system designed in this paper based on data mining, the average satisfaction of the four recommendations is evaluated.

In the experiment, when the system recommends, if the users put it in favorites or place an order, it is deemed that users are satisfied with the recommendation results; if the user no longer needs to recommend after selecting, it is deemed that he is dissatisfied with the result; if the user clicks in to view the recommended products, but does not place an order, it is considered as normal [8]. The experiment is divided into two parts. The 1st part tests the accuracy of the system, that is, the user's satisfaction with the products recommended by the system. The 2nd part is the recommendation rate, that is, to test the coverage of products recommended by the system. The 2nd part checks the coverage of the three recommendation algorithms (including the proportion of users' ideal commodities) when 90, 120 and 200 items are taken out, and the results are shown in Table 1:

Table 1. The coverage of four recommended algorithms

	content-based	behavior-based	collaborative filtering	integration algorithm
90 items	77.4%	86.3%	81%	90.1%
120 items	75%	82%	77.8%	90.2%
200	72.6%	83.4%	75%	89.9%

The results of the 1st part show that with the increase of the number of users, the satisfaction of each recommendation is higher and higher. In the case of the same number of users, the behavior-based and content-based recommendation is similar, and the satisfaction of collaborative filtering recommendation is higher than that of the two recommendations [9]. However, after the integration of the three recommendations, the satisfaction is significantly improved. The 2nd part of the experiment shows that with the increase of the number of goods, the recommendation coverage of all strategies will decrease, but for the same number of items, the coverage of the integration algorithm is significantly higher than that of other strategies. To sum up, the system based on data mining and integration algorithm has significantly improved the recommendation rate and accuracy.

5   Conclusion

In e-commerce activities, compared with traditional marketing methods, personalized marketing is more targeted because it can carry out precise marketing according to the individual differences. Personalized recommendation technology is the key of e-commerce recommendation system. The recommendation technology based on data mining is based on users' habits, hobbies and interests, which can more easily recommend appropriate products, and thus improve the number of visits, clicks and orders on the website. The personalized recommendation system based on data mining explored and designed in this paper can not only effectively solve the problem of huge and messy information in the recommendation system, but also realize the personalized presentation of items, which has great application research value. However, there are still many aspects to be improved. For example, the flexibility of the recommendation system needs to be further verified, the adjustment of rating types and the corresponding calculation need to be further improved, and the fusion of the recommendation lists generated by the three algorithms is relatively stiff, which needs further improvement.

References

1. Mobasher, B., Cooley, R., Srivastava, J.: Automatic personalization based on Web usage mining. Commun. ACM **43**(8), 142–143 (2000)
2. Yang, F.: Research on E-Commerce Personalized Recommendation Technology Based on Data Mining. Xi'an University of Electronic Science and Technology, Xi'an (2008). (in Chinese)
3. Pei, L.: Research on E-Commerce Recommendation System Based on Web Data Mining. Tongji University, Shanghai (2006)
4. Qu, T.: Research and Implementation of Web Data Mining Technology in E-Commerce System. University of Electronic Science and Technology, Chengdu (2011). (in Chinese)
5. Wang, W.: E-Commerce Personalized Recommendation Technology Based on Data Mining. University of Electronic Science and Technology, Chengdu (2014)
6. Guo, X.: Big data precision marketing based on recommended algorithms. Inf. Technol. Stand. **05**, 40–41 (2019). (in Chinese)
7. Liu, F.: Design and Implementation of E-Commerce Personalized Recommendation Algorithm. Jiangsu University, Nanjing (2010). (in Chinese)

8. Li, J.: Application of e-commerce personalized information automatic recommendation algorithm based on big data technology. Autom. Technol. Appl. **10**, 38–39 (2021). (in Chinese)
9. Nascimento, G., Correa, R.F.: Evaluation of selection criteria for noun phrases with relevance for information retrieval. Transnormal **30**(2), 179–184 (2018)

How Digital Change and Innovation in the Workplace Affect Front-Line Employee Retention: A Cross-Sectional Study Based on the Aged Care Industry

Ying Wang, Yuting Feng, and Changyong Liang[✉]

Hefei University of Technology, Hefei 230009, Anhui, China
cylianghfut@163.com

Abstract. In order to understand the retention of front-line employees in the process of digital technology change and innovation, this study uses the information system continuation theory and job demand-resource theory to build a framework, and conducts a cross-sectional survey of the post-use stage of digital technology. The focus is on the relationship between digital technology quality factors and continued trust, distrust, job engagement, job burnout and retention intentions. The results showed that continued trust in digital technology was the strongest predictor of retention intention. Job burnout and distrust were not important to retention intentions. The results also show that the quality factor of digital technology is an important antecedent of continued trust and distrust.

Keywords: post-use phase · digital technology · quality factors · continuous trust · distrust · retention intention

1 Introduction

Like other aging countries, China's aged care industry is facing the same shortage of front-line workers. Retaining front-line service professionals is an indispensable task. Digitalization has now been recognized as an effective solution to address the aging population and overcome the shortage of front-line employees. More and more scholars are proposing to use the advantages of emerging technology to attract and retain talent (Acemoglu & Restrepo 2020).

We found that the COVID-19 pandemic has accelerated digital change and innovation in the aged care industry. It has also fundamentally changed the way frontline workers deliver services (Bolton et al. 2018). Especially during crises, digital technologies are of considerable use in helping front-line employees with disease surveillance, data analysis, diagnosis, access to health information, and education and support, reducing their work stress and stimulating their ability to achieve their goals (Markowitz 2020).

However, as the frequency of digital technology use increases, some employees find that the effects promised by the technology do not match the actual results. They often experience problems such as interruptions in system information or poor information quality (Puranik, Koopman, & Vough 2020). Quality factors are key to ensuring the continuous use of front-line employees, and the continuous use of digital technologies is a key point that influences digital change and innovation in the workplace. In recent years, despite the continued digital change and innovation in the service industry, we know very little about the association between technology quality factors and front-line employee retention, especially in the post-use phase of digital technology (i.e., sustained use of digital technology). Previous empirical studies have also tried to reveal the role of digital technology support in attracting and retaining elderly care talents (Wang et al. 2022). On the contrary, due to the unexpected negative consequences of digital technology in the workplace, such as technical pressure, information overload (Sarabandi et al. 2018) or interruption, psychological stress (D'Arcy et al. 2014), will affect the personal well-being of nursing interns, resulting in excessive impact, resulting in increased willingness of nursing interns to leave.

Summarizing the previous literature, we found that research in the post-use phase of digital technology is lacking. With the uncertainty of the COVID-19 pandemic and the sense of vulnerability that technology creates in employees, some scholars have found that employee trust is particularly important in digital work environments (Rudolph et al. 2021). However, trust is a two-stage process that includes initial and continuous trust. As it develops over time, continuous trust is more likely to influence employees' further use. Therefore, the success of digital change and innovation in the workplace requires ensuring continuous trust in digital technology among front-line employees. Continuous trust helps to promote work engagement (Nicolaou, Ibrahim, & Van Heck 2013). Recently, build continuous trust is an important but unstudied issue. In the past, scholars have mainly focused on initial trust, in which case the antecedents and effects of continuous trust have been largely ignored (Zhou 2012). Moreover, few studies have empirically investigated how changes in continuous trust affect employees' work status and behavioral outcomes. This is an important issue for front-line employees in the aged care industry.

We also found that digital technology acts as a double-edged sword and that the quality of the technology may lead to distrust of the technology through employees. According to research, distrust can causes anxiety and job burnout among individuals (Fujimoto, Ferdous, Sekiguchi, & Sugianto 2016). Distrust in the work environment can determine employee performance and turnover. In short, continuous trust and distrust as distinct constructs can co-exist. In the context of this research, it is important to understand the impact of continuous trust and distrust in digital technologies.

Currently, there is a gap in the literature regarding the combination between digital technology changes in the workplace and innovation and front-line employees' retention intention in the workplace. Based on this, the main objective of this study is to understand how digital technology quality, continuous trust and distrust affect front-line employees' work engagement, job burnout, and retention intentions, focusing primarily on the post-use phase of digital technology.

2 Theoretical Framework and Hypothesis

2.1 Information System Continuance Theory (ISCT)

ISCT which is widely used to explain the continued use of information technology by individuals beyond the implementation stage (Bhattacherjee 2001). It is thus clear that individuals are not using information technology for the first time. The theory assumes that individuals' expectations of a product or service change over time. We found that ISCT has been used to study individuals' continuous trust. In contrast to initial trust, continuous trust is formed by individuals over time. Continuous trust has been less studied in information systems research. Especially in digital work environments, employees' continuous trust in digital technologies is particularly important. Continued trust in technology not only affects their behavior toward technology, but may further affect their state and behavior at work. At present, scholars have called for using the advantages of technology to attract and retain employees, but from the perspective of employees, there is still a research gap to explore how the continuous trust in digital technology affects their work status and behavior.

2.2 Continuous Trust and Distrust

Trust is a dynamic development process that includes initial trust and continuous trust, and this paper focuses on continuous trust. Compared to continuous trust, initial trust is particularly important when users purchase products and services at one time. Continuous trust is more related to personal activities that repeat over time, such as using digital technology at work. McKnight developed a scale to measure continuous trust (McKnight & Choudhury 2006). Previously, some scholars analyzed and compared trust with continuous trust, and measured the role of continuous trust in information systems (Hoehle *et al.* 2012). Based on the relevant literature, we consider continuous trust and distrust as two different constructs (Lewicki, McAllister, & Bies 1998). Continuous trust characteristics include continuous faith, confidence, and assurance in digital technology and also employees' expectations of the efficiency, reliability, and effectiveness of given technological devices and technological systems. Distrust is a negative expectation of employees towards digital technology, characterized by suspicion, wariness, and fear of digital technology (Lewicki et al. 1998).

2.3 Job Demands-Resources Theory (JD-R)

The Job Requirements-Resources (JD-R) model can be used as a theoretical framework to integrate the two perspectives of job engagement and job burnout (Barbier, Hansez, Chmiel, & Demerouti 2013). In the context of this paper, we argue that digital technology as a job resource facilitates front-line employees to achieve their job goals, while quality factors influence their continuous trust and distrust in digital technology.

2.4 Quality Factor and Continuous Trust and Distrust

Information quality refers to the completeness, accuracy, comprehensibility, timeliness, and security of information output from digital technology-driven devices (Abbasi, Sandran, Ganesan, & Iranmanesh 2022). System quality reflects the technical characteristics of digital technology-driven devices, including reliability, ease of use, flexibility, and responsiveness. Service quality responds to users' perceptions and value judgments of digital technology services and the performance of the entire service system, including assurance and personalization. In online health platforms, users find that the quality of information varies, and if the platform consistently maintains valuable, high-quality information it helps to gain continued trust from users. With frequent human-computer interactions at work, the stability of system operation and low failure rates contribute to the continued trust of employees. With the further use of technology, Service quality affects the continuous trust of users and further affects their loyalty.

Information quality affects individual judgment, and underprivileged information quality may also generate faithless beliefs. System usefulness can be considered a major factor in distrust. When service quality does not meet an individual's expectations is prone to mistrust. Therefore, we propose the following hypothesis.

H1a: Information quality has a positive effect on the continuous trust in digital technology

H1b: Information quality has a negative effect on distrust in digital technology

H2a: System quality has a positive effect on the continued trust in digital technology

H2b: System quality has a negative effect on distrust in digital technology

H3a: Service quality has a positive effect on the continued trust in digital technology

H3b: Service quality has a negative effect on distrust in digital technology.

2.5   Continuous Trust, Distrust and Work Engagement, Job Burnout

Continuous trust as an organizational principle can enhance employee enthusiasm and cooperation. Work engagement is defined as a positive work-related emotional state characterized by energy, dedication, and focus. We found short amount of literature on the relationship between continuous trust and work engagement. However, it has been demonstrated that, trust affects employee attitudes and behaviors and that employee trust helps to promote work engagement. Burnout is often conceptualized as a chronic stress syndrome that includes chronic feelings of exhaustion, negative attitudes toward work, and reduced professional effectiveness (Christina Maslach & Jackson 1981). Trust can improve productivity as well as performance and reduce burnout.

Distrust is thought to produce anxiety and stress and to lead to severe behavioral responses. Vigor or Robustness is a characteristic of an individual's positive emotional state. Therefore, employees' loss of vigor at work means that they will be less engaged in their work. Distrust is also feeling of individual frustration that affects behavior (Elbeltagi & Agag 2016). In healthcare settings, nurses' doubts about technical equipment capabilities and measurement parameters can create negative emotions at work leading to burnout. Therefore, we propose the following hypothesis.

H4: Continuous trust has a positive effect on work engagement

H5: Continuous trust has a negative effect on job burnout

H6: Distrust has a negative effect on work engagement

H7: Distrust has a positive effect on job burnout.

2.6 Continuous Trust, Distrust, and Retention Intention

Trust is an important predictor of behavioral intentions. Once trust is established, then the relationship between the parties can last longer by overcoming uncertainty. Distrust plays a key role in reducing behavioral intentions as an outcome of decision avoidance. Therefore, we propose the following hypothesis.

H8: Continuous trust has a positive effect on retention intention

H9: Distrust has a negative effect on retention intention.

2.7 Work Engagement, Job Burnout, and Retention Intention

Retention intention is the willingness of employees to stay in the organization. Existing research suggests that increased work engagement plays a critical role in increasing retention intentions. Burnout has also been identified as a significant factor influencing nurse retention (Christina Maslach & Jackson 1981). Therefore, we propose the following hypothesis.

H10: Work engagement has a positive effect on retention intention

H11: Job burnout has a negative effect on retention intention.

3 Measures

Information quality, System quality, Service quality questions were adapted from the scale developed by Abbasi et al. (Abbasi, Sandran, Ganesan, & Iranmanesh 2022). The continuous trust item measures and the distrust item measures, we used the McKnight et al. scale (McKnight & Choudhury, 2006); Work engagement was measured based on the scale of et al. (Balducci, Fraccaroli, & Schaufeli 2010). Job burnout measured through a scale developed by Maslach & Jackson (Christina Maslach & Jackson 1981); Retention intention in the workplace is based on the Chinese version of the Willingness to Stay in the Workplace Scale translated and revised by domestic scholars Tao Hong et al. (Tao & Wang 2010). And all survey items were administered on a five-point Likert scale ranging from 1 (strongly disagree) to 5 (strongly agree). 580 valid questionnaires were finally returned.

3.1 Analysis Method

This study uses the partial least squares structural equation modeling (PLS-SEM) approach. Next, SPSS was used to come in for descriptive statistical analysis.

3.2 Sample and Data Collection

The purpose of this study was to determine the factors that contribute to the retention intention of front-line employees in the aged care industry. The population studied was those who have used digital technology in their work in elderly services. The data were collected through online and offline questionnaires, using the WenJuanXing platform online. Participants were informed before the questionnaire began that this study was based on a managerial perspective and no personal information was collected from participants, such as names, addresses, cell phone numbers, etc. The data were used for academic purposes only and were completely confidential. Participants signed an informed consent form and then spent 20–30 min to complete the questionnaire. The study started in June 2022. 833 questionnaires were distributed to 13 elderly institutions, and after eliminating invalid questionnaires, 580 valid questionnaires were finally returned, with a return rate of 69.6%. Details of the sample characteristics are shown in Table 1.

Table 1. Sample structure

Demographic variable		Number	Percentage (%)
Gender	Male	82	14.1
	Female	498	85.9
Age	18–24	123	21.2
	25–35	371	64
	≥36	86	14.8
Education level	Less than technical secondary school	93	16
	Technical secondary school	231	39.8
	College or above	256	44.2
Monthly personal income (RMB)	≤4000 RMB	68	11.7
	4001–5000 RMB	249	42.9
	5001–6000 RMB	150	25.9
	≥6001 RMB	113	19.5
Working years	0–6 months	108	18.6
	6 months to 1 year	168	29
	1–2 years	187	32.2
	≥2 years	117	20.2

4 Results

4.1 Measurement Model Evaluation

In this study, the CR value is higher than the specified value of 0.7, it indicates that the model construct is reliable (Hair, Sarstedt, & Ringle 2019). As shown in the Table 2, the minimum value of factor loadings for this study was 0.76 and AVE values were greater than 0.5, both of which met the requirements specified by Hair et al. and therefore were suitable for an exploratory study (Hair et al. 2019). Scholars proposed to use the heterozygosity-monotrait ratio to measure discriminant validity (HTMT). As shown in the Table 3. According to the HTMT criterion, which satisfied the specified requirements.

Table 2. Results of convergent validity and reliability

Items	Mean	Standard deviation	Factor loading range	CR	Cronbach's Alpha	AVE
Information quality (IQ)	3.843	1.128	0.783–0.859	0.832	0.888	0.665
System quality (SYQ)	3.823	1.090	0.793–0.862	0.846	0.896	0.684
Service quality (SQ)	3.867	1.074	0.764–0.852	0.876	0.909	0.668
Continuous trust (CTR)	4.011	1.112	0.782–0.868	0.865	0.908	0.712
Distrust (DTR)	2.312	1.216	0.812–0.917	0.853	0.91	0.773
Work engagement (WE)	3.872	1.031	0.760–0.834	0.859	0.898	0.639
Job burnout (JB)	2.342	1.237	0.795–0.912	0.89	0.924	0.754

Abbreviations: AVE: Average variance extracted; CR: Composite reliability

Table 3. HTMT

	DTR	IQ	JB	RI	SQ	SYQ	CTR	WE
DTR								
IQ	0.476							
JB	0.861	0.521						
RI	0.435	0.79	0.437					
SQ	0.435	0.789	0.495	0.843				
SYQ	0.462	0.776	0.502	0.77	0.782			
CTR	0.456	0.794	0.486	0.87	0.807	0.788		
WE	0.39	0.78	0.463	0.801	0.801	0.737	0.753	

Note: IQ: information quality; SYQ: system quality; SQ: service quality; CTR: continue trust; DTR: distrust; WE: work engagement; JB: job burnout; RI: retention intention.

4.2 Structural Model Evaluation

As shown in Table 4 and Fig. 1, the results indicate that information quality ($\beta = 0.271$, $p < 0.001$), system quality ($\beta = 0.265$, $p < 0.001$) and service quality ($\beta = 0.344$, p

< 0.001) have significant positive effect on continuous trust. Therefore, we supported H1a, H2a and H3a. However, interestingly, we found a significant negative effect of information quality ($\beta = -0.204$, p < 0.05) and system quality ($\beta = -0.175$, p < 0.05) on distrust, but no significant effect of service quality on distrust, thus supporting H1b and H2b, and H3b was rejected. Furthermore, we found a significant positive effect of continuous trust on work engagement ($\beta = 0.615$, p < 0.001) and retention intention ($\beta = 0.503$, p < 0.001), but a significant negative effect on job burnout ($\beta = -0.15$, p < 0.001), thus, supporting H4, H8 and H5. Similarly distrust had a significant negative effect on work engagement ($\beta = -0.096$, p < 0.05), with a significant positive effect on job burnout ($\beta = 0.698$, p < 0.001), but distrust had no significant effect on the retention intention in the job. Therefore, we supported H6 and H7 and H9 was rejected. The results showed that work engagement had a significant positive effect on the retention intention ($\beta = 0.346$, p < 0.001) and therefore supported H10. However, we found that job burnout was not significant on the retention intention. Therefore, H11 was not supported. In addition, continuous trust, distrust, work engagement, job burnout, and retention intention explained variance (R^2) of 0.606, 0.213, 0.434, 0.594, and 0.633.

Table 4. Path coefficient and hypotheses

Hypotheses	Paths	Beta	T-value	P-value	Decision
H1a	IQ -> CTR	0.271	4.935	0	Supported
H1b	IQ -> DTR	−0.204	3.197	0.001	Supported
H2a	SYQ -> CTR	−0.175	4.461	0	Supported
H2b	SYQ -> DTR	0.265	2.567	0.011	Supported
H3a	SQ -> CTR	0.242	5.229	0.001	Supported
H3b	SQ -> DTR	−0.279	1.932	0.054	Not supported
H4	CTR -> WE	0.615	14.366	0	Supported
H5	CTR -> JB	−0.15	3.968	0	Supported
H6	DTR -> WE	−0.096	2.579	0.01	Supported
H7	DTR -> JB	0.698	20.792	0	Supported
H8	CTR -> RI	0.503	9.635	0	Supported
H9	DTR -> RI	−0.096	1.48	0.139	Not supported
H10	WE -> RI	0.346	6.177	0	Supported
H11	JB -> RI	−0.155	0.675	0.5	Not supported

4.3   Common Method Bias

To control this, we conducted Harman's single factor test. For this reason, we conducted exploratory factor analysis on multiple subjective variables in all studies to assess

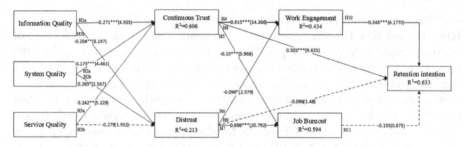

Fig. 1. Structural model test results

whether one or a single factor accounted for the majority of the covariance between variables, which indicates that there are a large number of common method variances (Podsakoff et al. 2003). The analysis revealed several factors, none of which accounted for more than 50% of the covariance between variables (the highest covariance attributable to a single factor was 42.621%) (Podsakoff et al. 2003). Therefore, any potential deviation of the variance of the common method is likely to be small and unlikely to affect our results.

5   Discussion

The results showed that information quality, system quality, and service quality positively influenced the continuous trust of front-line employees (H1a, H2a, and H3a). In the past, during the initial phase of trust, it was confirmed that the information, system and service quality of mobile technology had a significant impact on initial trust (Zhou 2012). Given this we argue that technology quality is an important factor throughout the developmental stages of employee trust, both in the first interaction with the technology and in the post-use phase. We found that with further use of digital technology, employees expect complete, accurate, easily understood, and timely information. Particularly in night care, the quality of data transmitted by digital devices (e.g., smart mattresses) influences front-line employees' confidence in their ability to monitor at night, which builds continuous trust in digital technology. Likewise, the reliability and stability of the system to meet the needs of the staff can increase their continuous trust. Particularly during the COVID-19 pandemic, the use of disinfection robots to perform routine disinfection or cleaning service tasks can meet employees' expectations and increase belief in the effectiveness of the technology, which in turn creates continuous trust. Among other things, we also found that service quality had the greatest impact on continuous trust, which may be due to the fact that in the post-use phase of digital technology, employees are more concerned about the positive impact that service quality brings to their work. We know that service quality is beneficial to employees' perceptions of service performance (Roses, Hoppen, & Henrique 2009). The success of service interactions is important to the job. As an example, intelligent assistants are increasingly assisting front-line staff, such as IBM's Watson, which can assist physicians with diagnoses and facilitate collaboration between healthcare professionals in geriatric care, and if Watson can consistently maintain quality service, then healthcare professionals will trust the reliability and competence of digital technology in their work, which in turn creates ongoing trust. In summary, the information, system and service quality of digital technology are missing in the workplace, and the quality factor not only ensures safe and efficient elderly care services, but also increases front-line employees' expectations of the effectiveness and reliability of digital technology.

In terms of retention intention, our results suggest that continuous trust has a direct and positive effect on retention intention and that continuous trust is a key determinant of retention intention (H8). This may be due to the following: the sample size in this paper is focused on young people who have obtained nursing education or vocational training. These individuals are unique in that they are the first generation of the digital age, often early adopters of technology, and they prefer to use technology to meet their job needs. The effective integration of technology with elderly care services increases their trustworthiness. For example, millimeter wave radar for 24 h/7d indoor detection of elderly falls helps assist front-line employees in monitoring the elderly over time. This system, which combines radar, wireless communication, and data processing technologies to locate and alert in a timely manner, can alert attention to the elderly's movements, notify of falls, and help manage dangerous situations as needed. The continuous trust in digital technology among front-line employees has led them to believe in the career prospects of elderly care and to continue working. Particularly during the COVID-19 crisis, the advantages offered by technology helped to foster the career identity of employees. Traditional care services such as turning, defecation, and bathing used to be done by smart technology now, employees believe that the changes brought by technology can give them abundant time resources to provide high quality services, continuous trust in digital technology can provide a new perception of elderly care work, and career identity can enhance the willingness to stay in the job has been mentioned by different scholars. Thus, in summary, front-line employees' trust in the reliability and validity of digital technology is an important predictor of retention intentions.

In terms of distrust, although it has been discussed earlier that service quality is the most important factor in continuous trust (H3a), our study did not confirm the effect of service quality on distrust (H3b). This may be due to the fact that trust and distrust are not opposites and low trust does not equal distrust, they are two different constructs (McKnight & Choudhury 2006). In the context of this paper's study, employees are more likely to be skeptical of technology because of issues such as incomplete information or system disruptions, and to use it cautiously in their retirement efforts, thus distrusting it.

In terms of retention intentions, our results show that distrust and job burnout do not have a significant effect on retention intentions (H9 and H11). Although the negative effects caused by distrust can lead to the occurrence of retention intentions (Elbeltagi & Agag 2016), the study of job burnout in relation to employees' retention intention has been validated by different scholars (Özkan 2022). However, the reason for the gap between our analysis and the previous results may be that this paper focuses on the elderly care service context, where for front-line employees, the work in elderly services is repetitive, monotonous and daily faced with elderly clients, with high workload and intensity, even though the use of technology fails to meet employees' expectations and high job burnout, front-line employees indicate that they are more concerned about the continuing education and promotion strategies provided by the organization, generous compensation, and organizational or family support. Especially during the COVID-19 pandemic, adequate equipment and supplies and a safe work environment were important factors influencing retention intention.

5.1 Practical Implications

Research has shown that quality factors are the basis for continuous trust, which requires digital technology providers to implement quality improvement programs to increase the continuous trust of front-line employees in digital devices. Organizational managers should be aware of the impact of work engagement on retention and develop mechanisms for commitment and assurance of technology quality. At the same time, suppliers should improve quality characteristics to enhance continuous trust and thus influence work engagement to promote retention.

5.2 Limitations and Future Research

The generalizability of the findings is limited. Future studies could test the model of this study again in other countries or industries. The sample size maybe biased. Future research will need to expand with the large sample size and compare the different impacts of digital change and innovation on front-line employees of different ages.

6 Conclusion

To our knowledge, this study is the first to examine the impact of digital change and innovation in the workplace on front-line employee retention. The focus points are on the relationship between qualitative factors on front-line employees' continuous trust, distrust, work engagement, job burnout, and retention intention in the workplace in the post-use phase of digital technology. This study provides a starting point for researchers to further investigate the study of digital technology change and innovation on retention intention.

References

Abbasi, G.A., Sandran, T., Ganesan, Y., Iranmanesh, M.: Go cashless! Determinants of continuance intention to use E-wallet apps: a hybrid approach using PLS-SEM and fsQCA. Technol. Soc. **68**, 101937 (2022)

Acemoglu, D., Restrepo, P.: Robots and jobs: evidence from US labor markets. J. Polit. Econ. **128**(6), 2188–2244 (2020)

Balducci, C., Fraccaroli, F., Schaufeli, W.B.: Psychometric properties of the Italian version of the Utrecht Work Engagement Scale (UWES-9): a cross-cultural analysis. Eur. J. Psychol. Assess. **26**(2), 143 (2010)

Barbier, M., Hansez, I., Chmiel, N., Demerouti, E.: Performance expectations, personal resources, and job resources: how do they predict work engagement? Eur. J. Work Organiz. Psychol. **22**(6), 750–762 (2013)

Bhattacherjee, A.: Understanding information systems continuance: an expectation-confirmation model. MIS Q. 351–370 (2001)

Bolton, R.N., et al.: Customer experience challenges: bringing together digital, physical and social realms. J. Serv. Manag. **29**(5), 776–808 (2018)

D'Arcy, J., Gupta, A., Tarafdar, M., Turel, O.: Reflecting on the "dark side" of information technology use. Commun. Assoc. Inf. Syst. **35**, 109–118 (2014)

Elbeltagi, I., Agag, G.: E-retailing ethics and its impact on customer satisfaction and repurchase intention: a cultural and commitment-trust theory perspective. Internet Res. **26**(1), 288–310 (2016)

Fujimoto, Y., Ferdous, A.S., Sekiguchi, T., Sugianto, L.-F.: The effect of mobile technology usage on work engagement and emotional exhaustion in Japan. J. Bus. Res. **69**(9), 3315–3323 (2016)

Hair, J.F., Sarstedt, M., Ringle, C.M.: Rethinking some of the rethinking of partial least squares. Eur. J. Mark. (2019)

Hoehle, H., Huff, S., Goode, S.: The role of continuous trust in information systems continuance. J. Comput. Inf. Syst. **52**, 1–9 (2012)

Lewicki, R.J., McAllister, D.J., Bies, R.J.: Trust and distrust: new relationships and realities. Acad. Manag. Rev. **23**(3), 438–458 (1998)

Markowitz, J.: Virtual treatment and social distancing. Lancet Psychiatry **7**(5), 388–389 (2020)

Maslach, C., Jackson, S.E.: The measurement of experienced burnout. J. Organiz. Behav. **2**(2), 99–113 (1981)

McKnight, D.H., Choudhury, V.: Distrust and trust in B2C e-commerce: do they differ? Paper Presented at the Proceedings of the 8th International Conference on Electronic Commerce: The New E-Commerce: Innovations for Conquering Current Barriers, Obstacles and Limitations to Conducting Successful Business on the Internet (2006)

Nicolaou, A.I., Ibrahim, M., Van Heck, E.: Information quality, trust, and risk perceptions in electronic data exchanges. Decis. Supp. Syst. **54**(2), 986–996 (2013)

Özkan, A.H.: The effect of burnout and its dimensions on turnover intention among nurses: a meta-analytic review. J. Nurs. Manag. **30**(3), 660–669 (2022)

Podsakoff, P.M., MacKenzie, S.B., Lee, J.-Y., Podsakoff, N.P.: Common method biases in behavioral research: a critical review of the literature and recommended remedies. J. Appl. Psychol. **88**, 879 (2003)

Puranik, H., Koopman, J., Vough, H.C.: Pardon the interruption: an integrative review and future research agenda for research on work interruptions. J. Manag. **46**(6), 806–842 (2020)

Roses, L.K., Hoppen, N., Henrique, J.L.: Management of perceptions of information technology service quality. J. Bus. Res. **62**(9), 876–882 (2009)

Rudolph, C.W., et al.: Pandemics: implications for research and practice in industrial and organizational psychology. Ind. Organiz. Psychol. **14**(1–2), 1–35 (2021)

Sarabandi, J., Carter, M., Compeau, D.: 10 years of research on technostress creators and inhibitors: synthesis and critique. In: Twenty-Fourth Americas Conference on Information Systems, New Orleans, United States (2018)

Tao, H., Wang, L.: Revision of the Chinese version of the nurses' willingness to stay in the job questionnaire. Acad. J. Second Mil. Med. Univ. **31**, 925–927 (2010)

Wang, Y., Xie, C., Liang, C., Zhou, P., Lu, L.: Association of artificial intelligence use and the retention of elderly caregivers: a cross-sectional study based on empowerment theory. J. Nurs. Manag. (2022)

Zhou, T.: Understanding users' initial trust in mobile banking: an elaboration likelihood perspective. Comput. Hum. Behav. **28**(4), 1518–1525 (2012)

A Case Study of Collaborative Learning Within a Digitalization Learning Environment

Xiaoxia Wang[(⊠)]

School of Traffic and Transportation, Beijing Jiaotong University, Beijing 100044, People's Republic of China
xxwang@bjtu.edu.cn

Abstract. The Covid-19 epidemic ushered in a new era of hybrid learning. After the Covid-19 pandemic, information technology (IT) acceptance is no longer a problem. And given that it is the "postdigital", technology-related constructs should be updated and devoted to creating a lifelong agile learning environment (LE). The research question is how to manage collaborative learning (CL) activities through online integrated platforms to better serve outcome-based education (OBE). This research reviews the digital transformation advancement in learning management systems and points out that the digitalization LE breeds postdigital learning, which is based on IT "affordance" and well organization and distribution of course resources. When led by OBE, this paper employs qualitative synthesis research and to foster personal development summarizes the appropriate method for managing CL activities as student-centered lifelong learning, organization of role-based activities, and all-around assessment. Finally, the findings are a conceptual framework for student-centered learning within digitalization LE and an illustration of a curriculum with a customized *Feishu* of ByteDance performing CL. The contribution involves learning in less structured environments, such as an advanced enterprise collaboration and management platform, which prompts creative and innovative approaches to uncertainty and change. As a result, the practical implication facilitates students to find both their will and their own creative and exploratory ways of lifelong learning.

Keywords: Student-Centered Learning · Collaborative Learning · Lifelong Learning

1   Introduction and Background

"Teaching in the Age of Covid-19" [1] allows a longitudinal tracking of 3 years of experience. And the latest collection in 2022 consists of 67 textual testimonies and 65 workspace photographs submitted by 69 authors from 19 countries. During the very first Covid-19 lockdowns, web-based materials, online seminars, and virtual conferences are used extensively, coping with feeling disconnected as well. With renewed danger from Covid variants being minimized, the restrictions have suddenly gone, especially in China mainland. It's a high probability event that workspaces go back to the pre-pandemic classroom. When we understand that we just have to live with the virus, everyone is first responsible for their health. If students or teachers cannot present in person either because of our safety or self-'care', namely the duty to look out for and after ourselves, hybrid learning (HL) across a variety of platforms, a new compensatory routine, has permitted the resilience to carry out various academic activities.

Technology Acceptance Model (TAM) is typically used when studying adoption. But for now, after the Covid-19 pandemic, adoption is no longer part of the problem. Nowadays, we have multiple options for accessing knowledge. When learning management systems (LMS) are considered a basic "infrastructure", almost every online learning platform could provide. There are the following cases. (1) Open Course Ware Consortium begins with MIT in 2001 following the Creative Commons license. (2) Open video courses offered by Harvard, Oxford, Yale, etc., accessing via Netease and Sina. (3) China's high-quality resource-sharing courses in 2012 and shared by the iCourse platform, are traced to the construction of high-quality courses in the "Teaching Quality and Teaching Reform Project of Colleges and Universities" carried out by the Ministry of Education from 2003 to 2010. (4) Massive Open Online Courses (MOOCs) started in 2008 and broke out in 2012, such as edX, Coursera, Udacity, and OpenLearning. (5) *Xuetang* spearheaded by Tsinghua University, provides learners with high-quality courses from elite universities and training in functional career skills with industrial partners. The impulses and instincts that lead students to enroll in MOOCs originated from autonomous intrinsic motivation, such as self-development, reputation, and perceived usefulness. Perceived satisfaction is a different reason, including quality, entertainment value, and usefulness. MOOCs offer not only accredited certification but also a systematic curriculum designed for tailored programs.

In general, an inclusive and accessible agile learning environment (LE) through an online integrated solution should provide the following basic functions: (1) releasing resources, such as course introduction, syllabus, teaching calendar, evaluation methods and marks, learning guide, teaching units, course chapters, and textbooks; (2) organizing interactive activities, which includes Q&A, questionnaires, exercise assignments, test papers, and discussion, etc. For instance, *Rain Classroom* integrates teaching tools into *PowerPoint* and *WeChat* panoramic data collection, carrying out a formative evaluation and multi-channel interaction. Furthermore, *Rain Classroom* Professional Edition provides functions such as pushing materials, recording voice, audio and video live broadcasts, and teacher-student interaction through *WeChat*, etc.

The application of information technology (IT) should serve educational objectives. And given that it is the "postdigital", technology-related constructs should be updated and devoted to creating a lifelong LE. When a collaborative society is a trend, cooperative work is emerging. Hence, applying the working mode to the learning mode, the earlier the better. This helps to serve lifelong learning and simultaneously carry out peer learning. Table 1 lists some popular collective writing tools.

Outcome-based education (OBE), also called achievement-oriented education, ability-oriented education, goal-oriented education, or demand-oriented education, namely the construction concept of the curriculum system is built on results-oriented, student-oriented, and reverse thinking. The syllabus of each course should be developed according to OBE. So far, all kinds of MOOCs, namely typical learning platforms, have partly been unable to support "student-centered learning" very well. Education is not merely the learning of knowledge, but also the training of learning methods and habits, which is especially important for students who major in e-commerce. To address this shortcoming, the research question is the way to manage collaborative learning (CL) activities to better serve OBE. Hence, adjusting an online integrated teamwork tool is the potential solution, which offers a seamless connection between learning and work.

Table 1. Popular collective writing tools

Apps	Features	
Google Docs	Assistive to write faster with fewer errors based on built-in intelligence	Save time with spelling and grammar suggestions, voice typing, and quick document translation
	Thoughtfully and seamlessly connect to other Google Apps	Reply to comments directly from *Gmail*, embed charts from *Google sheets*, and easily share via *Google meet*
	Bring collaboration and intelligence to other file types, making them instantly editable	e.g. microsoft word files and PDFs
Tencent Docs	A historical version can be traced and cross *QQ/WeChat* platform collaboration	
	Set the viewing range of the document independently Add the link validity period and watermark, and prohibit others from copying/exporting/generating copies	
Jinshan education version	Class stewards	Small programs, web terminals, effective message notifications
	Create and join classes Announcements Homework management	Regular notifications Homework: remind to hand in, distribute, collect, and correct
Evernote	Easy content collection, sort orderly data (intelligent search), clip, search, templates, lists, super notes (drag and drop of various modules), OCR scan, mind map, desktop notes, markdown	
Youdaoyun	e.g. tag, plus star	

The remainder of the paper proceeds as follows. Section 2 reviews a digitalization LE breeds postdigital learning, which is based on IT "affordance" and well organization and distribution of course resources. Section 3 employs qualitative synthesis research and to foster personal development presents the appropriate method for managing CL activities accompanying detailed guidelines. Section 4 presents a conceptual framework for student-centered learning within a digitalization LE and illustrates a curriculum with a customized *Feishu* performing CL. *Feishu* is an innovative enterprise collaboration and management platform developed by ByteDance. Section 5 concludes with a discussion that includes limitations and recommendations for future research.

2 Literature Review

This research review focused on online digital learning from 2020 to 2022, specifically in the field of digital transformation development in LMS.

2.1 Digitalization LE and Postdigital Learning

The criteria for educational innovation were functionality, flexibility, and accessibility. Innovations go through the planning of activities, teaching techniques, and assignments. As a driving force of innovations, IT introduces infinite opportunities for revolutionizing student-centered [2] education. The progress of the college and university classroom environment inventory has the relationship and system dimensions of personalization, involvement, friendly cohesiveness, satisfaction, task orientation, innovation, and individualization [3].

The design of attractive LE requires knowledge of the factors influencing student learning and perceptions. The TAM holds that an individual's behavioral intention to use a system determines their real use of the technology and is shaped by two beliefs: (1) perceived usefulness, the degree to which the person believes the LMS will improve their performance; and (2) ease of use, the degree to which they believe that using the LMS will be effortless [4].

The term postdigital is intended to acknowledge that learning through digital technology now takes center stage and pervades our daily lives, which is to untangle the impact of the digital on diverse systems and relationships as well. Bring your own device [5] enables students to participate and interact in both formal and informal LE, and access, share, co-create, and even merge learning resources in ways that are beyond imagining [6] with a range of digital learning techniques regardless of their location or time constraints [7].

2.2 Technology Affordances

The word "affordance" refers to the opportunities performed by an environment to an individual that prompt or encourage specific actions. Notwithstanding that most of today's children are growing up in the technology-condensed world, it's inevitable to raise awareness among key stakeholders to get the necessary learning facilities ready, develop digital literacy, and flexibly switch between online or offline learning modes if necessary.

The very foundation of e-learning is preparing the mandatory access requirements of the infrastructure and skills. Firstly, we have interactive digital devices, such as desktop computers with poly cameras, laptops, tablets, smartphones. Then choose and install the proper APPs which may be slightly different across a variety of platforms, for instance, Android, APP Store, Mac, Windows, Android HD, ipad HD, car, TV, UWP, Microsoft App store, etc.

How affordances of technology are generated and what effects they have are related to the material and cultural associations connected with the technology. Students become attuned to these affordances for goal-oriented actions when scaffolding is offered. To facilitate the enactment of certain behaviors [8], the amount and type of support affect students' ability to perform tasks, thus affecting their learning experience as well. For example, clearly-defined guidance enabling a structured flexible schedule promotes the opportunity for resolving tensions and holding a balance between the subject study requirements and work commitments.

2.3 Organization and Distribution of Course Resources

Many students expressed support for the availability of on-demand and pre-loaded material rather than being provided just in time. Self-paced learning through "self-service" APPs contributes to the maintenance of and improving pre-learning effects.

Student engagement was influenced by the quality, relevance, timeliness, and conciseness of the adequate supporting material pertinent to the subject [3]. LMS facilitates easy-to-transfer digital portfolios, which comprise a collection of documents and evidence of a teacher's knowledge, skills, and experience [9].

3 Research Methods: Managing Activities to Foster Personal Development

Qualitative synthesis research is a method that consolidates the output of different qualitative studies to create new subject knowledge [10]. Thereby generating increased levels of understanding of managing teaching activities and greater research finding generalizability on the student-centered lifelong learning within a digitalization LE.

3.1 Flexi-Path Learning Objectives

Led by OBE, instructors individually treat extreme diversity among students based on ability, skill levels, interest, rate of work, etc. Improve necessary capabilities based on individualization, both domain-specific knowledge and skill development [11] listed in Table 2.

Table 2. Promoting personal skill development

Reflective/critical thinking	Coordinating with others	Creativity thinking	Multicultural and empathy
Complex problem solving	Communication and negotiation	Innovative and anticipatory	Inter- and multidisciplinary
Judgment and decision-making	Collaborative/cooperation	Entrepreneurial	Emotional intelligence
Holistic and systems thinking	People management		Service orientation
Cognitive flexibility	Facilitating and project management		

In China, a curriculum should follow "the Guidelines for Ideological and Political Construction of University Curriculum (JiaoGai [2020] No. 3)". It's a strategic measure to give effect to the fundamental task of establishing morality and cultivating people. What, how, and for whom to cultivate people is the fundamental issue of schooling. To implement the fundamental task of establishing morality and cultivating people, we must integrate value shaping, knowledge imparting, and ability cultivation into one. To integrate values into knowledge teaching, ability training, and help students shape a correct outlook on the world, life, and values, which is the proper meaning and essential content of talent training. Let students master the law of development of things, understand the truth of the world, enrich their knowledge, increase their knowledge, shape their character, and strive to become socialist builders and successors with all-around development of morality, intelligence, physique, beauty, and labor.

Lifelong Learning within Learning Space. In the context of postdigital learning, particular degrees and diplomas are becoming less important than the capacity to change, learn, and adapt to a changing landscape over a lifetime. Therefore, the view of education is undergoing profound changes from transactional (trading time for a diploma) to transformative (time of exploration). Thus, a curriculum becomes a creation and a composition of educational experience that is complex, multidirectional, and multi-layered, and students think differently [6].

In the postdigital, lifelong learning may prompt distress and disjunction. It's important to help learners to agree on the existence and importance of various disjunctions, such as narrative, ontological, conceptual, and epistemological [6]. Key capacities for navigating learning space are active resilience and hope, including will-finding and way-finding. The driving forces for the movement were the learners' inner motivation for learning to improve practices, originating from the perceived meaning of the practical experience.

Student-Centered Learning. Students feel more accountable for their learning. Personalized learning includes inquiry learning, problem-solving, and project-based learning [12]. Inquiry learning encourages students to find out and construct information by themselves instead of having teachers serve as knowledge providers. The general phase of the inquiry cycle includes orientation, conceptualization, investigation, conclusion, and discussion.

3.2 The Clarity and Organization of Activities that Foster Refection

By studying the relationships among the cognitive, affective, and potential behavioral components of students' attitudes toward technology in a Swedish context, students' interest in technology should be stimulated through engaging tasks [13].

Cost-effective and useful ubiquitous CL, certain kinds of peer-to-peer learning, support ubiquitous task orientation activities, such as synthesizing, analysis, presentation, discussions, or problem-solving [14]. CL permits transparent cooperation and improves achievement by empowering the social negotiation space of group members, increasing effective coordination between the activity states, the possibility of mediation in inter-activity, and enabling students to better collaboration performance in groups supporting social face-to-face communication.

Quick Connectivity Opportunities for Incisive Interactive Feedback.
Personalization means the opportunity that individual students have to interact with
the instructor and the concern for students' welfare, which is embodied in facilitating
effective and timely interaction and an active efficient communication mechanism. The
nature of interactivity, namely the capacity for bidirectional communication, is set in the
context of the teacher and the student, between the students themselves as well. Equity
and constructive feedback allow students to confirm that they were on the right track.

Learning-by-Doing and Peer Co-Production: Knowledge Socialism [15]. As pro-
ducers or "prosumers", students play a more active role. Collective writing experiments
conducted between 2016 and 2022, allowed contributors to choose their supportive role.
Co-authors use a shared document to engage with the text and benefit from collective
insights and perspectives (fluid further thoughts). This kind of self-regulation has its
built-in peer review mechanism due to openness, which is subject to others' instant,
ongoing, dynamic 'criticism' and leads to high-quality outputs.

Role-Based Interaction [8]. Distinct roles students played represented different social
statuses in the group (as Table 3), which led to trade-offs in orientation to individual
consciousness and collective rules. Moreover, a stable action orientation within groups
during inquiry facilitates proper internal coordination, and that close interaction does
not always lead to efficient collaboration.

Table 3. Categories and examples of roles in a team

Types of roles in a team	Categories	Examples
Shaper, implementer, completer/finisher, coordinator, resource investigator, team worker, plant, monitor/evaluator, and specialist	Formative	An order supervisor
	Functional	Recorder, motivator, clarifier, interpreter, and consensus seeker
	Summative	Summarizer and creator
	Promotive	Reason requests and principal giving

Role-based interaction includes role emergence, role coordination, and group structure caused by role-related interaction patterns. The emerging role perspective addresses
student agency and the regulation of their learning activity so that participating students perform a different action orientation and develop different learning preferences
in their group work. The scripted perspective stresses the importance of designed roles
in supporting group interactions and improving students' learning outcomes.

3.3 Assessment: Peer Quality Enhancement and Control

The continuous pressure for efficient instruction and assessment had implemented a pedagogy of structured peer critiques, which aimed to: (1) encourage student interaction, (2)

emulate the effects of multiple stakeholder perspectives on multidisciplinary planning, and (3) have students practice their new knowledge in an early and influential social learning exchange [3].

4 Results: A CL Curriculum within a Digitalization LE via Customized *Feishu*

4.1 A Framework: Student-Centered Learning within Digitalization LE

Based on Sects. 2 and 3, Fig. 1 introduces a conceptual framework to illustrate the general idea of student-centered learning within a digitalization LE.

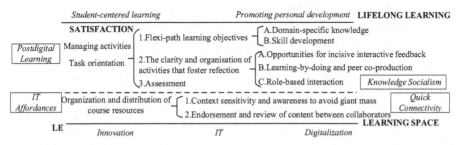

Fig. 1. Student-centered learning within digitalization LE

First, when IT is already becoming "affordance", it's possible to well organize and distribute course resources [3]. As a result, a digitalization LE is emerging, which will breed postdigital learning. Then, built on the core concept of OBE, the essential issue of teaching is to foster people and promote personal development [11], which relies on managing CL activities and carrying out knowledge socialism [15].

4.2 Illustrated a Curriculum with a Customized *Feishu* Performing CL

Learners' perceptions are shaped by explicit scripts in gaining knowledge. Scripts are tailored to the collaboration skills and roles of group members, which can be divided into internal by group and external by a teacher or other facilitator, the latter explicitly imposed on learners as a guiding structure to prompt them to act, which include induced, instructed, trained, prompted, follow-me. Specifically, interactive scripts are designed such that the roles of participants, the actions they engaged in, and the sequence of events they participate in trigger specific cognitive, sociocognitive, and metacognitive processes, thus ensuring that the intended learning takes place.

The standard configuration of rapid CL product functions based on multi-terminal synchronization: (1) traditional approaches, such as instant messaging, calendar, mailbox, cloud disk; (2) video conference, clever notes, open platform, thought notes; (3) efficiently create and seamlessly collaborate on online documents synchronized in real-time and from any device to build ideas together. (4) file/folder sharing, cloud collaboration space, defining team knowledge base, offer knowledge star map. (5) privacy and

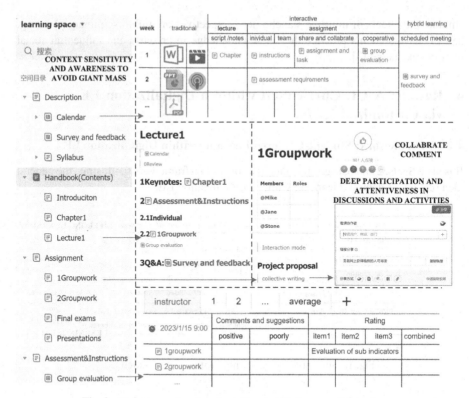

Fig. 2. Endorsement and review of content between collaborators

encrypt the document securely. Figure 2 presents the endorsement and review of content between collaborators via *Feishu*.

On the left side, the learning space well organizes the following materials: (1) the course description; (2) a course handbook containing aims or intended learning outcomes; (3) group assessment requirements. All these scripts are context sensitive and ready for searching.

When unfolding the specific script, it looks like on the right side. (1) A teaching calendar is filled with interactive lecture scripts and a schedule of assignments. (2) Each lecture script organizes each teaching section; (3) Group worksheets are developed to conduct collective writing. (4) A formative assessment is to evaluate process quality, supplementing a self-reporting questionnaire that assesses reflective thinking in solving problems. All these scripts can be edited together in real time with easy sharing, and user comments, suggestions, and action items to keep things moving. Or use @-mentions to pull relevant people, files, and events into specific online docs for rich collaboration.

When learners can understand the positive consequences of using this system, they are more likely to enjoy it.

5   Discussion and Conclusions

Definite positive results of intensive technology use will remain. There are more extensive technology-related support and awareness of the possibilities of hybrid technology-rich working. Teaching has "pivoted" to hybrid, which should not be considered as just a stopgap.

Postdigital learning needs to encourage students to interrogate both new knowledge and the learning space in which it is delivered. The curriculum should be about the development of inclusivity, equality, and critical pedagogy. This may involve learning in less structured environments and prompts creative and innovative approaches to uncertainty and change. Teachers need to ensure students continue to understand the importance of disjunction as a component of finding both their will and their own creative and exploratory ways of lifelong learning [6].

The limitation of this research, are (1) focusing on "student-centered learning" and serving teachers' interactive teaching, which might not consider the need for supervision to evaluate teaching quality; and (2) a potential payment demand for the commercial edition, not only because of premium features but also the upper limit trigger due to the number of users or storage space.

Acknowledgment. This research was supported by the undergraduate education reform project of "Logistics Distribution under the Internet Environment" (textbook) and the postgraduate education reform project of "Managerial Economics" (core course), School of Traffic and Transportation, Beijing Jiaotong University; Key Laboratory of Transport Industry of Big Data Application Technologies for Comprehensive Transport, Beijing Jiaotong University, Beijing, China.

References

1. Jandrić, P., Martinez, A.F., Reitz, C., et al.: Teaching in the age of Covid-19—The new normal. Postdigit. Sci. Educ. **4**(3), 877–1015 (2022)
2. Scott, J.L., Knezek, G., Poirot, J.R., et al.: Attributes of learning organizations: measuring personalized online learning and alternative credentials as part of a learning culture. TechTrends **67**(1), 54–67 (2023)
3. Joiner, K.F., Rees, L., Levett, B., Sitnikova, E., Townsend, D.: Learning environment of a distance and partly-distance postgraduate coursework programs. Learn. Environ. Res. **24**(3), 423–449 (2020). https://doi.org/10.1007/s10984-020-09335-w
4. Pozón-López, I., Higueras-Castillo, E., Muñoz-Leiva, F., Liébana-Cabanillas, F.J.: Perceived user satisfaction and intention to use massive open online courses (MOOCs). J. Comput. High. Educ. **33**(1), 85–120 (2020). https://doi.org/10.1007/s12528-020-09257-9
5. Nuhoğlu Kibar, P., Gündüz, A.Y., Akkoyunlu, B.: Implementing bring your own device (BYOD) model in flipped learning: advantages and challenges. Technol. Knowl. Learn. **25**(3), 465–478 (2019). https://doi.org/10.1007/s10758-019-09427-4
6. Ball, J., Savin-Baden, M.: Postdigital learning for a changing higher education. Postdigit. Sci. Educ. **4**(3), 753–771 (2022)
7. Peramunugamage, A., Ratnayake, U.W., Karunanayaka, S.P.: Systematic review on mobile collaborative learning for engineering education. J. Comput. Educ. **10**(1), 83–106 (2023)

8. Wang, C., Li, S.: The trade-off between individuals and groups: role interactions under different technology affordance conditions. Int. J. Comput.-Supp. Collab. Learn. **16**(4), 525–557 (2021)

9. Chye, S.Y.L.: Towards a framework for integrating digital portfolios into teacher education. TechTrends **65**(5), 818–830 (2021). https://doi.org/10.1007/s11528-021-00646-0

10. Skinner, R.J., Nelson, R.R., Chin, W.: Synthesizing qualitative evidence: a roadmap for information systems research. J. Assoc. Inf. Syst. **23**(3), 639–677 (2022)

11. Brosens, L., Raes, A., Octavia, J.R., et al.: How future proof is design education? A systematic review. Int. J. Technol. Des. Educ. (2022)

12. Al-Samarraie, H., Shamsuddin, A., Alzahrani, A.I.: A flipped classroom model in higher education: a review of the evidence across disciplines. Educ. Tech. Res. Dev. **68**(3), 1017–1051 (2019). https://doi.org/10.1007/s11423-019-09718-8

13. Svenningsson, J., Höst, G., Hultén, M., et al.: Students' attitudes toward technology: exploring the relationship among affective, cognitive and behavioral components of the attitude construct. Int. J. Technol. Des. Educ. **32**(3), 1531–1551 (2022)

14. Aljawarneh, S.A.: Reviewing and exploring innovative ubiquitous learning tools in higher education. J. Comput. High. Educ. **32**(1), 57–73 (2019). https://doi.org/10.1007/s12528-019-09207-0

15. Jandrić, P., Luke, T.W., Sturm, S., et al.: Collective writing: the continuous struggle for meaning-making. Postdigit. Sci. Educ. (2022)

A Study on the Influence Mechanism of Self-sacrificial Leadership on Employee Engagement-Based on Dual Identity Perspective

Tingting Wang and Fengqin Diao[✉]

School of Economics and Management, China University of Geosciences (Wuhan), Wuhan, Hubei, China
115899232@qq.com

Abstract. The self-sacrificial leader, who puts the collective interest first and is willing to postpone or sacrifice personal interests in order to achieve organizational goals, plays an important role in maintaining smooth operations and overcoming corporate crises in today's complex and changeable information age. The effective enhancement of employee engagement can also bring positive impact to individuals and organizations. Based on social identity theory, this paper will explore the mechanism of self-sacrificial leadership on employee engagement and its dimensions from the perspective of dual identity: leader identification and organizational identification. The findings show that: Self-sacrificial leadership can positively influence employee engagement. Leader identification and organizational identification are the mediating variables in the path of the influence of self-sacrificial leadership on employee engagement, and the mediating effect of leader identification is more significant. Leader identification can influence organizational identification, and the multiple mediating effect is significant in the path of the influence of self-sacrificial leadership on employee engagement. Cognitive engagement, affective engagement and behavioral engagement are all consistent with the above hypotheses when used as dependent variables.

Keywords: Self-sacrificial Leadership · Employee Engagement · Leader identification · Organizational Identification

1 Introduction

The world is undergoing profound changes ever seen in a century, and with the rapid development of new technologies, the market environment is full of change and uncertainty. As a pivotal role in an organization, the behavior and attitudes of leaders have a significant impact on the development of the organization, while the relationship between leaders and employees needs to maintain a new balance. Self-sacrificial leadership is a leadership style that postpones or gives up personal interests, benefits or privileges in order to achieve the mission and collective interests of the organization, it often postpones or sacrifices self-interest, such as the exercise of power, the division of labor and the distribution of rewards [1], in order to serve the collective interests and promote

Y. Tu and M. Chi (Eds.): WHICEB 2023, LNBIP 480, pp. 95–107, 2023.
https://doi.org/10.1007/978-3-031-32299-0_9

the achievement of organizational goals. The spirit of collectivism and the concept of sharing hardships often lead the organization to overcome difficulties, and is needed for enterprises to avoid risks and develop steadily in information age.

"Dedication" is one of the core values of Chinese socialism, and it is the requirement of an individual's attitude towards work. "Engagement" is defined as the positive integration of the individual in the work from physical, cognitive and emotional aspects [2]. Employees are the mainstay of the companies, governing the existence and development of the organization, and both individuals and organizations can derive positive results from a high level of employee engagement. Employee engagement provides motivation for employees to adopt more positive attitudes and behaviors in the organization, and also provides a sustainable competitive advantage for the organization in today's complex and changing information age.

According to leadership theory, leaders are able to influence employees' behavioral concepts through their perceptions, motivations, and competencies. Many studies have focused on the effects of self-sacrificial leadership on various aspects of employees, such as promoting employee creativity [3], improving work performance [4], etc. While the influencing mechanism of self-sacrificial leadership on employee engagement and its dimensions remain to be explored, and there is no research on the effectiveness of self-sacrificial leadership from the perspective of both extra-role identities, leader identification and organizational identification. Therefore, based on social identity theory, this study focuses on uncovering the internal influence mechanism of self-sacrificial leadership on employee engagement from both leader identification and organizational identification perspectives, and discusses the differences in the influence of different dimensions of engagement in order to provide suggestions for improving employee engagement and find a balance in leadership-employee relations, as well as providing valuable references for companies to maintain a balanced internal organizational environment and promote development In the current changeable era.

2 Theories and Hypotheses

2.1 Self-sacrificial Leadership and Employee Engagement

Self-sacrificial leadership is manifested as sacrificing oneself in order to achieve the organizational mission and set up personal example, which has the following characteristics: out of individual willingness, giving up or postponing personal interests, and aiming at achieving collective interests or goals [5]. Many studies have demonstrated that self-sacrificial leadership can have a positive impact on employees' perceptions or behaviors. Specifically, self-sacrificial leaders' selfless values and behaviors express that leaders value the interests of organizational members, so that employees can recognize the leaders and are willing to demonstrate positive work performance. According to the social learning theory, the collectivism concept of self-sacrificial leaders can easily be used as a role model to motivate employees to exhibit similar concept. And combined with the "reciprocity principle" of social exchange theory, when the self-sacrificial leaders sacrifice personal interests to serve the organization and its members, the members will have the belief to return leaders and show more positive states.

Kahn (1990) pointed out that employee engagement refers to the degree to which organizational members combine their personal emotions, abilities and other resources with their work roles [6], and classified engagement into three dimensions: cognitive engagement, affective engagement and behavioral engagement, where cognitive engagement is characterized by attention and immersion in the work, affective engagement is characterized by positive reactions in the work, and behavioral engagement is characterized by the effort put in the work. Some studies have shown that positive leaders have higher virtue, and subordinates will have a higher sense of trust and satisfaction with their leaders, thus showing a more dedicated work status [7]. Self-sacrificial leaders, as people who are willing to self-sacrifice for the benefit of the collective, can make employees feel supported and valued, satisfy their personal expectations, make them willing to work in a more positive state. The self-sacrificial leadership can create a role model that makes subordinates willing to follow them, and moreover, it can make employees feel obligated to reciprocate the sacrifice of the leader based on reciprocity, and meet the expectations of the leader to complete the work within the role with a higher level of dedication. Therefore, the following hypothesis is proposed.

H1: Self-sacrificial leadership has a positive effect on employee engagement (including cognitive engagement, affective engagement, and behavioral engagement).

2.2 Leader Identification as a Mediator

According to social identity theory, in order to reduce uncertainty or enhance their self-worth, individuals often define and categorize themselves in comparison with groups or others, and establish an emotional connection with the target object [8], that is, generate identity. The process of social identity generally includes social-classification and self-reinforcement. Social-categorization is the process of defining and categorizing oneself and the group, in which the similarity between individuals and the group is strengthened. Self-reinforcement is the process of accelerating this similarity and increasing dissimilarity to the external groups, in which individuals will actively exhibit behaviors that are consistent with the group and will also exhibit positive and proactive behaviors in order to increase the dominance of the group to which they belong.

Leader identification is the employee's connection to the leader and the degree to which the employee overlaps with the values and goals of leaders. In general, leader identification is catalyzed when leadership styles maintain or enhance employees' self-esteem, satisfaction of needs, and self-improvement of meaning [9]. Studies have proved that self-sacrificial leadership can make employees develop emotional attachment, and promote the formation of leader identification [4]. The dedication and collectivism of self-sacrificial leaders can make employees feel respected and valued, and thus willing to establish an emotional connection with the leader, that is, to improve employees' identification with the leader and show consistent behaviors with the leader.

When the behavioral state of the leader catalyzes employees to develop leader identification, which leads to a strong sense of belonging and psychological attachment to the leaders [10], employees will more actively associate themselves with the leaders in a consistent manner, translate identification into psychological motivation, and perform positive behaviors expected of leaders, such as increasing work engagement [11]. The higher virtues of self-sacrificial leaders can inspire employees to form identification with their leaders, and the higher the employees' leader identification, the more they tend to combine the attitude and behavior of leaders with themselves and maintain consistency, strive to achieve organizational goals and promote organizational development, and they are more willing to give feedback on more positive states, which can also result in higher engagement. Therefore, the following hypothesis is proposed.

H2: Self-sacrificial leadership has a positive effect on leader identification.

H3: Leader identification plays a mediating role in the influence of Self-sacrificial leadership on employee engagement (including cognitive engagement, affective engagement, and behavioral engagement).

2.3 Organizational Identification as a Mediator

Organizational identification is the cognitive or emotional association of organizational members with their identification as members of the organization and reflects the degree of integration and recognition of the individual to the organization. Generally speaking, employees are more likely to identify with the organization that brings them a higher sense of security, self-realization and belonging [12]. The self-sacrificial leader, as the agent of the organization, is loyal to the organization's goals and mission, and to a certain extent represents the organization's values and behavioral norms, thus being able to influence employees' personal concepts such as enhancing organizational identification [12]. Self-sacrificial leaders put the development of organization and organizational member's interests first and emphasize the overall awareness, which can make employees feel a sense of security and belonging brought by the organization, as well as the self-worth of individuals in the organization, they are willing to include individuals in the organization and thus increase their identification with the organization.

According to the social identity theory, the higher the employees' identification with the organization, the easier it is to link themselves closely with the organization, employees will incorporate organizational development and goals into their personal goals, and will be more willing to show a more active and proactive state for the development of the organization. Most studies on organizational identification also agree that organizational identification can have positive effects on employees, such as promoting subordinate taking charge [13]. High organizational identification enables employees to align their attitudes or behaviors with the organization and align the interests and development of the organization to the interests and development of the individual, driving employees to work hard to achieve organizational goals, employees will do their jobs better and show more positive and dedicated states and behaviors. Therefore, the following hypotheses are proposed.

H4: Self-sacrificial leadership has a positive effect on organizational identification.

H5: Organizational identification plays a mediating role in the influence of Self-sacrificial leadership on employee engagement (including cognitive engagement, affective engagement, and behavioral engagement).

2.4 Leader Identification and Organizational Identification

The typical manifestations of social identity are organizational identification and leader identification, that is, the emotional connection of employees to organizations or leaders.

Leader as part of the organization, employees support for the leader can be expanded to generate support for the organization, positive leadership style can also make employees produce follower effect and maintain a high sense of support and trust for the organization. Sluss et al. (2018) pointed out in their research that when the supervisor is perceived to be prototypical, Leader identification is more likely to generalize to organizational identification through affective, cognitive, and behavioral mediating mechanisms [14]. The collectivist value of the self-sacrificial leader is highly representative of the organization, and can effectively facilitate the transformation of leader identification to organizational identification, so that employees link the individual, the leader, and the organization as one, and thus show the attitude and behavior conducive to the development of the organization. Therefore, the following hypotheses are proposed.

H6: Leader identification can promote employees' organizational identification, which in turn affects employee engagement (including cognitive engagement, affective engagement, and behavioral engagement).

In summary, the research model of this study is shown in Fig. 1 below.

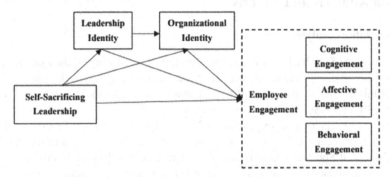

Fig. 1. Research model

3 Methods

In this study, data were collected through questionnaire method, the questionnaire scale is suitable for employees to fill in and the respondents anonymously evaluate the leaders and personal feelings. Pre-survey was conducted before the formal survey and the questions were optimized based on the analysis results. After the formal research, a total of 320 questionnaires were collected, of which 273 were valid, with an effective rate of 85.3%. The collected data were processed, analyzed, establish regression model and hypothesis tested using SPSS and AMOS soft.

The questionnaire scales used in this study are all mature scales that have been tested by domestic and foreign scholars, with appropriate modifications for the Chinese context. All scales were scored by Likert 7 points. The measurement of self-sacrificial leadership was based on a 5-item unidimensional scale developed by Cremer et al. [15], which is suitable for employees to fill in, and has been verified by domestic scholars for many times with good reliability and validity, the scale questions include "My leader will make personal sacrifices for the good of the organization". Leader identification was measured using the unidimensional leader identification scale developed by Kark et al. [16], which was modified to have seven items, and the scale questions included "I trust my leader a lot". The organizational identification scale was based on the unidimensional six-item scale introduced by Mael et al. [17], with question such as "I care about what people think of the company I work for". Regarding the scale of employee engagement, this paper draws on the three-dimensional employee engagement measurement scale adapted by Ma [18], which has 13 items, including "I think it is my duty to do my job well", etc.

According to the final data collection statistics, the respondents came from more than 20 provinces, covering various types of positions and business nature. In terms of gender, 51.3% were female and 48.7% were male; in terms of age, 25.6% were under 25 years old, 44.7% were between 26 and 30 years old, 20.1% were between 31 and 35 years old, and 9.5% were over 35 years old; in terms of working years, 18.7% were under one year, 34.1% were 1–3 years old, 33.7% were 4–6 years old, and 13.5% were over 7 years old; in terms of education, 34.8% were college education or below, 49.1% were bachelor degree, and 49.1% were graduate degree or above.

4 Data Analysis and Results

4.1 Reliability Analysis

In this study, the Cronbach-α was used to measure the reliability of the questionnaire. Among them, the coefficients of self-sacrificial leadership (SL), leader identification (LI), organizational identification (OI) and employee engagement (EE) were 0.807, 0.818, 0.780, and 0.888, and the coefficients of cognitive engagement (CE), affective engagement (AE), behavioral engagement (BE) in engagement were 0.743, 0.759, 0.756, all of which exceeded 0.7. The value of KMO statistic was 0.932 and the result of Bartlett's Test of Sphericity approximated 0, indicating that the data in this study were suitable for factor analysis. Next, the structural validity test was conducted using Amos, and the four-factor model containing second-order dimensions was validated by factor analysis. And the fit indicators were as follows: $\chi^2/df = 1.659 < 3$, IFI = 0.920, TLI = 0.908, CFI = 0.919, which were all greater than 0.9, and RMSEA = 0.049 < 0.08, indicating that each variable has high structural. The combined reliability values CR for SL, LI, OI, CE, BE and AE were 0.797, 0.820, 0.767, 0.757, 0.755 and 0.739, all of which exceeded 0.7, indicating that the reliability coefficients of the questionnaire were good and basically meets the requirements of the research. In addition, the results of unrotated factor analysis showed that the total variance of the first factor interpretation was 36.91%, less than 40%, indicating that there was no serious homologous variance problem in the data in this study.

4.2 Correlation Analysis

Correlation analysis was first performed using SPSS, and the correlation coefficients, means, and standard deviations of all variables are shown in Table 1 below. The results indicate that the independent variables, mediating variables and dependent variables are significantly correlated with each other, which initially supports the research hypothesis of this study.

Table 1. Descriptive statistics and correlation analysis results

	SL	LI	OI	EE
Self-sacrificial leadership	1			
Leader identification	.673**	1		
Organizational identification	.615**	.657**	1	
Employee engagement	.688**	.796**	.708**	1
Mean value	5.33	5.30	5.34	5.42
Standard deviation	1.028	.927	.821	.901

Note: *p < 0.05, **p < 0.01, ***p < 0.001.

4.3 Direct and Mediating Effects Tests

Next, the direct and mediating effects were tested by constructing regression models for the variables of self-sacrificial leadership (SL), leader identification (LI), organizational identification (OI) and employee engagement (EE) to verify the main hypotheses of this study. The results of the regression analysis are shown in Table 2 below.

Table 2. Regression analysis of self-sacrificial leadership, leader identification, organizational identification and employee engagement

Variables	Models							
	LI		OI		EE			
	Model1	Model2	Model3	Model4	Model5	Model6	Model7	Model8
1. Gender	−0.192	−0.019	0.055	0.063	.015	0.026	−0.007	0.011
2. Age	0.095	−0.038	−0.066	−0.049	−.066	−0.045	−0.040	−0.034
3. Seniority	−0.113	−0.037	−0.119*	−0.102	−.030	−0.010	0.018	0.014
4. Education	−0.147	−0.010	−0.028	−0.024	−.056	−0.51	−0.450	−0.045
5. Nature of business	0.046	−0.075 *	−0.043	−0.010	−.068 *	−0.026	−0.050	−0.024
SL		0.578 ***	0.552 ***	0.300 ***	.540 ***	0.221 ***	0.317 ***	0.151 **
LI				0.438 ***		0.552 ***		0.449 ***
OI							0.404 ***	0.235 ***
R2		0.466	0.414	0.510	0.492	0.682	0.611	0.716
F		38.733	31.288	39.472	43.000	81.310	59.439	83.129

Note: *p < 0.05, **p < 0.01, ***p < 0.001.

As shown in the table above: Model 2 shows that self-sacrificial leadership has a significant positive effect on leader identification ($\beta = 0.578$, P < 0.001). Model 3 shows that self-sacrificial leadership has a significant positive effect on organizational identification ($\beta = 0.552$, P < 0.001). Model 4 shows that the positive influence of leader identification on organizational identification is significant ($\beta = 0.438$, p < 0.001), and the positive effect of self-sacrificial leadership on organizational identification is reduced but still significant ($\beta = 0.300$, p < 0.001), indicating that leader identification plays a partial mediating effect in the positive effect of self-sacrificial leadership on organizational identification. Model 5 shows that self-sacrificial leadership has a significant positive effect on employee engagement ($\beta = 0.540$, P < 0.001). Model 6 shows that the positive effect of leader identification on employee engagement is significant ($\beta = 0.552$, p < 0.001), and the positive effect coefficient of self-sacrificial leadership on employee engagement is reduced but still significant ($\beta = 0.221$, p < 0.001), indicating that leader identification plays a partial mediating effect in the positive effect of self-sacrificial leadership on employee engagement. Model 7 shows that the positive effect of organizational identification on employee engagement is significant ($\beta = 0.404$, p < 0.001), and the positive effect of self-sacrificial leadership on employee engagement is reduced but still significant ($\beta = 0.317$, p < 0.001), indicating that organizational identification plays a partial mediating effect in the positive effect of leader identification on employee engagement ($\beta = 0.449$, p < 0.001). Model 8 shows that that the positive effect of leader identification on employee engagement is significant ($\beta = 0.449$, p < 0.001), and the positive effect of organizational identification on employee engagement is significant ($\beta = 0.235$, p < 0.001), and the positive effect of Self-sacrificial leadership on employee engagement is reduced but still significant ($\beta = 0.151$, p = 0.001), indicating that leader identification and organizational identification play the multiple mediating effect in the positive effect of self-sacrificial leadership on employee engagement.

Table 3. The bootstrapping test of self-sacrificial leadership and employee engagement

Paths	β	LLCI	ULCI	r
Ind1: SL-LI-EE	0.259	0.187	0.344	47.96%
Ind2: SL-OI-EE	0.070	0.024	0.145	12.96%
Ind3: SL-LI-OI-EE	0.060	0.024	0.109	11.11%
Direct effect	0.151	0.075	0.227	27.96%
Total	0.540	0.467	0.612	

The bootstrapping test was used to further verify the mediating effect of leader identification and organizational identification in the influence of self-sacrificial leadership on employee engagement. As the results shown in Table 3, the 95% confidence intervals of the influence effects of each path do not include 0, that is, self-sacrificial leadership can influence employee engagement through the mediating effect of leader identification, organizational identification, and the multiple mediating effect of leadership identification-organizational identification. And according to the proportion of influence effects, self-sacrificial leadership are more likely to positively influence employee engagement through the mediating effect of leader identification, followed by the direct effect influence on employee engagement, the effect influenced through the mediating path of organizational identification and the multiple mediating path of leader identification-organizational identification accounts for a smaller percentage.

4.4 Hypothesis Testing of the Dimensions of Employee Engagement

In order to further explore the different effects of the dimensions of engagement in this research, cognitive engagement (D1), affective engagement (D2), and behavioral engagement (D3) were introduced into the model as dependent variables and constructed regression analysis models. The analysis results are shown in Table 4 below.

As the results shown in Table 4 above, the direct effects of self-sacrificial leadership on cognitive engagement, affective engagement, and behavioral engagement are all significant. When leader identification and organizational identification are introduced into the model, both of them can positively influence employee engagement, and direct effect coefficients of self-sacrificial leadership are all reduced but still significant, indicating that leader identification and organizational identification can play the partial mediating effect and multiple mediating effect in the influence of self-sacrificial leadership on the dimensions of engagement.

The bootstrapping test was used to further verify the mediating effects of leader identification and organizational identification in the influence of self-sacrificial leadership on cognitive, affective, and behavioral engagement. As the results shown in Table 5, the 95% confidence intervals of the influence effects of each path do not include 0. That is, self-sacrificial leadership can influence cognitive engagement, affective engagement, and behavioral engagement through the mediating effect of leader identification, organizational identification, and the multiple mediating effect of leader identification-organizational identification. According to the proportion of influence effects, Self-sacrificial leaders are more likely to positively influence the dependent variable through the mediating effect of leader identification, followed by the direct effect influence on employee engagement, the effect influenced through the mediating path of organizational identification and the multiple mediating path of leader identification-organizational identification accounts for a smaller percentage, and gradually decreases with the change of cognitive, affective, and behavioral engagement.

Table 4. Regression analysis of self-sacrificial leadership, leader identification, organizational identification and engagement dimensions

Variables	Models											
	CE				AE				BE			
	Model 5a	Model 6a	Model 7a	Model 8a	Model 5b	Model 6b	Model 7b	Model 8b	Model 5c	Model 6c	Model 7c	Model 8c
1. Gender	0.045	0.055	0.020	0.036	0.030	0.040	0.008	0.024	−0.050	−0.093	−0.069	−0.048
2. Age	−0.108	−0.088	−0.078	−0.073	−0.009	0.011	0.018	0.023	−0.078	−0.058	−0.055	−0.049
3. Seniority	0.001	−0.020	−0.055	0.051	−0.097	−0.078	−0.050	−0.053	−0.007	0.028	0.047	0.043
4. Education	0.051	−0.045	−0.064	0.063	−0.130*	−0.125**	−0.119*	−0.119**	0.007	−0.064	−0.060	−0.61
5. Nature of business	−0.025	−0.014	−0.006	0.017	−0.035	−0.028	−0.050	−0.026	−0.094	−0.050	−0.079*	−0.049
SL	0.521***	0.218***	0.272***	0.127**	0.573***	0.273***	0.351***	0.199***	0.541***	0.204***	0.352***	0.160***
LI		0.525***		0.393***		0.520***		0.412***		0.583***		0.518***
OI			0.450***	0.303***			0.401***	0.246***			0.342***	0.147**
R	0.408	0.565	0.542	0.616	0.440	0.572	0.531	0.601	0.438	0.619	0.510	0.630
F	30.516	49.184	44.872	52.901	34.793	50.563	42.936	49.645	34.573	61.416	39.496	56.148

Note: $*p < 0.05$, $**p < 0.01$, $***p < 0.001$.

Table 5. The bootstrapping test of self-sacrificial leadership and the dimensions of engagement

Dimensions		Paths				
		Ind1 SL-LI-CE	Ind2 SL-OI-AE	Ind3 SL-LI-OI-BE	Direct effect	Total
CE	β	0.227	0.090	0.077	0.127	0.521
	LLCI	0.137	0.038	0.039	0.035	0.439
	ULCI	0.325	0.167	0.129	0.220	0.603
	r	43.57%	17.27%	14.78%	24.38%	
AE	β	0.238	0.074	0.062	0.199	0.573
	LLCI	0.153	0.025	0.021	0.097	0.487
	ULCI	0.327	0.157	0.125	0.301	0.657
	r	41.5%	12.91%	10.82%	34.73%	
BE	β	0.300	0.044	0.037	0.160	0.541
	LLCI	0.210	0.002	0.002	0.066	0.458
	ULCI	0.402	0.110	0.083	0.254	0.623
	r	55.45%	8.13%	6.84%	29.57%	

5 Discussion

5.1 Conclusion

Self-sacrificial leadership can effectively motivate the generation of employee engagement in enterprises. Previous studies have not yet explored the impact of self-sacrificial leadership on employee engagement. This study proves that the leader who is able to make self-sacrifices for the benefit of his organization and employees will win the recognition of employees, as well as inspiring them by example, which positively affects employees' engagement and related dimensions such as cognitive engagement, affective engagement, and behavioral engagement.

Self-sacrificial leadership can positively influence employees' engagement through leader identification and organizational identification, and can also promote employees' organizational identification through the multiple mediating effects of leader identification-organizational identification. Based on the social identity theory, this paper attempts to introduce two extra-role identity variables, leader identification and organizational identification, into the model of the effect of self-sacrificial leadership on employee engagement, and the results show that, self-sacrificial leadership mainly enhances employees' positive perceptions and leader identification through personal values and behaviors of making personal sacrifices for the public good, so that employees can keep their own attitudes and behaviors consistent with their leaders. At the same time, as an agent of the organization, the leader's own performance will also make the organizational characteristics show similarity, so the employees' organizational identification will be stimulated along with the leader identification, and the employees will be willing to subsume themselves into the organization and show positive behaviors.

The effects of self-sacrificial leadership on cognitive, affective, and behavioral engagement are consistent with the hypotheses of this research, and the proportion of mediating effects and multiple mediating effect of the path where organizational identification is located gradually decreases with changes in cognitive, affective, and behavioral engagement. The paper argues that employees' affective engagement and behavioral engagement need affective or behavioral giving as performance, still have some differences with the actual psychological will of employees, and employees may inhibit the actual occurrence of certain pay based on personal or situational factors such as ability mismatch or protecting personal resources [19]. Leader identification is an intuitive psychological perception of self-sacrificial leaders, and employees tend to align themselves directly with their leaders more than with the organization. Therefore, when leader identification and organizational identification are introduced simultaneously, organizational identification is more likely to be inhibited by external factors or employees' internal willingness than leader identification, thus the positive effects on affective and behavioral engagement is reduced.

5.2 Practical Implications

For leaders, they need to sacrifice personal interests for the sake of organizational goals and employees' interests to some extent, such as daring to take on more difficult tasks at work, actively sacrificing their personal time to lead employees to accomplish corporate goals, giving up the privileges they have as leaders, etc., make employees feel valued from their leaders and thus willing to behave in a more positive manner; Self-sacrificial leaders should weaken the traditional commanding and authoritarian leadership style, and effectively promote the formation of their leader identification by influencing the psychological state of employees. It should also strive to improve its representation in the organization, and promote the development and transformation of organizational identification; Leaders should strengthen communication with employees, and promptly find out the reasons that cause inconsistency between employees' psychological state and actual performance, such as whether employees feel that they have received a personal loss of benefits, whether they have generated greater pressure in their work, etc., and promptly communicate with employees to solve the problem, so as to avoid the actual occurrence of inhibiting employees' dedicated emotions and behaviors.

For companies, when recruiting or selecting leaders, they can focus on leaders with the spirit of self-sacrifice, the internal training of enterprises can also focus on the cultivation of leaders of all ranks with the concept of " Collective priority", this type of leadership can play an important role in promoting the formation of employee dedication; The organization should create a corporate culture, and synchronize with self-sacrificial leadership to effectively protect the interests of employees, to make employees really feel valued and inspire them to have organizational identification and show higher dedication to accomplish the mission of the organization; In daily work, incentive system can be developed to encourage and support employees, so as to better promote the actual occurrence of employee engagement emotion and behavior.

References

1. Yeon, C.: On the leadership function of self-sacrifice. Leadersh. Q. **9**(4) (1998)
2. Hu, S., Wang, Y.: Concepts, measurements, antecedents and consequences of work engagement. Adv. Psychol. Sci. **22**(12), 1975–1984 (2014). (in Chinese)
3. Xu, Z., Li, X., Sun, X., Cheng, M., Xu, J.: The relationship between self-sacrificial leadership and employee creativity: multilevel mediating and moderating role of shared vision. Manag. Decis. **60**(8) (2022)
4. Li, Y., Zhang, W., Long, L.: How self-sacrificial leadership influences subordinates' work performance: the mediating roles of strategic orientation and supervisor identification. Acta Psychol. Sin. **47**(05), 653–662 (2015). (in Chinese)
5. Zhang, H., Ling, W.: Research on self-sacrifice behavior of managers. Hum. Resour. Dev. China **11**, 9–13 (2010). (in Chinese)
6. Kahn, W.A.: Psychological conditions of personal engagement and disengagement at work. Acad. Manag. J. **33**(4) (1990). (in Chinese)
7. Yan, Y., Zhang, J., Akhtar, M.N., Liang, S.: Positive leadership and employee engagement: the roles of state positive affect and individualism-collectivism. Curr. Psychol. (New Brunswick, N.J.) (2021, prepublish)
8. Zhang, Y., Zuo, B.: Social identity theory and it's development. Adv. Psychol. Sci. **03**, 475–480 (2006). (in Chinese)
9. Chen, L., Liu, S., Hu, X.: Leader humble behavior and follower proactive behavior: a social identity perspective. J. Manag. Sci. China **25**(02), 104–115 (2020). (in Chinese)
10. Cui, Z., Liu, P., Yang, F., Liu, R., Yang, Z.: Study on the relationship between spiritual leadership and employees' positive followship behavior from the integrated perspective of leader identification and self-determination. Chin. J. Manag. **18**(11), 1649–1658 (2021). (in Chinese)
11. Zhang, Z., Gu, Y.: The influence mechanism of person-supervisor fit on R&D employee job engagement. Sci. Technol. Progr. Policy **34**(4), 134–139 (2017). (in Chinese)
12. Cao, Z., Wang, T., Song, Y.: Can self-sacrificial leadership promote unethical pro-organizational behavior? the mediating role of organizational Identification and Its boundary conditions. Hum. Resour. Dev. China **36**(06), 21–32 (2019). (in Chinese)
13. Li, R., Zhang, Z.-Y., Tian, X.-M.: Can self-sacrificial leadership promote subordinate taking charge? The mediating role of organizational identification and the moderating role of risk aversion. J. Organiz. Behav. **37**(5) (2016)
14. Sluss, D.M., Ployhart, R.E., Cobb, M.G., Ashforth, B.E.: Generalizing newcomers' relational and organizational identifications: processes and prototypicality. Acad. Manag. J. **55**(4) (2012)
15. De Cremer, D., van Knippenberg, D.: Leader self-sacrifice and leadership effectiveness: the moderating role of leader self-confidence. Organiz. Behav. Hum. Decis. Process. **95**(2) (2004)
16. Ronit, K., Shamir, B., Chen, G.: The two faces of transformational leadership: empowerment and dependency. J. Appl. Psychol. **88**(2) (2003)
17. Mael, F., Ashforth, B.E.: Alumni and their alma mater: a partial test of the reformulated model of organizational identification. J. Organiz. Behav. **13**(2) (1992)
18. Ma, S.: Research on the Relationship between Pay Equity, Employee Engagement and Job Performance. Shandong University (2018). (in Chinese)
19. Yin, J., Wang, H., Huang, M.: Empowering leadership behavior and perceived insider status: the moderating role of organization-based self-esteem. Acta Psychol. Sin. **44**(10), 1371–1382 (2012). (in Chinese)

Impact of Data Breach on IT Investment: Moderating Role of Buyer-Supplier Relationship

Meirong Zhou[1], Miao Hu[2(✉)], and Shenyang Jiang[3]

[1] Zhejiang University, Hangzhou, Zhejiang, China
[2] Soochow University, Suzhou, Jiangsu, China
humiao@suda.edu.cn
[3] Tongji University, Shanghai, China

Abstract. Data breach is a typical IT failure in the process of digitalization, and it helps firms recognize their shortages of IT security capabilities, influencing their IT investment. Drawing from failure learning theory, this study analyzes the influences of data breach on the firm's IT investment and examines the moderating effect of firms' position in the buyer-supplier relationship. Based on data from Compustat, PRC, ITRC, and CI Tech databases in 2009–2016, this study uses a fixed-effect model to analyze the relationships among data breach, buyer-supplier relationship, and firm's IT investment. This study finds that a data breach increases a firm's IT investments. When a firm plays a role as a dependent supplier in the supply chain, the positive effect of data breach on IT investment is weakened. However, when a firm's position in the buyer-supplier relationship is a principal customer, the positive effect of data breach on IT investment is strengthened. Our findings provide practical guidance for firms to better understand and respond to data breaches and improve their IT security capabilities.

Keywords: Data Breach · IT Investment · Failure Learning · Buyer-Supplier Relationship

1 Introduction

Digitalization plays an important role in promoting economic development and business efficiency. However, data security issues may occur during the process of digitalization, causing economic and reputation losses that can even threaten firms' survival [1]. According to failure learning theory, managers consider IT security when making investment decisions after a data breach event. The data breach event sends a signal to firms that their IT capabilities need improvement to deal with data security threats. As data security issues may result from a defective IT infrastructure, firms can prevent data security accidents by increasing IT investment and updating their IT infrastructure [2]. Additionally, firms will allocate more resources to ensure the security of their information systems. Although IT investment improves firms' IT capabilities, new IT implementation may increase data workload and data security risks. Firms may be more risk-averse after data breaches and prefer a more conservative IT investment approach, such as adopting a tight IT investment budget [3]. Therefore, data security issues affect firms' IT investment decisions. However, the relationship between data breach and IT investment has not received much attention in the current literature. To address this gap, this study explores whether firms' concerns about data security issues will promote or inhibit their IT investment decisions after a data breach event.

We argue that a firm's IT investment behavior after data breaches may be affected by its position in the supply chain. In a buyer-supplier relationship, firms can be dependent suppliers or principal customers [4]. Dependent suppliers refer to firms that rely heavily on their dominant customers in sales, while principal customers refer to customers in a dominant position in a buyer-supplier relationship [4]. According to failure learning theory, a firm's failure-solving motivation is affected by its resources and sensitivity to failure after experiencing a failure. Therefore, we propose that firms' attitudes and behaviors after a data breach event are determined by their financial constraints and sensitivity to data breaches, which are influenced by their positions in the supply chain. Compared with principal customers, dependent suppliers are upstream in a supply chain relationship and are less affected by financial constraints and pressures from stakeholders. Firms playing the role of dependent suppliers in a buyer-supplier relationship will increase their IT investments to ensure data security after data breaches.

The study empirically analyzes the relationship between data breaches and IT investment and examines the moderating effects of the buyer-supplier relationship based on failure learning theory. We collect data breach events from the Privacy Rights Clearinghouse (PRC) and the Identity Theft Resource Center (ITRC), IT investment data from the Computer Intelligence (CI tech) database, and buyer-supplier relationship data from Compustat, and use a fixed-effect model. Our findings show that firms increase their IT investments after data breaches. Moreover, when firms play the role of dependent suppliers in the supply chain, the positive effect of data breach on IT investment is weakened. However, firms as principal customers are more likely to increase their IT investment after data breaches.

This study has two main contributions. First, it enriches research on data security. Scholars have analyzed the influences of data security on CIO turnover, social responsibility, customer loyalty, and outsourcing of security services [5, 6]. Firms' concerns about data security issues make IT investment decisions either conservative or proactive. This study is the first to analyze the influences of data breach on firms' IT investment behaviors. Second, it enriches the theoretical boundaries of failure learning by analyzing the moderating role of supply chain factors. Previous research has focused on the impact of the buyer-supplier relationship on firm decision-making [7]. We draw upon failure learning theory to examine the moderating role of a firm's position in the supply chain network (i.e., dependent suppliers or principal customers) on the relationship between data breach and firms' IT investment behaviors.

In the next section, we review the literature and develop hypotheses. Section 3 describes the methodology. Section 4 presents the results. The final section of this study discusses the results, implications and limitations.

2 Theory and Hypotheses Development

2.1 Failure Learning and Data Breach

Firms face various failures in their daily operations, such as technical mistakes and product development failures. These failures cause economic losses and have a negative impact on the firm's reputation. However, learning from failures is an essential way for firms to optimize their production process, improve product quality and production efficiency. Therefore, failure learning has become a key research issue in the field of organizational learning. Scholars have focused on failure learning in areas such as product recall, project failure, bankruptcy, medical malpractice, and accidents [8].

A firm's failure learning is defined as the process by which firms identify errors or failure events, analyze the failures to find out their main causes, and search for and implement solutions to prevent similar errors or failures in the future [9]. The learning mechanisms can be clustered into three categories: opportunity to learn, motivation to learn, and ability to learn [9]. Opportunity to learn refers to the scope of information and the time that allows firms to learn from failure events. Motivation to learn refers to the resource levels (e.g., attention and operational investments) that firms devote to failure learning activities. Ability to learn refers to the capacity to identify failures, understand their causes, and implement solutions to prevent future failures [10].

Data breaches are typical failure events that help firms recognize the shortcomings of their data security capabilities and management. After experiencing a data breach event, firms analyze the causes of the breach and implement corresponding solutions to prevent future data breaches. IT failures are a result of the failures of the complex interactions of technical and structural elements in the systems. In fact, it is challenging to identify the causes of these failures and propose corresponding solutions. However, as emphasized by Pearson and Mitroff [11], firms should "systematically and continuously search for potential breaks before they are too big to fix". We argue that IT investment is the firm's solution to prevent future data breaches after systematically evaluating its data security capabilities.

2.2 The Impact of Data Breach on IT Investment

Digitization has become one of the important sources of firms' competitive advantages. Data security issues occur in the process of digitization and have become one of the most serious threats to firms. Data breach is a typical data security issue and is defined as the destruction of data integrity, availability, and confidentiality when accessing confidential or sensitive information without authorization. Data breaches help firms proactively prevent the losses of digital assets in the future. Drawing on the failure learning theory, firms will conduct a comprehensive analysis of their own IT assets, threats, and vulnerabilities after suffering from data breach events [2]. When firms find that the causes for IT failure are the defective or backward IT framework, firms will make decisions to improve the present situation, e.g., updating the security management process and IT architecture. According to the failure learning theory, data breach reflects the potential weaknesses of a firm's IT. In this case, firms may invest more resources to fix the IT loopholes, enhance the stability of information systems, and prevent data breach problems that may occur in the future.

First, data breach increases firms' IT security awareness. If firms are not fully aware of IT security threats and do not take corresponding countermeasures, IT security threats cannot be effectively avoided. With the improved IT security awareness, firms can identify the most valuable digital assets that need to be protected or are threatened by security risks. Firms will upgrade their data security implementations. Firms with higher IT security awareness will also allocate more resources to protect the IT security environment, e.g., increasing IT investment in IT security, prioritizing IT security when designing IT systems, identifying and analyzing security issues more effectively, and implementing more appropriate IT security solutions.

Second, firms will strategically allocate more resources to ensure the stability of their IT systems. The improvement of data security capabilities and reliability of system configuration must rely on the understanding of the information system environment and the assessment of the availability of IT investments. Managers need to systematically check the IT status, regularly update software and hardware, and better design the system. Many prior studies have found that firms will increase their IT investments. Hence, we hypothesize the following:

H1. Data breaches will increase a firm's IT investments.

2.3 The Moderating Role of Firm's Position in the Buyer-Supplier Relationship

A firm's position in the supply chain network (i.e., principal customer or dependent supplier) may moderate the relationship between data breaches and IT investments. A firm is considered a dependent supplier if its sales are mainly purchased by several dominant customers. A firm is viewed as a principal customer if its purchases occupy a large proportion of a supplier. According to failure learning theory, a firm's behavior after IT failures is affected by the firm's sensitivity to data breaches (opportunity to learn) and the resources needed to solve the failures (ability to learn) [9]. When a firm plays the role of principal customer in the buyer-supplier relationship, it is in a dominant position and has stronger bargaining power compared with its buyer [4]. When firms have more bargaining power, they can gain more economic benefits from the buyer-supplier relationship [3]. Moreover, a firm as a principal customer will require its dependent suppliers to increase relationship investments, e.g., accounts receivable and inventory holdings [7]. The higher the level of dependence the firm has on its customers, the more resources the firm has to invest in the supply chain relationship. In this case, the firm has a high level of financial constraints. When firms have financial constraints, they may not have enough available resources to fix existing data deficiencies after experiencing a data breach event. A data breach helps firms increase awareness of IT security management and find out the defects of current software and hardware equipment. Firms will increase investments in IT security and fix the defective IT facilities. However, firms may feel pressure because they suffer from high levels of financial constraints. That is, firms may recognize the causes of IT failure but have limited resources for implementing preventing future IT failures. According to the failure learning theory, a firm's motivation to learn from data breaches is reduced if they do not have enough resources and investments for data security improvement [12].

Second, compared with principal customers, dependent suppliers are usually far away from end consumers in the buyer-supplier relationship. Therefore, the dependent suppliers' reputation losses caused by data breaches are much lower than those caused by principal customers. Firms as dependent suppliers are less sensitive to data breach events. Managers in these firms may think that the cost of data security improvement is much higher than that caused by a data breach event; hence, managers are less willing to increase IT investments for improving their data security capabilities after a data breach event. Therefore, we propose the following research hypothesis:

H2a: When a firm is a dependent supplier in the buyer-supplier relationship, the positive impact of data breaches on the firm's IT investment is weakened.

Firms as principal customers are more likely to increase their IT investments after a data breach event. First, firms playing a role as principal customers in a buyer-supplier relationship have fewer financial constraints [13]. These firms can ask their suppliers to take on the operational costs through using market power and thus have enough investments for their data security management [13].

Second, firms playing a role as principal customers directly face end consumers, who are highly concerned about IT security and privacy. Therefore, data breaches cause serious economic and reputation losses to these firms [6]. From a stakeholder perspective, IT investments reflect the firm's attitude and concern to IT security problems, enhance stakeholders' confidence in the firm, and improve the reputation of IT security [5]. Specifically, a data breach event results in low levels of customer trust, which further affects customers' purchasing behavior [14]. The circumstance is more serious for firms who are closer to end customers. Therefore, considering the serious damages of reputation, firms will increase IT investments to regain customers' trust after a data breach event. Building upon these arguments, we put forward the below research hypothesis:

H2b: When a firm is a principal customer in the buyer-supplier relationship, the positive effect of data breaches on firm's IT investment is strengthened.

3 Research Method

3.1 Data

To empirically analyze the relationship between data breaches and IT investment, we analyzed a panel dataset from 2009 to 2016 with yearly firm-level observations. Specifically, we collected firms' financial information from the Compustat database and data breach information from the PRC and ITRC databases. We obtained information on firms' IT investments from the CI-Tech database and supplemented missing data by searching firms' websites and other sources. In total, we obtained 13,068 firm-year observations, including 938 data breaches and 512 different firms, with 179 firms experiencing multiple data breaches.

3.2 Measures

We use the logarithm of IT investment as a proxy variable for a firm's IT investment. The IT investments include annual IT spending, safety technology investment expenditure, and non-safety technology investment expenditure. The independent variable data breach is a dummy variable. We denote the variable as 1 if the firm has a data breach event; otherwise, it is 0. A firm is denoted as a dependent supplier in the buyer-supplier relationship if the firm reports any customer who purchases more than 10% of total sales. The customer is denoted as a principal customer. When a firm is viewed as a dependent supplier, we code the variable dependent suppliers as 1; otherwise, it is coded as 0. When a firm is viewed as a principal customer, we code the variable principal customer as 1; otherwise, it is coded as 0. When a firm plays the role of both principal customers and dependent suppliers in the supply chain network [4, 13], we code variables principal customer and dependent supplier as 1.

We control for several factors that might influence the firm's investment decisions. First, firm size may affect firms' investment decisions. Specifically, compared with SMEs, large firms invest more intensively [15]. Therefore, we control for firm size by constructing the natural logarithm of the annual total asset value (millions of dollars). Second, firm profitability determines whether the firms have enough resources for digitalization investment. Therefore, we control for return on assets (ROA), which is equal to net income divided by total assets. We also control for earnings per share, which is measured by the ratio of profit to total equity. A firm's debt ratio and capital expenditure determine the available funds for IT investment. We use the asset liability ratio to measure the firm's debt ratio. Capital expenditure is measured by the sum of cash paid for the acquisition of fixed assets, intangible assets, and other long-term assets. In addition, firms with strong R&D capabilities are willing to engage in digitalization and fix data security failures [16]. Therefore, we control for R&D investments with the logarithm of the firm's R&D expenses (millions of dollars). Firms with lean operations usually have fewer available resources for IT investments. Therefore, we use unabsorbed slack and absorbed slack as controls. Environmental factors also influence firm's decision [17]. In line with Keats and Hitt [18], we use environmental affluence and environmental dynamics as controls. We add the firm and year fixed effect in all models.

3.3 Model Specification

To estimate the impact of data breaches on firms' IT investments, we use the following model:

$$IT\ investment_{it} = \beta_1\ Post\ Breach_{it} + \beta_2 Principal\ customer_{it}$$
$$+ \beta_3\ Dependent\ supplier_{it} + X_{it} + Firm\ FE + Year\ FE + \varepsilon_{it} \qquad (1)$$

To further examine the moderating effects of a firm's position in the buyer-supplier relationship on the relationship between data breaches and IT investment, we use the following model:

$$IT\ investment_{it} = \beta_1\ Post\ Breach_{it} + \beta_2\ Principal\ customer_{it} + \beta_3\ Dependent\ supplier_{it}$$
$$+ \beta_4\ Principal\ customer_{it} \times Post\ Breach_{it} + \beta_5\ Dependent\ supplier_{it} \times Post\ Breach_{it}$$
$$+ X_{it} + Firm\ FE + Year\ FE + \varepsilon_{it} \tag{2}$$

where *IT investment*$_{it}$ refers to the IT investment of firm i in year t; *Post Breach*$_{it}$ takes the value 1 if firm i has a data breach in year t and 0 otherwise. *Principal customer*$_{it}$ = 1 takes the value 1 if firm i plays a role of principal customer in the buyer-supplier relationship in year t, 0 otherwise. *Dependent supplier*$_{it}$ takes the value 1 if firm i t is viewed as a dependent supplier in year and 0 otherwise. X_{it} represents the control variable. *Firm FE* and *Year FE* represent the firm-level fixed effect and time fixed effect, respectively. ε_{it} is the error term.

4 Empirical Results

4.1 Main Results

Table 1 reports the estimated effect of a data breach on IT investment using Eqs. (1) and (2). In Model 1, the coefficient of the data breach is significant and positive ($\beta =$

Table 1. Impact of data breach on IT investment

	Dependent variable: IT Investment			
	Model 1	Model 2	Model 3	Model 4
Data breach	0.321***	0.219***	0.365***	0.263***
	[0.069]	[0.081]	[0.079]	[0.092]
Data breach × Principal customer		0.222**		0.216**
		[0.102]		[0.103]
Data breach × Dependent supplier			−0.214*	−0.202*
			[0.121]	[0.121]
Principal customer	−0.053	−0.075*	−0.054	-0.075*
	[0.039]	[0.040]	[0.039]	[0.040]
Dependent supplier	0.056	0.056	0.066*	0.065*
	[0.040]	[0.040]	[0.040]	[0.040]
Controls	Included	Included	Included	Included
Firm fixed	Included	Included	Included	Included
Year fixed	Included	Included	Included	Included
Observations	11039	11039	11039	11039
Adj R^2	0.460	0.460	0.460	0.460

Note: ***, **, * indicate that the parameter estimates are significant at the statistical level of 1%, 5%, and 10%, respectively; the values in brackets are the standard errors of cluster adjustment at the firm level

0.321 p < 0.01), indicating that firms increase their IT investment after a data breach. Therefore, Hypothesis 1 is supported. Model 2 shows that the interaction coefficient of the data breach and principal customer is significant and positive ($\beta = 0.222$, p < 0.05). The result suggests that firms playing a role as principal customers in the buyer-supplier relationship are more likely to increase IT investment after a data breach event, which supports Hypothesis 2b. In Model 3, we also find a significant and negative interaction coefficient of the data breach and dependent supplier ($\beta = -0.214$, p < 0.10), indicating that firms playing a role as dependent suppliers in the buyer-supplier relationship are less likely to increase IT investment after a data breach event. Therefore, Hypothesis 2a is supported. Model 4 is the full model.

4.2 Robustness Checks

To demonstrate the robustness of these results, we have used an alternative measure of data breaches. Data breaches can be classified into two types: internal data breaches and external data breaches. Internal data breaches are caused by internal factors such as employee errors or internal information system failures, while external data breaches are caused by external factors such as hacker attacks or physical theft. The results of the impact of internal and external data breaches on IT investment are presented in Table 2. As shown in Model 1, the coefficient of internal data breach is 0.395 (p < 0.001). In Model 2, the coefficient of external data breach is 0.291 (p < 0.001). Model 3 is the full model. The results indicate that both internal and external data breaches increase a

Table 2. Alternative measurement of data breach

	Model 1	Model 2	Model 3
Internal data breach	0.395***		0.372***
	[0.095]		[0.096]
External data breach		0.291***	0.269***
		[0.073]	[0.073]
Principal customer	-0.055	−0.053	−0.052
	[0.039]	[0.039]	[0.039]
Dependent supplier	0.057	0.056	0.055
	[0.040]	[0.040]	[0.040]
Controls	Included	Included	Included
Firm fixed	Included	Included	Included
Year fixed	Included	Included	Included
Observations	11,039	11,039	11,039
Adj R^2	0.459	0.459	0.460

Note: ***, **, * indicate that the parameter estimates are significant at the statistical level of 1%, 5%, and 10%, respectively; the values in brackets are the standard errors adjusted by firm-level clustering firm's IT investment. Additionally, we find that there is no significant difference in the impact of internal data breach and external data breach on IT investment (F (1,1911) = 0.67, p > 0.10). Moreover, analyzing the impact of external data breaches on IT investment helps alleviate the endogeneity problem caused by reverse causality and further confirms the robustness of our findings, as external data breaches are exogenous to the firm's investment behavior.

4.3 Additional Analysis

We estimated the impact of data breaches on the efficiency of IT investment allocation, i.e., over-investment and under-investment. We defined over-investment as a firm's IT investment exceeding the industry average, while under-investment as a firm's IT investment being lower than or equal to the industry average. We measured over-investment by the difference between a firm's IT investment and the industry average, setting it as 1 if the value was negative. We measured under-investment by the difference between a firm's IT investment and the industry average, setting it as 1 if the value was positive. IT

Table 3. Over-investment and under-investment

	Over IT investment		Under IT investment	
	Model 1	Model 2	Model 3	Model 4
Data breach	0.351***	0.229***	−0.189***	−0.120**
	[0.053]	[0.064]	[0.036]	[0.057]
Data breach × Dependent supplier		−0.092		0.002
		[0.094]		[0.061]
Data breach × Principal customer		0.288***		−0.141***
		[0.082]		[0.051]
Dependent supplier	−0.011	−0.036	0.013	0.026
	[0.026]	[0.027]	[0.025]	[0.026]
Principal customer	0.030	0.035	−0.041	−0.041
	[0.023]	[0.023]	[0.029]	[0.029]
Controls	Included	Included	Included	Included
Firm fixed	Included	Included	Included	Included
Year fixed	Included	Included	Included	Included
Cons	−0.059	−0.057	0.205***	0.203***
	[0.066]	[0.066]	[0.077]	[0.077]
Observations	12,890	12,890	12,890	12,890
Adj R^2	0.154	0.155	0.146	0.146

Note: ***, **, * indicate that the parameter estimates are significant at the statistical level of 1%, 5%, and 10%, respectively; the values in brackets are the standard errors adjusted by firm-level clustering investment was estimated by dividing the firm's total IT budget by its total assets. The industry average IT investment was measured by the average value of IT investment in the double-digit SIC industry. The results of the impact of data breaches on over-investment and under-investment are presented in Table 3. Model 1 shows that the coefficient of data breach is significant and positive for over-investment ($\beta = 0.351$, $p < 0.01$). Model 3 indicates that data breach has a significant negative impact on under-investment ($\beta = -0.189$, $p < 0.01$). In Model 2 and Model 4, the interaction coefficients of data breach and dependent supplier are not significant ($\beta = -0.092$, $p > 0.10$ and $\beta = 0.002$, $p > 0.10$, respectively). However, in Model 2, the interaction coefficient of data breach and principal customer for over-investment is significant and positive ($\beta = 0.288$, $p < 0.01$), while in Model 4, the interaction coefficient of data breach and principal customer for under-investment is significant and positive ($\beta = -0.141$, $p < 0.01$). Overall, our results suggest that data breaches have a dual effect on IT investment allocation efficiency. On one hand, data breaches lead firms to increase their IT investments, resulting in higher IT investment than other firms in the same industry (over-investment). On the other hand, data breaches have a negative impact on under-investment. Furthermore, when a firm plays the role of a principal customer, the double-edged effect of data breaches is strengthened.

5   Discussion and Conclusion

In this study, we empirically analyze the influence of data breaches on IT investment and the moderating effect of a firm's position in the supply chain based on data from Compustat, PRC, ITRC, and CI Tech databases from 2009–2016. We find that firms increase their IT investments after a data breach event, consistent with prior studies [10]. Data breaches help firms recognize their defective information systems and inadequate IT capabilities, leading them to update their information system infrastructure and improve IT. Our findings also indicate that IT failures such as data breaches do not hinder a firm's digitalization process, as they continue to invest in IT to address deficiencies in their IT architecture and security technology capabilities.

Furthermore, we find that a firm's position in the supply chain affects its IT investment after a data breach. In a buyer-supplier relationship, a principal customer purchases a large amount of products and services from a dependent supplier, who must invest resources to maintain the relationship. This leads to an unequal relationship between buyers and suppliers, with dependent suppliers having limited resources for IT investments and being less sensitive to IT security. Therefore, the positive influence of data breach on IT investment is weakened for firms playing the role of dependent suppliers. Conversely, when a firm is a principal customer, the positive influence of data breach on IT investment is strengthened.

Our findings contribute significantly to the literature on failure learning and supply chain management. We explore the impact of data breaches on IT investment based on failure learning theory, with data breaches being a typical IT failure in the firm's digitalization process. Despite the economic losses caused by data breaches, firms can learn from them and identify their IT capabilities' shortcomings [9]. Our findings confirm that failure learning can improve firms' operations.

Second, this study adds boundary conditions for failure learning. Previous studies have mainly focused on the moderating role of knowledge, experience, resources, and capabilities on failure learning [8–10]. Few scholars have paid attention to the role of a firm's position in the supply chain on failure learning. We propose that firms as dependent suppliers are in the upstream of the supply chain and suffer from financial constraints; therefore, their motivation to increase IT investment is reduced after a data breach event. The empirical results of this study prove that a firm's failure learning process is affected by the buyer-supplier relationship.

Our study has significant practical implications for firms learning from their failures. First, the process of digitalization may cause IT failures, e.g., data breaches. However, the occurrence of data breaches does not reduce a manager's IT investments. Instead, managers can learn from these IT failures and recognize the shortage of their IT capabilities. Therefore, managers should view the data breach event as an opportunity for improving their IT capabilities. Specifically, to prevent the occurrence of similar IT failures in the future, managers should create a learning culture and build a learning organization. Moreover, managers should increase internal integration to improve the understanding of the causes of the IT failure and actively seek solutions. Second, managers should consider their positions in the supply chain when increasing IT investment after a data breach event. When firms are principal customers in the buyer-supplier relationships, they will increase more IT investments for improving their IT capabilities. However, when firms play a role of dependent suppliers in the supply chain, they may not have enough resources for IT investments, and the failure learning effect is reduced. These firms can collaborate with their supply chain partners to improve their IT capabilities and security management.

A key limitation of our study is that we collected data from Chinese firms. Different national cultures may influence the firm's attitudes towards data breaches. Future research can use worldwide data to reexamine the arguments in this study. Second, we focus on the influences of data breaches on a firm's IT investment. IT investment is one of a firm's responses to IT failures. Future research can focus on other firm behaviors after a data breach event, e.g., human resource management, IT strategy.

References

1. Syed, R.: Firm reputation threats on social media: a case of data breach framing. J. Strateg. Inf. Syst. **28**(3), 257–274 (2019)
2. Salge, T.O., Kohli, R., Barrett, M.: Investing in information systems: on the behavioral and institutional search mechanisms underpinning hospitals' is investment decisions. MIS Q. **39**(1), 61–90 (2015)
3. Shi, W., Connelly, B.L., Cirik, K.: Short seller influence on firm growth: a threat rigidity perspective. Acad. Manag. J. **61**(5), 1892–1919 (2018)
4. Cen, L., Maydew, E.L., Zhang, L., Zuo, L.: Customer–supplier relationships and corporate tax avoidance. J. Financ. Econ. **123**(2), 377–394 (2017)
5. Lending, C., Minnick, K., Schorno, P.J.: Corporate governance, social responsibility, and data breaches. Financ. Rev. **53**(2), 413–455 (2018)
6. Janakiraman, R., Lim, J.H., Rishika, R.: The effect of a data breach announcement on customer behavior: evidence from a multichannel retailer. J. Mark. **82**(2), 85–105 (2018)

7. Cen, L., Chen, F., Hou, Y., Richardson, G.D.: Strategic disclosures of litigation loss contingencies when customer-supplier relationships are at risk. Account. Rev. **93**(2), 137–159 (2018)

8. Kim, J.Y., Miner, A.S.: Vicarious learning from the failures and near-failures of others: evidence from the US commercial banking industry. Acad. Manag. J. **50**(3), 687–714 (2007)

9. Dahlin, K.B., Chuang, Y.T., Roulet, T.J.: Opportunity, motivation, and ability to learn from failures and errors: review, synthesis, and ways to move forward. Acad. Manag. Ann. **12**(1), 252–277 (2018)

10. Benaroch, M., Chernobai, A.: Operational IT failures, IT value-destruction, and board-level IT governance changes. MIS Q. **41**(3), 729–762 (2017)

11. Pearson, C.M., Mitroff, I.I.: From crisis prone to crisis prepared: a framework for crisis management. Acad. Manag. Perspect. **7**(1), 48–59 (1993)

12. Bentley, F.S., Kehoe, R.R.: Give them some slack—they're trying to change! The benefits of excess cash, excess employees, and increased human capital in the strategic change context. Acad. Manag. J. **63**(1), 181–204 (2020)

13. Cen, L., Dasgupta, S., Elkamhi, R., Pungaliya, R.S.: Reputation and loan contract terms: the role of principal customers. Rev. Finance **20**(2), 501–533 (2015)

14. Dai, R., Liang, H., Ng, L.: Socially responsible corporate customers. J. Financ. Econ. **142**(2), 598–626 (2020)

15. Kim, K., Mithas, S., Kimbrough, M.: Information technology investments and firm risk across industries: evidence from the bond market. MIS Q. **41**(4), 1347–1367 (2017)

16. Cheng, Z.J., Rai, A., Tian, F., Xu, S.X.: Social learning in information technology investment: the role of board interlocks. Manag. Sci. **67**(1), 547–576 (2021)

17. Kobelsky, K.W., Richardson, V.J., Smith, R.E., Zmud, R.W.: Determinants and consequences of firm information technology budgets. Account. Rev. **83**(4), 957–995 (2008)

18. Keats, B.W., Hitt, M.A.: A causal model of linkages among environmental dimensions, macro organizational characteristics, and performance. Acad. Manag. J. **31**(3), 570–598 (1988)

The Influence of Benefit Appeals in CSR Communication on Consumers' Willingness to Co-creation

Xiaoping Liu$^{(\boxtimes)}$, Yingqian Liang, and Shiyu Wang

College of Economics and Management, Chongqing University of Posts and
Telecommunications, Chongqing 404100, China
liuxiaoping@cqupt.edu.cn

Abstract. Based on the background of corporate social responsibility (CSR) communication, this study aims to explore the role of different types of CSR interest appeal information (self-benefit vs. others-benefit) in CSR communication
of different consumers on social media, and mainly discuss consumers' willingness to participate in CSR co-creation. A total of 288 valid questionnaires were
obtained through an online experiment. The moderating effect of consumer values was verified by "floodlight" analysis and the moderated mediating effect of
consumer trust was verified by the Process program. Self-enhancement values
have a congruent effect with CSR communication benefit appeals. Specifically,
benefit appeals characterized by self-benefit generate higher consumer trust and
willingness to co-create value among individuals with high self-enhancement values (vs. low self-enhancement values). CSR credibility and brand trust have a
continuous mediating effect in the interaction between self-enhancement values
and benefits appeals, while the interaction between self-transcendence values and
benefits appeals is not significant. Understanding how consumer values influence
consumer responses to CSR social media posts with different interest claims can
provide marketers with useful guidance on how to creatively segment customers
and curate appropriately targeted messages to effectively connect with consumers
on CSR campaigns.

Keywords: CSR Communication · Benefit Appeal · Consumers' Trust · CSR
Value Co-creation · Personal Values

1 Introduction

Corporate social responsibility refers to the economic, legal, ethical, and philanthropic
responsibilities that companies take on social issues while creating profits, and can
be seen as an investment in capital, the environment, and stakeholder relations. CSR
communication means that companies anticipate stakeholder expectations, articulate
CSR policies, social and environmental issues, and truthful and transparent information
about their interactions with stakeholders [1]. Only a complete understanding of CSR
behavior can eliminate information asymmetry and enable stakeholders to make correct

© The Author(s), under exclusive license to Springer Nature Switzerland AG 2023
Y. Tu and M. Chi (Eds.): WHICEB 2023, LNBIP 480, pp. 120–130, 2023.
https://doi.org/10.1007/978-3-031-32299-0_11

value judgments about CSR activities, thereby improving their relationship with the company and promoting consumer participation in CSR value creation.

Co-creation social responsibility is the identification and satisfaction of consumers' demands by companies that invite them to participate jointly in social responsibility activities [2]. As a new model of responsibility, co-creative social responsibility completely overturns the traditional CSR communication method, which breaks the top-down corporate-centered model and turns it into an interactive consumer-centered model [3]. The report of The 20th Communist Party Congress mentions "building a community of social governance in which everyone is responsible, everyone does his or her part, and everyone enjoys it". Public participation is crucial to the successful implementation of CSR activities and the creation of social value, and how to get consumers to actively participate has become a common concern for both academia and enterprises.

However, gaining public participation is challenging due to the lack of public attention and low awareness of CSR activities. While there is a large social marketing literature documenting the role that informational appeals play in persuading audiences, there is no clear evidence of the effectiveness of different types of appeals [4]. Companies still face the challenge of how to increase consumer willingness to engage, and understanding why consumers engage in specific pro-social behaviors is critical for social marketing scholars and companies, and further research is still needed on the relationship between message appeals and consumer engagement delivered through social media platforms. Therefore, this paper focuses on CSR communication and CSR co-creation to explore the boundary conditions and internal mechanisms of the influence of interest claims in information appeals on consumer participation in CSR co-creation. Our research questions are as follows: (1) whether different benefit appeals have different effects on the different consumers? (2) whether consumer trust has an indirect effect on co-creation willingness?

2 Theoretical Basis and Research Hypotheses

2.1 CSR Benefit Appeal and Consumer Value Co-creation Willingness

Well-communicated CSR activities not only increase their trust but also trigger their affection for the brand and their willingness to buy. Although the value of CSR communication is to spread the message, companies must recognize CSR as an important strategy and key culture. For CSR programs to be effective, different types of appeals designed to elicit more favorable consumer responses can be used strategically in marketing messages [5]. Research on the empathy-altruism hypothesis suggests that other-benefit claims will promote consumer pro-social behavior more than self-benefit claims [6]. However, some researchers have expressed doubts about the validity of "other-help" appeals and emphasized that people are more likely to be persuaded by "self-help" appeals. The validity of self-interest appeals can be explained by social exchange theory, which suggests that pro-social behavior is driven by various forms of self-interest and is directed at the pursuit of personal interests [7]. At present, there is no academic conclusion on whether there is a difference in the impact of CSR benefit claims on consumers, and its post-effectiveness studies have largely focused on a single dimension of consumers' purchase intentions.

With the service-led logic gradually replacing the traditional commodity-led logic, the co-creation of value with consumers is becoming an essential marketing practice for companies [8]. CSR co-creation means that companies encourage consumers to participate in the design and implementation of CSR activities and to interact, share and cooperate with them on CSR activities [9].

Compared with traditional unilateral CSR activities conducted by enterprises, co-creative CSR activities can achieve a "triple-win" result: for society, it can improve the governance system and enhance people's well-being; for enterprises, it can enhance brand reputation and increase consumers' willingness to purchase and recommend; for consumers, they can get the entertainment experience or spiritual satisfaction of helping others. The willingness to CSR co-create value will develop when customers receive benefits and psychological satisfaction that exceed the cost of time, physical effort, and energy [10]. Value co-creation includes three dimensions: interaction, relationship, and knowledge sharing. Therefore, this paper defines consumers' willingness for CSR co-creation as the extent to which consumers are willing to interact, share and cooperate with the company in CSR co-creation activities conducted by the company.

In the process of CSR value creation, the two different claims reflect two different direct values of CSR, and consumers, after fully considering the external values and their own needs, will be more willing to participate in CSR co-creation by assessing the different claims shown in the CSR communication messages of the company and believing that participating in CSR co-creation activities with different claims can satisfy their basic physical or psychological needs [8].

2.2 The Effect of Consistency Between Social Values and Benefit Appeals

Consumers' value perceptions and attitudes toward CSR value co-creation activities are influenced by social values. Individuals with different values differ in their motivation to pay attention, and different social values trigger their differentiated [9]. According to Schwartz's [11] social value theory, consumers have self-transcendent social values such as universality, benevolence, tradition, and security, and self-enhancement social values such as power, achievement, enjoyment, and excitement. The two different types of social values reflect consumers' different levels of concern for self, others, and society, which directly influence their perceptions of CSR behaviors and, in turn, their perceptions and attitudes toward CSR activities [12]. Self-improvement values emphasize the pursuit of personal success and happiness and match the concept of self-interested CSR activities. In contrast, self-transcendence values emphasize promoting the well-being of others and transcending self-interest, matching the concept of altruistic-appealing CSR activities, and consumers will be more likely to respond positively when their personal values are aligned with the CSR concept [12], with both extrinsic information and intrinsic motivation driving individuals to participate in value co-creation. For companies, it is necessary to clarify what behavioral strategies to adopt to show that they share common values and goals with consumers, and thus stimulate consumers' willingness to co-create values.

Researchers have argued that individuals have two inconsistent values at the same time, and self-transcendence values and self-enhancement values were analyzed as two independent dimensions in the study of employee co-border behavior and task performance [13]. Therefore, this study uses two opposing values as two independent moderating variables, assuming that consumers with strong self-transcendence values are more likely to respond to CSR messages that focus on the interests of others, while consumers with strong self-improvement values are more likely to respond to CSR messages that focus on their interests. Therefore, this research proposes the following:

H1: Self-benefit appeals generate a higher willingness to co-create values among individuals with high self-enhancement values (vs. low self-enhancement values).

H2: Other-benefit appeals generate a higher willingness to co-create values among individuals with high self-transcendent values (vs. low self-transcendent values).

2.3   The Mediating Role of CSR Credibility and Brand Trust

Trust is a major determinant of relational commitment and trust builds long-term relationships between firms and consumers [14], so consumer trust is defined not only as the consumer's belief that the product or service offered by a company is trustworthy, but is also considered to be the consumer's belief that its long-term interests will be met [15]. From the perspective of products and services as well as long-term benefits, the consumer trust involved in the field of CSR research can be viewed as two dimensions, namely CSR credibility and brand trust.

When consumers perceive that companies have sincere and positive intentions to improve the welfare of members of society, they will reciprocate in the form of trust [16]. The level of consumer-perceived CSR is by influences consumer CSR trust, which in turn influences consumer responses, while trust will eventually also lead to cooperation [14]. In previous studies, consumer trust often plays a mediating role in the process of CSR's influence on consumer behavior. Although exposure to various CSR appeals can enhance message credibility [5], there is a lack of research on the extent to which self/altruistic benefit appeals used in CSR communication trigger perceived CSR credibility, which further influences consumers' trust in the brand and thus their willingness to co-create value, the role of this mechanism is still lacking. Therefore, this paper selects consumer trust as the mediator of benefits claim and value co-creation in CSR communication and subdivides consumer trust into CSR credibility and brand trust. Therefore, this research proposes the following:

H3: CSR credibility mediates the interaction between interest claims and social values and consumer willingness to co-create

H4: Brand trust mediates the interaction between interest claims and social values and consumers' willingness to co-create

H5: CSR credibility and brand trust play a continuous mediating role in the interaction of interest appeals and social values in influencing consumers' willingness to co-create

Thus, we can derive a conceptual framework as shown in Fig. 1:

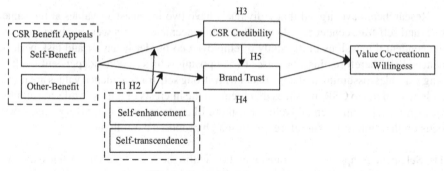

Fig. 1. Conceptual framework

3 Methodology

3.1 Design and Data Collection

In this study, a one-factor (CSR benefit claim: self-interest vs. altruism) between-group experiment was used to select a CSR co-creation campaign for recycling empty bottles being conducted by a real-life skincare company. Based on the CSR advertisement released by the company, two materials were prepared regarding the studies of Wei and Jung [17], and the materials included text and pictures. The Self-benefit claim focuses on the shopping cost savings to consumers from participating in recycling empty bottles, while the Other-benefit claim focuses on the environmental benefits of participating in recycling empty bottles. All stimuli, including message presentation format, layout, font, color, and image typography, were the same in both questionnaires, except for the message and headline.

In this study, the online research platform was used to collect questionnaires, and 351 questionnaires were collected. After excluding invalid questionnaires (including short response time, incomplete completion, and consecutive selection of the same option), a total of 288 valid questionnaires were collected, with an effective rate of 82.08%, including 122 males (42.4%), and the age group was concentrated in 21–34 years old (70.1%), the highest education of the subjects was mainly undergraduate (63.9%), and the percentage of the subjects who sometimes and often paid attention to CSR information was 66.7%.

3.2 Procedure and Measure

The procedure for this experiment was that each subject received a questionnaire at random, which first contained an explanation of the terminology associated with the experiment. The subjects were randomly divided into two groups and then read the materials separately. The questionnaire consisted of three parts: the first part was a measure of consumers' personal values, the second part contained experimental materials and questions on each variable, and the third part consisted of questions on subjects' personal information and their level of concern about CSR information released by companies.

In this study, two items from [18]. White were used to assess the types of benefit claims in consumers' perceived materials. The previous item measured the extent of altruistic appeals in consumer perception of CSR communication: "To what degree is this appeal associated with looking out for the interests of others". The latter item measures the extent to which consumers perceive self-interested claims in CSR communications: "To what degree is this appeal associated with looking out for one's own interests?". The latter item was reverse-coded for this study and then averaged to form a score of interest as a manipulation check.

Consumer personal values were measured concerning [19]. Schwartz Schwartz's study, using five self-transcending values scales and five self-enhancing values scales, respectively, and further specifying the meaning of each value by providing additional explanatory phrases in parentheses, while randomly arranging the ten question items to avoid subjects' perception of the true purpose of the experiment. Following Schwartz's suggestion, respondents were first asked to ask themselves, "What values are important guiding principles for me in my life?" Then the values scale was filled out.

The self-transcendent values scale includes social justice (eliminating injustice and helping the weak), broad-mindedness (tolerating different ideas and beliefs), loyalty (being loyal to friends and the community), honesty (being truthful and sincere), helpfulness (working for the well-being of others) (Cronbach's $\alpha = 0.727$). The self-improvement values scale includes success (achieving set goals), ambition (the pursuit of power, fame, etc.), power (having more or less control compared to others), maintaining a public image (maintaining one's image in front of outsiders), and having influence (having influence over others and things) (Cronbach's $\alpha = 0.712$).

Three items were used to measure consumer CSR trustworthiness [14], including "The CSR co-creation activities conducted by this company are very dependable", "The CSR co-creation activities conducted by this company are high integrity", " This company's CSR co-creation activities are very competent" (Cronbach's $\alpha = 0.742$).

Four items were used to measure consumer brand trust [20], including: " I have trust in this brand", 'I feel confidence in the brand", " This brand gives me a trustworthy impression", "it's a brand name that meets my expectations" (Cronbach's $\alpha = 0.818$).

Six items to measure consumer value co-creation intentions [10], including: "I am willing to use or purchase the products involved in this CSR activity", "I intend to purchase the products involved in the CSR campaign at some point in the future", "I would like to participate in the CSR activities conducted by the company", "I would like to make suggestions to this CSR activity that will help improve the service", "I would recommend the CSR campaign and brand products to my friends and family", "I would like to share the CSR campaign and brand products on social media" (Cronbach's $\alpha = 0.870$). All questions were on a 7-point Likert scale.

3.3 Pre-test

After the questionnaire items were designed, this study first asked experts in the field of CSR to assist in making corrections to the question items to confirm the correct design of the scale for this study and to optimize the details of the experimental materials based on the suggestions. A small-scale pre-experiment was then conducted with the aim of conducting a preliminary test of the interest claim scenario manipulation by analyzing data from the responses of 30 undergraduate economics subjects from a university in Chongqing after reading the material, and the perceived interest scores of the others-benefit appeal group were significantly higher than those of the self-benefit appeal group. ($M_{Other-benefit} = 4.483$, $SD_{Other-benefit} = 0.812$, $M_{Self-benefit} = 3.598$, $SD_{Other-benefit} = 1.113$, $t = 3.478$, $P = 0.001 < 0.01$), that states that the manipulation regarding benefit claims meets expectations and can be used in formal experiments.

4   Results

Manipulation tests: The results of the manipulation test using the independent samples t-test showed that the perceived benefit claims of the others-benefit appeal group were significantly higher than those of the self-benefit appeal group ($M_{Other-benefit} = 4.9854$, $SD_{Other-benefit} = 1.0199$, $M_{Self-benefit} = 3.5861$, $SD_{Other-benefit} = 1.0950$, $t = 11.188$, $P = 0.000 < 0.01$).

Hypothesis testing: Multiple regression analysis was used to test H1 and H2, standardizing the two values variables separately. Consumer value co-creation intentions were regressed on claim type (self-benefit appeal $= 1$, other-benefit appeal $= 2$), self-enhancement values, and two-way interaction. The regression results showed that the interaction term between interest claim type and self-improvement values was significant ($b = -0.328$, $t = -3925$, $p = 0.000 < 0.01$). The regression of consumers' willingness to co-create values on claim type, self-transcendent values, and two-way interaction. The regression results showed that the interaction term between benefit claim type and self-transcendent values was not significant ($b = 0.024$, $t = 0.257$, $p = 0.798 > 0.01$) and the moderating effect of self-transcendent values were not significant.H2 did not hold.

Since consumers' personal values are a continuous variable, in order to measure the boundary conditions of the moderating effect of self-enhancement values to test the effect of claim type at different levels of self-enhancement values, the Johnson-Neyman method is used in this paper to calculate the significance of the moderating effect, which is significant above point 6.0271 and below point 5.2273 for self-enhancement values (see Table 1). self-benefit (vs. other- benefit) appeals led to higher willingness to value co-creation among individuals with higher self-transcendent values (see the right-hand section of Fig. 2). In contrast, other-benefit (vs. self-benefit) appeals elicited a higher willingness to value co-creation among individuals with relatively low self-transcendent values (see the left-hand section of Fig. 2), supporting H1.

Since the interaction between consumer self-transcendent values and benefit claims is not significant, only the moderated mediating effects of consumer trust (CSR credibility and brand trust) under self-enhancement values are analyzed next. This study used the PROCESS programs Model 8 and Model 85 to examine the mediating effects being moderated, with gender age, education level, and degree of concern for CSR as control variables.

Table 1. The conditional effect of interest claim type on consumers' willingness to co-create CSR under self-improvement values

self-enhancement	Effect of Benefit Appeal Type	se	t	p	LLCI	ULCI
1.2000	2.0481	0.4158	4.9260	0.0000	1.2296	2.8665
1.5053	1.9046	0.3855	4.9404	0.0000	1.1457	2.6635
1.8105	1.7611	0.3554	4.9558	0.0000	1.0616	2.4606
2.1158	1.6176	0.3253	4.9720	0.0000	0.9772	2.2581
2.4211	1.4742	0.2955	4.9886	0.0000	0.8925	2.0559
2.7263	1.3307	0.2659	5.0046	0.0000	0.8073	1.8541
3.0316	1.1872	0.2366	5.0178	0.0000	0.7215	1.6529
3.3368	1.0437	0.2078	5.0237	0.0000	0.6348	1.4527
3.6421	0.9003	0.1796	5.0128	0.0000	0.5467	1.2538
3.9474	0.7568	0.1525	4.9635	0.0000	0.4566	1.0569
4.2526	0.6133	0.1271	4.8268	0.0000	0.3632	0.8634
4.5579	0.4698	0.1046	4.4905	0.0000	0.2639	0.6758
4.8632	0.3264	0.0875	3.7304	0.0002	0.1541	0.4986
5.1684	0.1829	0.0791	2.3106	0.0216	0.0271	0.3387
5.2273	0.1552	0.0788	1.9685	0.0500	0.0000	0.3104
5.4737	0.0394	0.0823	0.4785	0.6326	0.1227	0.2015
5.7789	−0.1041	0.0959	1.0851	0.2788	0.2929	0.0847
6.0271	−0.2207	0.1121	1.9685	0.0500	0.4414	0.0000
6.0842	−0.2475	0.1163	2.1287	0.0341	0.4765	−0.0186
6.3895	−0.3910	0.1405	2.7823	0.0058	0.6677	−0.1144
6.6947	−0.5345	0.1670	3.2009	0.0015	0.8632	−0.2058
7.0000	−0.6780	0.1947	3.4816	0.0006	1.0613	−0.2947

As shown in Table 2 mediating effect of CSR credibility indicates that the confidence interval does not contain 0 (LLCI = −0.2532, ULCI = −0.0177) at high self-improvement values (+1SD) and does not contain 0 (LLCI = 0.0792, ULCI = 0.4234) at low self-improvement values (−1SD). The mediating effect of brand trust indicates that the confidence interval does not contain 0 (LLCI = −0.1917, ULCI = −0.0329) at high self-improvement values (+1SD) and does not contain 0 (LLCI = 0.0399, ULCI = 0.2801) at low self-improvement values (−1SD). Sequential mediation effects indicated that the confidence interval did not contain 0 (LLCI = −0.1217, ULCI = −0.0056) at high self-improvement values (+1SD) and did not contain 0 (LLCI = 0.0372, ULCI = 0.213) at low self-improvement values (−1SD), and H3, H4, and H5 partially held.

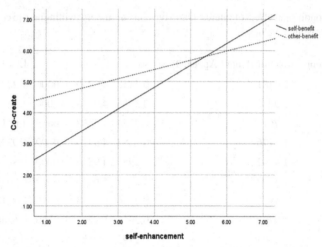

Fig. 2. Interactive effects of interest claim types and self-enhancement values on willingness to co-create CSR values

Table 2. Moderated mediating effect of interest claim type on the willingness of CSR co-creation

self- enhancement	Effect of benefit Appeal Type	SE	LLCI	ULCI
Benefit Appeal → CSR Credibility → Co-create				
4.3932 (−1SD)	0.2548	0.0875	0.0792	0.4234
5.2104	0.0621	0.0384	−0.0139	0.1370
6.0277 (+1SD)	−0.1306	0.0604	−0.2532	−0.0177
Benefit Appeal → Brand Trust → Co-create				
4.3932 (−1SD)	0.1573	0.0608	0.0399	0.2801
5.2104	0.0232	0.0276	−0.0300	0.0795
6.0277 (+1SD)	−0.1108	0.0405	−0.1917	−0.0329
Benefit Appeal → CSR Credibility → Brand Trust → Co-create				
4.3932 (−1SD)	0.1231	0.0445	0.0372	0.2130
5.2104	0.0300	0.0195	−0.0066	0.0715
6.0277 (+1SD)	−0.0631	0.0292	−0.1217	−0.0056

5   Conclusions

Existing research has focused on exploring the impact of CSR co-creation on consumer behavior in terms of value types, value frameworks, and interaction types, while why consumers engage in CSR co-creation is a common concern among academics and companies. This paper explores the mechanisms by which interest appeals influence consumers' willingness to co-creating values in CSR communication. The results of this paper confirm the congruent effect of consumers' self-enhancement values and benefits appeals while finding that self-transcendent values do not have a moderating role in CSR communication benefit appeals. This paper also explores the internal mechanisms of action that influence consumers' willingness to participate, divides consumer trust into CSR trust and brand trust in the CSR field, and confirms their mediating roles separately. In summary, these findings provide important theoretical and practical implications for the design of CSR messages and branding strategies in social media marketing.

The theoretical contributions of this study include the following points. First, previous studies have not focused on the wide application of benefit appeals in CSR communication and lacked discussions on the productive effects of CSR benefit appeals from the perspective of consumer co-participation. Therefore, this study contributes to the study of CSR communication and value co-creation by examining the different effects and boundary conditions of different types of interest appeals. Secondly, this study explores the internal processing mechanisms of CSR messages in CSR communication under social media where consumers face different interest claims and finds further useful references to the relationship marketing literature through the separate mediating roles and sequential mediating mechanisms of CSR credibility and brand trust. Finally, this study found that self-transcendent values do not have a moderating role in CSR communication benefit claims, which may be because while individuals with self-transcendent values emphasize the welfare of others over personal interests, at the same time concern for the interests of others does not imply a lack of concern for self. At the same time, this study was conducted in China, where Chinese people may generally have high self-transcendence values due to the influence they receive from traditional Confucian culture, among others.

The results of this study provide some practical implications for companies to effectively communicate with consumers about CSR activities on social media and to promote consumer engagement in CSR value creation. First of all, the findings of this paper provide some solutions to the problem of "who to say" and "how to say" for CSR activities. Companies should pay attention to the constructive characteristics of their target groups, and marketers should not simply rely on one advertising appeal in different contexts but should choose the right appeal to effectively match consumers with different psychological motivations. Secondly, when designing the content of CSR activities, attention should be paid to the impact of the appeal on consumers' perceived trust including the credibility of the CSR activities themselves as well as the trust in the company to avoid consumers' perception that the company is conducting CSR activities for their benefit, resulting in lower trust and thus lowering consumers' willingness to co-create value.

The limitations of this study provide insights for future research. First, using only a sample of Chinese consumers in this study, we confirmed the significant moderating effect of self-enhancement values and the insignificant effect of self-transcendence values. This result may receive the influence of different cultural and identity motivations, and subsequent studies could conduct cross-cultural research to comprehensively analyze the internal influencing mechanisms that affect consumers' messages about different interest claims in CSR communication and extend the findings to different consumer groups and social contexts to provide additional insights into business practices. Secondly, this study used the experimental method of blurring real brand names. There are studies that prove that different brands and industries affect different consumer responses to CSR benefit claims, and future studies should consider various brand names, including virtual brand names, to enhance the validity of the findings.

References

1. Chu, S.C., Chen, H.T., Gan, C.: Consumers' engagement with corporate social responsibility (CSR) communication in social media: evidence from China and the United States. J. Bus. Res. **110**, 260–271 (2020)
2. Lane, A.B., Devin, B.: Operationalizing stakeholder engagement in CSR: a process approach. Corp. Soc. Responsib. Environ. Manag. **25**(3), 267–280 (2018)
3. Grönroos, C., Voima, P.: Critical service logic: making sense of value creation and co-creation. J. Acad. Mark. Sci. **41**(2), 133–150 (2012)
4. Yap, J.E., Zubcevic-Basic, N., Johnson, L.W., et al.: Mental health message appeals and audience engagement: evidence from Australia. Health Promot. Int. **34**(1), 28–37 (2019)
5. Fernández, P., Hartmann, P., Apaolaza, V.: What drives CSR communication effectiveness on social media? A process-based theoretical framework and research agenda. Int. J. Advert. **41**(3), 385–413 (2021)
6. Gershon, R., Cryder, C., John, L.K.: Why prosocial referral incentives work: the interplay of reputational benefits and action costs. J. Mark. Res. **57**(2), 394–394 (2020)
7. Jaw, C., Chi, K.J., Li, G.J.: Is kindness invaluable? The impact of benefit and cost on prosocial behavior intentions. Asia Pac. J. Mark. Logist. (2022). Ahead-of-print (ahead-of-print)
8. Zhang, L., Zhu, N., Wang, H.: Influence of co-creation signals on observers' co-creation willingness: a self-determination theory perspective. Front. Psychol. **13** (2022)
9. Zhengxiang, W., Tingting, G.: The influencing mechanism of interactive route on consumers' participation willingness of virtual CSR value co-creation. J. Cent. Univ. Finance Econ. **40**(8), 119–128 (2022). (in chinese)
10. Wenming, Z., Fengxuan, H., Lingyan, B.: Factors affecting value co-creation behavior in the sharing economy: the case of online car-hailing. Nankai Bus. Rev. **23**(5), 183–193 (2020). (in chinese)
11. Schwartz, S.H.: Are there universal aspects in the structure and contents of human values. J. Soc. Issues **50**(4), 19–45 (1994)
12. Min, T., Qinglong, X., Yi-Ni, C.: The impact of activity mode of customer engagement in CSR on consumer response: the mediating effect of consumer-brand identification. Front. Sci. Technol. Eng. Manag. **39**(5), 37–44 (2020). (in Chinese)
13. Mingming, C., Yi, S., Dan, L.: The effects of boundary spanning behavior on employee's task performance: based on the multiple moderation of values. Bus. Manag. J. **40**(8), 72–88 (2018). (in Chinese)
14. Hunt, R.M.M.S.D.: The commitment-trust theory of relationship marketing. J. Mark. **58**(3), 20–38 (1994)
15. Kollat, J., Farache, F.: Achieving consumer trust on Twitter via CSR communication. J. Consum. Mark. **34**(6), 505–514 (2017)
16. Aljarah, A.: The nexus between corporate social responsibility and target-based customer citizenship behavior. J. Sustain. Tour. **28**(12), 2044–2063 (2020)
17. Wei, X.Y., Jung, S.J.: Benefit appeals and perceived corporate hypocrisy: implications for the CSR performance of fast fashion brands. J. Prod. Brand Manag. **31**(2), 206–217 (2022)
18. White, C.R.: Allometric analysis beyond heterogeneous regression slopes: use of the Johnson-Neyman technique in comparative biology. Physiol. Biochem. Zool. **76**(1), 135–140 (2003)
19. Schwartz, S.H.: Universals in the content and structure of values: theoretical advances and empirical tests in 20 countries. Adv. Exp. Soc. Psychol. **25**, 1–65 (1992)
20. He, Z., Liu, S., Ferns, B.H., et al.: Pride or empathy? Exploring effective CSR communication strategies on social media. Int. J. Contemp. Hosp. Manag. **34**(8), 2989–3007 (2022)

The Influence of Marketing Stimuli and Contextual Factors on Consumers' Intention to Make Impulse Purchases in Live E-Commerce

Yi Chen and Wenwen Yue[✉]

Wuhan University of Technology, Wuhan 430070, China
y19730530@126.com

Abstract. Impulse purchase is a prevalent consumer behaviour, and consumers' willingness to consume on impulse is even stronger in live e-commerce context. Based on the S-O-R model, the study explores the mechanism of the factors influencing consumer's impulse purchase intention in live e-commerce from five dimensions: price discounts and time limits of marketing stimuli, interaction, opinion leaders, atmospheric cues of contextual factors. Meanwhile, a structural equation model is constructed in combination with flow theory. Data were collected through questionnaires, and SPSS 22.0 and AMOS 21.0 were used to analyse the data of sample. It shows that price discounts, time limits, interaction, opinion leaders and atmospheric cues all positively associate with impulse purchase intentions, with the flow experience playing a mediating role in this process. The results suggest that platforms can design engaging atmospheric cues; operators can innovate live-streaming gameplay and optimise incentives; and consumers should spend rationally according to their actual needs. The study contributes to an understanding of S-O-R theory application in live e-commerce context, and enriches the research on the antecedent variables of impulsive purchase intention and its formation mechanism.

Keywords: Live E-commerce · Impulsive Purchase intention · Flow Experience · S-O-R Model

1 Introduction

With the development of the mobile internet, live e-commerce has broken the bottleneck of traditional e-commerce platforms and become the most convenient and efficient marketing method nowadays. CNNIC report shows that by the end of 2021, the scale of live e-commerce users reached 463 million in China, accounting for 55.1% of online shopping users, and the scale of live e-commerce transactions reached 456.12 billion yuan, which indicates that most consumers prefer to shop in live e-commerce. In live e-commerce context, real-time interaction, rich audio-visual methods, multi-dimensional product display and immersive shopping experience could fully satisfy consumers' social needs [1]. The stimulation of different factors leads to changes in customers' internal emotional and cognitive states, making them more likely to make impulse purchases.

Impulse purchase is an unplanned and irrational consumer behaviour, with 83% of consumers in the live stream experiencing impulse buying. As a result, how to stimulate consumers to generate impulse purchase intentions has become an crucial concern for enterprises to formulate marketing strategies [2]. Throughout previous research, scholars have focused on the factors influencing online impulse purchases, mainly about website factors, anchor features and consumers' characteristics, with little literature considering the impact of marketing stimuli and contextual factors. Moreover, the research on live e-commerce mostly revolves around consumers' motivation to participate and purchase behaviour, while studies on consumers' psychological states and impulse consumption are not in-depth enough to systematically explain the reasons for consumers' impulse purchase intentions.

Therefore, based on S-O-R theory, this study combines the characteristics of e-commerce live streaming with marketing stimuli and contextual factors, uses flow experience as a mediator to construct a structural equation model of consumers' impulse purchase intention, and explores the formation mechanism of consumers' impulse purchase intention in live e-commerce, so as to enrich the theoretical research on live e-commerce context and consumers' purchase behaviour. It also increases the empirical research in related fields, with a view to providing practical suggestions for e-commerce live platforms, related practitioners and consumers.

2 Theoretical Foundation and Research Hypothesis

2.1 S-O-R Theoretical Model

Mehrabian and Russell (1974) proposed the S-O-R theoretical model in which factors involved in person's interaction with the external environment stimulate the internal state of individuals, leading to corresponding responses and actions [3]. Eroglu et al. (2001) first applied the theory to online shopping scenario to investigate the relationship between online consumer behaviour and the online environment, suggesting that different online shop atmospheres (S) have different effects on consumers' internal states (O) and consequently on their shopping outcomes (R) [4]. Chopdar (2020) verified the impact of various characteristics of mobile commerce APP on consumers' repeat purchase intention and satisfaction experience through impulsive purchase behavior and perceived value [5]. Related studies have shown that S-O-R theory could be used to better explain the intrinsic mechanisms by which external factors create stimuli for consumers. Meanwhile, marketing stimuli and contextual factors have a certain impact on consumers' behavioral intentions in live e-commerce. Therefore, price discounts, time limits are selected as two critical elements of marketing stimuli, and interactions, opinion leaders, atmospheric cues are selected as three significant elements of contextual factors, which together constitute the external stimuli variable (S). In the meantime, the flow experience is chosen as the internal state of the organism (O), and the consumer's impulse purchase intention is taken as the response (R) to explore the internal influencing mechanism. The research model shown in Fig. 1.

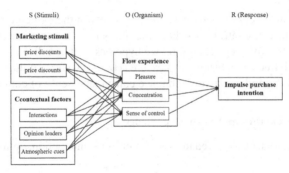

Fig. 1. Research model

2.2 Marketing Stimuli and Flow Experience

The flow theory was proposed by Csikszentmihalyi (1975). In the flow experience, consumers are immersed physically and mentally in what they like to do, reaching a state of full concentration, forgetting themselves, and being internally pleasurable. This study uses Koufaris' three-dimensional segmentation method to take pleasure, concentration and control as internal emotional expression. Meanwhile, the marketing stimuli are explored in two dimensions: price discounts and time limits.

According to the type of discounts, price discounts can be divided into direct discounts (reducing sales prices to provide consumers with certain goods or services) and indirect discounts (adding value to the original price to make consumers feel worthwhile). Wang (2014) suggested that the positive effect of price discounts on pleasure was not significant, but price discounts can have an impact on consumer pleasure through consumers' arousal in group purchase situations [6]. Wu et al. (2020) proposed that the price advantage of online purchases triggers consumers' satisfaction when purchasing products, and further enhances consumers' transaction utility by generating more positive emotions [7]. In live e-commerce contexts, instant discounts can increase price attractiveness, increase attention to the live room by enhancing consumer pleasure [6] and briefly disconnecting from reality, resulting in flow that influences consumers' impulse purchase decisions. Otherwise, the control over one's own behaviour is reduced and there is an unconscious desire to consume at the pace of the anchor. Therefore, we hypothesise that in live e-commerce, price discounts positively influence consumers' pleasure (H1a), positively influence consumers' concentration (H1b), and negatively influence consumers' sense of control (H1c).

Time limits mean that products can only be purchased within an effective time, and supply is often less than demand. Time constraints make full use of information asymmetry to manipulate consumer psychology [8], which put a degree of pressure to consumers [9], forcing them to make decisions in a short time. Zhu et al. (2021) found that in contexts with high transaction utility, time pressure accelerates one's cognitive processing under the effect of pleasure, which in turn promotes consumers' online impulsive buying tendency through situational experiments [10]. During online purchases, the time limit of promotion shortens the time for consumers to think and process information, and consumers' own anxiety and tension due to the perceived opportunity costs increase their excitement and attention, thus affecting the quality of their purchase decisions [11] and triggering a loss of control. Whether time limits may have similar utility in live e-commerce is worth exploring. Therefore, we hypothesise that in live e-commerce, time limits positively influence consumers' pleasure (H2a), positively influence consumers' concentration (H2b), and negatively influence consumers' sense of control (H2c).

2.3 Contextual Factors and Flow Experience

The contextual factors are explored in three dimensions: interaction, opinion leaders and atmospheric cues.

Interaction refers to the process of information exchange between consumers, the anchor and other viewers. In live streaming, interaction is real-time, with social engagements achieved through a virtual medium where viewers are free to express their opinions and also able to receive timely feedback signals. The strong sense of participation satisfies consumers' social needs [12] and brings favourable emotional experience to users, resulting in a state of pleasurable emotions and focus, weakening the sense of control over oneself. Research on interactivity in live e-commerce is gradually expanding. Sun et al. (2019) asserted that interactivity is a critical condition provided by information technology in live broadcast, and verified the significant impact of interactive behavior on purchase intention [13]. Fan (2022) incorporates pop-ups into live streaming in e-commerce and demonstrated that flow experiences mediate the relationship between pop-up interactions and consumers' impulsive purchase [14]. This study attempts to explore interaction as an antecedent variable of the flow experience with live e-commerce features. Therefore, we hypothesise that in live e-commerce, interaction positively influences consumers' pleasure (H3a), positively influences consumers' concentration (H3b), and negatively influences consumers' sense of control (H3c).

Opinion leaders refer to anchors and influential external guests in live e-commerce, including groups such as netizens, celebrities and entrepreneurs. The professionalism and authority of them make their opinions more persuasive. Feng (2020) put forward that the more consumers trust opinion leaders, the easier their attitudes and behaviors will be shaken, reducing their sense of control over themselves [2]. Furthermore, opinion leaders are attractive in terms of appearance, personality and talent, making consumers immersed in the viewing process, the opinions and propositions expressed provide guidance for consumers' decision-making. Research has been conducted from the perspective of anchor characteristics, with Jpark (2020) suggesting that consumers tend to develop positive emotions towards attractive anchors and transfer this positive attitude to commodities [15]. Wei (2022) proposed that flow experience plays a mediating role between anchor attractiveness and consumers' impulse purchase intention [16]. However, anchors just act as representatives of opinion leaders. Therefore, from the perspective of opinion leaders, we hypothesise that in live e-commerce, opinion leaders positively influence consumers' pleasure (H4a), positively influence consumers' concentration (H4b), and negatively influence consumers' sense of control (H4c).

Atmospheric cues focus on environmental, functional and layout elements, such as colour and sound, and are used to influence consumers' senses, thereby increase their interest. Studies related to online shopping have shown that ambient cues contribute to the generation of consumers' positive emotions. Xiang et al. (2016) confirmed that the variety of product displays helps to increase consumers' visual appeal, creating the illusion of personal experience, compensating for tactile deficits, and evoking positive emotional responses in PC-based shopping [17]. Zhang (2020) demonstrated that visual appeal can positively influence consumers' impulsive purchase intentions by affecting perceived pleasure in mobile shopping situations [18]. When consumers are satisfied with the atmospheric elements, they might develop the flow experience. Therefore, we hypothesise that in live e-commerce, atmospheric cues positively influence consumers' pleasure (H5a), positively influence consumers' concentration (H5b), and negatively influence consumers' sense of control (H5c).

2.4 Flow Experience and Impulse Purchase Intentions

Previous researches have studied impulse purchase behavior more than intentions and tendencies since behaviors actually occurs and can be identified and measured. Beatty & Ferrell (1998) proposed that favourable emotion has a positive associate with impulsive purchase intentions, and they argued that if an individual's emotional response becomes strong, the likelihood of an impulsive purchase occurring is greatly increased [19]. But it is worth noting that the occurrence of behavior stems from the activation of purchase intentions, and the results of behaviors can be inferred from individual behavioral intentions to a certain extent. From the emotional and cognitive perspective, impulsive purchase intention refers to the tendency of consumers to spend in haste when their emotions fluctuate, regardless of the consequences.

Current research on the flow experience focuses more on pleasure and arousal, and the exploration of concentration and control is not deep enough. Zhang (2020) suggested that when consumers' emotions are aroused and pleasure dominates, they overestimate their needs and financial strength, and are prone to impulsive purchase intentions [18]. Specifically in live e-commerce, consumers are stimulated by external factors to generate a strong emotional response and increase their urgent purchase needs and ideas [3]. Therefore, we hypothesise that in live e-commerce, pleasure positively influences impulse purchase intentions (H6a), concentration positively influences impulse purchase intentions (H6b), and control negatively influences impulse purchase intention (H6c).

3 Empirical Analysis

3.1 Variable Measurement

The variables were measured by the five-level Likert scale, with items mainly referring to mature scales at home and abroad. Appropriate modifications were made on the basis of the pre-investigation to make them more in line with the live e-commerce context. The reference sources for the scale are shown in Table 1.

3.2 Data Collection and Sample Analysis

This study was conducted among people aged 18 and above who had watched live e-commerce and purchased products in the past two months. Online questionnaire was

Table 1. Research scale

Variables	Items	References
Price discounts	3	Rook et al. (1987)
Time constraints	3	Inman et al. (1996)
Interaction	3	Meng (2012)
Opinion leaders	3	Meng (2012); Chen & Lin (2018)
Atmospheric cues	5	Floh et al. (2013); Gong (2019)
Pleasure	4	Koufaris (2002); Chen & Lin (2018); Ghani et al. (1991)
Concentration	3	
Sense of control	2	
Impulse purchase intention	4	Beatty et al. (1998); Gong et al. (2019)

distributed by WeChat and e-mail. From August 4, 2022 to August 17, 2022, a total of 512 questionnaires were returned, excluding those who did not meet the age requirement and shopping experience, and invalid questionnaires that took less than one minute to fill in.

The sample shows that the age group of 18–34 years old accounts for more than 70% of the population, indicating that young people are passionate about adventure and willing to accept this new form of live e-commerce; the proportion of females participating in live shopping is higher than that of males; the respondents' occupation is relatively evenly distributed, with more private sector workers and students, make up 32.16%; More than one-half of the participants had an average monthly income between 5,000 and 10,000 RMB (52.12%), indicating that the main audience of e-commerce live streaming is the middle and high-income group, who have certain consumption capacity.

3.3 Analysis of Reliability and Validity

The results of the reliability analysis show that the cronbach's coefficients for nine variables are above 0.8, indicating that the reliability of this questionnaire is favourable. Meanwhile, the correlation coefficients of the corrected items of each item meet the requirement of higher than 0.5, and there is no significant increase in cronbach's alpha after deleting this item, suggesting that the internal consistency and stability of the scale is high (Table 2).

The results of the validity analysis show that the KMO value is 0.872 and the significance of bartlett's spherical test was 0, which proved that the scale was suitable for factor analysis. Secondly, the principal component analysis extracted nine factors with eigenvalues above 1, the cumulative variance contribution is approximately 73.32%, and all factor loadings are above 0.5, indicating that the scale has good structural validity. Next, AMOS 21.0 is used to conduct the validation factor analysis. The combined reliability (CR) of each variable is higher than 0.8 and the average variance extracted (AVE) exceed the accepted level of 0.5, with the figure of opinion leader and sense of control above 0.7, suggesting that each item could explain the dimension to a large extent, while

Table 2. Results of reliability and convergent validity analysis

Variables	Item	CITC	Item removed from Cronbach's Alpha	Standardised factor loadings	CR	AVE	Cronbach's Alpha
Price discounts	A1	0.651	0.79	0.747	0.83	0.62	0.825
	A2	0.663	0.776	0.765			
	A3	0.744	0.696	0.847			
Time constraints	B1	0.711	0.807	0.798	0.854	0.662	0.853
	B2	0.738	0.784	0.819			
	B3	0.728	0.792	0.823			
Interaction	C1	0.709	0.738	0.814	0.828	0.617	0.827
	C2	0.686	0.76	0.787			
	C3	0.659	0.787	0.754			
Opinion leaders	D1	0.804	0.86	0.866	0.903	0.757	0.902
	D2	0.829	0.841	0.897			
	D3	0.789	0.874	0.846			
Atmospheric cues	E1	0.659	0.855	0.725	0.876	0.587	0.872
	E2	0.681	0.85	0.753			
	E3	0.665	0.853	0.719			
	E4	0.692	0.849	0.738			
	E5	0.808	0.818	0.882			
Pleasure	F1	0.593	0.788	0.69	0.818	0.529	0.816
	F2	0.623	0.774	0.711			
	F3	0.705	0.734	0.768			
	F4	0.626	0.773	0.737			
Concentration	G1	0.682	0.716	0.761	0.809	0.586	0.807
	G2	0.653	0.74	0.757			
	G3	0.646	0.749	0.778			
Sense of control	H1	0.783	/	0.869	0.878	0.783	0.878
	H2	0.783	/	0.901			
Impulse purchase intention	I1	0.588	0.764	0.677	0.804	0.508	0.801
	I2	0.595	0.76	0.687			
	I3	0.705	0.703	0.802			
	I4	0.575	0.77	0.678			

the square root (diagonal) of the AVE of each variable is greater than the correlation coefficient between the variables, proving that the convergent and discriminant validity of this study is ideal.

3.4 Correlation Analysis

Pearson correlation analysis shows that the correlation coefficients between price discounts, time limits, interaction, opinion leaders, atmosphere cues and impulse purchase intention are all above 0, indicating that there is a significant positive correlation, and the intensity is interaction > atmosphere cues > price discounts > opinion leaders > time limits. Price discounts, time limits, interaction, opinion leaders, atmosphere cues are positively correlated with pleasure and concentration, but negatively correlated with sense of control; Similarly, there is a significant positive correlation between pleasure, concentration and impulse purchase intention, and the correlation coefficient between sense of control and impulse purchase intention is less than 0, which means there is a significant negative correlation, and the intensity is sense of control > concentration > pleasure.

3.5 Model Checking and Path Analysis

In order to analyse the mechanism of "marketing stimuli, contextual factors - flow experience - impulse purchase intention", a structural equation model is constructed by AMOS 21.0 as shown in Fig. 2. According to the data in Table 3, all indexes of χ^2/df, AGFI, TLI, NFI, CFI and RMSEA are excellent except the AGFI of $0.875 < 9$, which indicates that the research data have a favourable fit with the model.

Table 3. The goodness-of-fit index of the model

Fitting index		χ^2/df	GFI	AGFI	TLI	NFI	CFI	RMSEA
Fitting standard	Good	<3	>0.8	>0.8	>0.8	>0.8	>0.8	<0.08
	Excellent	<2	>0.9	>0.9	>0.9	>0.9	>0.9	<0.05
Model index		1.693	0.890	0.911	0.951	0.904	0.958	0.040

According to the results of each standardized path coefficient, it can be seen that price discounts have a significant impact on pleasure ($\beta = 0.218$, $p < 0.001$), but the positive effect of time limits on pleasure is not significant ($\beta = 0.084$, $p = 0.132 > 0.05$), so H1a is valid and H2a is invalid. The standardized path coefficients of interaction, opinion leaders and atmosphere cues to pleasure are 0.193, 0.154 and 0.184, respectively, and the P values are all lower than 0.01, indicating that interaction, opinion leaders and atmosphere cues have significant positive effects on pleasure, so H3a, H4a and H5a are valid; Price discounts have a significant impact on concentration ($\beta = 0.147$, $p = 0.016 < 0.05$), time limits have a significant impact on concentration ($\beta = 0.244$, $p < 0.001$), interaction has a significant impact on concentration ($\beta = 0.178$, $p < 0.01$), opinion leaders have a significant impact on concentration ($\beta = 0.132$, $p = 0.021 <$ 0.05), atmosphere cues have a significant impact on concentration ($\beta = 0.156$, $p = 0.01 < 0.05$), so H1b–H5b are valid; The standardized path coefficients of price discounts, time limits, interaction, opinion leaders and atmosphere cues to sense of control are -0.154, -0.261, -0.137, -0.120 and -0.145 in turn, and the P values are all lower than 0.05, which indicates that price discounts, time limits, interaction, opinion leaders and atmosphere cues have significant negative effects on sense of control, so H1c-H5c are valid; The standardized path coefficients of pleasure, concentration and control on impulse purchase intention are 0.157, 0.226 and -0.304, respectively, and the P values are all lower than 0.05, which indicates that pleasure and concentration have significant positive effects on impulse purchase intention, and control has significant negative effects on impulse purchase intention, so H6a–H6c are valid.

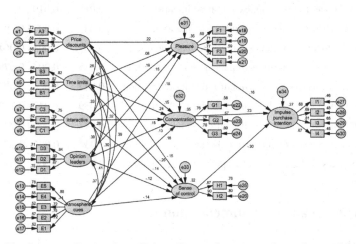

Fig. 2. Normalised path coefficient diagram for structural equation models

3.6 Analysis of Mediating Effects

Mediating effects are assessment through the bias-corrected bootstrap method. Repeated samples are taken 5000 times with a confidence interval level of 95%. The results are shown in Table 4. It can be seen from the data that the effect value of time limits on impulse purchase intention through the mediating effect of pleasure is 0.013, and the 95% confidence interval is $[-0.006, 0.039]$, which contains 0, $p > 0.05$, so pleasure cannot mediate the effect of time constraints on consumers' impulse purchase intention. Similarly, pleasure plays a mediating role in the process of price discounts, interaction, opinion leaders and atmosphere cues on consumers' impulse purchase intention, while concentration and control play a mediating role in the process of price discounts, inter-action, opinion leaders and atmosphere cues on consumers' impulse purchase intention. This is mutually confirmed with the results of the previous structural equation model analysis.

Table 4. Bootstrap mediated effects test

Path	Effect	Bias - Corrected 95% CI		
		lower	upper	p
Price discounts-Pleasure-Impulse purchase intention	0.034	0.004	0.078	0.021
Time limits-Pleasure-Impulse purchase intention	0.013	−0.006	0.039	0.204
Interaction-Pleasure-Impulse purchase intention	0.03	0.003	0.073	0.024
Opinion leaders-Pleasure-Impulse purchase intention	0.024	0.001	0.054	0.037
Atmosphere cues-Pleasure-Impulse purchase intention	0.029	0.003	0.068	0.022
Price discounts-Concentration-Impulse purchase intention	0.033	0.001	0.074	0.045
Time limits-Concentration-Impulse purchase intention	0.055	0.019	0.100	0.001
Interaction-Concentration-Impulse purchase intention	0.04	0.007	0.094	0.006
Opinion leaders-Concentration-Impulse purchase intention	0.03	0.003	0.064	0.032
Atmosphere cues-Concentration-Impulse purchase intention	0.035	0.004	0.078	0.014
Price discounts-Sense of control-Impulse purchase intention	0.047	0.008	0.092	0.019
Time limits-Sense of control-Impulse purchase intention	0.079	0.042	0.120	0.000
Interaction-Sense of control-Impulse purchase intention	0.042	0.002	0.092	0.039
Opinion leaders-Sense of control-Impulse purchase intention	0.036	0.006	0.07	0.016
Atmosphere cues-Sense of control-Impulse purchase intention	0.044	0.009	0.088	0.011

4   Conclusion and Recommendation

4.1   Conclusion

Through empirical analysis, the following conclusions are drawn: (1) In live e-commerce, consumers' internal psychological states are influenced by marketing and contextual factors, which ultimately manifest in their motivation and behaviour. Both marketing stimuli (price discounts and time limits) and contextual factors (interaction, opinion leaders and atmospheric cues) are positively associated with impulsive purchase intentions; both price discounts and contextual factors positively affect consumer pleasure and concentration, and negatively affect consumers' sense of control; while time limits have a no significant effect on consumer pleasure, probably because making decisions in a shorter time is more intensive, consumers are in a tense atmosphere, and find it difficult to relax. (2) The flow experience partially mediates the relationship between marketing stimuli and contextual factors and impulsive purchase intentions. Pleasure can not mediate between time limits and impulse purchase intentions; pleasure plays a mediating role in the influence of price discounts, interactions, opinion leaders and atmospheric cues on impulse purchase intentions; concentration and sense of control mediate between marketing stimuli and contextual factors and impulse purchase intentions.

The theoretical contribution of this study is to expand the research perspective on consumer purchasing behaviour in the context of e-commerce. Based on the flow theory, the internal state and feelings of consumers watching e-commerce live broadcasts are studied more carefully in the psychological level, and explores the mechanism between marketing stimuli and contextual factors and consumers' impulsive purchase intentions from the aspects of pleasure, concentration and sense of control. It makes up for the lack of research on the changes in consumers' internal emotions and the correlation between emotions and consumer behavior. In addition, it enriches the research on the antecedent variables of impulsive purchase intention and its formation mechanism.

4.2 Practical Insights

For e-commerce platforms, design engaging atmospheric cues. The platform should take ease of use as the first principle, provide diverse ways of presenting information, and meet consumers' requirements for detail, novelty and accuracy of content. Secondly, the design of the appearance of the live platform should be pleasant and up-to-date, focusing on the balance and harmony of the display interface to create a excellent visual experience which could attract the consumer's eye. In addition, the development of more interactive efficiency, real-time feedback auxiliary interactive features to extend the focus time.

For live operators, they should innovate live broadcast gameplay and optimise incentive mechanisms. Input characterised scenarios around live streaming themes. Regular or irregular changes in live-streaming themes can effectively enhance consumers' individual experiences and maintain a sense of freshness between consumers and live-streaming. Continued consumer attention is more likely to elicit the flow experience, thus enhancing consumers' impulsive purchase intentions. Make full use of random prize draws, coupon distribution, and limited time sales to provide intermittent stimulation to attract consumers' attention and stimulate impulse purchase desire. Furthermore, the appropriate combination of some games or performance sessions, with special guests of celebrities or other well-known personalities is a usual means, and can also open up new ideas from a cultural perspective.

For consumers, they should use their risk awareness and return to rationality. Consumers are supposed to obtain more information about products, improve their discernment and weaken the impact of information asymmetry and impulsiveness; establish a rational consumption concept according to their own strengths and actual needs, and reduce unnecessary waste; pay attention to protecting their rights and interests, utilise the law as a shield and be wary of infringements such as false advertising.

References

1. Fei, M., Tan, H., Peng, X.: Promoting or attenuating? An eye-tracking study on the role of social cues in e-commerce livestreaming. Decis. Support Syst. **142**, 113466 (2021)
2. Feng, J., Lu, M.: An empirical study on impulsive purchase intention of live marketing in the era of mobile internet. Soft Sci. **34**(12), 128–133+144 (2020). (in Chinese)
3. Tak, P., Gupta, M.: Examining travel mobile app attributes and its impact on consumer engagement: an application of SOR framework. J. Internet Commer. **20**(3), 293–318 (2021)

4. Eroglu, S.A., Machleit, K.A., Davis, L.M.: Atmosphericqualities of online retailing: a conceptual model and implications. J. Bus. Res. **54**(2), 177–184 (2001)
5. Chopdar, P.K., Balakrishnan, J.: Consumers response towards mobile commerce applications: SOR approach. Int. J. Inf. Manag. **53**(8), 1–12 (2020)
6. Wang, Q.Z., Yao, Q., Ye, Y.: Research on the mechanism of price discount and number of buyers on consumers' impulse purchase intention in online group purchase scenario. J. Manag. Eng. **28**(04), 37–47 (2014). (in Chinese)
7. Wu, L., Chiu, M.L., Chen, K.W.: Defining the determinants of online impulse buying through a shopping process of integrating perceived risk, expectation-confirmation model, and flow theory issues. Int. J. Inf. Manag. **52**, 102099 (2020)
8. Sundstrom, M., Hjelm-Lidholm, S., Radon, A.: Clicking the boredom away - exploring impulse fashion buying behavior online. J. Retail. Consum. Serv. **47**, 150–156 (2019)
9. Sohn, H.K., Lee, T.J.: Tourists' impulse buying behavior at duty-free shops: the moderating effects of time pressure and shopping involvement. J. Travel Tour. Mark. **34**(3), 341–356 (2017)
10. Zhu, Y.M., Zhang, J.M.: A study of the effect of time pressure on online impulse buying: moderation of transaction utility and perceived risk. Bus. Econ. Manag. **07**, 55–66 (2021). (in Chinese)
11. Wu, Y., Xin, L., Li, D., et al.: How does scarcity promotion lead to impulse purchase in the online market? A field experiment. Inf. Manag. **58**(1), 103283 (2021)
12. Sun, K., Liu, L.C., Liu, C.L.: Emotional perspective on impulsive purchase intention of live e-commerce consumers. China Circ. Econ. **36**(01), 33–42 (2022). (in Chinese)
13. Sun, Y., Shao, X., Li, X., et al.: How live streaming influences purchase intentions in social commerce: an IT affordance perspective. Electron. Commer. Res. Appl. **37**, 100886 (2019)
14. Fan, Y.J., Liu, J.: Pop-up interaction, online product display and consumers' impulsive purchase behavior-mediated by presence and flow experience. J. Harbin Univ. Commer. **184**(03), 78–89 (2022). (in Chinese)
15. Jpark, H.J., Lin, L.M.: The effects of match-ups on the consumer attitudes toward internet celebrities and their livestreaming contents in the context of product endorsement. J. Retail. Consum. Serv. **2**, 1–6 (2020)
16. Wei, J.F., Li, M.N., Liu, B.P.: The influence of anchor characteristics on consumers' impulse purchase intention in e-commerce live streaming. China Circ. Econ. **36**(04), 32–42 (2022). (in Chinese)
17. Xiang, L., Zheng, X., Lee, M.K.O., et al.: Exploring consumers' impulse buying behavior on social commerce platform. Int. J. Inf. Manag. **36**(3), 333–347 (2016)
18. Zhang, W., Yang, T., Zhang, W.K.: A study on the mechanism of mobile shopping contextual factors on impulsive purchase intention. Manag. Rev. **32**(02), 174–183 (2020). (in Chinese)
19. Beatty, S.E., Ferrell, E.M.: Impulse buying: modeling its precursors. J. Retail. **74**(2), 169–191 (1998)

How Older Adults' Moments Sharing in SNS Contributes to Their Subjective Well-Being?

Ru Zhang, Wenlong Liu[(✉)], Yi Jiang, and Shenghui Sang

Nanjing University of Aeronautics and Astronautics, Nanjing 211106, China
willenliu@nuaa.edu.cn

Abstract. The purpose of this study is to investigate the effects of older adults' moment sharing behavior on their hedonic, social, self-esteem gratification, and subjective well-being by using the theory of use and gratification. By adopting a questionnaire survey, 226 valid samples were collected and further analyzed using PLS-SEM, to reveal the antecedents of gratification in social media use and the effect of gratification on older adults' subjective well-being. Results show that older adults' moment sharing behavior has positive effect on hedonic, social, self-esteem gratification, and subjective well-being. Social gratification and self-esteem gratification have positive effect on subjective well-being. Social isolation moderates the effects of older adults' moment sharing behavior on their perceived hedonic, social, as well as self-esteem gratification. This study broadens the research on subjective well-being of older adults by linking their social media use with the theory of use and gratification. This work was supported by the National Social Science Foundation of China (Grant No. 20CGL055).

Keywords: Older adult's moment sharing behavior · Hedonic gratification · Social gratification · Self-esteem gratification · Subjective well-being

1 Introduction

The core functions of WeChat are three social applications based on acquaintances, including instant messaging, circle of friends, and public account self-media (Yi'nan Wang, Nie, Li, & Zhou 2018). Among them "Moments" is WeChat's brand name for its social feed of friends' updates. Moments allows users to post images, post text, post comments (A. Whiting & D. Williams 2013), share music, share articles, and post "likes". The use of social media can give users a sense of gratification. When using social media, there is a sense of hedonic gratification that comes from entertaining, browsing, and spending time [1]. In the process of using social media, the user can reduce boredom, and entertain myself and it has been a habit for them (Sheldon et al. 2017). What's more, the reason people can feel pleasure and gratification from social media may be that people can temporarily escape the things they don't want to face and divert their attention [2].

Another kind of gratification is social gratification. Users can find out what their friends are doing, inform themselves about social events, set up dates with friends,

Y. Tu and M. Chi (Eds.): WHICEB 2023, LNBIP 480, pp. 143–155, 2023.
https://doi.org/10.1007/978-3-031-32299-0_13

discuss school activities, and hang out with their friends [3]. It greatly assists to build social relationships, find more career opportunities and be familiar with subjective norms [2]. In addition, some people derive self-esteem from their use of social media (Sheldon et al. 2017). The process of using social media is the process of self-discovery of users, and the process of seeking their social status (Jin, Zhang, Wang, & An 2020; Raza et al. 2020). They expect to be able to enhance their social status and authority in the community [3].

The adoption of social networking sites by the older adult continues to lag behind the adoption of social networking sites by the young (Xie & Jaeger 2008; Xie, Watkins, Golbeck, & Huang 2012). As people age, older people may experience more social exclusion [4], because retirement can lead to dramatic changes in later life, and older people begin to disengage from society. Recently, older adults have shown a special enthusiasm for adopting social media in daily life. Social media enable older adult people to connect with a larger network of contacts to observe friends and family members' status updates, and to express themselves to others online, which may play a role in promoting happiness in old age. So it's worth investigating how social media has changed the lives of these people (Rui, Yu, Xu, & Cui 2018).

This paper is structured as follows. The next section provides a theoretical background. The research model and hypotheses are then developed in Sect. 3. Section 4 describes the research methodology, followed by data analysis in Sect. 5. Section 6 discusses the results, and Sect. 7 concludes the paper with a focus on the theoretical and practical implications as well as the research limitations.

2   Theoretical Background

The rapid development of global social media has changed the way individuals share information [5]. Researchers have used many theories and frameworks to explain individuals' willingness to use social media sites (SNS). Among all the theories, the most commonly used one is the use and gratification theory (U&G theory).

The U&G theory can clarify the psychological needs of people to use specific media (Cheung & Lee 2009). U&G theory focuses on explaining the psychological value of media users' participation in specific media use behaviors [6]. This theory studies how the audience uses media and what kind of gratification they get (A. Whiting & D. Williams 2013). People actively choose and use media according to their own needs (Hongxiu Li, Liu, Xu, Heikkilä, & van der Heijden 2015), It emphasizes that positive motivation and active use of media content can meet individual needs (A. Whiting & D. Williams 2013).

The U&G theory includes the use of traditional media and new media. In the early stages of its development (around the 1950s–1980s), this theory focused on traditional media (A. Whiting & D. Williams 2013) radio broadcasts, newspapers (Elliott & Rosenberg 1987), and television (Babrow 1987). Recently, more and more scholars apply it to the study of new media, especially social media (Leung 2013; Y. Li, Yang, Zhang, & Zhang 2019; Anita Whiting & David Williams 2013), Microblogging (Gan & Li 2018; I. L. B. Liu, Cheung, & Lee 2016) Instagram (Sheldon et al. 2017), and WeChat (Gan 2016; Gan & Li 2018; Sun et al. 2016).

Prior studies have categorized the gratifications gained when using different media. For example, (Sheldon et al. 2017) holds the opinion that users can obtain Content gratification, social gratification, process gratification, and technology gratification when they use Instagram [7]. In recent years, researchers have also identified different types of gratifications associated with using a variety of social media. A study by [8] revealed social gratification (socializing), hedonic gratification (entertainment), self-esteem gratification (self-status seeking), and information gratification (information) were gained when college students use Facebook. Another study on the students by [2] found hedonic gratification (escape), technology gratification (ease of use), information gratification (information seeking), and social gratification (social relationships, career opportunities, education, subjective norms) were derived from the use of Facebook of students.

In China, WeChat is the most popular instant messaging tool, and more and more scholars have paid attention to the gratification brought by the use of WeChat. Another study by [9] found hedonic gratification, social gratification, utilitarian gratification, and technology gratification were derived from the use of WeChat. In summary, U&G theory has been applied to identify what kind of gratification can be obtained by the WeChat users (Table 1).

Table 1. Summary of the related studies

Context	Measure	Samples	U&G Typology	Source
Facebook	Survey	1,715 college students	**Social gratification** (socializing); **hedonic gratification** (entertainment); **self-esteem gratification** (self-status seeking); **information gratification** (information)	(Park et al. 2009)
Facebook	Survey	431 Facebook users	**Hedonic gratification** (to reduce boredom, to fill my free time, habit, to entertain myself); **social gratification** (to find out what my friends are doing, to inform myself about social events, to set up meetings and dates with friends, to discuss school activities, to hang out with my friends); **information gratification** (to share the content I like)	(A. Whiting & D. Williams 2013)

(*continued*)

Table 1. (*continued*)

Context	Measure	Samples	U&G Typology	Source
Facebook	Survey	280 students	**Hedonic gratification** (escape); **technology gratification** (ease of use); **information gratification** (information seeking); **social gratification** (social relationships, career opportunities, education, subjective norms)	(Raza et al. 2020)
Facebook	Survey	314 respondents	**Self-esteem gratification** (self-discovery, social enhancement value); **hedonic gratification** (entertainment value); **technology gratification** (instrumental value); **information gratification** (informational value); **social gratification** (interpersonal interconnectivity)	(Lin et al. 2020)
Microblogging and WeChat	Survey	368 Chinese university students	**Hedonic gratification; affection gratification; information gratification;** social gratification	(Gan & Li 2018)
Microblogging	Survey	230 users	**Content gratification; social gratification; process gratification; technology gratification**	(I. L. B. Liu et al. 2016)
Instagram	Survey	402 users	**Social gratification** (self-promotion, social Interaction); **hedonic gratification** (diversion); **information gratification** (documenting, Creativity)	(Sheldon et al. 2017)
WeChat	Survey	215 active friendship group members	**Social gratification** (social value); **hedonic gratification** (hedonic value); **self-esteem gratification** (self-discovery value); **information gratification** (informational value)	(Sun et al. 2016)
WeChat	Survey	297 WeChat users	**Hedonic gratification; social gratification; utilitarian gratification; technology gratification**	(Gan & Li 2018)

3   Research Model and Hypotheses

3.1   Older Adults' Moment Sharing Behavior and Subjective Well-Being

Due to the convenient access to the Internet and mobile phones, WeChat is popular among people of all ages, from teenagers to the older adult (Yi'nan Wang et al. 2018). Furthermore, according to the report by Tencent, 64.4% of the 61 million older WeChat users in China (Harwit 2016) have the experience of posting original moments. WeChat is an important alternative communication channel for the older adult in China. [10] reviewed the history and recent development of WeChat, and believed that WeChat is an important technology for users who "seek intimate, personal and local oriented communication" (Rui et al. 2018). Subjective well-being is an overall assessment of a person's quality of life according to self-determination criteria (Gerson, Plagnol, & Corr 2016; Rui et al. 2018). Powerful social networks can improve the quality of life of the older adult (Cornejo, Tentori, & Favela 2013). Participating in SNSs can increase older adults' social activities and social ties, and help them to reduce social isolation, and improve their well-being (Aarts, Peek, & Wouters 2015). In short, using WeChat moments to share content can help the older adult improve their life gratification and happiness [11]. Drawing on the above literature, this study proposes the following hypothesis.

Hypothesis 1. The older adults' moment sharing behavior in SNS has a positive effect on their subjective well-being.

3.2   Older Adults' Moment Sharing Behavior and U&G

According o the Uses and Gratification Theory (U&G theory), expected psychological values can motivate media users to participate in specific media use behaviors. UGT has been widely used in understanding users' IT adoption behaviors. Learning benefits, social benefits, self-esteem benefits, and hedonic benefits were identified for explaining users' commitment and loyalty to the online brand community (Kuo & Feng 2013). Hedonic value, social value, informational value, and technology value were used to understand users' continuance intention towards social media [12]. Meanwhile, social value, hedonic value, self-discovery value, and informational value were used to predict a member's intention to act collectively within the group in social commerce context (Gan & Li 2018; A. Whiting & D. Williams 2013). Considering the self-presentation feature of moment sharing behavior, this study adopts hedonic gratification, social gratification, and self-esteem (Dholakia et al. 2004; Kuo & Feng 2013; Park et al. 2009) gratification as the benefits that older adults can achieve by posting moments in SNSs.
Drawing on the above literature, this study proposes the following hypothesis.

Hypothesis 2. The Older adults' moment sharing behavior in SNS positively influences their hedonic gratification (2a), social gratification (2b), and self-esteem gratification (2c).

3.3 Mediating Role of Gratification Between U&G and Subjective Well-Being

Hedonic gratification is related to the fulfilment of hedonic expectations (Park et al. 2009; Raza et al. 2020; A. Whiting & D. Williams 2013). Perceived enjoyment, the main indicator of hedonic gratification, is examined to be one of the key motivators influencing individuals' use of social media since they can perceive enjoyment, pleasant and fun during the usage process(Gallego, Bueno, & Noyes 2016; Gan & Li 2018). In the process of using social media, social media users share pictures, post-self-portraits, forward content, and other behaviors, which belong to a kind of entertainment (Coto et al. 2017), and can obtain the feeling of enjoyment and pleasure.

Through WeChat moment, users can find emotional support through communication and interaction with friends and relatives(Chen et al. 2019). By displaying self-image on social networking sites, people can obtain social support from online friends [13]. Studies showed that social support has a direct beneficial effect on mental health outcomes, regardless of the stress a person is experiencing (Cohen & Wills 1985; Savelkoul, Post, de Witte, & van den Borne 2000). Perceived social support helps to provide material or information. These materials or information can increase people's sense of happiness and belonging in the face of stressful life events, improve self-esteem and self-confidence, increase positive emotions, suppress negative emotions, and prevent the decline of subjective well-being (J. Kim & Lee 2011; Z. Liu, He, Wang, & Jiang 2020; X. Wang 2016).

The fulfilment of self-esteem needs leads to a specific feeling of well-being (C.-M. Chiu, Huang, Cheng, & Sun 2015). In an online environment, it refers to members' status and reputation in their community (Kuo & Feng 2013). Posting moment is an opportunity for older adults' to demonstrate their life, resource, view of a certain event, and even the ability to use this technology (Nambisan & Baron 2009). Older people want to maintain their role as providers in the family and contribute more to family relationships than they receive attention from relatives (Cornejo et al. 2013; Hutto et al. 2015). Drawing on the above literature, this study proposes the following hypothesis.

Hypothesis 3. The older adults' perceived hedonic gratification (3a), social gratification (3b), and self-esteem gratification (3c) positively contribute to their subjective well-being.

Hypothesis 4. The older adults' perceived hedonic gratification (4a), social gratification (4b), and self-esteem gratification (4c) play an intermediary role in older adult's moment sharing behavior and subjective well-being.

3.4 The Mediation Effect Hypothesis

The Older adult share their lives on social networks, a record of their daily lives. The older adult can interact with their relatives and friends in sharing behavior, thus they can get social gratification and self-esteem gratification (Dickens, Richards, Greaves, & Campbell 2011). WeChat gives older adult more opportunities to communicate. The older adult share their daily life with WeChat, which makes the older adult get the gratification of sharing [10], older adult can get pleasure from sharing on social networks.

Older adult can get social support by interacting with friends and relatives on social networks and by developing a self-image (Ramirez-Correa, Grandon, Ramirez-Santana, & Belmar Ordenes 2019). When older adult feel social support, they can increase their sense of well-being and belonging, increasing positive emotions while suppressing negative ones (Barker 2009).

Therefore, based on the above discussion of hedonic gratification, social gratification, and self-esteem gratification, it can be expected that hedonic gratification, social gratification, and self-esteem gratification have a moderate effect between older adults' moment sharing behavior and subjective well-being, and there was a mediating effect.

The use of WeChat in daily life can affect the subjective well-being of the older adult [14]. The real-time sharing behavior of the older adult on the social platform can make the older adult obtain hedonic gratification, and when the older adult feel happy, it will have a positive impact on subjective well-being. When people get self-esteem gratification from social networks, they are more likely to participate. Research shows that individuals with low levels of social support often experience loneliness and low self-esteem, leading to lower life gratification. As a controllable factor, self-esteem has a certain influence on life gratification [15]. The social support and self-esteem of the old people affect their life gratification.

Drawing on the above literature, and proposes the following hypotheses:

Hypothesis 5. Social isolation will moderate the effects of older adults' moment sharing behavior on their perceived hedonic gratification (5a), social gratification (5b), self-esteem gratification (5c), as well as subjective well-being (5d).

Based on the above hypotheses, the research model is developed in Fig. 1.

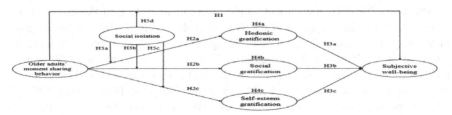

Fig. 1. Research model.

4 Research Methodology

4.1 Construct Measurement

The research model consists of six constructs, including the older adult's moment sharing behavior, hedonic gratification, social gratification, self-esteem gratification, subjective well-being, and social isolation. All the constructs were measured using multiple-item scales. The survey questionnaire is developed by adopting mature measures from previous studies and adjusting them to fit the research context of WeChat. The items of the older adult's moment sharing behavior were adapted from (Chen et al. 2019; Gan & Li 2018). The items of hedonic gratification were adapted from (Gan & Li 2018). The items of social gratification were adapted from (Gan & Li 2018; Kuo & Feng 2013; Sun et al. 2016). The items of self-esteem gratification were adapted from (Dholakia et al. 2004; Kuo & Feng 2013; Park et al. 2009). The items of subjective well-being were adapted from (Diener, Emmons, Larsen, & Griffin 1985). The item of social isolation was adapted from (Cornwell & Waite 2009; Nicholson 2009). All items were measured with a seven-point Likert scale, ranging from "strongly disagree (1)" to "strongly agree (7)".

4.2 Data Collection

The questionnaire was mainly collected offline, mainly for the older adult, mainly related to the location of Nanjing, a total of 226 valid questionnaires were collected. In the questionnaire collection, most of the older people we met couldn't see the paper questionnaire we provided because of their health, so we would ask the older people in the form of a question and answer, and fill in the data directly into the questionnaire star. After collecting a questionnaire, we will give two packs of disposable masks to the respondents as a token of our appreciation.

According to the time series age division standard, the old people in our country are divided into 45–59 years old pre-senile period, that is, middle-aged and old people, 60–89 years old, that is what we call the older adult, 90–99 years of life and 100 years of age or more of the longevity of the stars, that is, the longevity of the older adult. In this paper, the age is divided into 45–49 years old, 50–59 years old, 60–69 years old and 70 years old or above. The demographics characteristics of the questionnaires collected in this article are shown in Table 2. A total of 226 valid questionnaires were collected, of which 46.02% were women and 53.98% were men. 29.65% of the questionnaires were collected in the age group of 45–49 years, followed by 43.36% in the age group of 50–59 years, followed by 25.66% in the age group of 60–69 years, with the fewest questionnaires collected in the age group of 70 years and over, only 3(1.33%). Among the data collected, 191(84.52%) were married and their spouses were still alive. Marital status also affected the subjective well-being of the older adult. In the survey, 106 older adult people used WeChat several times a day. We also measured the size of the social network of the older adult, using the number of WeChat Friends of the older adult as a control variable affecting subjective well-being.

5 Data Analysis

5.1 Measurement Model

Convergent validity measures whether items can effectively reflect their corresponding factor. To assess reliability and validity using PLS, researchers typically calculate a block of indicators' composite reliabilities (CR), average variance extracted (AVE). Interpreted like a Cronbach's alpha internal consistency reliability estimate, composite reliability of 0.70 or greater is considered acceptable for research. The AVE measures the variance captured by the indicators relative to measurement error, and it should be greater than 0.50 to justify using a construct. As shown in Table 3 the values of Cronbach's Alpha, AVE, and CR (Peterson & Kim 2013) all exceed the thresholds of 0.7, 0.5, and 0.7, respectively. Thus, the convergent validity of the measurement model was confirmed.

We also assessed the measurement model by conducting a discriminant validity test. As shown in Table 3, the squared root value of the AVE was greater than that of related facets, which indicated the discriminant validity of this instrument.

The study reports the loading and cross-loading of all measures in the model. Searching down the columns, one can see that the item loadings in their corresponding columns

Table 2. Descriptive statistical analysis of data

Construct	Items	Mean	SD	VIF (<4)	Factor Loading
OAMSB	OAMSB1	5.053	1.480	2.169	0.825
	OAMSB2	5.013	1.474	1.867	0.796
	OAMSB3	5.310	1.424	2.236	0.847
	OAMSB4	5.013	1.444	1.920	0.796
	OAMSB5	5.208	1.471	1.851	0.788
HG	HG1	5.372	1.235	1.688	0.752
	HG2	5.310	1.263	1.526	0.745
	HG3	5.442	1.182	1.780	0.777
	HG4	5.270	1.344	1.590	0.770
	HG5	5.288	1.287	1.487	0.713
SEG	SEG1	5.066	1.424	1.884	0.803
	SEG2	5.013	1.416	1.802	0.781
	SEG3	5.407	1.256	1.781	0.782
	SEG4	5.173	1.439	1.930	0.802
	SEG5	5.358	1.408	1.819	0.789
SG	SG1	5.389	1.279	1.537	0.724
	SG2	5.367	1.195	1.542	0.710
	SG3	5.442	1.201	1.785	0.780
	SG4	5.500	1.224	1.572	0.744
	SG5	5.442	1.204	1.854	0.809
SI	SI1	5.080	1.440	2.432	0.860
	SI2	4.805	1.658	2.205	0.817
	SI3	4.527	1.727	2.316	0.841
	SI4	4.916	1.626	3.264	0.915
	SI5	4.522	1.780	2.186	0.798
SWB	SWB1	5.310	1.213	1.958	0.824
	SWB2	5.469	1.141	1.577	0.752
	SWB3	5.496	1.161	1.660	0.754
	SWB4	5.354	1.219	1.691	0.767
	SWB5	5.084	1.333	1.464	0.698

Note: OAMSB: Older adult's moment sharing behavior, HG: Hedonic gratification, SEG: Self-esteem gratification, SG: Social gratification, SI: Social isolation, SWB: Subjective well-being.

are all higher than the loadings of the items used to measure the other constructs. Furthermore, when searching across the rows, one finds the item loadings to be higher for their corresponding constructs than for others. Therefore, our measurements satisfy the two criteria for discriminant validity (Table 2).

Table 3. Results of reliability test and validity test

	Cronbach's Alpha	Composite Reliability	Average Variance Extracted	EMSB	HG	SEG	SG	SI	SWB
OAMSB	0.869	0.905	0.657	**0.810**					
HG	0.807	0.866	0.565	0.768	**0.752**				
SEG	0.810	0.868	0.569	0.645	0.726	**0.754**			
SG	0.851	0.893	0.627	0.745	0.702	0.698	**0.792**		
SI	0.816	0.872	0.577	0.717	0.740	0.728	0.765	**0.760**	
SWB	0.903	0.927	0.718	0.208	0.141	0.120	0.180	0.109	**0.847**

Note: The Bold portion is the square root of AVE. OAMSB: Older adult's moment sharing behavior, HG: Hedonic gratification, SEG: Self-esteem gratification, SG: Social gratification, SI: Social isolation, SWB: Subjective well-being.

5.2 Structural Model

The results of the path coefficients and the corresponding levels of significance. Figure 2 depicts the results of the path coefficients and the corresponding levels of significance. The model explained 66.9% of the variance of the subjective well-being when sharing their moment, indicating that it has good explanatory power. The results show that the older adult's moment sharing behavior has a significant effect on hedonic, social,

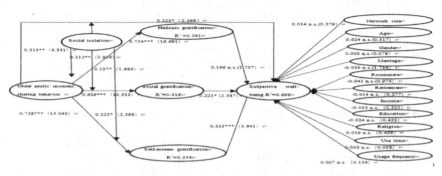

Notes: *p<0.05, **p<0.01, ***p<0.001

Fig. 2. The results estimated by PLS

self-esteem gratification and subjective well-being. Subjective well-being is also significantly affected by social gratification and self-esteem gratification. Social isolation moderates the relationships between older adult's moment sharing behaviors and social gratification.

As shown in Table 4 older adult's moment sharing behavior do not affect subjective well-being through hedonic gratification, while it can affect subjective well-being through social gratification and self-esteem gratification.

Table 4. Mediation effect

Variable	SPF	SD	T	P	2.5%	97.5%
OAMSB → HG → SWB	0.036	0.022	1.637	0.102	-0.005	0.079
OAMSB → SG → SWB	0.139	0.060	2.319	0.020	0.037	0.270
OAMSB → SEG → SWB	0.243	0.069	3.495	0.000	0.108	0.381

Note: OAMSB: Older adult's moment sharing behavior, HG: Hedonic gratification, SEG: Self-esteem gratification, SG: Social gratification, SWB: Subjective well-being.

6   Discussion

As shown in Fig. 2, older adult's moment sharing behavior has a significant effect on hedonic gratification, social gratification, self-esteem gratification and subjective well-being. Social gratification and self-esteem gratification have a significant effect on subjective well-being. The results also show that, social isolation will moderate the effects of older adult' s moment sharing behavior on their perceived hedonic gratification, social gratification, as well as self-esteem gratification. Social isolation doesn't moderate the effects of older adults' moment sharing behavior on subjective well-being. Education background, age and other control variables have no effect on the subjective well-being of the older adult.

Older people pay more attention to themselves in life, most of them live a solitary life, this time the older adult need to accompany, communication and recognition rather than pleasure. Therefore, when using social software, the older adult pay more attention to social satisfaction and self-esteem satisfaction, and hedonic satisfaction can not affect the executive well-being of the older adult.

When the older adult feel social isolation in their lives, they will feel lonely, which will affect the sharing behavior of the older adult in WeChat moments, hedonic gratification, where the comments and likes that older people receive in their social networks affect older people, social gratification, as well as self-esteem gratification [16].

6.1   Theoretical Implications

From a theoretical viewpoint, the factors that affect the subjective well-being of the older adult after using social network services are put under the use and gratification theory, which broadens the scope of the use and gratification theory. It provides a new perspective to study the influence of older adults' moment sharing behavior on the relationship between older adults' moment sharing behavior and hedonic gratification, social gratification, and self-esteem gratification.

In this paper, we examined the positive effects of older adults' moment sharing behavior, social gratification, and self-esteem gratification on the subjective well-being of older adults in social networks. Social network service providers should pay attention to the development of the function, provide a multi-channel sharing function for the older adult, enhance the contact between the older adult and relatives, and enhance the social gratification and self-esteem gratification of the older adult, which will increase the subjective well-being of the older adult.

This study found that different factors affect the subjective well-being of the older adult, the older adult in the social network sharing behavior will affect the subjective well-being, and the sharing behavior of the older adult can also enhance the subjective well-being of the older adult through social gratification and self-esteem gratification.

6.2 Practical Implications

The social gratification and self-esteem gratification of the older adult in the sharing behavior of social networks can affect subjective well-being. Enterprises should pay attention to the social gratification and self-esteem gratification of the older adult, only in this way can effectively increase the subjective well-being of the older adult. [11] said that when older adult share content in WeChat moments, will improve subjective well-being. Companies should pay attention to the needs of the older adult for social software, the older version of social software interface settings are more concise, provide a platform to show personal ability, and pay attention to the display function of moment sharing module, making older people feel cared for by their friends can satisfy their social and self-esteem contentment.

Social isolation can regulate the sharing behavior, social gratification, and self-esteem gratification of the older adult, and thus affect subjective well-being. Enterprises should pay attention to the social needs and self-esteem needs of the older adult in social networks to reduce the sense of isolation of the older adult. The social network used by the older adult has certain requirements on product quality, usage smoothness, and aging adaptation. Enterprises should make aging adaptation products to make it more convenient for the older adult to use the social network.

7   Conclusions and Limitations

The sharing behaviors of the older adult in social networks has significant effects on hedonic gratification, social gratification, self-esteem gratification, and subjective well-being, the effect of hedonic gratification on subjective well-being was not significant. Social isolation plays a moderating role in sharing behaviors and hedonic gratification, social gratification, and self-esteem gratification, but not in sharing behavior and subjective well-being.

This study bears several limitations that future researchers might need to address further. First, since the samples are from China and not random samples from the population, the findings should be applied conservatively. Future research might try other countries before generalizing the conclusions.

Second, while this study is aimed at the result of the older adult mobile users adopting WeChat moments, the proposed model did not explore some other obstructive factors, such as privacy risk and data security risk, which would impede the older adult mobile users from adopting WeChat moments. Given this fact, future researchers can increase the number of samples in different groups and conduct analyses based on the larger samples, to verify the correctness of the group analysis results from this study.

References

1. Kim, B., Kim, Y.: Facebook versus Instagram: how perceived gratifications and technological attributes are related to the change in social media usage. Soc. Sci. J. **56**(2), 156–167 (2019)
2. Raza, S.A., et al.: Drivers of intensive Facebook usage among university students: an implications of U&G and TPB theories. Technol. Soc. **62** (2020)
3. Lin, T.C., et al.: Drivers of participation in Facebook long-term care groups: applying the use and gratification theory, social identification theory, and the modulating role of group diversity. Health Inform. J. **26**(1), 513–527 (2020)
4. Urbaniak, A., Walsh, K.: The interrelationship between place and critical life transitions in later life social exclusion: a scoping review. Health Place **60**, 102–134 (2019)
5. Ng, M.: Factors influencing the consumer adoption of Facebook: a two-country study of youth markets. Comput. Hum. Behav. **54**, 491–500 (2016)
6. Sun, Y., et al.: Does social climate matter? On friendship groups in social commerce. Electron. Commer. Res. Appl. **18**, 37–47 (2016)
7. Sheldon, P., et al.: A cross-cultural comparison of Croatian and American social network sites: exploring cultural differences in motives for Instagram use. Comput. Hum. Behav. **75**, 643–651 (2017)
8. Park, N., Kee, K.F., Valenzuela, S.: Being immersed in social networking environment: Facebook groups, uses and gratifications, and social outcomes. Cyberpsychol. Behav. Soc. Netw. **12**(6), 729–733 (2009)
9. Gan, C., Li, H.: Understanding the effects of gratifications on the continuance intention to use WeChat in China: a perspective on uses and gratifications. Comput. Hum. Behav. **78**, 306–315 (2018)
10. Harwit, E.: WeChat: social and political development of China's dominant messaging app. Chin. J. Commun. **10**(3), 312–327 (2016)
11. Zhou, J.: Let us meet online! Examining the factors influencing older Chinese's social networking site use. J. Cross Cult. Gerontol. **34**(1), 35–49 (2019)
12. Li, H., et al.: Disentangling the factors driving users' continuance intention towards social media: a configurational perspective. Comput. Hum. Behav. **85**, 175–182 (2018)
13. Lee, K.T., Noh, M.J., Koo, D.M.: Lonely people are no longer lonely on social networking sites: the mediating role of self-disclosure and social support. Cyberpsychol. Behav. Soc. Netw. **16**(6), 413–418 (2013)
14. Rui, J.R., et al.: Getting connected while aging: the effects of WeChat network characteristics on the well-being of Chinese mature adults. Chin. J. Commun. **12**(1), 25–43 (2018)
15. Kapıkıran, Ş: Loneliness and life satisfaction in Turkish early adolescents: the mediating role of self esteem and social support. Soc. Indic. Res. **111**(2), 617–632 (2012)
16. Courtin, E., Knapp, M.: Social isolation, loneliness and health in old age: a scoping review. Health Soc. Care Community **25**(3), 799–812 (2017)

Video Going Viral: Subjective Emotional Clash vs. Objective Emotional Assertion

Jiang Wu[1,2(✉)], Yaxuan Yang[1,2], Pu Sun[1,2(✉)], and Mengxi Zhang[1,2]

[1] School of Information Management, Wuhan University, 299 Bayi Road, Wuhan 430072, China
{00030050,2014301200207}@whu.edu.cn
[2] Center for Studies of Information Resources, Wuhan University, 299 Bayi Road,
Wuhan 430072, China

Abstract. As online video has gradually become the main channel for information dissemination and marketing advertising, it is necessary to determine which factors will affect the diffusion of video on the website further. The research goal of this paper is to explore what kind of title can help online videos attract more views. The research takes 49989 videos in bilibili as the research object, analyzes the relationship between the emotional polarity expressed in the title text and the number of views the video gets, and explores the role of personal pronouns play in the relationship. The results show that no matter whether the video titles contain positive or negative emotions, the video titles with higher polarity of these emotions can get more attention. In addition, those video titles that use personal pronouns also get more attention. Simultaneously, the use of personal pronouns moderates the impact of title's sentiment polarity. The conclusion provides guidance for video publishers who produce content and helps them get more attention.

Keywords: Viewership · Virality · Video diffusion · Emotion polarity · Personal pronouns

1 Introduction

With the rapid development of mobile internet devices and high-speed networks, people can now watch online videos anytime and anywhere. Online video has become an increasingly powerful information transmission medium in daily life. Currently, tens of thousands of videos are uploaded online every day, resulting in information explosion and information overload. Understanding factors affecting online popularity can assist content creators in developing attractive content and aid content consumers in coping with information overload [1]. Viral videos can quickly capture the attention of viewers and gain immense popularity in a short period. Advertisers and content providers will benefit from understanding what makes videos popular and identifying them early. Some scholars discussed the reasons for the popularity of video through empirical analysis or case studies, taking different popular videos as samples, including the scale of the network, the connectivity of the network, video content quality, external video reviews, and the author's characteristics [2]. For political videos, the credibility of political information is one of the impact indicators [3]. In addition, there is a Matthew effect of information in video dissemination, which means videos that get more attention in the pre-video period and interact with viewing and commenting will also get more attention in the later period.

As video platforms that rely on user-generated content, YouTube, bilibili and so on, have a lot of "UP" and "Youtuber" (channel owners and video uploaders) who upload original or unoriginal videos to communicate with viewers and present their experiences, and express their opinions, and feelings. The immersive watching experience incur viewers' emotional responses in the comments area, evoking either empathy or revulsion [4]. Guadagno et al. demonstrate, through a dynamic illustration of video-induced emotions, that the emotional characteristics of videos will cause them to be popular [5]. The title and cover of the video are exposed features, especially the emotions in the title can be easily perceived. Therefore, this work examines the effects of video emotions expressed in titles on the diffusion effect of the video itself using bilibili as the research environment. In essence, the video title, as a narrative text, is a microcosm of the video content, and the narrative effect will be affected by many factors. Several academics have emphasized that the existence of recognizable characters. Personal pronouns in the text, is a necessary condition for narrative transmission [6].

In this study, we explored the relationship between the emotional polarity expressed in the video title and the popularity of the video based on bilibili video view data. Furthermore, we investigated the role personal pronouns play in moderating the effect of the emotional polarity of the title on video plays. The results show that, whether positive or negative, the emotion of text transmission can effectively improve the effect of video diffusion, expanding the scope of the original research on user-generated content video. Interestingly, the first-person pronouns weaken the amount of attention brought by negative emotions in our sample. And the combination of second-person pronouns and the positive title does not work very well. In addition, due to the existence of fan stickiness, those users are more likely to be recommended by the platform to watch videos posted by the people they follow. Based on this situation, we analyzed the interaction between the number of followers and their emotions. The results shows that negative emotions spread faster in the channels of users with more followers, while the influence of follower scale on views is heterogeneous between using positive title and using negative title, which extends the existing research conclusions to a certain extent.

2 Literature Review and Theoretical Foundation

2.1 Literature Review

The use of social media websites is increasing in the 21st century. A large number of viral videos have emerged through the sharing and dissemination of users [7]. Social media provides many opportunities for individuals and enterprises. Enterprises can expand the audience area and their brand influence through social media. Individuals can obtain fans and material incentives. Therefore, it is of great significance for enterprises and individuals to explore what characteristics of videos can help them transmit in a virality to achieve higher popularity.

Many scholars use Youtube videos as samples to explore. Broxon et al. (2010) analyzed the reasons for the high popularity of videos from the perspective of video click, they found that in the process of production popularity maturity completion, those videos that get the viewing amount through independent click are different from those videos that get the viewing amount through more sharing [7]. From the perspective of social network and diffusion theory, Liu et al. (2012) believe that the characteristics that affect the video diffusion effect include: the size and connectivity of the video publisher's social network, the quality and external evaluation of the video itself, and the author's characteristics. For videos that spread knowledge and political information, the credibility of video content is a significant factor affecting the popularity of videos [2]. Li et al. (2021) verified this conclusion against the background of COVID-19. Compared with Youtube, bilibili has functions such as danmuku, which enables users to communicate asynchronously [3]. Based on these features, Yan et al. (2020) use the billili video as a sample to track the whole life cycle of the video and believe that the active and simple participation of users and some features of video publishers play different roles in different stages of the video [8]. In addition, the number of views in the early stage is an essential parameter for the popularity of videos [9].

Many scholars have explored the relationship between video diffusion and viral transmission from the perspective of its emotion. As we said earlier, persuasion will affect the spread of political videos. Some scholars have explored the characteristics of persuasion and believed that ethos is the best, followed by logos and pathos. English et al., (2011) explored the relationship between the persuasive factors (sources of thoughts, logos, and pathos) of different characteristics of political videos and viral transmission of videos [10]. For video ads that need to arouse users' love and sympathy, the different emotions conveyed by videos will affect users' attitudes towards this ad and the whole brand [11]. Videos that can effectively awaken viewers' emotional resonance are more likely to get high transmission [12].

Through the literature review, we found that in the research on video advertising, emotional arousal and emotion-related research was mentioned more. While the research on user-generated content video was less. Therefore, this paper intends to explore the relationship between video emotion transmission and video popularity. The video title and cover features are important factors to attract users to click for the first time and they are also the beginning and important premise for users to share after watching. Therefore, this paper will study the video title and cover features to explore the relationship between their transmission features and video popularity.

The use of personal pronouns can effectively affect the emotions expressed in sentences. In the field of marketing, research has proved that different use of personal pronouns can affect the helpfulness of online reviews [13, 14]. In the same sentence, using the first-person pronouns rather than not using personal pronouns expresses the subjectivity of the text to a certain extent. Similarly, in the video title, the use of the first-person pronouns expresses video uploaders' own point of view to a certain extent. The second-person pronouns can form a self-reference, allowing viewers to shift their perspective to themselves. If they refresh relevant memories or experiences, they will respond positively to the information.

Therefore, this paper explores the role of personal pronouns in video titles as well. In the way of empirical analysis, we discuss the impact of the title's subjective opinion expression VS objective fact statement on the video diffusion effect.

2.2 Theoretical Foundation

Emotions as Social Information Theory. Van Kleef (2009) created the Emotions as Social Information (EASI) paradigm based on the notion that emotion is information [15]. He believed that emotion is a type of social information. In social interactions, individuals interpret the emotional expressions of others as a sort of information, which influences their conduct or attitude after internalizing and inferring emotional reactions. In this paper, we regard the video publisher as the expression of emotion, and the audiences as the observer. Through the emotional expression of the title and the use of personal pronouns, we can affect the emotional reaction and reasoning of the observer, thus affecting the user's behavior.

Narrative Transportation Theory. According to narrative transmission theory, when individuals focus their attention and immerse themselves in the act of reading a tale, they are transmitted from the real world to the virtual one described by the story and experience a powerful feeling of presence and emotional response [16]. Immersive reality and narrative identification are fundamental components of the narrative transmission persuasion mechanism [4]. This unique psychological process has a significant impact on the attitude and behavior change of the audience. For instance, finance media can improve the image through the narrative transmission of video, while text can expand the imaginative space by expression of multiple meanings. In narrative transmission, they will actively imagine the story's future progression and generate appropriate hypotheses.

With the acceleration of society, many short videos and short texts are flooding people's lives, but this does not affect the process of people's immersion in stories. In this study, when users see a video title, they will understand the emotion and character conveyed by the title text. Then they are involved in the corresponding narrative environment, resulting in corresponding emotional resonance or emotional repulsion. The use of personal pronouns has changed the effect of narrative transmission to some extent. Text without personal pronouns is more objective, and users rarely bring it into their own or "UP" perspective. Based on the above, the use of personal pronouns in the title will affect the effect of narrative transportation. At the same time, the use of different personal pronouns may also have a corresponding effect on the emotion conveyed, and then affect the user's behavior.

3 Hypotheses Development

3.1 Video Title Emotions

According to the theory that emotion is social value, emotion, as a clue, affects how individual information is processed and processes. To be specific, the emotion contained in the text will infect other users, causing them to pay attention to the video, thereby increasing the video transmission effect. According to the negative bias idea [17], negative items will have a more enormous impact on an individual's psychological state and decision-making behavior than good or neutral things [18]. The emotions represented by video title text will impact video diffusion. Consequently, this study suggests the following hypotheses:

H1a: The positive polarity of video title has a beneficial effect on the video views.

H1b: The negative polarity of a video's title has a beneficial effect on the video views.

H1c: The negative polarity of the title's text has a greater impact on the video views than the positive polarity.

3.2 Personal Pronouns Use

Using personal pronouns will help the reader visualize distinct characters and enhance the narrative effect. We discuss the application of various personal pronouns. Typically, the first-person pronouns (such as "I" and "we") make the text more genuine and empathic. "UP" evokes inner resonance in others by describing own experience, engaging users in the "UP" narrative scene, resonating with the emotions conveyed in the narrative, causing users to pay attention to the video, and subsequently affecting the video transmission. The use of second-person pronouns (such as "you") shifts the focus of expression to users, makes users feel cordial, and increases their interest in watching [19]. Based on the preceding discussion, this paper proposes the following hypotheses:

H2a: The use of personal pronouns increases the video views.

H2b: The use of first-person pronouns in video titles increases the transmission effect of both positive and negative emotions on viewers, thereby increasing the video views.

H2c: The use of second-person pronouns in video titles increases the transmission effect of positive video emotions on viewers thereby increasing the video views. While it decreases the transmission effect of negative emotions thereby decreasing the video views.

4   Methodology

4.1   Empirical Samples

Since its inception in 2009, bilibili has evolved into a highly viscous content culture community and pop-up video platform, offering users live streaming, animation, games, documentaries, and self-produced variety shows.

This research crawls user-generated videos on the bilibili using Python. Since video views and other indicators fluctuate significantly and dynamically in the early stages of a video's distribution, picking the most recently published videos will make it simple to analyze the elements influencing video dissemination impacts. In this work, the freshly published films on April 1, 2022, serve as the research object, with the period from April 1 to April 17 constituting the observation window. Video titles, video covers, video plays, video owner data, video length, etc., were gathered for each video, along with the tags of the partition where the video was stored, which included life, food, movie, etc. The collection includes 49,989 genuine video data.

4.2 Data and Variables

As dependent variables, the number of video views measures the popularity of video and the level of video diffusion. Both text and images can transmit corresponding emotions; however, video titles are more capable of transmitting explicit emotional polarity than video covers, so our independent variables are the positive/negative polarity expressed in the titles. For sentiment polarity, we created emotion dictionary utilizes Dalian Polytechnic University's emotion vocabulary book question bank and Tencent's open-source word vectors. Their affective polarity is manually marked before being calculated by the affective lexicon and compared with an accuracy rate of 86.6%, which is applicable.

In addition to examining the role of emotional polarity in video text narrative transmission, we counted the personal pronouns in the titles (I, we; you) as independent variables for studies three. Although these words represent only a small portion of the text in the overall titles, it will produce a different reference. It will affect the user's behavior. We control several factors that may influence the effect of video dissemination, which are mainly all information video viewers can receive before watching. First, we obtain picture clarity and the picture information entropy from the video preview. For picture entropy, the larger information entropy represents the average amount of information contained in the picture (The specific formula is (1)). Second, we also calculate the amount of information contained in the title by measuring its information entropy (the specific formula is (2)).

$$H = -\sum\nolimits_{i=0}^{255} P_{ij} log p_{ig} \tag{1}$$

$$H(x) = -\sum\nolimits_{i=1}^{n} p(x_i) log p(x_i) \tag{2}$$

Finally, we also manage information about the publisher, such as the number of followers, their level, the number of videos they have uploaded, etc. Additionally, variables such as the video's duration and creativity are regulated. See Table 1 for names and definitions.

Before constructing a regression model, it is essential to comprehend the distribution of the variables, which is then used to determine the application of models and the treatment of variables. The description results are shown in Table 2. It's clear that the variance of our ViewNum is much higher than its mean. Our dependent variable is an over-dispersed count outcome variable. The negative binominal regression should be used to test for the connections between the regressand and regressors.

Before conducting the formal regression analysis, we performed correlation analysis and multiple covariance tests on the variables. After we tested for multicollinearity, the average covariance $VIF = 1.25$, which indicates no absence of multicollinearity between variables (Table 3).

Table 1. Variable description

Dimension	Name	Symbol	Definition
Dependent Variable	View	ViewNum	Cumulative number of video plays as of the moment of data collection for the current period
Independent Variable	Positive polarity	PosPol	Weighting the positive words in the title results in a score
	Negative polarity	NegPol	Weighting the negative words in the title results in a score
	Pronouns with and lacking	IfPron	Whether the personal pronouns are used in video title(used = 1;non-used = 0)
	First-person pronouns	First_Pron	Whether a first-person pronouns is used in video title(used = 1;non-used = 0)
	Second-person pronouns	Second_Pron	Whether a second-person pronouns is used in video title(used = 1;non-used = 0)
Control Variable	User's Level	UserLevel	User level, divided into 0–6 levels
	Follower	Follower	Number of users' followers
	VideoNum	VideoNum	The total number of user-published video contributions up to the time of data collection
	Duration	Duration	The length of the video
	Type	Type	The channel that the video is on
	Picture Clarity	Clarity	Calculate the average gradient value of grayed-out images based on image data
	Picture Entropy	PicEntro	The absolute value of two-dimensional information entropy is calculated based on the number of images

(continued)

Table 1. (*continued*)

Dimension	Name	Symbol	Definition
	Text Entropy	TxtEntro	The absolute value of one-dimensional information entropy is calculated according to the amount of text information

Table 2. Summary statistics

Variable	Obs.	Mean	Std. Dev.	Min	Max
ViewNum	49,989	3488.13	56196.72	0	5603837
PosPol	49,989	2.07	2.78	0	28
NegPol	49,989	1.61	2.92	0	28
IfPron	49,989	0.15	0.36	0	1
First_Pron	49,989	0.093	0.291	0	1
Second_Pron	49,989	0.068	0.252	0	1
UserLevel	49,989	3.52	1.54	0	3
Follower	49,989	5230.56	68949.95	0	6763106
VideoNum	49,989	1994.64	17206.46	0	274454
Duration	49,989	613.42	4953.23	1	438536
Clarity	49,989	643.63	1230.82	0	45130.51
PicEntro	49,989	5003.65	3833.40	63.92	163889.90
TxtEntro	49,989	3.62	1.04	0	6.06

4.3 Model Specification

Our estimation aims to investigate the relationship between the polarity of emotion transmitted by video titles and video dissemination measured by views through empirical analysis and to discuss how the existence of personal pronouns moderate such emotion carryover and then influences the video views. To examine this relationship, we employ a negative binominal regression (NBR) model because our dependent variable – ViewNum is an over-dispersed count outcome variable. The specific model displays as follow.

$$\ln(ViewNum) = \beta_0 + \beta_1 PosPol + \beta_2 NegPol + \beta_3 UserLevel$$
$$+ \beta_4 ln(Follower + 1) + \beta_5 ln(VideoNum + 1) + \beta_6 ln(Duration) \qquad (3)$$
$$+ \beta_7 ln(Clarity + 1) + \beta_8 PicEntro + \beta_9 TxtEntro + \beta_{10} Type\_Dummy + \varepsilon$$

Table 3. Multicollinearity test

Variable	1	2	3	4	5	6	7	8	9	10	11	12
1 ViewNum	1.000											
2 PosPol	0.007	1.000										
3 NegPol	0.216***	0.081***	1.000									
4 First_Pron	0.006	0.044***	0.072***	1.000								
5 Second_Pron	0.019***	0.052***	0.095***	0.152***	1.000							
6 UserLevel	0.056***	0.030***	−0.011**	0.007	0.028***	1.000						
7 ln(Follower + 1)	0.133***	0.064***	0.088***	0.004	0.040***	0.416***	1.000					
8 ln(VideoNum + 1)	0.028***	0.062***	0.070***	0.037***	0.010*	0.181***	0.632***	1.000				
9 ln(Duration)	0.015***	0.022***	0.018***	0.035***	0.030***	0.180***	0.268***	0.103***	1.000			
10 ln(Clarity + 1)	−0.001	0.020***	−0.011**	0.041***	0.040***	0.039***	−0.003	0.036***	0.111***	1.000		
11 PicEntro	−0.002	−0.029	−0.007	−0.006	−0.007	0.042***	0.064***	0.010	0.136***	0.236***	1.000	
12 TxtEntro	0.024***	0.236***	0.263***	0.124***	0.125***	0.120***	0.330***	0.234***	0.278***	0.080***	0.043***	1.000
VIF	1.02	1.02	1.03	1.03	1.04	1.24	2.10	1.71	1	1.10	1.10	1.37

Notes: *** $\rho < 0.001$, ** $\rho < 0.01$, * $\rho < 0.05$

Based on the main model, we further examined the effect of the use of personal pronouns and the interaction with affective polarity on video diffusion effects.

$$
\begin{aligned}
\ln(ViewNum) = {} & \alpha_0 + \alpha_1 PosPol + \alpha_2 NegPol + \alpha_3 First\_Pron \\
& + \alpha_4 Second\_Pron + \alpha_5 First\_Pron * PosPol + \alpha_6 First\_Pron \\
& * NegPol + \alpha_7 Second\_Pron * PosPol + \alpha_8 Second\_Pron * NegPol \\
& + \alpha_9 UserLevel + \alpha_{10} \ln(Follower + 1) + \alpha_{11} \ln(VideoNum + 1) \\
& + \alpha_{12} \ln(Duration) + \alpha_{13} \ln(Clarity + 1) + \alpha_{14} PicEntro + \alpha_{15} TxtEntro \\
& + \alpha_{16} Type\_Dummy + \varepsilon
\end{aligned}
\tag{4}
$$

4.4 Results

The estimation results of Eq. (3) and (4) are presented in Table 4 (Model 1&3). The impact of the emotional polarity of video titles, as determined by the NBR model, on the volume of playback is seen in Table 4's first column (Model 1). In light of this, we base on Model 1 and add the variable of whether personal pronouns occur (Model 2). The estimated findings are displayed in the second column of Table 4; Finally, we addressed the moderating effect of personal pronouns in the transmission of emotional polarity (Model 3). The coefficients of most control variables are significant, indicating that the control variables we choose are reasonable.

For model 1, the positive and negative emotional polarities of video title both have a positive impact on video viewing amount ($\beta_1 = 0.015$, $\rho < 0.001$, SE = 0.003; $\beta_2 = 0.064$, $\rho < 0.001$, SE = 0.006), which supports H1a and H1b. No matter positive or negative, a more emotional video title seems to be more attractive to viewers so videos with such a title have significantly more views. And H1c is supported as well. Given that the coefficient of NegPol is larger than that of PosPol ($\beta_1 < \beta_2$), a video title with a negative emotional tendency has a greater impact on the video's popularity than a positive title at the same sentiment polarity. So far, our first hypothesis has been fully supported.

As mentioned earlier, in order to explore the role of personal pronouns in emotional transmission, we first create classified dummy variables based on whether there are personal pronouns, and add them to Model 1 for estimation. However, the result shows that the impact of personal pronouns on video views is insignificant. ($\rho > 0.005$). There are two possible reasons for the current result – the video views have nothing to do with personal pronouns in titles, or the effects of personal pronouns in titles mix so that their effects are vague. So we explore more details in Model 3.

Results from Model 3 tell us that the use of first-person pronouns in video titles itself does not have a significantly different impact on viewer's propensity to watch the video. Similarly, the coefficient of the interaction term "First_Pron*PosPol" is insignificant as well. It is interesting to see that, if the negative emotion is conveyed from the first-person perspective, its effectiveness will be weakened ($\alpha_6 = -0.079$, $\rho < 0.001$). Otherwise, the use of second-person pronouns in video titles attracts more views ($\alpha_4 = 0.227$, $\rho < 0.001$). However, the positive impacts of positive title and second-person pronouns won't be fully achieved if the positive emotion is conveyed from the perspective of second-person ($\alpha_7 = -0.026$, $\rho < 0.05$). It seems that the positive emotion in titles is not so

Table 4. Estimated results of main effect and adjustment effect

	Model 1		Model 2		Model 3	
	Coef.	SE	Coef.	SE	Coef.	SE
_cons	3.850***	(0.246)	3.864***	(0.246)	3.824***	(0.246)
PosPol	0.015***	(0.003)	0.015***	(0.003)	0.017***	(0.004)
NegPol	0.064***	(0.003)	0.064***	(0.003)	0.074***	(0.036)
IfPro	-	-	−0.030	(0.024)	-	-
First_Pron	-	-	-	-	0.038	(0.044)
Second_Pron	-	-	-	-	0.227***	(0.051)
UserLevel	−0.038***	(0.006)	0.038***	(0.006)	−0.03***	(0.006)
ln(Follower + 1)	0.791***	(0.004)	0.791***	(0.004)	0.789***	(0.004)
ln(VideoNum + 1)	−0.492***	(0.005)	−0.493***	(0.005)	−0.492***	(0.005)
ln(Duration)	0.006	(0.008)	0.005	(0.008)	0.005	(0.008)
ln(Clarity + 1)	−0.136***	(0.006)	−0.136***	(0.006)	−0.0139***	(0.006)
PicEntro	0.0001***	(0.000)	0.000***	(0.000)	0.000***	(0.000)
TxtEntro	0.260***	(0.009)	0.262***	(0.010)	0.259***	(0.010)
First_Pron*PosPol	-	-	-	-	−0.000	(0.011)
First_Pron*NegPol	-	-	-	-	−0.079***	(0.001)
Second_Pron*PosPol	-	-	-	-	−0.026*	(0.012)
Second_Pron*NegPol	-	-	-	-	−0.019	(0.010)
Type_dummy	Control		Control		Control	
Pseudo-R2	0.0816		0.0816		0.0817	
Log.Lik	−296791.49		−296778.56		−296743.85	
Observations	49989		49989		49989	

Notes: Table entries for three models are a NBR regression analysis, with regression coefficients in the left, and standard errors in parentheses. *** $\rho < 0.001$, ** $\rho < 0.01$, * $\rho < 0.05$

persuasive if the presence of second-person pronouns imposes that positive emotion on viewers, which to some extent limits viewer's interest in watching the video. Overall, H2 has been partially supported.

5   Heterogeneity Analysis

To a large extent, the number of followers determines the baseline of views. It is because of strong fan stickiness that internet celebrities usually get higher viewing times and a better diffusion effect. Therefore, to further explore possible heterogeneity, we conducted further regression analysis based on the number of followers, emotional polarity, and their interaction.

Interestingly, through the estimated results, we found that videos with only negative emotional titles were better spread and received higher viewing volume under the high number of followers ($\beta = 0.003$, $\rho < 0.001$). For these fans, compared with the videos title full of positive emotions ($\beta = -0.010$, $\rho < 0.001$), they have higher curiosity about videos with negative emotional titles. As we said earlier, negative emotional titles are more attractive to people than positive emotional titles on the whole.

6 Robustness Check

On the bilibil website, many videos are original, and many are carried from other websites. Bilibil has labeled these videos differently, so that users can effectively distinguish them. This situation gives users a certain advanced expectation of the videos they watch, which affecting the persuasiveness of the video titles to users involuntary. Therefore, we redo our research methods for those original video samples to further verify the conclusions of this paper and enhance their robustness. The results are almost consistent with our previous research, which indicates that the research conclusions in this paper are robust($\alpha_1 = 0.015$, $\rho < 0.001$; $\alpha_2 = 0.072$, $\rho < 0.001$; $\alpha_3 = 0.098$, $\rho < 0.05$; $\alpha_4 = 0.223$, $\rho < 0.001$; $\alpha_5 = -0.038$, $\rho < 0.001$; $\alpha_6 = 0.801$, $\rho < 0.001$; $\alpha_7 = -0.468$, $\rho < 0.001$; $\alpha_8 = -0.008$, $\rho > 0.05$; $\alpha_9 = -0.138$, $\rho < 0.001$; $\alpha_{10} = 0.000$, $\rho < 0.001$; $\alpha_{11} = 0.226$, $\rho < 0.001$; $\alpha_{12} = 0.006$, $\rho > 0.05$; $\alpha_{13} = -0.083$, $\rho < 0.001$; $\alpha_{14} = -0.021$, $\rho > 0.05$; $\alpha_{15} = -0.022$, $\rho < 0.05$;).

7 Discussion and Conclusion

Our research has made some theoretical contributions. First of all, this study examined the impact of user-produced video title emotion on video popularity, which is an important factor that has not been studied enough in the dissemination of user produced content videos. We found that explicit positive and negative emotions in video titles can affect users' interest in clicking in.

Secondly, we found that videos using personal pronouns in video titles had a significant impact on amount of plays. But unlike what we thought, personal pronouns strengthen emotions and then attract more clicks and views, our results were surprising. Viewers show indifference to video uploaders' negative emotions unless the uploader is an internet celebrity with many followers. On the other side, users are attracted by video titles with second-person pronouns on average, and it is better to keep objective when titling the video for maximum views. In addition, from the heterogeneity analysis, we also found that people prefer small "UP" (bilibili video uploader with small amount of subscribers) to express positive emotions in video titles than influencer to do.

As users produce content videos and enterprise video ads, promotional videos, etc., they need to gain higher popularity and attention. Then benefit from the videos. Therefore, it is essential for individuals and enterprises to deal with video to make it look more attractive to the audience. We found that both positive and negative video titles can effectively improve the early viewing volume and popularity of video. Therefore, when making and sharing videos, we need to pay attention to the form of emotional expression of video titles.

About the defects and prospects of our research. The video we chose is a node video, so more nodes should be added to mitigate the related problems caused by time. At the same time, we believe that the title is a critical element to attract users to watch videos for the first time. For those videos that have a certain amount of viewing, we lack the impact of the title element on the later popularity of videos. In addition, as a very important attraction element, we only introduce some extractable variables of the picture into it, lacking research on the emotional transmission of the picture, which is also what we want to study in the future. In addition, the location of personal pronouns will further affect the transmission of the overall emotion, and our research also lacks an in-depth exploration of the location of personal pronouns.

Acknowledgement. This research was supported by the National Natural Science Foundation of China under Grant 71874131.

References

1. Kong, Q., Rizoiu, M.A., Wu, S., Xie, L.: Will this video go viral: explaining and predicting the popularity of Youtube videos. In: Companion of the The Web Conference 2018 on the Web Conference 2018 - WWW 2018, pp. 175–178 (2018)
2. Liu Thompkins, Y., Rogerson, M.: Rising to stardom: an empirical investigation of the diffusion of user-generated content. J. Interact. Mark. **26**(2), 71–82 (2012)
3. Li, H.O.Y., Bailey, A., Huynh, D., Chan, J.: YouTube as a source of information on COVID-19: a pandemic of misinformation? BMJ Glob. Health **5**(5), e002604 (2020)
4. Oksanen, A., et al.: Pro-anorexia and anti-pro-anorexia videos on YouTube: sentiment analysis of user responses. J. Med. Internet Res. **17**, e256 (2015)
5. Guadagno, R.E., Rempala, D.M., Murphy, S., Okdie, B.M.: What makes a video go viral? An analysis of emotional contagion and Internet memes. Comput. Hum. Behav. **29**(6), 2312–2319 (2015)
6. van Laer, T., de Ruyter, K., Visconti, L.M., Wetzels, M.: The extended transportation-imagery model: a meta-analysis of the antecedents and consequences of consumers narrative transportation. J. Consum. Res. **40**(5), 797–817 (2014)
7. Broxton, T., Interian, Y., Vaver, J., Wattenhofer, M.: Catching a viral video. In: 2010 IEEE International Conference on Data Mining Workshops, pp. 296–304 (2010)
8. Yan, L., Cha, N., Cho, H., Hwang, J.: Video diffusion in user-generated content website: an empirical analysis of Bilibili. In: 2019 21st International Conference on Advanced Communication Technology (ICACT), pp. 81–84 (2019)
9. Aggrawal, N., Arora, A., Anand, A., Dwivedi, Y.: Early viewers or followers: a mathematical model for YouTube viewers' categorization. Kybernetes **50**(6), 1811–1836 (2021)
10. English, K., Sweetser, K.D., Ancu, M.: YouTube-ification of political talk: an examination of persuasion appeals in viral video. Am. Behav. Sci. **55**(6), 733–748 (2011)
11. Eckler, P., Bolls, P.: Spreading the virus: emotional tone of viral advertising and its effect on forwarding intentions and attitudes. J. Interact. Advert. **11**(2), 1–11 (2011)
12. Nelson Field, K., Riebe, E., Newstead, K.: The emotions that drive viral video. Australas. Mark. J. **21**(4), 205–211 (2013)
13. Wang, F., Karimi, S.: This product works well (for me): the impact of first-person singular pronouns on online review helpfulness. J. Bus. Res. **104**, 283–294 (2019)
14. Lei, Z., Yin, D., Zhang, H.: Focus within or on others: the impact of reviewers' attentional focus on review helpfulness. Inf. Syst. Res. **32**, 801–819 (2021)

15. Kleef, G.A.V.: How emotions regulate social life: the emotions as social information (EASI) model. Curr. Dir. Psychol. Sci. **18**(3), 184–188 (2009)
16. Green, M.C., Brock, T.C.: The role of transportation in the persuasiveness of public narratives. J. Pers. Soc. Psychol. **79**(5), 701–721 (2000)
17. Rozin, P., Royzman, E.B.: Negativity bias, negativity dominance, and contagion. Pers. Soc. Psychol. Rev. **5**(4), 296–320 (2001)
18. Liu, Y., Song, Y., Sun, J., Sun, C., Chen, X.: Understanding the relationship between food experiential quality and customer dining satisfaction: a perspective on negative bias. Int. J. Hosp. Manag. **87**, 102381 (2019)
19. Cruz, R.E., Leonhardt, J.M., Pezzuti, T.: Second personal pronouns enhance consumer involvement and brand attitude. J. Interact. Mark. **39**, 104–116 (2017)

Understanding First-Aid Learning Intention Through Using Social Media: Perceptions from External Emergency Events and Individual Internal Changes

Huijing Guo[1]([✉]), Xifu Wang[2], Xiaoxiao Liu[3,4], and Xiaofeng Ju[1]

[1] School of Management, Harbin Institute of Technology, Harbin 150001, China
guo_huijing@163.com
[2] Healthcare Simulation Center, Guangzhou First People's Hospital, Guangzhou 510180, China
[3] School of Management, Xi'an Jiaotong University, Xi'an 710049, China
[4] China Institute of Hospital Development and Reform, Xi'an Jiaotong University, Xi'an 710049, China

Abstract. Emergency events, such as out-of-hospital cardiac arrest, are China's leading causes of mortality. However, witnesses of emergencies are seldom trained with first-aid measures before emergency events happens. Relative to traditional offline first-aid training methods, social media greatly enhanced audiences' interest in first-aid learning in a more entertaining, time-saving, and labor-saving way. Based on Construal Level Theory (CLT), this study aims to understand the impact of external emergencies (past emergencies experience) on individual internal change (psychological distances) and subsequently generate first-aid learning intention through using social media. As emergencies are severe but not widespread, this study only examines social and spatial dimensions of psychological distance (PD) to broaden the application scenarios of CLT. At the same time, we apply prosociality to measure the individual difference. This study conducts a survey in a first-aid popularization account on Sina Weibo. 348 participants, who had never learned first-aid knowledge and skills before, engaged. Results prove that both PDs and prosociality may be impacted by external emergency experiences, then promote related learning intention. This study also finds that prosociality moderates the relationship between spatial distance and related learning intention. This study roots in an emergency context and broadens the application of CLT in first-aid learning. At the same time, since first-aid training is usually hard to grasp and residents usually do not need complex skills to rescue people in emergency events, we applied social media as our learning context in this study to lower the threshold of first-aid education.

Keywords: First-aid learning intention · Emergency events · Past experience · Psychological distances · Construal Level Theory · Prosociality · Social media

1 Introduction

Emergency events, such as out-of-hospital cardiac arrest, are the leading causes of mortality worldwide. In China, cardiac arrest causes more than 550 thousand sudden deaths yearly, and 70%–80% of cardiac arrest events occur outside hospitals [1] without physicians nearby taking rescue measures. At the same time, less than 1% of witnesses are trained with first-aid knowledge and skills in China [2]. First-aid learning has shown increasing values in reducing mortality and improving prognosis due to cardiac arrest [3].

Various resources have been invested in first-aid education, but more progress has yet to be made. Traditional offline first-aid training could only serve a small number of learners, showing inefficiency in relieving cardiac arrest in China. Under this circumstance, social media could be one of the indispensable channels for popularizing scientific information to maximize the scope of popularization. Social media greatly enhanced audiences' interest in first-aid education through a more entertaining way in various forms, such as pictures and videos, providing valuable insights through innovative content generation [4]. At the same time, first-aid learning in social media has shown to be time-saving and labor-saving with solid publicity results.

This study aims to understand the influencing factors of online first-aid learning intention in social media and conducts an empirical analysis with a survey through a first-aid education account on Sina Weibo, one of China's most popular social media platforms. Results give insights to understand the external emergencies promote individual internal change, and finally impact online social media. First, our findings provide evidence that past emergency event experiences could narrow social and spatial dimensions of PDs, then the spatial distances could generate first-aid learning intention through using social media. Second, this study prove that past emergency event experiences generate prosociality, and then facilitate first-aid learning intention through using social media, consistent with our reasoning. At last, we also find that prosociality moderate the relationship between spatial distance for future emergencies and first-aid learning intention through using social media. This study roots in an emergency context and broaden the application of CLT in first-aid learning intention. At the same time, since first-aid training is usually professional and hard to grasp and residents usually do not need complex skills to rescue people in emergency events, we applied social media as our learning context in this study to lower the threshold of first-aid education.

2   Literature Review

2.1   Construal Level Theory and Psychological Distances

CLT is a psychological theory that applied to describe the PDs toward the event are remote or close [5, 6], then PDs may impact the extent to which cognitive thinking about an event is abstract or concrete and guide behaviors referring to the events experienced [7]. Most existing studies adopted CLT to understand the project failure and skills learning context. These studies confirmed that project failure experience may narrow PDs and then promote learning to prevent another failure in the future [8]. For emergency contexts, multiple studies adopted CLT, such as climate disasters. Still, seldom studies have tried to facilitate first-aid learning, which is essential to facilitate the future behaviors of people with emergency event experiences. From the perceptions of the construal level, when people have undergone emergencies, they will have close PDs, and the construal level for emergency events is low.

2.2   First-Aid Learning Intention Through Using Social Media

Generally, an individual's learning intention is defined as the proximal determinant of engaging in learning activities [9]. This intention is a robust predictor for actual learning behaviors [10]. Various indicators could impact individual learning intentions, such as the learner's characteristics, the learning activity's characteristics, and social context [11]. To better understand the first-aid learning intention, we consider the individual psychological factors (PDs), individual differences (prosociality), and the social context of emergency events in this study.

At the same time, first-aid learning through using social media lowers the threshold of traditional offline first-aid professional education. The typical learning mode for first-aid training is proficiency in a face-to-face manner. However, only a few residents need this systematic training to give a helping hand in emergencies. With the fast demand for education needs, limited offline resources become a learning barrier. Social media could integrate learning sources to meet many individuals' learning needs.

3   Hypotheses Development and Research Model

The past experience, which may generate emotions and feelings, could be viewed as an external event that impacts the internal change rather than a direct experience [8]. Under various experiences, individuals may generate different mental models, such as PDs [12]. After integrating past experiences into individual cognitive change, people could stimulate learning behaviors to prevent adverse events from happening in the future [12]. Like other experiences, the past emergency experience could give residents a sense of the consequences of emergencies, generate recognition of a future emergency event, and stimulate subsequence learning behaviors [13]. We also adopt prosociality as a personal trait in our research model. In this study, we explore the impact of past emergency experiences on first-aid learning intention through two internal changes, mental change (PDs) and individual differences (prosociality).

3.1   Impact of Mental Changes on First-Aid Learning Intention

Based on CLT, existing studies illustrated that past experience could change all four dimensions of PDs: spatial distance (here), temporal distance (now), social distance (self), and uncertainty (certainty) [8]. When an event locates at a relatively remote spatial distance, occurs in a more distant future, happens to others more unfamiliar than oneself, and takes place with a lower probability, the PDs of this event that occurred in the future may be remote.

Unlike the experience examined in most studies, emergency events are severe but not widespread, resulting in consideration of temporal and uncertainty dimensions of PDs that are insignificant in this context. In this study, we broaden the application of CLT in the emergency context by examining the impact of spatial and social dimensions of PDs, which leads to the hypothesis below:

H1a: Past emergency experience negatively relates to social distance toward a future emergency event.

H1b: Past emergency experience negatively relates to spatial distance toward a future emergency event.

At the same time, CLT emphasizes that PDs could change the mental construal of an event and predict behaviors toward the future event [7]. People with a close social distance in emergency events are more sensitive to the risks posed by the circumstances, resulting in engaging in activities to prevent occurrences of future emergencies. First-aid learning could be one of the most effective preventive measures. At the same time, social media lower the threshold of first-aid education to meet the individual need of specific first-aid learning demands.

On the other hand, spatial distance focused on how far people perceived the emergency event would happen based on their current location. People with a close spatial distance in emergency events always have little time to respond to this event, leading to a desire for skilled first-aid measures. Under these circumstances, spatial distance will influence first-aid learning intention through using social media. Then we propose the hypothesis below:

H2a: Social distance in future emergencies negatively relates to first-aid learning intention through using social media.

H2b: Spatial distance in future emergencies negatively relates to first-aid learning intention through using social media.

3.2 Impact of Individual Difference on on First-Aid Learning Intention

Prosociality can be seen as the individual differences that guide future behaviors to benefit others without considering self-benefit [14], containing helping, sharing, comforting, rescuing, and so on [15]. One reason for introducing prosociality in our research model is that the motivation to help others is paramount for emergency and first-aid learning contexts. At the same time, research has illustrated that experience can explain prosociality in adulthood [16], for people could catch the need for help. Emergencies are situations in desperate need of help from witnesses. Under these circumstances, people may promote their prosociality under emergencies.

H3: Past emergency events positively relate to prosociality.

The behaviors produced by past emergency experiences may be subjective and dissimilar from the characteristics of people groups [17]. When prosociality is high, people will stimulate their ability to meet others' needs and take action to benefit others. Then, when prosociality is high, the relationship between PDs and first-aid learning intention through using social media enhances.

H4: Prosociality positively relates to first-aid learning intention through using social media.

3.3 Moderating Role of Prosociality on the Relationship Between Psychological Distances and First-Aid Learning Intention

People with high prosociality are intended to benefit or help an individual or group [18]. When prosociality is high, the mental construal of an emergency event would be changed; then, the impact of PDs and first-aid learning intention through using social media will be enhanced. Hence, we hypothesize that:

H5a: Prosociality negatively moderates the relationship between social distance in future emergencies and first-aid learning intention through using social media.

H5b: Prosociality negatively moderates the relationship between spatial distance in future emergencies and first-aid learning intention through using social media.

3.4 Research Model

Based on the hypothesis mentioned above, we build the research model shown in Fig. 1. At the same time, this study controls age, gender, education, and living with old adults. Age, gender, and education may impact learning behaviors. In the emergency context, people living with senior adults may have concerns that ultimately influence first-aid learning behaviors.

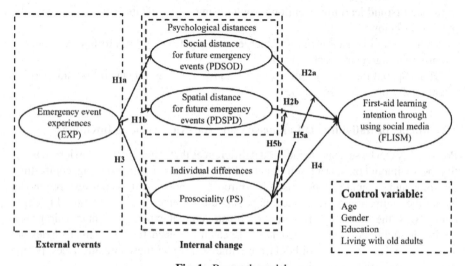

Fig. 1. Research model.

4   Research Methodology

4.1   Data Collection

To test the hypothesis, we conducted a survey online to collect data through an emergency popularity account (Jizhen Yeying) on Sina Weibo, one of China's most popular social media platforms. This account aims to publish emergency popularity articles and post first-aid skills videos for years. This account was built by a doctor working at a large 3a hospital in Guangdong province with years of emergency treatment experience. Before the survey was conducted, the number of followers exceeded one million.

Before the final questionnaire was distributed, we conducted a preliminary survey with existing measurement items, which were modified by our research context. Each item was first translated into Chinese, and then we translated it back into English. After that, a pilot study was conducted to ensure the clarity of every question. Ultimately, we distributed this questionnaire to social media users who were adults. In total, 804 participants were engaged. We excluded 456 participants who learned first-aid knowledge and skills before filling in this questionnaire, leaving 348 samples.

4.2 Measures

This study examined past emergency experience through using a single item of "How many emergencies have you experienced through using social media?" (never = 0, one time = 1, and more than 2 times = 2). The items for PDs (social distance and spatial distance toward future emergencies) were adopted from the scales of Spence et al. (2012) [19] on a 5-point Likert scale (5 stands for a relative far distance). Besides, we also use the scales which were validated and used in prior studies to measure prosociality [14] and first-aid learning intention through using social media [20] on 5-point Likert scales, and the numerical scores ranging from 1 (strongly disagree) to 5 (strongly agree). The measurement of these items is shown in Table 1 as follows.

4.3 Demographic Analysis

Table 2 shows the demographic statistics results. First, the majority of the participants were female (74.4%). Second, among all the participants, almost half were aged between 25 and 34 (45.6%); other participants were located between the ages of 18–24 and 35–44; only two were older adults above 54. At last, most of the participants were college or university graduates.

5   Results

5.1 Measurement Model

This study first examines the construct reliability and validity by reporting the item loading, average variance extracted (AVE), composite reliability (CR), and Cronbach's alpha (CA), as shown in Table 3. The item loadings were all above 0.7. Besides, the AVE was between 0.596–0.703, the CR at 0.904–0.943, and the CA between 0.860–0.932, exceeding the recommended thresholds of 0.5, 0.7, and 0.7, respectively. The discriminant validity of the constructs and concepts is shown in Table 4. The results showed satisfactory discriminant validity of the measurements.

5.2 Structural Model

Figure 2 presents the results of our research model. Past emergency experience significantly negatively impacts two PDs. The path coefficient of the relationship between past emergency experience and social distance is -0.091 (t = 1.832, p < 0.1), and the path coefficient of the relationship between past emergency experience and spatial distance is -0.160 (t = 3.231, p < 0.01), supporting H1a and H1b. Then, past emergency experience significantly positively impacts prosociality with the path coefficient of 0.039 (t = 1.826, p < 0.1), supporting H2.

PDs show a diverse significance in first-aid learning intention through using social media. Social distance does not significantly impact first-aid learning intention (t = 0.929, p > 0.1), rejecting H3a, and spatial distance significantly negatively impacts first-aid learning intention with a path coefficient of −0.234 (t = 3.398, p < 0.01), supporting H3b. At the same time, prosociality significantly positively impacts first-aid learning intention through using social media with a path coefficient of 0.354 (t = 5.803, p < 0.01), supporting H4.

At last, prosociality shows a significantly positive moderating role in the relationship between social distance and first-aid learning intention through using social media (β = 0.103, t = 2.281, p < 0.05), rejecting H5a, and a significant negative moderating role in the relationship between spatial distance and first-aid learning intention (β = −0.109, t = 1.969, p < 0.05), supporting H5b.

Table 1. Measurement scales.

Constructs	Items		Sources
Social distance toward future emergencies	PDSOD	Emergencies are not likely to have big impact on me	Spence et al. 2012
Spatial distance toward future emergencies	PDSPD	My living area is not likely to suffer emergencies	
Prosociality	PS1	I am pleased to help my friends/colleagues in their activities	Caprara et al. 2005
	PS2	I share the things that I have with my friends	
	PS3	I try to help others	
	PS4	I am available for volunteer activities to help those who are in need	
	PS5	I am emphatic with those who are in need	
	PS6	I help immediately those who are in need	
	PS7	I do what I can to help others avoid getting into trouble	
	PS8	I intensely feel what others feel	
	PS9	I am willing to make my knowledge and abilities available to Others	

(*continued*)

Table 1. (*continued*)

Constructs	Items		Sources
	PS10	I try to console those who are sad	
	PS11	I try to be close to and take care of those who are in need	
First-aid learning intention through using social media	FLISM1	I intend to look for information about first-aid courses and learning activities that I could participate in through using social media	Hazelzet et al. 2009
	FLISM2	I intend to participate in a first-aid learning activity within next year through using social media	
	FLISM3	Sometimes I think about following a first-aid training within the next year through using social media	
	FLISM4	I intend to talk with persons on social media about first-aid related courses or trainings that I could follow through using social media	

Table 2. Demographic statistics.

	Characteristics	Number	Percentage
Gender	Male	88	25.2%
	Female	260	74.7%
Age	18–24	69	19.8%
	25–34	159	45.6%
	35–44	91	26.1%
	45–54	27	7.7%
	>54	2	0.5%
Education	Senior high school graduate and below	23	6.6%
	College and university graduate	259	74.4%
	Master and Ph.D	66	19.0%

Table 3. Testing of reliability and convergent validity.

	Items	Item loading	Average Variance Extracted (AVE)	Composite Reliability (CR)	Cronbach's Alpha (CA)
Learning intention through using social media (LISM)	LISM1	0.846	0.703	0.904	0.860
	LISM2	0.824			
	LISM3	0.851			
	LISM4	0.833			
Prosocial (PS)	PS1	0.744	0.596	0.942	0.932
	PS2	0.728			
	PS3	0.844			
	PS4	0.757			
	PS5	0.770			
	PS6	0.806			
	PS7	0.822			
	PS8	0.733			
	PS9	0.817			
	PS10	0.753			
	PS11	0.704			

Table 4. Correlation analysis.

	EXP	PDSOD	PDSPD	PS	LISM
EXP	**1.000**				
PDSOD	−0.091	**1.000**			
PDSPD	−0.160	0.468	**1.000**		
PS	0.093	−0.461	−0.409	**0.772**	
LISM	0.080	−0.374	−0.411	0.490	**0.838**

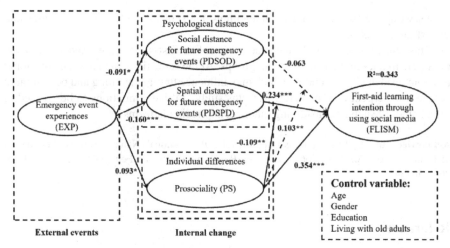

Fig. 2. Smart PLS analysis results (Note: *p < 0.05; **p < 0.01; ***p < 0.001).

6 Discussion

This study examines the influencing factors of first-aid learning intention through using social media other than offline learning intention. Results give insights to understand the external emergencies promote individual internal change, and finally impact online social media. First, our findings provide evidence that past emergency event experience could narrow social and spatial dimensions of PDs, then the spatial distances could generate first-aid learning intention. However, social distances of future emergencies could not generate first-aid learning. This finding is consistent with the definition of social distance which emphasizes the extent events affecting self and the nature of first-aid learning to benefit others. Second, this study prove that past emergency event experiences generate prosociality, and then facilitate first-aid learning intention through using social media, consistent with our reasoning. At last, we also find that prosociality moderate the relationship between spatial distance for future emergencies and first-aid learning intention through using social media.

7 Conclusion

This study investigates how external emergency experiences influence individual internal changes and ultimately facilitate first-aid learning intention through using social media. This study roots in an emergency context to build our research model. First, we broaden the application of CLT in first-aid learning intention by investigating the social and spatial dimensions of PDs. Emergency context is unique for the emergency events, usually severe but not widespread, leading to the consideration that the other two dimensions are meaningless. Second, we introduce an individual difference, namely prosociality, which usually guides people to benefit others to understand the influence path of first-aid learning intention. Third, since first-aid training is usually professional and hard to grasp and residents usually do not need complex skills to rescue people in emergency events, we applied social media as our learning context in this study to lower the threshold of first-aid education.

This study's results could help facilitate online first-aid learning and identify the high-potential target first-aid learning groups. At the same time, the government should promote residents' prosociality, which may influence first-aid learning and benefit more people in emergency events. However, this study still has limitations to be verified in future studies, such as considering other social media platforms.

Acknowledgement. This study is supported by the National Natural Science Foundation of China (72001170, 72032006) and China Postdoctoral Science Foundation (2022T150515, 2020M67343).

References

1. Qian, Y.F., Ren, Y.Q., Wang, L., et al.: Application of the modified basic life support training model in improving community residents' rescue willingness in Nantong City in China. Int. J. Clin. Pract. **2022**, 6702146 (2022). https://doi.org/10.1155/2022/6702146
2. Xu, F., Zhang, Y., Chen, Y.: Cardiopulmonary resuscitation training in China. JAMA Cardiol. **2**(5), 469–470 (2017). https://doi.org/10.1001/jamacardio.2017.0035
3. Kattan, A.E., AlShomer, F., Alhujayri, A.K., et al.: Current knowledge of burn injury first aid practices and applied traditional remedies: a nationwide survey. Burns Trauma **4**, 37 (2016). https://doi.org/10.1186/s41038-016-0063-7
4. Figueiredo, F., Almeida, J.M., Gonçalves, M.A., et al.: On the dynamics of social media popularity: a YouTube case study. ACM Trans. Internet Technol. (TOIT) **14**(4), 1–23 (2014). https://doi.org/10.1145/2665065
5. Trope, Y., Liberman, N.: Construal-level theory of psychological distance. Psychol. Rev. **117**(2), 440–463 (2010). https://doi.org/10.1037/a0018963
6. Soderberg, C.K., Callahan, S.P., Kochersberger, A.O., et al.: The effects of psychological distance on abstraction: two meta-analyses. Psychol. Bull. **141**(3), 525–548 (2015). https://doi.org/10.1037/bul0000005
7. Trope, Y., Liberman, N., Wakslak, C.: Construal levels and psychological distance: effects on representation, prediction, evaluation, and behavior. J. Consum. Psychol. **17**(2), 83–95 (2007). https://doi.org/10.1016/S1057-7408(07)70013-X
8. Liu, J., Geng, L., Xia, B., et al.: Never let a good crisis go to waste: exploring the effects of psychological distance of project failure on learning intention. J. Manag. Eng. **33**(4), 04017006 (2017). https://doi.org/10.1061/(ASCE)ME.1943-5479.0000513
9. Kyndt, E., Govaerts, N., Dochy, F., et al.: The learning intention of low-qualified employees: a key for participation in lifelong learning and continuous training. Vocat. Learn. **4**(3), 211–229 (2011). https://doi.org/10.1007/s12186-011-9058-5
10. Maurer, T.J., Weiss, E.M., Barbeite, F.G.: Model of involvement in work-related learning and development activity: the effects of individual, situational, motivational, and age variables. J. Appl. Psychol. **88**(4), 707–724 (2003). https://doi.org/10.1037/0021-9010.88.4.707
11. Boeren, E.: Understanding adult lifelong learning participation as a layered problem. Stud. Contin. Educ. **39**(2), 161–175 (2017). https://doi.org/10.1080/0158037X.2017.1310096
12. Bekebrede, G., Lo, J., Lukosch, H.: Understanding complex systems through mental models and shared experiences: a case study. Simul. Gaming **46**(5), 536–562 (2015). https://doi.org/10.1177/1046878115621463

13. Demuth, J.L., Morss, R.E., Lazo, J.K., Trumbo, C.: The effects of past hurricane experiences on evacuation intentions through risk perception and efficacy beliefs: a mediation analysis. Weather Clim. Soc. **8**(4), 327–344 (2016). https://doi.org/10.1175/WCAS-D-15-0074.1

14. Caprara, G.V., Steca, P.: Prosocial agency: the contribution of values and self-efficacy beliefs to prosocial behavior across ages. J. Soc. Clin. Psychol. **26**(2), 218–239 (2007). https://doi.org/10.1521/jscp.2007.26.2.218

15. Eagly, A.H.: The his and hers of prosocial behavior: an examination of the social psychology of gender. Am. Psychol. **64**(8), 644–658 (2009). https://doi.org/10.1037/0003-066X.64.8.644

16. Van Lange, P.A.M., De Bruin, E., Otten, W., et al.: Development of prosocial, individualistic, and competitive orientations: theory and preliminary evidence. J. Pers. Soc. Psychol. **73**(4), 733–746 (1997). https://doi.org/10.1037/0022-3514.73.4.733

17. Roppolo, L.P., Wigginton, J.G., Pepe, P.E.: Revolving back to the basics in cardiopulmonary resuscitation. Minerva Anestesiol. **75**(5), 301–305 (2009)

18. Hay, D.F.: Prosocial development. Child Psychol. Psychiatry Allied Discipl. **35**(1), 29–71 (1994). https://doi.org/10.1111/j.1469-7610.1994.tb01132.x

19. Spence, A., Poortinga, W., Pidgeon, N.: The psychological distance of climate change. Risk Anal. **32**(6), 957–972 (2012). https://doi.org/10.1111/j.1539-6924.2011.01695.x

20. Kyndt, E., Dochy, F., Onghena, P., et al.: The learning intentions of low-qualified employees: a multilevel approach. Adult Educ. Q. **63**(2), 165–189 (2013). https://doi.org/10.1177/0741713612454324

Impacts of Analyst Reports' Descriptions of Corporate Innovative Behavior on Stock Price Synchronicity

Wei Zhang[1(✉)], Yu-xia Zhao[1], Chen-guang Li[2], Yan-chun Zhu[3], and Xue-feng Li[1]

[1] School of Information, Central University of Finance and Economics, Beijing 100081, China
weizhang@cufe.edu.cn
[2] School of Insurance, Central University of Finance and Economics, Beijing 100081, China
[3] Business School, Beijing Normal University, Beijing 100875, China

Abstract. Using text analysis, in this study, we identified and quantified the textual contents of the enterprise innovation behavior descriptions in analyst reports, and we formed an information content index. Based on the views of information efficiency and noise trading theory, we analyzed the impact of the corporate innovation behavior descriptions in analyst reports on the stock price synchronicity, using the degree of information asymmetry as the moderating factor, and the heterogeneous beliefs of investors and noise trading as the mediating factors. Our empirical research results are as follows: (1) the corporate innovation behavior descriptions in analyst reports can inhibit the stock price synchronicity phenomenon, which is constrained by the degree of information asymmetry; (2) the analyst descriptions of corporate innovation behavior strengthen the heterogeneous beliefs of investors, thereby inhibiting the stock price synchronization; (3) noise trading has no mediating effect between the analyst descriptions of corporate innovation behavior and stock price synchronicity. This study provides favorable evidence for the information intermediary role of analysts, and it enriches the theoretical research on stock price synchronicity. It also provides a new research perspective for the application of text analysis in the fields of finance and accounting, and it enriches the research dimensions of the textual characteristics of analyst reports.

Keywords: Stock Price Synchronicity · Analyst Reports · Text Analysis · Corporate Innovation

1 Introduction

The price mechanism guides the allocation of resources in the capital market. However, the emergence of various anomalies in the capital market, such as the stock price synchronicity phenomenon, hinders the efficiency of the resource allocation. At this time, the price loses the function of the signaling mechanism, and investors cannot identify the true value of the enterprise through the price, which damages the operation efficiency of the capital market.

Y. Tu and M. Chi (Eds.): WHICEB 2023, LNBIP 480, pp. 182–193, 2023.
https://doi.org/10.1007/978-3-031-32299-0_16

Based on the view of information efficiency, Roll [1] points out that the integration of information at the enterprise level is the reason for the heterogeneity of stock price fluctuations. Noise trading theory holds that the fluctuation in the stock price is not entirely caused by information factors, especially in markets in which noise trading dominates. Noise deteriorates the efficiency of the information transmission, which causes the stock price to deviate from the true value of the enterprise and presents low stock price synchronicity [2].

The key influencing factor for the formation of stock price synchronicity is information asymmetry [3]. As one of the important corporate characteristics, the corporate innovation behavior is an important basis from which investors evaluate the corporate value. In reality, there is large information asymmetry between the internal and external investors in the enterprise innovation behavior information [4]. Analysts interpret the company's idiosyncratic information and transmit it to investors in the form of analyst reports to guide them in correct and rational investment decision making, which is a key link in improving the overall operational efficiency of China's capital market [5].

As for the impact of securities analysts on the stock price synchronicity, in the early research, which was based on the "information efficiency view", researchers focused on tracking the number of analysts, and they could not agree upon the relationship between the analysts and stock price synchronicity. In recent years, researchers have begun to focus on the impact of the textual content characteristics of analyst reports on the stock price synchronicity. Corporate innovation behavior is an important enterprise characteristic; however, scholars have not paid enough attention to the textual characteristics of the corporate innovation descriptions in analyst reports and their impacts on the stock price synchronicity.

On this basis, we evaluated the relationship between the corporate innovation behavior descriptions in analyst reports and the stock price synchronicity from the corporate microlevel perspective. Through the textual analyses of analyst reports, we constructed an information content index that describes the enterprise innovation behavior. Based on the views of information efficiency and noise trading theory, we took the degree of information asymmetry as the moderating factor and the heterogeneous beliefs of investors and noise trading as the mediating factors, and we analyzed the influence of the corporate innovation behavior descriptions in analyst reports on the stock price synchronicity. We provide favorable evidence for analysts as information intermediaries, discuss the mechanism of the role of securities analysts in stock price synchronicity, and thereby enrich the theoretical stock price synchronicity research.

2 Related Works

2.1 Stock Price Synchronicity

Stock price synchronicity refers to the phenomenon that the share price of a company simultaneously rises and falls on the stock market. When the stock price synchronicity is high, there is no difference in the stock price fluctuations among different enterprises, and the stock price does not reflect the real value of the enterprise, which thus damages the signal transmission mechanism of the stock price. Roll (1988) combined the fluctuation in the stock price with information content, proposed the explanation of "information efficiency" [1], and thereby established the logical starting point of stock price synchronicity research. Hutton et al. (2008) [6] found a substantial positive effect between the opacity of financial statements and the stock price synchronicity, which indicates that the stock price synchronicity is higher when the degree of the incorporation of the enterprise characteristic information into the stock price is low. As West [2] demonstrated, noise can exacerbate the volatility of share prices, which is reflected in lower stock price synchronicity.

2.2 Analyst Report

The analyst's report contains the analyst's opinion and judgment basis. In the early studies, researchers focused on quantitative results and adjustments to analyst reports. Kothari et al. (2002) [7] point out that the text that contains the analyst's analysis of industries, policies, corporate business, and risks is of great value to his or her research. Asquith et al. (2005) [8] classified the textual intonations in analyst reports, which created a precedent for research on the textual data of these reports. Subsequently, more researchers began to pay attention to the importance of the textual contents of analyst reports.

2.3 Corporate Innovation Behavior Information

Innovation is the core of the competitiveness of enterprises, and it is the key basis for the decision making of investors. James et al. (2016) [9] believe that the disclosure of R&D information by enterprises can send a signal of technological leadership to investors, which causes a positive market reaction. However, sometimes, to avoid infringement, free riding, and other acts, or considering the legal risks, enterprises will try to reduce the disclosure of their innovation information. From the content of enterprise innovation information disclosure, most researchers focus on the analysis of traditional financial data. Another form of innovation information is nonfinancial information, which includes the textual descriptions of an enterprise's innovation activities. Merkley et al. (2014) [10] demonstrated that the financial data of an enterprise has a limited ability to convey the value of the investment, and that textual information can be a good supplement to financial information.

3   Related Theories and Research Hypotheses

According to the efficient market hypothesis, in a strong efficient market, price fluctuations are mainly influenced by information factors. Based on the view of information efficiency, low stock price synchronicity is due to the integration of the corporate characteristics into the stock price [1]. According to the noise trading theory, when the fluctuation in the stock price is primarily affected by noise, the uncertainty faced by investors is higher, and the increase in information reduces their noise-trading behavior, which improves the synchronization of the stock price [11].

To sum up, the impact of the corporate innovation behavior descriptions in analyst reports on the stock price synchronicity is still an issue that requires empirical testing.

The direction of the impact is often related to the market conditions. Therefore, we propose the following hypotheses:

H1(a): The more the analyst report describes the innovation behavior of the enterprise, the lower the stock price synchronicity of the enterprise, other factors being equal;

H1(b): Under the condition that other conditions remain unchanged, the more the analyst report describes the innovation behavior of the enterprise, the higher the stock price synchronicity of the enterprise.

Enterprise innovation behavior is a kind of internal enterprise behavior, with individual differences, and it often involves large investments and high risks. To ensure their interests, enterprises tend to avoid the specific disclosure of their innovation behavior information, which is difficult for investors to grasp [12]. At present, the investors that are participating in China's capital market, on average, lack professional knowledge and information collection abilities, while analysts have professional knowledge and the ability to collect, process, and summarize information, which means that they can better interpret the financial, operational, and operating conditions of enterprises, and to some extent, ease the degree of information asymmetry between internal managers and external investors. When the degree of information asymmetry is high, investors increasingly rely on the information that is provided by analyst reports, which reduces the degree of noninformation transactions and the synchronization of stock prices. Therefore, we propose the following hypothesis:

H2: When an enterprise's degree of information asymmetry is high, the description of the enterprise's innovation behavior in the analyst report has a stronger negative impact on the stock price synchronicity.

The innovation behavior of enterprises is highly professional and vague, and it is difficult for investors to speculate on the innovation strength of the target enterprise from the perspective of the enterprise information disclosure. The corporate innovation behavior descriptions in analyst reports can enrich the information set used by investors, increase their heterogeneous beliefs, and substantially improve the valuation of the corporate innovation behavior on the stock market [13]. Therefore, we propose the following hypotheses:

H3: The corporate innovation behavior descriptions in analyst reports have a positive impact on the heterogeneous beliefs of investors;

H4: The heterogeneity beliefs of investors mediate between the analyst report enterprise innovation behavior descriptions and stock price synchronicity.

According to the efficient market hypothesis, there is a positive correlation between the efficiency of the stock market and the degree to which information is integrated into the stock price. However, when the stock market is full of noninformation factors (i.e., the impact of noise trading), the transmission mechanism of the information in the stock market is hindered, noise becomes the dominant factor in the stock price, and there is a positive correlation between the stock price synchronicity and information efficiency. In noisy trading markets, investors are more uncertain about corporate information. Lee et al. (2011) [11] found that the more frequent the noisy trading in the market, the lower the stock price synchronicity. Analyst reports provide descriptive information on corporate innovation behavior that reduces this uncertainty and improves the stock price synchronicity. Therefore, we propose the following hypotheses:

H5: Analyst report enterprise innovation behavior descriptions inhibit noise trading;

H6: Noise trading mediates between the corporate innovation descriptions in analyst reports and the stock price synchronicity.

4 Research Design

4.1 Data Selection

In this study, we selected nonfinancial listed companies from the Shanghai and Shenzhen A-shares from 2019 to 2021 as the research samples. We collected 70,695 analyst reports from Oriental Fortune. We collected the financial data of the companies involved and the stock market data from the CSMAR and Ruisi databases (www.resset.cn). To reduce the outlier interference on the results, we adopted the winsorization tail-shrinking method at the 1% and 99% levels for the main continuous variables. To further reduce the impact of noise, based on the research needs, we carried out the following treatments: (1) the enterprise-annualized treatment of the enterprise innovation behavior descriptions in analyst reports; (2) the elimination the sample data of the listed companies in the financial industry; (3) the elimination of analyst reports that track multiple enterprises at the same time; (4) the elimination of data on ST and *ST listed companies; (5) the elimination of samples with missing data for the main variables. We finally obtained 5,246 valid samples.

4.2 Text Analysis

In this study, we combined the LDA thematic model proposed by Blei et al. (2003) [14] and the HDP model proposed by Teh et al. (2006) [15] to construct the explanatory variable: the descriptive index of the analyst reports on the enterprise innovation behavior. First, we use the PDFminer library to parse the obtained analyst reports. Then, we performed word segmentation by combining common terms, such as "Jieba thesaurus" and "analysts' reports". In this study, we referred to the keywords provided by Li Yanqiong and Yao Yi (2020) [16], and we constructed a "keyword dictionary". By combining the LDA filter and HDP model, we conducted the text clustering analysis. The LDA theme model decomposes the document into the document theme matrix and theme feature word matrix. In this study, we manually screened the keywords of each topic generated by the LDA, we selected the topic that represented enterprise innovation, and we judged the probability of the "keyword dictionary" under this topic. If it was greater than 0.6, then the topic represented a description of enterprise innovation behavior information in analyst reports. To ensure the accurate identification of the topics, we set the number (n) of topics that the LDA topic model needed to provide a priori as an integer between 5 and 10, and under each topic number, we included the documents with the highest probabilities of containing the enterprise innovation topics in the training corpus of the subsequent HDP topic model. With the HDP model, we can avoid the setting of superparameters, and we can independently determine the number of topics that can be attributed to the document.

Finally, we quantified the enterprise innovation behavior descriptions. We summed up the probabilities of the innovation topics in the analyst reports in the enterprise and year dimensions, and we then standardized the value and adjusted it to a score with a mean of 50 and a standard deviation of 10, as shown in Eq. (1):

$$AnaInnov_{i,t} = 50 + 10 \times \left(\frac{AnaInnovProb_{i,t} - AnaInnovMean}{AnaInnovStd} \right) \qquad (1)$$

where $AnaInnov_{i,t}$ represents Year t of Enterprise i based on the corporate innovation indicators reported by analysts; $AnaInnovProb_{i,t}$ represents the sum of the probabilities that the analyst reports of Enterprise i were the subject of innovation in Year t; $AnaInnovMean$ represents the average value of the sum of the probabilities of innovation topics; $AnaInnovStd$ represents the variance in the sum of the probabilities of innovation topics.

4.3 Multivariate Regression Model

To test H1, we established the following regression model:

$$SYN_{i,t} = \alpha_0 + \alpha_1 AnaInnov_{i,t} + \alpha_2 Controls_{i,t} + \sum Year + \sum Ind + \varepsilon_{i,t} \qquad (2)$$

To test H2, we established the following regression model:

$$SYN_{i,t} = \alpha_0 + \alpha_1 AnaInnov_{i,t} + \alpha_2 ASY_{i,t} + \alpha_3 AnaInnov_{i,t} \times ASY_{i,t} \\ + \alpha_4 Controls_{i,t} + \sum Year + \sum Ind + \varepsilon_{i,t} \qquad (3)$$

According to the previous mediation effect test procedure, we established the following models to test H3 and H4 in this study:

$$SYN_{i,t} = \alpha_1 + c_1 AnaInnov_{i,t} + \sum d\, Controls_{i,t} + \sum Year + \sum Ind + \varepsilon_{i,t} \qquad (4)$$

$$HB_{i,t} = \gamma_1 + a_1 AnaInnov_{i,t} + \sum d\, Controls_{i,t} \\ + \sum Year + \sum Ind + \varepsilon_{i,t} \qquad (5)$$

$$SYN_{i,t} = \alpha'_1 + c'_1 AnaInnov_{i,t} + b_1 HB_{i,t} + \sum dControls_{i,t} \\ + \sum Year + \sum Ind + \varepsilon_{i,t} \qquad (6)$$

To test H5 and H6, we established the following models in the same way:

$$SYN_{i,t} = \alpha_2 + c_2 AnaInnov_{i,t} + \sum dControls_{i,t} + \sum Year + \sum Ind + \varepsilon_{i,t} \qquad (7)$$

$$NOISE_{i,t} = \gamma_2 + a_2 AnaInnov_{i,t} + \sum dControls_{i,t} \\ + \sum Year + \sum Ind + \varepsilon_{i,t} \qquad (8)$$

$$SYN_{i,t} = \alpha'_2 + c'_2 AnaInnov_{i,t} + b_2 NOISE_{i,t} + \sum dControls_{i,t} \\ + \sum Year + \sum Ind + \varepsilon_{i,t} \qquad (9)$$

where $SYN_{i,t}$ denotes the stock price synchronicity in Year t of Enterprise i, which we obtain by the logarithm of R^2 obtained by the regression of individual stock earnings and market earnings. According to the perspective of information efficiency, the higher the *SYN* value, the higher the stock price synchronicity.

AnaInnov$_{i,t}$ is a corporate innovation indicator that is based on analyst reports for Year *t* of Corporation *i*, and we calculated it using Eq. (1). *ASY$_{i,t}$* is the degree of asymmetry in the corporate information, and we measured it by the earnings management level (*AbsDA$_{i,t}$*) and liquidity level (*ILL$_{i,t}$*). We calculated the *AbsDA* using the modified Jones model, and we measured it in absolute terms by discretionary accruals. The *ILL* is a grouping of the stock liquidity. The degree of information asymmetry is higher when the annual turnover rate of the stock is lower than the median of all the samples. The *ILL* is recorded as 1 at this time; otherwise, it is recorded as 0. *HB$_{i,t}$* represents the heterogeneous beliefs of investors in Year *t* of Enterprise *i*, which is measured by constructing a turnover rate separation model to calculate the unexpected trading volume. *NOISE$_{i,t}$* represents the level of noise trading in Year *t* of Enterprise *i*. We used the previous calculation method for the reference, with the trend stationary test and ARMA fitting to the timeseries of the trading volume. After determining the appropriate hysteresis order, we obtained the residual sequence after the regression. We calculated the variance in the residual series, and we took its natural logarithm as the proxy variable of the noise transaction.

Control represents the following control variables: the size of the enterprise, level of debt (*lev*), book-to-market ratio (*bm*), annual turnover rate (*TurnOver*), proportion of institutional shareholders (*inshold*), return on total assets (*roa*), and whether B shares or H shares are issued (*crosslist*). *Year* and *Ind* represent the annual effect and industry effect, respectively.

5   Empirical Analysis Results

5.1   Impacts of Corporate Innovation Behavior Descriptions in Analyst Reports on Stock Price Synchronicity

We present the impacts of the enterprise innovation behavior descriptions in the analyst reports on the stock price synchronization in Table 1. We detected a substantial negative correlation between the contents of the enterprise innovation behavior descriptions in the independent variable analyst reports (*AnaInnov*) and the dependent variable, the stock price synchronicity (*SYN*). The regression coefficient was −0.012, and it was significant at 1%.

We preliminarily verified the research hypothesis H1(a) in this paper. The more the analyst report describes the innovation behavior of the enterprise, the greater the reduction in the stock price synchronization.

For the control variables, the stock turnover rate (*TurnOver*) had a substantial negative correlation with the stock price synchronicity (*SYN*), and there was a substantial positive correlation between the enterprise size (*Size*), book-to-market ratio (bm), and stock price synchronicity (*SYN*). The proportion of institutional shareholders (*inshold*) had a substantial positive correlation with the stock price synchronicity (*SYN*), which indicates that institutional investors can effectively promote the operation efficiency of the capital market, enhance the ability of stock prices to reflect specific information at the enterprise level, and thereby reduce the stock price synchronicity.

Table 1. Impacts of corporate innovation behavior descriptions in analyst reports on stock price synchronicity.

Variable	SYN
AnaInnov	-0.012^{***}
TurnOver	-0.051^{***}
size	0.202^{***}
lev	0.007
bm	0.218^{***}
inshold	-0.214^{***}
roa	-0.261
crosslist	-0.010
Constant	-6.211^{***}
Observations	5,246
R-squared	0.267
year FE	YES
industry FE	YES
r2_a	0.264
F	53.86

Note: *** indicates $p < 0.01$; ** indicates $p < 0.05$; * indicates $p < 0.1$

5.2 Moderating Effects of Information Asymmetry Degree

We added the information asymmetry variable to the above model. We added the interaction between the earnings manipulation level (AbsDA) and analyst corporate innovation behavior descriptions in Model 2. We added the interaction between the stock liquidity (ILL) and analyst corporate innovation behavior descriptions in Model 3. Due to the absence of some samples, we still subjected Model 1 to a regression test based on the dataset subjected to the adjustment effect test. We present the regression results in Table 2.

As can be seen from Table 2, the regression coefficient of the cross term *AnaInnov* × *ASY* to the dependent variable *SYN* is positive and significant at the levels of 5% and 1%, respectively, which indicates that the degree of information asymmetry moderates the relationship between the analyst corporate innovation behavior descriptions and the stock price synchronicity. However, contrary to H2, the degree of information asymmetry weakens the negative impact of the analyst reports on the stock price synchronicity, and we analyzed the possible reasons. First, when the degree of information asymmetry is large, it is difficult for analysts to identify the corporate innovation behavior. Information asymmetry weakens the role of analyst reports in the interpretation of the corporate innovation behavior information. Second, when the degree of information asymmetry

Table 2. Moderating effects of information asymmetry degree.

Variable	Model 1	Model 2	Model 3
AnaInnov	-0.011^{***}	-0.011^{***}	-0.015^{***}
AnaInnov × *ASY*		0.079^{**}	0.025^{***}
ASY(AbsDA)		-0.144	
ASY(ILL)			0.015
TurnOver	-0.037^{***}	0.077^{**}	-0.037^{***}
size	0.167^{***}	-0.036^{***}	0.169^{***}
lev	0.005	0.167^{***}	0.004
bm	0.450^{***}	0.005	0.446^{***}
inshold	-0.226^{***}	0.457^{***}	-0.231^{***}
roa	-0.360^{*}	-0.223^{***}	-0.383^{*}
crosslist	0.048	-0.275	0.054
Constant	-5.372^{***}	0.050	-5.967^{***}
Observations	3,768	3,768	3,768
R-squared	0.221	0.222	0.223
year FE	YES	YES	YES
industry FE	YES	YES	YES
r2_a	0.215	0.216	0.217
F	42.64	34.77	35.32

Note: *** indicates $p < 0.01$; ** indicates $p < 0.05$; * indicates $p < 0.1$

in the market is greater, the uncertainty faced by investors is higher, and they are unable to rationally judge the corporate innovation behavior information in the analyst report.

5.3 Mediating Effects of Heterogeneous Beliefs of Investors

Next, we considered the mechanism of the influence of the enterprise innovation behavior descriptions in analyst reports on the stock price synchronicity; that is, we tested the intermediary effects of the investors' heterogeneous beliefs. We tested the models established above in turn, and we present the regression results in Table 3. First, we tested Model 4, and the c_1 coefficient was significant. Then, we tested Model 5 and Model 6 in turn, and the model coefficients a_1 and b_1, respectively, were significant. The indirect effect confidence interval of the bootstrap test does not contain 0. The regression coefficient c'_1 of Model 6 was significant.

We verified H3 and H4 with the above empirical analysis results. The corporate innovation behavior descriptions in the analyst reports had a positive impact on the heterogeneous beliefs of investors, and the heterogeneous beliefs of investors mediated the impact of the analyst report corporate innovation behavior descriptions on the stock price synchronicity.

Table 3. Mediating effects of investors' heterogeneous beliefs.

Variable	Model 4	Model 5	Model 6
	SYN	*HB*	*SYN*
AnaInnov	-0.011^{***}	0.008^{**}	-0.010^{***}
HB			-0.108^{***}
size	0.188^{***}	-0.328^{***}	0.153^{***}
lev	0.008^{*}	0.034^{***}	0.011^{**}
bm	0.276^{***}	0.516^{***}	0.331^{***}
inshold	-0.107	0.361^{***}	-0.068
roa	-0.107	0.228	-0.083
crosslist	-0.017	0.181^{***}	0.002
Constant	-6.069^{***}	6.511^{***}	-5.368^{***}
Observations	4,464	4,464	4,464
R-squared	0.251	0.080	0.259
year FE	YES	YES	YES
industry FE	YES	YES	YES
r2_a	0.247	0.0744	0.255
F	44.09	50.78	45.15
Sobel test z value			-1.907
Indirect effect confidence interval (bootstrap)			$[-0.0169, -0.0001]$
Intermediate effect ratio			46.35%

Note: *** indicates $p < 0.01$; ** indicates $p < 0.05$; * indicates $p < 0.1$

5.4 Mediating Effects of Noise Trading

In this section, we examine the mediating effect of noise trading in the same way as we did the investors' heterogeneous beliefs in the previous section. The coefficient (b_2) of Model 9 was not significant. We conducted a Sobel test and bootstrap test, and the indirect effect of the noise trading was not substantial. However, according to the regression results of Model 8 in Table 4, the enterprise innovation information provided by analyst reports can restrain the noise trading and improve the operation efficiency of the capital market. We verified H5; however, we did not verify H6.

To ensure the robustness of the research results, we considered three aspects: (1) potential sample selection bias, (2) different stock price synchronicity measurement methods, and (3) firm fixed effects, and we conducted the robustness tests. The main research hypothesis of this paper is still valid.

Table 4. Mediating effects of noise trading.

Variable	Model 7	Model 8	Model 9
	SYN	NOISE	SYN
AnaInnov	-0.010^{***}	-0.050^{***}	-0.011^{***}
NOISE			-0.015
TurnOver	-0.046^{***}	0.622^{***}	-0.037^{***}
size	0.217^{***}	1.461^{***}	0.238^{***}
lev	0.007	-0.040^{***}	0.006
bm	0.190^{***}	-0.041	0.189^{***}
inshold	-0.194^{***}	-0.899^{***}	-0.207^{***}
roa	-0.303	-2.619^{***}	-0.342
crosslist	-0.013	-0.552^{***}	-0.021
Constant	-6.604^{***}	-0.323	-6.608^{***}
Observations	4,942	4,942	4,942
R-squared	0.292	0.561	0.292
year FE	YES	YES	YES
industry FE	YES	YES	YES
r2_a	0.288	0.559	0.288
F	56.23	695.7	50.29
Sobel test z value			1.578
Indirect effect confidence interval (bootstrap)			[−0.0003, 0.0017]

Note: *** indicates $p < 0.01$; ** indicates $p < 0.05$; * indicates $p < 0.1$

6   Conclusion

Based on the views of information efficiency and noise trading theory, in this study, we analyzed the impact of the corporate innovation behavior descriptions in analyst reports on the stock price synchronicity. According to the results, we drew the following conclusions: (1) the corporate innovation behavior descriptions in analyst reports can restrain the stock price synchronicity; (2) due to the existence of information asymmetry, the signaling mechanism in the stock market is hindered, and the inhibitory effect of the analyst report corporate innovation behavior descriptions on the stock price synchronicity is weakened; (3) investors form heterogeneous beliefs based on the corporate innovation behavior information in analyst reports, which are transmitted to the stock prices through market transactions, which thus reduces the stock price synchronicity; (4) analyst corporate innovation behavior descriptions have a negative correlation with the noise trading level; however, the relationship between the noise trading and stock price synchronicity is not substantial. The conclusion supports the "information efficiency view", and it indicates that securities analysts can effectively mine corporate innovation behavior information. The textual contents of the reports of securities analysts contain incremental information, which can effectively alleviate the stock price synchronicity of enterprises.

Acknowledgement. This work was supported by National Natural Science Foundation of China (71874215, 71571191) and MOE (Ministry of Education in China) Project of Humanities and Social Sciences (15YJCZH081, 17YJAZH120, 19YJCZH253), Fundamental Research Funds for the Central Universities (SKZZY2015021). The funders had no role in study design, data collection and analysis, decision to publish, or preparation of the manuscript.

References

1. Roll, R.: R2. J. Financ. **43**(3), 541–566 (1988)
2. West, K.D.: Dividend innovations and stock price volatility. Econometrica **56**(1), 37–61 (1986)
3. Myers, S.C., Jin, L.: R-squared around the world: new theory and new tests. J. Financ. Econ. **79**(2), 257–292 (2006)
4. Han, P., Yue, Y.Y.: Economic consequences of information disclosure of enterprise innovation. Account. Res. **37**(01), 49–55+95 (2016). (in Chinese)
5. Zhang, Z., Yang, W.C.: Reputation model or information model: how do China securities analysts affect the market. Econ. Res. **51**(09), 104–117 (2016). (in Chinese)
6. Hutton, A.P., Marcus, A.J., Tehranian, H.: Opaque financial reports, r-square, and crash risk. J. Financ. Econ. **94**(1), 67–86 (2009)
7. Kothari, S.P., Laguerre, T.E., Leone, A.J.: Capitalization versus expensing: evidence on the uncertainty of future earnings from capital expenditures versus R&D outlays. Rev. Acc. Stud. **7**(4), 355–382 (2002)
8. Asquith, P., Mikhail, M.B., Au, A.S.: Information content of equity analyst reports. J. Financ. Econ. **75**(2), 245–282 (2005)
9. James, S.D., Shaver, J.M.: Motivations for voluntary public R&D disclosures. Acad. Manag. Discov. **2**(3), 290–312 (2016)
10. Merkley, K.J.: Narrative disclosure and earnings performance: evidence from R&D disclosures. Account. Rev. **89**(2), 725–757 (2013)
11. Lee, D., Liu, M.H.: Does more information in stock price lead to greater or smaller idiosyncratic return volatility. J. Bank. Financ. **35**(6), 1563–1580 (2011)
12. Xue, Y.K., Wang, Z.T.: Research on information disclosure of intangible assets and its value relevance. Account. Res. **22**(11), 40–47 (2001). (in Chinese)
13. Hong, H., Stein, J.C.: Differences of opinion, short-sales constraints, and market crashes. Rev. Financ. Stud. **16**(2), 487–525 (2015)
14. Blei, D.M., Ng, A., Jordan, M.I.: Latent Dirichlet allocation. J. Mach. Learn. Res. **3**(1), 993–1022 (2003)
15. Teh, Y.W., Jordan, M.I., Beal, M.J., Blei, D.M.: Hierarchical Dirichlet processes. J. Am. Stat. Assoc. **101**(476), 1566–1581 (2006)
16. Li, Y.Q., Yao, Y.: R&D narrative disclosure: is talk more really useless. Account. Res. **41**(02), 26–42 (2020). (in Chinese)

Understanding Users' Ask Intention on Paid Q&A Platform from the Perspective of Impression Management

Peiyao Liang[1,2], Mingyue Zhang[1,2(✉)], and Baojun Ma[1,2]

[1] Shanghai Key Laboratory of Brain-Machine Intelligence for Information Behavior, Shanghai 201620, China
zhangmy@shisu.edu.cn
[2] School of Business and Management, Shanghai International Studies University, Shanghai 201620, China

Abstract. With the widespread fusion of social media and knowledge economy, paid Q&A platform has become one of the most prominent ways for people to seek knowledge online. More and more users enroll as answerers to answer questions for gaining extra money, so it is necessary for them to find out ways to attract more askers in this competitive market. When investigating influential factors on the ask intention, most previous research focuses on the objective data displayed on answerers' accounts such as number of followers and price per question, while largely ignores the information that was voluntarily disclosed by answerers. In this regard, we draw from impression management theory to explore the role of answerers' self-image which is built through active information disclosure in this Q&A process. We constructed a cross-sectional dataset with 9,887 answerers on Weibo Q&A platform to test hypotheses. Using zero-inflated negative binomial model, we find that the congruence between answerers' self-image and their provided knowledge has a significant positive impact on knowledge seekers' ask intention. Particularly, the larger the congruence between those actively disclosed text information (i.e., biography) and picture information (i.e., avatar) and provided knowledge, the higher the askers' willingness to ask questions. Managerial implications on paid Q&A platforms are thus provided.

Keywords: Image Congruence · Paid Q&A Platform · Ask Intention · Biography and Avatar · Topic Taxonomy

1 Introduction

Paid Q&A platform is one of the knowledge payment platforms which has become popular in recent years. Since 2016, the scale of users in this platform has shown a trend of rapid growth in China, which is expected to exceed 572 million in 2023 [1]. There are mainly two types of knowledge payment platforms, knowledge-owner oriented and knowledge-asker oriented. The knowledge-owner oriented platform means that knowledge is proactively provided by the knowledge owners such as Zhihu Live, while the knowledge-seeker oriented platform emphasizes on questions raised by knowledge askers such as paid Q&A platforms. We investigate on the latter one because the successful operation of knowledge payment platforms depends on the demands rather than the supply [2] and paid Q&A platforms exactly focus on the knowledge askers demand.

To survive in so many competitors, keeping the asking frequency at a high level to promote a large number of active user base is of great importance [2]. Before raising questions, knowledge seekers usually need to recognize that the specific answerer can provide high-quality knowledge [3]. With the cost-benefit consideration, they are more cautious and care more about the quality of service [4], thus collecting the relevant information of the answerers as much as possible to reduce the information asymmetry [5]. After that, they can select a more suitable answerer to solve their questions. Therefore, whether the answerers have disclosed appropriate information to make them more attractive for certain questions is a prerequisite for being asked. Previous literature has shown that in social media, users disclose personal information to build image and increase credibility [6], which is called impression management where users can take text and picture information as effective ways of showing ideal image.

Previous research about answerers' self-image on paid Q&A platforms is limited to objective data on their accounts such as the number of followers and likes, rather than the information disclosed by the answerers including text and pictures [3, 7]. What's more, few research has considered the attribute of knowledge that askers seek, which is the important factor that affect which kind of answerers will be chosen. Particularly, although some factors that influence the ask intention have been proposed in prior studies [2, 3], there is a lack of research digging into whether there exists any difference in such effects under different types of knowledge sought by askers. On this basis, we aim to fill these two gaps by analyzing the congruence between answerers' disclosed information and their provided knowledge. Such congruence shows the suitability between answerers' self-image and knowledge sought by askers [8]. Thus, we propose:

1. How does the congruence between the attribute of knowledge sought by askers and the answerers' self-image reflected from the text and picture information disclosed by themselves affect the ask intention?
2. For different types of knowledge sought by the askers, will the above congruence affect the ask intention in a different way?

In the following sections, we first reviewed related studies and introduce the theoretical underpinnings of this research, based on which four hypotheses are proposed. Then we describe the cross-sectional dataset from Weibo Q&A and the zero-inflated negative binomial model. The empirical results indicate that the congruence between self-image presented by answerers and the attribute of knowledge sought by askers has a significant influence on the ask intention. For different types of knowledge, the congruence accordingly has different effects. Finally, we conclude the paper.

2 Literature Review

2.1 The Willingness to Ask Questions on Paid Q&A Platform

For paid Q&A platforms, it is important to keep the platform users active by encouraging users to constantly raise questions or provide answers, which is the key to stand out from

Table 1. Factors influencing askers' willingness to ask questions on paid Q&A platforms

Perspective	Reference	Factors/Independent Variables	Theory
Asker	Zhao et al. [2]	Financial benefit, social support, self-enhancement, entertainment (measured by questionnaire)	Social exchange and social capital theory
	Gu and Liu [9]	Performance expectancy, facilitating conditions, trust towards answerer/platform, long tail effect	Unified theory of acceptance and use of technology
Answerer	Zhao et al. [3]	Ability (number of answers, has tagged or not), benevolence (times of free sharing), integrity (has page/link or not), reputation (number of followers/likes)	Trust theory
	Shi et al. [7]	Perceived credibility of free content/content creators, perceived likability of content creators, perceived quantity of participants (measured by questionnaire)	Information foraging theory
	Daradkeh et al. [10]	Information quality of product description (number of words/pictures in each answer) and knowledge producer credibility (number of followers/live sharing/information disclosed)	Information adaption model
Answerer	This study	Congruence between the knowledge sought by askers and the answerers' self-image presented by text and picture information disclosed	Impression management

competitors. Askers' willingness to ask questions is the starting point to maintain a high level of active user base [2], thus studying the factors that affect it is necessary. Table 1 shows the extrinsic factors that have been explored in prior studies.

Given the two research streams (i.e., from the perspective of askers vs. answerers), yet the understanding from the perspective of answerers primarily focuses on objective data about their accounts, few has explored the impact of answerers' self-image on the ask intention. Thus, our study focuses on the information proactively disclosed by the answerers which is crucial to build their self-image. At the same time, we also take into account the types of knowledge that askers are seeking, so that we can link answerers' self-image with the knowledge askers are seeking and explore whether the influence will be different under different types of knowledge.

2.2 Impression Management and Information Disclosed

Impression management refers to people creating or maintaining an ideal image in the minds of others by presenting appropriate information about themselves, which can maintain the congruence between the desired image and the current one and please the audience [11].

On online communities, self-disclosure is a way of impression management. By disclosing personal information, users establish their images in order to manage the desired image in others' minds. Research has shown that some information cues on Weibo platform such as gender, nickname style, and account avatar are quite helpful to predict the users' credibility [6, 12]. However, the existing literature only considers users' image reflected from the disclosed information alone, while largely ignores the congruence between the image of the information discloser and the corresponding context. In this study, we aim to integrate the context on paid Q&A platform when exploring the role of answerers' self-image, that is, the attribute of knowledge sought by askers.

3 Hypothesis Development

3.1 Congruence Based on Text Information

Paid Q&A platform implements topic taxonomy to systematically organize the questions and answers, where answerers need to present a corresponding image to attract askers' attention. For example, the biography is one of the most conspicuous text information on the answerer listing page, reflecting the answerers' self-image [13]. Task-technology fit theory (TTF) suggests that when the information technology matches the tasks that users must finish, it is more likely to have a positive impact on individual performance [14]. Based on TTF, a high congruence between the self-image presented by the answerers' text information and the attribute of knowledge sought by askers will show a good match between answerers and knowledge required [8]. This good match reflects that the answerers are more likely to provide a better answer [8, 14]. Therefore, when askers recognize this high congruence, they would regard the answerer as a good match with the knowledge such that the answerer is capable of providing high-quality and professional answers [14]. Thus, the askers are more prone to choose the specific answer, resulting in a higher willingness to ask questions. Hence, we hypothesize:

H1. Based on text information, the larger the congruence between the knowledge sought by askers and the answerers' self-image which is reflected from biography, the higher the askers' willingness to ask questions.

3.2 Congruence Based on Picture Information

On the basis of workplace attire, we divide the topics into two parts. One is 'outwardly oriented' topic, the other is 'non-outwardly oriented' topic. As a non-verbal form of communication, attire can reflect the corresponding professional image [15]. Therefore, our study defines the following topics as the 'outwardly oriented' topic: medical and health, real estate, law, and finance; The remaining topics are defined as 'non-outwardly oriented' topic including internet, sports, entertainment, etc. Given that for 'outwardly oriented' topic, the judgment of the service provider's professionality will be affected by the workplace attire [16], the answerers' picture information such as avatar will be first visually and quickly analyzed by the askers. According to the TTF, when the self-image reflected from the picture information is more congruent with the attribute of knowledge askers seek, the answerer matches the knowledge more [14]. Then it is more likely that the answerer will be chosen due to the higher possibility to provide a better answer, which results in the higher askers' willingness to ask questions.

However, for the 'non-outwardly oriented' topic, the judgment of the service provider's professionality does not depend on the workplace attire. Therefore, the self-image congruence raised by picture information is not important to the judgment of professionality [16], resulting in little influence on the askers' willingness to ask questions. Instead, if the answerer discloses the picture information with a high congruence on knowledge askers require, the asker will notice this prominent event and then make a judgment of 'non-compliance behavior' [17]. This phenomenon can be explained as a decrease in credibility due to the behavior contrary to practices within the community [17]. Therefore, for the 'non-outwardly oriented' topic, if the congruence between the answerers' self-image and the knowledge required is higher, the answerers' 'non-compliance behavior' will render the askers to doubt their credibility for deliberate persuasion, which reduces the askers' willingness to ask questions. Hence, we hypothesize:

H2a. Based on picture information, for the 'outwardly oriented' topic, the higher the congruence between the knowledge sought by askers and the answerers' self-image reflected from avatar, the higher the askers' willingness to ask questions.

H2b. Based on picture information, for the 'non-outwardly oriented' topic, the higher the congruence between the knowledge sought by askers and the answerers' self-image reflected from avatar, the lower the askers' willingness to ask questions.

3.3 Moderating Roles of Volume of Information and Smile

Strangers who meet for the first time would gather nonverbal cues to know each other to reduce uncertainty on online community [5]. Further, reducing uncertainty can reduce perceived risk, which in turn reduces the number of nonverbal cues that users need [18]. Therefore, for the answerer who discloses less volume of text information, the asker has a higher uncertainty when making the selection decision. The perceived risk increases, so the asker needs more information about the answerer. As a result, the influence of self-image congruence is more significant. Therefore, we hypothesize:

H3. Based on text information, the volume of information has a substitution effect on the influence of the congruence between the knowledge sought by askers and the answerers' self-image on the askers' willingness to ask questions.

As to picture, a smiling face can create familiarity and kindness [19]. As one of the three components of trust, kindness increases trust and thus the likelihood of being chosen [3, 19]. On paid Q&A platforms, picture information including a smile is more reflective about the answerers' kindness, which enhances the credibility of them and increases the askers' willingness to ask questions [3]. Therefore, for 'outwardly oriented' topic, smile can show the kindness of answerer. At this time, the higher the congruence between the answerers' self-image and knowledge sought by askers, the higher the credibility will be due to the kindness. For 'non-outwardly oriented' topic, a smile brings a cordial and friendly image. Then the lower congruence between the knowledge sought by askers and answerers' self-image is, the higher credibility of the answerers will be, so the kindness brought by the smile this time enhances negative relationship of the congruence on ask intention. Therefore, we hypothesis:

H4. Based on picture information, whether there is a smile has a reinforcement effect on the influence of congruence between the knowledge sought by askers and the answerers' self-image on the askers' willingness to ask questions.

4 Research Design

4.1 Data

The dataset is constructed from Weibo Q&A module (see Fig. 1). The *Fiddler* tool is used to obtain the data of 9,896 answerers, including the biography, avatar, number of answers, etc. Subsequently, the image recognition tool Clarifai API[1] is used to further extract the specific content in each avatar. After data cleaning, we select 9,887 answerers to construct a cross-sectional dataset.

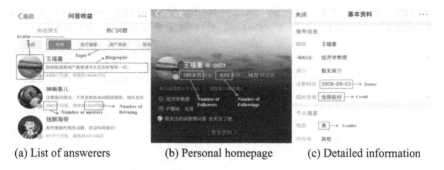

(a) List of answerers   (b) Personal homepage   (c) Detailed information

Fig. 1. Example page of Weibo Q&A

---

[1] https://clarifai.com/clarifai/main/models/general-image-recognition.

4.2 Variables

In terms of dependent variable, instead of the number of questions raised, the number of answers is used to measure askers' ask intention for the unobservable data on Weibo Q&A [20]. As to the independent variables, the knowledge sought by askers is presented by the topic name. We extract the nouns in the biography and get the specific words of content in the avatar using Clarifai API. Then, use Word2vec to vectorize the topic name, the nouns in biography, and the specific words in avatar. Next, based on the vectorization, we calculate the maximum cosine similarity between the nouns in biography and the topic name for congruence based on text information. Also, we calculate the average cosine similarity between the specific words of content read by Clarifai API in avatar and the topic name for congruence based on picture information [10]. In terms of volume of information, text length of biography is used to measure it [20]. To determine if there is a smile, we use Face++[2] to obtain the score of smiling in the avatar. If score is more than 50, then there is a smiling in avatar. The corresponding description of the variables are shown in Table 2.

4.3 Empirical Models

Since the dependent variable is the number of answers, we use a nonlinear model for empirical analysis. By examining the statistical characteristics of dependent variable, we find that the variance is much greater than the mean, showing a significant skewed distribution. As to the numerical distribution of dependent variable, nearly half are zero, so we adopt Zero-Inflation Negative Binomial (ZINB) model specified as follows.

$$Question_{num} = c_1 + \alpha_1 Bio\_similarity + \beta_1 Avatar\_similarity + \gamma_1 \boldsymbol{Controls} \\ + \varepsilon_1 \tag{1}$$

$$Question_{num} = c_2 + \alpha_2 Bio\_similarity + \beta_2 Avatar\_similarity + \alpha_3 Bio\_length \\ + \beta_3 Avatar\_smile + m_1 Bio\_simi\_length \\ + m_2 Avatar\_simi\_smile + \gamma_2 \boldsymbol{Controls} + \varepsilon_2 \tag{2}$$

Model 1 is for H1 and H2. Model 2 is for the H3 and H4. **Controls** is a vector containing nine control variables presented in Table 2. ε_1 and ε_2 are the random error terms.

---

[2] https://www.faceplusplus.com.cn/face-detection/.

Table 2. Definition and measurement of variables

Type	Variable	Definition	Measurement
Dependent Variable	Question_num	Number of being asked	Number of answers
Independent Variable	Bio_similarity	Congruence between biography and topic	Maximum cosine similarity between nouns in biography and topic name using Word2vec
	Avatar_similarity	Congruence between avatar and topic	Average cosine similarity between words extracted from avatar and topic name using Word2vec
Moderating Variable	Bio_length	Length of biography	Number of characters in biography
	Avatar_smile	Smile or not	Score of smiling in avatar by Face++ 1 if > 50; 0 otherwise
Control Variable	Listen_num	Number of listening	Number of times the answers were viewed
	Avatar_color	Attributes of avatars in color	Average value of hue, saturation, brightness, contrast, clarity, and colorfulness of avatars
	Face	Face or not	Face in avatar by Face++. 1 if there is. 0 if not
	Credit	Credit level	1 for 'excellent credit'; 0 for 'common credit'
	Askprice	Price for asking	Price for asking
	Tenure	Duration since accounts created	In the measure of years
	Gender	Gender	1 for male and 0 for female
	Followernum	Number of followers	Number of followers
	Followingnum	Number of followings	Number of followings

5 Analysis and Results

We test the four hypotheses using above two ZINB models with Stata 15. The results of the ZINB regression analysis are shown in Table 3.

Model 1 shows that for all answerers, the coefficient of the similarity between the nouns in biography and the topic name is 1.183 ($p < 0.01$), which is significantly positive, so hypothesis 1 is supported. As to the avatar, for both the 'outwardly oriented' topic

Table 3. Regression Results

Question_num	(1) Model 1 (all)	(2) Model 1 (outwardly)	(3) Model 1 (non-outwardly)	(4) Model 2 (all)	(5) Model 2 (outwardly)	(6) Model 2 (non-outwardly)
Bio_similarity	1.183***	1.006***	0.740***	0.582***	0.215	0.394**
	(0.106)	(0.241)	(0.108)	(0.145)	(0.309)	(0.133)
Bio_length				0.0453***	0.0513***	0.0311***
				(0.00730)	(0.0145)	(0.00671)
Bio_simi_length				-0.0514**	-0.0944*	-0.0308
				(0.0174)	(0.0429)	(0.0172)
Avatar_similarity	-2.718***	8.107**	-2.680***	-2.390***	7.503**	-2.358***
	(0.546)	(2.773)	(0.543)	(0.571)	(2.437)	(0.550)
Avatar_smile				-0.0635	-0.357	0.170
				(0.124)	(0.214)	(0.117)
Avatar_simi_smile				-0.419	13.24*	-2.596*
				(1.273)	(6.448)	(1.241)
Listen_num	0.0000847***	0.0000329**	0.0000626***	0.0000827***	0.0000326**	0.0000610***
	(0.0000182)	(0.0000126)	(0.0000163)	(0.0000179)	(0.0000121)	(0.0000160)
Avatar_color	0.0191	-0.289	0.243	0.0461	-0.312	0.178
	(0.342)	(0.609)	(0.411)	(0.330)	(0.574)	(0.387)
Face	0.451***	0.352*	0.140	0.443***	0.467*	0.0693
	(0.0755)	(0.146)	(0.0797)	(0.105)	(0.181)	(0.0846)

(continued)

Table 3. (*continued*)

Question_num	(1) Model 1 (all)	(2) Model 1 (outwardly)	(3) Model 1 (non-outwardly)	(4) Model 2 (all)	(5) Model 2 (outwardly)	(6) Model 2 (non-outwardly)
Credit	1.062***	1.825***	0.483***	1.034***	1.835***	0.444***
	(0.106)	(0.234)	(0.122)	(0.112)	(0.203)	(0.133)
Askprice	0.0000568	0.0000737	0.0000526	0.0000568	0.0000472	0.0000706
	(0.0000442)	(0.0000548)	(0.0000685)	(0.0000441)	(0.0000433)	(0.0000696)
Tenure	0.0315	0.0925**	0.0158	0.0349*	0.0995**	0.0126
	(0.0175)	(0.0334)	(0.0197)	(0.0173)	(0.0320)	(0.0195)
Gender	0.345***	0.00681	0.265**	0.308**	−0.0999	0.260**
	(0.0919)	(0.225)	(0.0823)	(0.104)	(0.246)	(0.0828)
Followernum	5.76e−08**	0.000000509***	3.06e−08*	6.13e−08**	0.000000514***	3.03e−08*
	(2.00e−08)	(0.000000109)	(1.46e−08)	(2.06e−08)	(0.000000111)	(1.40e−08)
Followingnum	0.0000528	−0.0000288	0.000130*	0.0000404	−0.0000371	0.000103*
	(0.0000325)	(0.0000246)	(0.0000590)	(0.0000322)	(0.0000233)	(0.0000473)
_cons	0.338	−4.845***	1.629***	−0.0719	−4.820***	1.379***
	(0.375)	(1.353)	(0.408)	(0.399)	(1.228)	(0.413)
inflate						
Listen_num	0.000000596*	−0.000000254	−19.47***	0.0000117**	−0.00000535***	−19.83***
	(0.000000241)	(0.000000323)	(0.0763)	(0.0000045)	(0.00000137)	(0.0763)
_cons	−19.30***	−29.77***	1.452***	−41.63***	−28.88***	1.448***
	(0.0443)	(0.0786)	(0.0518)	(9.115)	(0.0851)	(0.0519)
N	9887	2429	7458	9887	2429	7458

Standard errors in parentheses

* $p < 0.05$, ** $p < 0.01$, *** $p < 0.001$.

and the 'non-outwardly oriented' topic, the coefficients of the independent variables are significant respectively (8.107, $p < 0.05$; -2.68, $p < 0.01$), which means the self-image congruence reflected from avatar has different effects on the ask intention when the knowledge sought by askers is different, so hypothesis 2a and 2b are supported.

From Model 2, for all answerers, as to the moderating effect of information volume, the coefficient of the interaction term is -0.0514 ($p < 0.05$), which is significantly negative. Since the coefficient of the moderating variable is significantly positive (0.0453, $p < 0.01$), the volume of information has a substitute effect on the influence of the congruence on the ask intention, so hypothesis 3 is supported. As to the smile in avatar, the coefficient of interaction term is significantly positive (13.24, $p < 0.1$) under 'outwardly oriented' topic while it is significantly negative (-2.596, $p < 0.1$) under 'non-outwardly oriented' topic. Given that the main effects under these two topics are different, positive under 'outwardly oriented' topic and negative under the other one, the smile in avatar has a reinforcement effect on the influence of congruence on the ask intention. Therefore, hypothesis 4 is supported.

6 Discussions

6.1 Conclusion

This study mainly discusses the influence of the answerers' image on askers' willingness to ask questions on paid Q&A platforms from two dimensions, that is, biography and avatar. There are three main conclusions. First, the congruence between the biography and the topic has a positive impact on the askers' willingness to ask questions, with the length of the biography having a substitution effect on it. Second, the congruence between the avatar and the topic has a significant impact on the askers' willingness to ask questions for both 'outwardly oriented' topic and 'non-outwardly oriented' topic. Third, if the avatar contains a smile, it will strengthen the influence of the congruence between the avatar and the topic on the askers' willingness to ask questions.

6.2 Implications

For theoretical contributions, first, we extend impression management from traditional social media context to paid Q&A platforms [6], focusing on the individual information disclosed by answerers on the paid Q&A platform. Second, previous literature mainly applied image congruence to marketing and explore the congruence between consumer image and brand image. We further extend it to knowledge payment platforms, linking user image with the context and exploring the influence of answerer image congruence on askers' willingness to ask questions. We also find that the self-image congruence effects vary on the type of knowledge. Finally, the positive effect of self-image congruence on performance found in previous research does not always exist. When the self-image congruence is deliberately emphasized by the answerers, it will lead to a decrease in credibility due to 'non-compliant behavior'. For the practical implications, it provides guidance to answerers on how to effectively disclose information to attract attention. Also, a recommendation mechanism can be established based on answerers' disclosed information so that the traffic of those who can attract askers can be increased, thereby increasing the probability of being asked and improving the user activity.

6.3 Limitations and Future Research

First, our study is based on the Weibo Q&A. Future research can replicate our models in other paid Q&A platforms like Zhihu.com and test the generalizability of our findings. Second, Word2vec method is used to measure the two main independent variables. This method belongs to machine learning which is based on statistical reasoning, so the accuracy of the similarity calculated is limited by the preconditions. Future research can enhance the preconditions to improve the accuracy of the calculation. Third, we only study the influencing factors of ask intention from the perspective of answerers, not the askers. Further research can be conducted from the perspective of the askers through other research methods, such as experiments and questionnaires.

Acknowledgement. This work was supported by the National Natural Science Foundation of China [grant number 72272101, 71802024, 72172092, 71772017], the Innovative Research Team of Shanghai International Studies University [grant number 2020114044] and the Fundamental Research Funds for the Central Universities [grant number 2019114032].

References

1. Report on knowledge payment industry in China. https://www.iimedia.cn/c400/85595.html. Accessed 10 Jan 2023
2. Zhao, Y., Peng, X., Liu, Z., Song, S., Hansen, P.: Factors that affect asker's pay intention in trilateral payment-based social Q&A platforms: from a benefit and cost perspective. J. Assoc. Inf. Sci. Technol. **71**, 516–528 (2020)
3. Zhao, Y., Zhao, Y., Yuan, X., Zhou, R.: How knowledge contributor characteristics and reputation affect user payment decision in paid Q&A? An empirical analysis from the perspective of trust theory. Electron. Commer. Res. Appl. **31**, 1–11 (2018)
4. Gao, K., Yang, Y., Qu, X.: Diverging effects of subjective prospect values of uncertain time and money. Commun. Transp. Res. **1**, 100007 (2021)
5. Berger, C.R., Calabrese, R.J.: Some explorations in initial interaction and beyond: toward a developmental theory of interpersonal communication. Hum. Commun. Res. **1**, 99–112 (1975)
6. Bovey, J.: Tweeting is believing? Understanding microblog credibility perceptions. Nurs. Stand. **19**, 30–31 (2005)
7. Shi, X., Zheng, X., Yang, F.: Exploring payment behavior for live courses in social Q&A communities: an information foraging perspective. Inf. Process. Manag. **57**, 102241 (2020)
8. Wang, X., Wong, Y.D., Chen, T., Yuen, K.F.: Adoption of shopper-facing technologies under social distancing: a conceptualisation and an interplay between task-technology fit and technology trust. Comput. Hum. Behav. **124**, 106900 (2021)
9. Gu, J., Liu, L.: Investigating the determinants of users' willingness to pay for answers on Q&A platforms. In: Communications in Computer and Information Science, pp. 13–20 (2019)
10. Daradkeh, M., Gawanmeh, A., Mansoor, W.: Information adoption patterns and online knowledge payment behavior: the moderating role of product type. Information **13**, 1–23 (2022)
11. Baumeister, R.F.: The Self in Social Psychology. Psychology Press (1999)
12. Yang, X., Hu, D., Robert, D.M.: How microblogging networks affect project success of open source software development. In: Proceedings of the Annual Hawaii International Conference on System Sciences, pp. 3178–3186 (2013)

13. Huurne, M., Moons, J., Ronteltap, A., Corten, R.: How linguistic features of seller profiles in the sharing economy predict trustworthiness. Open Sci. Framework Prepr., 1–44 (2017)
14. Goodhue, D.L., Thompson, R.L.: Task-technology fit and individual performance. MIS Q. **19**, 213–236 (2014)
15. Furnham, A., Chan, P.S., Wilson, E.: What to wear? The influence of attire on the perceived professionalism of dentists and lawyers. J. Appl. Soc. Psychol. **43**, 1838–1850 (2013)
16. Sampson, E.: Dressing for success. Women Manag. Rev. **5**, 20 (1990)
17. Jiang, Y., Ho, Y.-C., Yan, X., Tan, Y.: What's in a "Username"? The effect of perceived anonymity on herding in crowdfunding. Inf. Syst. Res. **33**, 1–17 (2022)
18. Tan, X., Wang, Y., Tan, Y.: Impact of live chat on purchase in electronic markets: the moderating role of information cues. Inf. Syst. Res. **30**, 1248–1271 (2019)
19. Peng, L., Cui, G., Chung, Y., Zheng, W.: The faces of success: beauty and ugliness premiums in e-commerce platforms. J. Mark. **84**, 67–85 (2020)
20. Chen, W., Cheng, Y., Li, J.: A causal configuration analysis of payment decision drivers in paid Q&A. J. Data Inf. Sci. **6**, 139–162 (2021)

How Do We Trust AI Service? Exploring the Trust Mechanism in AI Service

Ao Chen and Jinlin Wan[✉]

School of Information, Central University of Finance and Economics, Beijing 100098, China
jinlinwan@cufe.edu.cn

Abstract. AI services have been widely used by consumers, and trust is a key factor impact them to continuously use AI services. However, due to the intelligent feature, trust in AI service is different from other trust. So, we explore how do users trust AI services and willingly continue to use them. In this paper, we have two studies: in Study 1, we encode user comments of AI service products according to grounded theory, and identify the multilevel dimensions of AI service trust antecedent (AISTA); in Study 2, we use empirical data collected through a survey to develop and test an AI service trust mechanism model based on Study 1. The results indicate that anthropomorphism, perceived intelligence-interactivity, service adaptation and coolness influence affect-based and cognition-based trust to different degrees, thus promoting the continuous use behavior of AI services. This paper extends the research scope of trust literature and contributes to the practice of AI product design.

Keywords: Trust · AI service · Grounded theory

1 Introduction

With the sustained development of artificial intelligence (AI) technology, AI service have been integrated various industries such as tourism, medical and home [1]. And it is more and more common in daily life [1, 2], including smart speaker, intelligent voice assistant and other products. According to the "Global Semi-annual Artificial Intelligence Tracking Report" by IDC, the business scale of the global AI service market in 2021 reached $24 billion, with a year-on-year growth of 22.4% compared to 2020. The use of AI to carry out service innovation has become prevailing trend. In a user survey on smart speaker conducted by Strategy Analytics, a market research agency, nearly 60% of users believed that they trusted smart speaker and became dependent on them. Hence, Trust is a key factor influence continued use of AI services. Previous studies have extensively discussed platform trust and interpersonal trust, and it has been proved that service quality, consumer attitude and external environment can affect user trust [3]. However, the process of trust formation in AI services is different. On the one hand, AI service products can timely update the service form according to the specific demand of users, and possess the characteristics of intelligent interaction and anthropomorphism [4]. On the other hand, during the interaction, people may develop the affective empathy towards the AI service. Therefore, trust in AI services is not the same as trust between humans and machines, or interpersonal trust. To extend the theoretical perspective of trust in AI services, the research question of this study is: what the factors influence user trust in AI services?

This research is divided into two studies. In Study 1, we undertake an in-depth study of the AI service trust antecedent (AISTA). Considering these antecedents may have difference influence on AI service trust and then impact users' continuous use, we combine two different types of trust to build an AI service trust mechanism model to examine it in Study 2.

2 Theoretical Background

2.1 AI Service

AI service is defined as providing users with personalized and agile service based on AI technology through deep mining of massive data and business intelligence analysis. Compared with the traditional service, the AI service has the advantage of dynamically adapting to the environment and can better fit the demands of consumers. AI services gradually become the focus of human-computer interaction research, especially its technical characteristics. Several studies suggests that the intelligent interaction of AI services can be regarded as a process of constant interaction and adaptation between human intelligence and machine intelligence [4]. However, there are few researches related trust in the field of AI service, so it is very necessary to investigate trust in the context of AI.

2.2 Trust Mechanism

Trust means that the truster believes and is willing to rely on the trustee, even under certain risk conditions, which is a kind of psychological state, including the trust belief and the trust intention [5].

Trust mechanism explains how trust is formed. The previous studies mainly investigate the trust mechanism in two streams. One stream is to study the platform trust generated by users using e-commerce or online services. The researchers find the degree of customer trust on the platform depends on whether the institutional guarantee of the platform is effective [6]. Moreover, social support, customer review quality may positively influence trust in e-commerce. Another is to study the interpersonal trust in social relationship. In this context, the trust mechanism between strangers usually goes through the transition from initial trust to mature trust, which is dynamic [7]. A study on online social networks points out that the more similar users are, the more frequently they interact with each other, and certain social emotion may be generated, thus deepening interpersonal trust [8].

Trust in AI services seems to be conceptually different from previous trust and is likely to capture a broader scope. Due to the features of intelligence and dynamic adaptation, user trust antecedents are more complex. For example, some studies suggest that although users may not be willing to trust the algorithm behind chatbot, when chatbot deals with creative tasks, people may perceive stronger task solving ability, resulting in a higher degree of trust [4]. Another study focuses on the dual humanness perception in conversational AI products, and emphasizes the human-like nature of AI products, including speaking like a person and listening like a person, both of which can affect user trust [9]. In addition, user perceived communication quality of AI service agents are also important in shaping users initial trust.

However, two challenges inhibit the adoption of existing studies to explain trust in the context of AI service. First, different from the traditional service, the AI service has the attributes of intelligent interaction and technical integration, such as intelligent speakers with more interactive algorithms. The platform trust and interpersonal trust cannot fully reflect the features of human-computer interaction. Second, people may also form emotions towards human-like AI devices, and how such affective attributes affect the formation of trust is a topic worth investigating. To address this gap, we apply the grounded theory to explore the multilevel dimensions of AISTA, which can promote the theoretical development of the trust mechanism.

3 Study 1: Exploring the Multilevel Dimensions of AISTA

Study 1 adopts the grounded theory method, which is suitable for discovering rules from phenomena and sorting out data. In this part, we formulate the coding scheme, which include the concepts that may be related to the trust antecedents and the characteristics of AI services. Then, we encode the user comments of AI service products in three layers, refining multilevel dimensions of AISTA.

3.1 Data Collection and Preprocessing

To study the trust antecedents in the context of AI service from a comprehensive perspective, we compiled web crawler programs based on pycharm 2021 to mine user comments of AI service products on seven well-known shopping and information sharing platforms (such as Weibo and Jingdong). In particular, web crawler programs used AI service experience as a keyword in order to more accurately crawl relevant content. There are differences between various products and brands, which can have potentially vital information. Therefore, these user comments come from different AI products, including sweeping robot, intelligent voice assistant, smart speaker and so on. For the same category of products, there are also different brands, such as smart speaker brands including XiaoaiClassmate, TmallGenie and DuSmart. The data collection lasted from November 2021 to October 2022. Then, the repeated comments of the same user were deleted and only one comment was retained, while the comments unrelated to the research topic were removed. We finally obtained 427 pages of textual data with a total of 14,688 real user comments.

3.2 The Results of Text-Coding

We import the obtained text data into Nvivo11, and then follow the paradigm of grounded theory for open coding, axial coding and selective coding. The AISTA framework consisting of four second-order constructs (selective codes) and ten first-order constructs (axial codes) is established (Table 1).

Anthropomorphism. Many users claim that they experience the characteristics of anthropomorphism from AI devices when interacting with them. Anthropomorphism is a key construct for understanding people's trust to AI products. Most users express a positive attitude towards that AI products provide services like people. We also find that conversational AI gives users a warm feeling, and this anthropomorphic empathy increases the sense of intimacy in service delivery [10]. During human-computer interaction, people can easily apply the social scripts and trust expectations of human-human interaction. Thus, they tend to find the robot friendlier and the interaction easier. For example, smart speakers have their own anthropomorphic social cues, such as voices and names. In addition, users believe that chatbots form anthropomorphic personality style and have their own temper in the process of responding to users, which may contribute to effective communication in various aspects.

Perceived Intelligence-Interactiviy. AI services with intelligence-interactiviy allow users to avail information and help make their choices. The text data implies that users perceive the intelligence-interactiviy of AI products in engagement and timeliness, which may impact them to trust AI services [11]. Compared with traditional services, customers can easily enjoy more high-quality services in AI interaction. Furthermore, some customized functions even exceed user expectations, such as dialect recognition. Existing evidence shows that if consumers perceive a high level of innovation performance of AI devices, they are likely to develop emotional connection and trust, even rely on the AI service. One of the aspects the users satisfy with AI chatbots most is quick responsiveness. Anytime customers make requests to AI chatbots, they receive feedback immediately. On the other hand, The expectancy fit is also a factor in evaluating AISTA, due to the fast learning ability of AI service products, they can exceed the expectations of users and provide great experience.

Service Adaptation. Customers with different technology capabilities may still need different levels of assistance to adapt to the AI service. Our results indicate that service adaptation is a significant part of AISTA. This antecedent suggests aspects of the institutional environment designed in a way to minimize barriers for consumers to use AI services. First, whether the service are easy to adapt determines how receptive customers are to the use of AI devices in service encounters, such as the threshold of configuration process. Therefore, if users believe that using products will require too much effort, negative emotions will be generated [1]. Second, researchers also argue that facilitating service-use conditions tends to influence users' technology trust due to the effect of improving the sense of security [12]. Thus, in order to maintain the stable customer relationship, it is necessary for AI service enterprises to provide instruction books and customer service guidance.

Coolness. Our text study suggests that AI products offer some quite novel functions and fascinating appearance that appeal to lots of consumers, which inspired us to generalize the concept of coolness. Coolness is considered a user-based positive perception of advanced products. Further, we believe that the new function novelty and attractive appearance of AI service products, which contribute to the coolness, may influence user trust and subsequent behavior [13]. For example, while the regular speaker is just a tool for audio output, the smart speaker can also be used as a controller for IoT products in family in addition to playing music. On the other hand, consumers usually form their impressions about a AI device quickly by assessing its physical attractiveness such as lovely color and comfortable shape. Users prefer products that can be well integrated into the home environment style, as they perceive them to be more able to accomplish tasks assigned and elicit affective interactions.

Table 1. The definitions of constructs from the grounded theory

Selective and axial codes	Definition
A. Anthropomorphism	AI service products have a wide range of human-like characteristics in physical appearance, mental state or behaviors
A1. Anthropomorphic social cue	Users can perceive AI service products' anthropomorphic social cue, such as name, voice, logicality
A2. Anthropomorphic personality	AI service products have their own personality and temper when responding
A3. Anthropomorphic empathy	Users can perceive AI service products' emotional cognition ability and intimacy when interacting
B. Perceived intelligence-interactiviy	AI service products can meet users' interaction needs in intelligent, timely and personalized way
B1. Perceived innovation performance	Users can perceive better, richer and more innovative AI services
B2. Quick responsiveness	Users can get a timely response from AI service products at any time
B3. Expectancy fit	The high level of fitness between users' expectancy and AI service product' performance
C. Service adaptation	The process of users adapting to AI services is friendly
C1. Easy to adapt	Users can easily learn how to adapt to using AI services
C2. Facilitating service-use condition	The availability of assistance that helps users effectively use and interact with AI service products
D. Coolness	AI service products have the characteristics of novelty, attraction and speciality
D1. New function novelty	Users are interested in the novel functions of AI service products when interacting with them
D2. Attractive appearance	The attractiveness of AI service products towards users in terms of appearance

4   Study 2: Building the AI Service Trust Mechanism Model

To examine trust in AI service, we integrate previous framework with continuous use intention using affect-cognition-behavior framework [14]. Following the discussion of AISTA above, all constructs are defined in Study 1, Table 1.

4.1   Research Hypotheses

Trust and the Continuous Use of AI Services. Continuous use of the service is a behavior of user trust in the service provider. In the context of AI services, expressing a general trust intention to depend on AI services means that users are already willing to engage in a positive relationship with AI devices [5]. On the one hand, affect-based trust denotes the belief that the empathy generated by users in the interaction process of AI services. AI service products with anthropomorphism and coolness will inspire users' warm and friendly emotional attachment such as intimacy which promotes the continuous use of the AI service [10]. Hence, we hypothesize the following:

H1: Affect-based trust is positively related to the intention of continuous use towards AI services.

In terms of cognition, cognition-based trust refers to user assessments of the matching degree of AI service products' needs from the perspective of benefits and costs. Cognition-based trust can significantly reduce consumer attitude towards the uncertainty of the AI service, and they believe that it can help them complete tasks efficiently, thus increasing their intentions to use AI services [4]. Hence, we hypothesize the following:

H2: Cognition-based trust is positively related to the intention of continuous use towards AI services.

Anthropomorphism and Trust. Anthropomorphism is defined as the attribution of human-like characteristics, behaviours or mental states to non-human entities [10]. The anthropomorphic cues of chatbots affects perceived social presence, which promotes user trust and behaviors. For example, when the AI service product has moderate humanoid characteristics such as human-like voice and the ability to understand human language, users may demonstrate high degree of cognition-based trust [9]. Moreover, if the intelligent assistants have its own personality, it will activate the users' social attraction, which in turn reinforce cognitive or affective trust in these AI devices. On the other hand, it logically follows that similar to the empathetic employee who can get great service performance, the existence of empathy in the relation between AI service products and consumers can increase acceptance and trust towards these. Hence, we hypothesize the following:

H3–H5: Anthropomorphic social cue, anthropomorphic personality, anthropomorphic empathy are positively related to affect-based trust (H3a–H5a) and cognition-based trust (H3b–H5b).

Perceived Intelligence-Interactivity and Trust. Perceived intelligence-interactiviy is defined as the intelligent extent to which a person thinks that a particular technology reacts to a person's request or behavior. When people evaluate a product, they typically make judgment based on function. Relative to common devices, AI products offer more efficient and innovative performance based on the powerful Q&A database and self-learning system. Therefore, users perceive innovation performance in AI products, which may lead to emotional attachment to the technology [11], thus maintaining the high level of trust. Previous studies have shown that chatbots can fit customers' needs in time through their quick response capabilities [2]. That is, when customers accept high service quality, they perceive that AI service surpass expectancies, enhancing their trust and credibility in AI services. Hence, we hypothesize the following:

H6–H8: Perceived innovation performance, quick responsiveness, expectancy fit are positively related to affect-based trust (H6a–H8a) and cognition-based trust (H6b–H8b).

Service Adaptation and Trust. Service adaptation means that users can easily adapt to the service, and the effort required in the process is acceptable. Previous studies have revealed that as long as users believe the AI service robot is easy to use, they may perceive the robot as minimizing their costs such as time and attention, thereby increasing their trust towards AI techniques. In addition, facilitating service-use conditions make users feel familiarity to services. The familiarity leads users to believe that the AI services is positive and well ordered [15]. Therefore, we argue that continuous positive attitudes can form an affect-based trust about the reliability of the service-use conditions. Hence, we hypothesize the following:

H9–H10: Easy to adapt, facilitating service-use condition are positively related to affect-based trust (H9a–H10a) and cognition-based trust (H9b–H10b).

Coolness and Trust. Coolness refers to the extent to which a new product is novel, appealing, fascinating and attractive [13]. Coolness is thought to be important in determining the success of the AI service products, translating into the users' intention to use service. For instance, Users are not only curious about the new function novelty of AI products, but also have active affective reactions to attractive appearance, including positive surprise [13]. A study has suggested that users can be drawn to unique technology products, showing that the feelings of enjoyment, identity, and differentness can be attained via the possession and purchase of cool devices. Therefore, AI service products based on novel functions and appearance are likely to lead users to form positive cognitions heuristically, thus quickly building initial trust. Hence, we hypothesize the following:

H11–H12: New function novelty, attractive appearance are positively related to affect-based trust (H11a–H12a) and cognition-based trust (H11b–H12b).

4.2 Methodology

Smart speakers are currently the most representative products of AI services and have become indispensable for many users' lives. Users can use smart speakers to experience a variety of AI services, including IoT, anthropomorphism interaction and online shopping. Therefore, we selected smart speaker users for our online survey.

Questionnaire Design. We mainly adapted measures for the constructs used in this study from those appearing in previous studies. We adapted the measurement scales of anthropomorphic social cue, anthropomorphic personality, anthropomorphic empathy and quick responsiveness from Chen et al. [2]. Perceived innovation performance, expectancy fit, easy to adapt and facilitating service-use condition were drawn from organizational and IS literature [1, 10, 12]. We adapted the items for new function novelty from Im et al. [13], those for affect-based trust and cognition-based trust from Wang et al. [14], and those for intention to continuously use AI services from McKnight et al. [15]. All responses were given on a seven-point Likert scale. A few reverse questions were designed to delete inattentive responses. The demographic information part asked questions related to gender, age, brand and so on.

Data Collection. We collected the data for this study from smart speaker users. Most users come from XiaoaiClassmate and TmallGenie, which are the top two brands in the market. We also designed simple questions in the questionnaire to choose people who have actually used the smart speaker. After receiving the responses, we checked the data for invalid responses (such as those for which all questions had the same answer, those with the same IP address and those completed in less than 5 min). We had 403 valid responses out of 441 completed surveys. The demographic of respondents shows that 55.8% were male and 44.2% were female. More than 50% respondents used smart speakers frequently, and the average age was below 30 years.

Data Analysis and Results. We used the principal components analysis to test the convergent and discriminant validities of the constructs. The KMO statistic for our sample was 0.961, indicating that the data were appropriate for factor analysis. We eliminated an item that cannot meet the factor loading requirement. At last, all indicators loaded on the expected factors, and all the factor loadings were above 0.7.

Measurement Model. The data were further analyzed using structural equation modeling by two stage, as recommended by literature. We used SmartPLS 3.3.9 to conduct the measurement model testing. First, we examined the measurement model for reliability and validity. The Cronbach's α values were greater than 0.7, and the composite reliability (CR) values were greater than 0.8, exhibiting good reliability (Table 2). The average variance extracted (AVE) values were all above 0.5, thus confirming good convergent validity. The square roots for the AVEs of all constructs were larger than their correlations with other constructs, which indicating the discriminant validity was acceptable (Table 3).

Hypothesis Testing. We tested the hypotheses using SmartPLS 3.3.9. The results suggested that the results of path coefficients support most of the assumptions, indicating that model was effective (Fig. 1). However, we found that anthropomorphic personality and easy to adapt had no influence on trust, so the hypothesis H4a, H4b, H9a and H9b were rejected. In addition, Expectancy fit had no significant relationship with cognition-based trust (H8b), and facilitating service-use condition had no significant relationship with affect-based trust (H10a). The explained variance for the dependent constructs was adequate (affect-based trust, 58.3%; cognition-based trust, 56.8% and intention of continuous use towards AI services, 32.7%).

Note: ns non-significant, *p < 0.05, **p < 0.01, ***p < 0.001.

Table 2. The results of the measurement model.

Construct	Item	Loading	Cronbach's α	CR	AVE
Anthropomorphic social cue	ASC1	0.915	0.889	0.931	0.819
	ASC2	0.909			
	ASC3	0.891			
Anthropomorphic personality	AP1	0.900	0.877	0.924	0.803
	AP2	0.897			
	AP3	0.890			
Anthropomorphic empathy	AE1	0.915	0.948	0.962	0.864
	AE2	0.961			
	AE3	0.916			
	AE4	0.926			
Perceived innovation performance	PIP1	0.938	0.930	0.956	0.878
	PIP2	0.940			
	PIP3	0.932			
Quick responsiveness	QR1	0.914	0.906	0.941	0.842
	QR2	0.919			
	QR3	0.920			
Expectancy fit	EF1	0.941	0.944	0.964	0.900
	EF2	0.964			
	EF3	0.941			
Easy to adapt	ETA1	0.907	0.880	0.926	0.807
	ETA2	0.894			
	ETA3	0.893			
Facilitating service-use condition	FSC1	0.935	0.935	0.959	0.886
	FSC2	0.934			
	FSC3	0.954			
New function novelty	NFN1	0.931	0.917	0.947	0.857
	NFN2	0.928			
	NFN3	0.919			
Attractive appearance	AA1	0.922	0.947	0.962	0.863
	AA2	0.933			
	AA3	0.953			

(*continued*)

Table 2. (*continued*)

Construct	Item	Loading	Cronbach's α	CR	AVE
	AA4	0.908			
Affect-based trust	AT1	0.861	0.841	0.904	0.759
	AT2	0.877			
	AT3	0.875			
Cognition-based trust	CT1	0.881	0.852	0.910	0.772
	CT2	0.875			
	CT3	0.879			
Intention of continuous use	ICU1	0.952	0.925	0.952	0.869
	ICU2	0.923			
	ICU3	0.921			

Table 3. The square roots of the AVEs and correlations between constructs.

	ASC	AP	AE	PIP	QR	EF	ETA	FSC	NFN	AA	AT	CT	ICU
ASC	0.90												
AP	0.44	0.90											
AE	0.50	0.44	0.93										
PIP	0.52	0.48	0.57	0.94									
QR	0.56	0.44	0.61	0.57	0.92								
EF	0.57	0.50	0.66	0.62	0.62	0.95							
ETA	0.52	0.41	0.58	0.55	0.52	0.63	0.90						
FSC	0.57	0.49	0.64	0.62	0.62	0.72	0.57	0.94					
NFN	0.48	0.36	0.56	0.56	0.51	0.56	0.51	0.53	0.93				
AA	0.52	0.50	0.65	0.62	0.61	0.66	0.60	0.66	0.55	0.93			
AT	0.55	0.43	0.62	0.61	0.61	0.65	0.55	0.60	0.58	0.65	0.87		
CT	0.55	0.45	0.62	0.60	0.59	0.61	0.52	0.64	0.57	0.62	0.40	0.88	
ICU	0.46	0.41	0.51	0.52	0.42	0.53	0.46	0.49	0.51	0.51	0.50	0.46	0.93

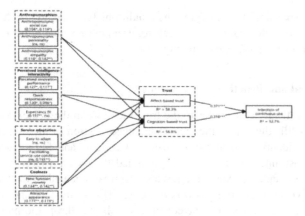

Fig. 1. The results of hypothesis testing.

5 Discussion

5.1 Discussion of Results

This paper investigates the AISTA based on grounded theory and empirically develops the trust mechanism in AI services. It is found that, for different trust antecedents, cognition-based trust and affect-based trust produce varying degrees of influence on the users' intention to use AI services. A few interesting findings appeared within our studies. First, we conclude that applying the grounded theory generates a better understanding of trust in the context of the AI service. Second, the four types of trust antecedents extracted play different roles in trust. AI service products show more coolness and perceived intelligence-interactivity, resulting in a higher sense of trust, while anthropomorphism contributes less to user trust. Third, under the framework of trust mechanism, we prove that affect-based trust and cognition-based trust have positive effects on the intention to continuously use AI services. In other words, the process of trust in AI services is different from that in traditional IS, and user willingness to use AI products may be more complicated.

The empirical results do not support a few hypothesis. On the one hand, anthropomorphic personality and easy to adapt are not related to trust. Recent study noted that AI service products can provide objective and correct functions, which are unlikely to contain personal emotions or prejudice like humans for different users. Whether it is an AI service product or not, the product being offered to the consumer is probably inherently easy to use. Therefore, it is difficult to determine the impact of these two antecedents on user trust. On the other hand, the relationship between expectancy fit and cognition-based trust is nonsignificant. When the AI service highly fit the needs of consumers, emotional attachment will be generated [11]. Trust largely depends on this social emotion, while the benefit emphasized by cognition-based trust has been ignored. In addition, the relationship between facilitating service-use condition and affect-based trust is also not significant. One reasonable explanation for this finding is that AI service providers are responsible for satisfying the conditions for users to use the service normally, such as after-sales guidance. Therefore, users believe this to be a basic service, which does not form an affective empathy.

5.2 Theoretical and Practical Implications

This study theoretically contributes to the trust literature in the context of AI services. First, this study fills the gap in the lack of the classification of the multilevel AISTA. Specifically, we identify ten first-order trust antecedents and further generalize four second-order trust antecedents by using grounded theory on a large number of user comment data. Second, we extend the research on trust mechanism to examine trust in the context of AI services from a new perspective. This study combines the characteristics of AI services to capture unique constructs such as anthropomorphism, perceived intelligence-interactivity and coolness. In addition, few studies in the IS literature have considered the role of affective connection in human-computer interaction. We redefine trust from two dimensions of affect-based trust and cognition-based trust, and test a AI service trust mechanism model.

This study also provides three practical implications for both AI service product' designers and managers. First, companies should focus on producing AI products with intelligence-interactivity and coolness to maximize user trust. Second, our research implies that users may be attracted to AI products because of their anthropomorphic sounds and names, but human-like personalities are not helpful in keeping users engaged. Hence, we argue that AI devices need to add anthropomorphic features appropriately to improve service performance. Third, we find the special role of affective attributes (such as attachment) in human-computer interaction trust. It recommends managers should understand the sources of the emotional resonance from the user by mining user data, which strengthen the level of affective trust and motivate the customer to continually use AI services.

5.3 Limitations and Directions for Future Research

We acknowledge several limitations of the present study. First, this study proposes the AISTA framework via the coding technique of grounded theory, but there might be other trust antecedents. Future research could refine other significant antecedents from other theoretical perspectives. Second, our results are specific to smart speaker users, because smart speakers are the most mainstream AI service products. Future study should extend our model to other types of AI service products to examine user trust mechanism and behaviors from different samples. Third, trust in this study includes both cognitive and affective aspects, so whether there is a transformation within trust is an interesting research topic. In the future, we can further explore the potential correlation between cognition-based trust and affect-based trust to increase the model's explanatory power.

Acknowledgement. This work was supported jointly by the grants of National Natural Science Foundation of China (71902204).

References

1. Gursoy, D., Chi, O.H., Lu, L., et al.: Consumers acceptance of artificially intelligent (AI) device use in service delivery. Int. J. Inf. Manag. **49**, 157–169 (2019)
2. Chen, Q., Gong, Y., Lu, Y., et al.: Classifying and measuring the service quality of AI chatbot in frontline service. J. Bus. Res. **145**, 552–568 (2022)
3. Oliveira, T., Alhinho, M., Rita, P., et al.: Modelling and testing consumer trust dimensions in e-commerce. Comput. Hum. Behav. **71**, 153–164 (2017)
4. Jiang, Y., Yang, X., Zheng, T.: Make chatbots more adaptive: Dual pathways linking human-like cues and tailored response to trust in interactions with chatbots. Comput. Hum. Behav. **138**, 107485 (2023)
5. McKnight, D.H., Cummings, L.L., Chervany, N.L.: Initial trust formation in new organizational relationships. Acad. Manag. Rev. **23**(3), 473–490 (1998)
6. Lu, B., Wang, Z., Zhang, S.: Platform-based mechanisms, institutional trust, and continuous use intention: the moderating role of perceived effectiveness of sharing economy institutional mechanisms. Inf. Manag. **58**(7), 103504 (2021)
7. Kim, D.Y., Kim, H.Y.: Trust me, trust me not: a nuanced view of influencer marketing on social media. J. Bus. Res. **134**, 223–232 (2021)
8. Bapna, R., Gupta, A., Rice, S., et al.: Trust and the strength of ties in online social networks: an exploratory field experiment. MIS Q. **41**(1), 115–130 (2017)
9. Hu, P., Lu, Y.: Dual humanness and trust in conversational AI: a person-centered approach. Comput. Hum. Behav. **119**, 106727 (2021)
10. Pelau, C., Dabija, D.C., Ene, I.: What makes an AI device human-like? The role of interaction quality, empathy and perceived psychological anthropomorphic characteristics in the acceptance of artificial intelligence in the service industry. Comput. Hum. Behav. **122**, 106855 (2021)
11. Kim, J., Kang, S., Bae, J.: Human likeness and attachment effect on the perceived interactivity of AI speakers. J. Bus. Res. **144**, 797–804 (2022)
12. Chi, O.H., Jia, S., Li, Y., et al.: Developing a formative scale to measure consumers' trust toward interaction with artificially intelligent (AI) social robots in service delivery. Comput. Hum. Behav. **118**, 106700 (2021)
13. Im, S., Bhat, S., Lee, Y.: Consumer perceptions of product creativity, coolness, value and attitude. J. Bus. Res. **68**(1), 166–172 (2015)
14. Wang, W., Qiu, L., Kim, D., et al.: Effects of rational and social appeals of online recommendation agents on cognition-and affect-based trust. Decis. Support Syst. **86**, 48–60 (2016)
15. McKnight, D.H., Choudhury, V., Kacmar, C.: Developing and validating trust measures for e-commerce: an integrative typology. Inf. Syst. Res. **13**(3), 334–359 (2002)

A Study into Sponsorship Disclosure on Video Sharing Platforms: Evidence from Bilibili

Chenwei Li and Huijin Lu[(✉)]

Xi'an Jiaotong-Liverpool University, Suzhou 215000, China
huijin.lu@xjtlu.edu.cn

Abstract. Sponsorship disclosure is becoming increasingly important in the marketing field and its business value deserves further exploration. This paper investigates how different types of sponsorship disclosure affects consumers' purchase intention through influencer trust in the context of video sharing platforms with evidence from Bilibili. Notably, as a distinguished feature of Bilibili, the differences between bullet screen and traditional user comments in their impacts on sponsorship disclosure and customer purchase intention are compared in terms of consumers' interactivity with the social media influencers. Based on the knowledge persuasion model and signaling theory, the results indicate that influencer trust mediates the relationship between sponsorship disclosure and consumers' purchase intention both for general and specific sponsorship disclosure, and interactivity positively moderates the relationship between sponsorship disclosure and consumers' purchase intention only for general sponsorship disclosure.

Keywords: Sponsorship Disclosure · Video Sharing Platform · Purchase Intention · Bilibili

1 Introduction

In the new era of Web 2.0, social media is developing rapidly and is witnessing the emergence of various types of user-generated content (UGC). UGC refers to a new type of web usage where users can display or provide their personalized created content to other users through online platforms. Leveraging UGC, traditional video websites are evolving into fashionable video sharing platforms allowing for intensive interpersonal interactions.

Nowadays, consumers on video sharing platforms are no longer passive content receivers but can actively express their views and feelings about products or services through content generation. Some of them become social media influencers, who are productive content creators with professional knowledge and skills in a certain area and have established credibility among a large social media audience thus may affect the decision making of their followers and consumers (Lou & Yuan 2019).

Marketers have recognized the value of social media influencers and began to promote brands and products through influencer marketing. However, as sponsored content is widespread, the credibility of social media influencers is in doubt and has caused

Y. Tu and M. Chi (Eds.): WHICEB 2023, LNBIP 480, pp. 220–232, 2023.
https://doi.org/10.1007/978-3-031-32299-0_19

controversy. To protect consumers, Federal Trade Commission (FTC) and other related institutions have regulated the use of sponsorship disclosure and tried to make influencer marketing transparent (Lee & Kim 2020).

Previous research on the impact of sponsorship disclosure has obtained conflicting results. Some scholars argued that sponsorship disclosure may lead to advertising recognition, thus negatively affect consumers' attitudes towards the brand and their purchase intention (De Veirman & Hudders 2020; De Jans et al. 2018). But some studies pointed out that social media influencers would be seen as sincere, open-minded and favorable if the sponsorship was disclosed (Hwang and Jeong 2016). Moreover, there is a lack of research examining sponsorship disclosure in the context of video sharing platforms (Boerman 2020), which deserves further attention. Thus, this paper tries to answer the research question:

RQ1: On video-sharing platforms, how does sponsorship disclosure affect consumers' purchase intention?

Additionally, sponsorship disclosure may in different forms. Past research has investigated the impact of simple sponsorship disclosure on consumer behavior (Pfeuffer & Huh 2021; Xie & Feng 2022), and further study about other types of sponsorship disclosure is needed. Thus, we try to address another research question:

RQ2: Does the impact of sponsorship disclosure on consumers' purchase intention change with the type?

As a typical example of video sharing platform, Bilibili has successfully engaged a large number of social media influencers and potential consumers through a wide range of user engagement and interaction, make it an idea platform for influencer marketing (Hu et al. 2016). Notably, Bilibili offers an innovative approach, bullet screen, for consumers to interact with social media influencers in addition to traditional user comments. Depending on the intensity of bullet comments, the degree of interactivity between social media influencers and consumers varies. Thus, we want to know:

RQ3: Whether and how does the degree of interactivity between social media influencers and consumers affect the impact of sponsorship disclosure?

2 Literature Review

This section reviews literature about sponsorship disclosure, influencer trust and interactivity with influencer.

2.1 Sponsorship Disclosure

Sponsorship disclosure refers to the commercial message that social media influencers communicate sponsorship content with consumers to help them identify the relationship between the influencer and the promoted brand (Boerman et al. 2014). Past literature has argued that sponsorship disclosure helps consumers build awareness of commercial nature of sponsored content, thereby increasing advertising recognition and persuasive knowledge recognition. For instance, Evans et al. (2017) argued that sponsorship disclosure will be easily perceived as advertising. Lee and Kim (2020) found that sponsorship disclosure stimulates persuasive knowledge when the disclosure lasts longer, which negatively affects brand attitudes. In addition, sponsored disclosure may lead to advertising skepticism and negatively affect brand attitudes and influencer credibility (De Veirman & Hudders 2020; Kim & Kim 2021). De Jans et al. (2018) also argued that sponsorship disclosure negatively affects consumers' purchase intention through emotional advertising literacy, influencer trustworthiness, and prosocial interaction. However, there are some conflicting findings. Colliander and Erlandsson (2015) argue that sponsorship disclosure will not affect the purchase intention of sponsored brand. Sah et al. (2018) argued that sponsor disclosure may generate greater trust in social media influencer's expertise and bring persuasive knowledge. But this positive effect decreases or even reverses as consumers' consideration of sponsorship disclosure deepens. Pfeuffer et al. (2021) suggested that for a sponsored product review on YouTube, changes in sponsorship disclosure do not appear to affect attitudes toward the product, brand and reviewer. This paper wants to clarify these confusions by investigating the impact of sponsorship disclosure on consumers' purchase intention.

It should be noted that different types of sponsorship disclosures may have different impacts on consumers. Past literature has roughly categorized sponsorship disclosure into general and specific sponsorship disclosure based on the specificity of the disclosure of the business relationship between social media influencers and the sponsored brand (Stubb et al. 2019). Since the research into the type of sponsorship disclosure is not sufficient, this paper focuses on general sponsorship disclosure and specific sponsorship disclosure and tries to reveal their impacts on consumers' purchase intention.

2.2 Influencer Trust

McKnight et al. (2002) defined trust as a psychological recognition of the trusted party's competence, benevolence, and honesty while being willing to trust the other party in a given scenario. We adopt this definition and apply it in the video sharing area to define influencer trust as consumers' trust in social media influencer and is mainly expressed as consumers' belief that social media influencers are honest, well-intentioned, and have the professional competence to meet their needs. On social media, trust is designated as a major component of how people relate to each other and share and receive information (Santiago et al. 2020). Social media influencers and consumers share and receive information from both parties through bullet screen, comments and so on, thus building trust, resulting in purchase intentions or the completion of business transactions (Dwidienawati et al. 2020). Therefore, trust in social media influencer could be a suitable mediator between sponsorship disclosure and consumers' behavioral intentions in influencer marketing.

2.3 Interactivity with Influencers

Although the definition of interactivity varies across areas and is constantly changing, their common perception is that interactivity is bidirectional (Rogers et al. 1986). Ha and James (1998) consider interactivity as the degree to which communicators and receivers respond and satisfy both communication needs. Following that, we define influencer interactivity as the degree to which consumers communicate with and get feedback from social media influencers through comments, bullet screen, etc., on social media. Morgan and Hunt (1994) argued that interactions affect credibility perceptions. Jun and Yi (2020) showed that influencer interaction affects brand trust through authenticity, emotional attachment, and brand loyalty. However, how the interactions exert effect remains unclear. That's one of the focuses in this paper.

3 Theoretical Foundation

This paper builds research model on the basis of persuasive knowledge model and signaling theory.

3.1 Persuasive Knowledge Model

Persuasive knowledge model assumes that people develop persuasive knowledge and use it to cope with the persuasive situations they encounter (Friestad & Wright 1994). Persuasive knowledge refers to the persuasive subjects' persuasive intentions, persuasive techniques, the effectiveness and appropriateness of persuasive techniques, and means of coping strategies to the persuasive target. The persuasion process is an interaction between the persuasion subjects and the persuasion targets. Persuasion knowledge can help people identify persuasive intent and prevent their attitudes and behaviors from being unduly influenced. In the field of marketing, consumers change their coping strategies, beliefs, attitudes, and choices after applying persuasive knowledge (Campbell & Kirmani 2008).

Regarding to sponsorship disclosure, persuasive knowledge will be activated if the consumers identify the sponsorship disclosure as with a persuasive intent. Several past studies have found that persuasive knowledge leads to negative product attitudes (Daniel et al. 2010; Mei-Ling et al. 2008) and lower perceived reliability of the persuasive subject (Campbell & Kirmani 2000; Stafford & Stafford 2002). It can elicit advertisement recognition thus activate advertisement suspicion (De Veirman & Hudders 2020; Boerman 2020; Kim & Kim 2020). Based on persuasive knowledge model, we believe that sponsorship disclosure may affect the influencer trust perceived by consumers.

3.2 Signaling Theory

Signaling theory is a body of theoretical work examining communication between individuals. It is based on information asymmetry in the interactions and leads to uncertainty and vulnerability. Signaler, signal and receiver are the three fundamental elements in the signaling theory (Rahman, Rodríguez-Serrano and Lambkin 2018).

In the online context, signaling theory is often used to test and predict the outcomes of online auctions, e-commerce, websites, and eWOM because information asymmetry is more pronounced online than offline (Boulding & Kirmani 1993; Helm & Mark 2007; Rao, Qu, & Rueckert 1999). Buyers can make effective inferences based on the critical information provided by sellers to reduce information asymmetry (Kirmani & Rao 2000; Benlian & Hess 2011; Chen & Gao 2019; Mavlanova, Benbunan-Fich, & Lang 2021). Signaling theory is suitable in the area of influencer marketing since consumers usually do not have sufficient information about the product and there is an information asymmetry between social media influencers and consumers. According to signaling theory, sponsorship disclosure can be used as information cues to reduce information asymmetry and affect consumers' perceptions and behavior.

4   Research Model and Hypothesis

Based on persuasive knowledge model and signaling theory, we propose our research model and discuss the corresponding hypotheses.

4.1   Research Model

The paper examines the relationship between general and specific sponsorship disclosure and consumer purchase intentions mediated by influencer trust. Interactivity with influencers acts as moderator between sponsorship disclosure and influencer trust. The research model is shown in Fig. 1.

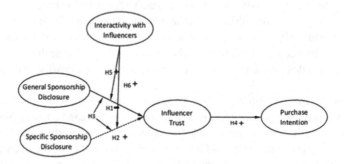

Fig. 1. Research model

4.2   Research Hypothesis

Sponsorship Disclosure and Influencer Trust

De Jans et al. (2018) argued that sponsorship disclosure increased affective advertising literacy for the adolescent population, which leads to negative attitudes toward the sponsor. According to the affective transfer mechanism, adolescents' assessment of influencer trustworthiness decreases. De Veirman and Hudders (2020) also concluded that sponsorship disclosure activates advertisement recognition, triggering consumer coping mechanisms that lead to more ad skepticism, and thus influencer trustworthiness is negatively affected. According to the persuasive knowledge model, consumers can easily activate ad recognition through general sponsorship disclosure without other messages (Lee & Kim 2020). When consumers identify the advertisement, they easily assume that the influencer is indeed marketing the product for commercial purposes, which activates persuasive knowledge and further decreases trust in the influencer. Thus, we posit:

H1: On the video-sharing platform, general sponsorship disclosure will lead to lower influencer trust.

When influencers disclose more sponsorship information, consumers begin to receive more signals. According to signaling theory, specific sponsorship disclosure indicates honesty of the social media influencer who are willing to unveil the sponsoring relationship with the brand. It also sends out a signal that social media influencers allow consumers to make their own informed choices and judgments, leading to higher perception of benevolence. As two important dimensions of trust (Sternthal et al. 1978), higher honesty and benevolence can strengthen consumers' trust in the social media influencer. Thus, we posit:

H2: On the video-sharing platforms, specific sponsorship disclosure will lead to higher influencer trust.

Consumers perceive influencers as respectful, caring, and following ethical principles when they perceive more honesty and benevolence (Pfeuffer & Huh 2021). Even if their persuasive knowledge is activated, they still perceive the influencer as trustworthy because positive signals attenuate the negative effects of persuasive knowledge and weaken consumers' perceptions of persuasive intent, resulting in relatively high levels of trust for influencers. Thus, we posit:

H3: On the video-sharing platforms, specific sponsorship disclosure will have higher impact on influencer trust than general sponsorship disclosure.

Influencer Trust and Purchase Intention

Trust in suppliers positively affects consumers' purchase intention in e-commerce (Gefen 2000). When a supplier conveys benevolence, honesty, and predictability in online transactions, consumers reinforce their beliefs about the supplier, resulting in trust-related behaviors such as purchases (McKnight & Chervany 2001). It has been well documented in the past literature that trust beliefs have a positive impact on trust intentions and increase consumers' online purchase intentions (To & Ho 2014; McKnight & Choudhury 2006). Thus, we posit:

H4: On the video-sharing platform, influencer trust will positively affect consumers' purchase intention.

Moderation Effect of Interactivity with Influencer

In e-commerce, brands communicate product information to consumers through interaction, and consumers learn about products by participating in the interactive process (Susan 2010). In this way, consumers are more likely to obtain valid information about the product thus reducing uncertainty. Higher interactivity between consumers and sellers can largely help consumers obtain relevant information for decision-making (Jiang et al. 2010). Information asymmetry persists when consumers receive general sponsored disclosure. Through interactions, consumers reduce their suspicion of the product being disclosed and of the influencer, and are more likely to perceive the general sponsored disclosure information to be reliable and accurate, thus reducing information barriers. Thus, we posit:

H5: Interactivity with influencer positively moderates the impact of general sponsorship disclosure on influencer trust that higher interactivity with influencer will lead to higher impact of general sponsorship disclosure on influencer trust.

Jun and Yi (2020) found that consumers' interaction with social media will increase brand trust in the influencer through authenticity and emotional attachment to the influencer. High interactivity leads to informational and emotional satisfaction for consumers. Thus, we suggest that high interactivity will promote the positive impact of specific sponsorship disclosure on influencer trust.

H6: Interactivity with influencer positively moderates the impact of specific sponsorship disclosure on influencer trust that higher interactivity with influencer will lead to greater impact of specific sponsorship disclosure on influencer trust.

5　Methodology

An online experiment was used in this study for data collection. It was presented via a web-based survey with assured anonymity.

5.1　Experiment Design

A 3 (type of disclosure: control with no disclosure, general disclosure and specific disclosure) × 2 (Interactivity with influencers: high vs. low) between-group experiment design was used. Participants who have experience in using video sharing platforms were invited to join the online experiment. The participants were asked to watch a video with product information and indicate their attitudes through answering a questionnaire. During the experiment, the participants were randomly assigned into six scenarios, which vary both in the types of product information, types of disclosed sponsorship information contained in the video, and levels of interactivity with social media influencer. In total, we have 328 valid answers (Table 1).

Table 1. Experimental conditions

	Low interactivity with influencer	High interactivity with influencer
No sponsorship disclosure	Condition 1	Condition 4
General sponsorship disclosure	Condition 2	Condition 5
Specific sponsorship disclosure	Condition 3	Condition 6

To enhance the validity of the experiment, product videos produced by real social media influencers who have a large engaged audience and have been published on the Bilibili platform were adopted for experiment. Meanwhile, to ensure the representativeness, product videos in the top four popular communities of Bilibili platform were adopted. Further, the videos were re-edited by removing product irrelevant content to avoid distractions. The details of the manipulation of sponsorship disclose are shown in Table 2. To save space, we will not provide the details of the manipulation of interactivity with influencer, which is mainly achieved by the intensity of bullet comments contained in each video clip. A manipulation check question was placed at the end of the questionnaire by asking the respondents in the treatment groups whether they have noticed the intended stimulus.

Table 2. Details of the manipulation of sponsorship disclose

No sponsorship disclosure

General sponsorship disclosure

Specific sponsorship disclosure

5.2 Measures

A 7-point Likert scale (1 = strongly disagree; 7 = strongly agree) was adopted for measures as shown in Table 3.

Table 3. Measures

Construct	Items		Sources
Interactivity with influencers	II1	The influencer is willing to have the video viewer communicate directly with him	Jun & Yi (2020); Luo (2016)
	II2	The influencer will respond effectively	
	II3	During the interaction with the influencer, the viewer will also receive interaction and feedback from other members	
	II4	I am willing to share my opinions and thoughts with the influencer	
Influencer trust	IT1	I believe that the content posted by the influencer is true	Mcknight et al. (2002); Ba & Pavlou (2002)
	IT2	I believe that the influencer keeps its promises and has a guarantee of credibility	
	IT3	I believe that the influencer does not deliberately deceive customers	
	IT4	I believe that the influencer is posting information about the product to help others understand a good product and not for commercial gain	
	IT5	I believe the influencer has experience with this product	
	IT6	I trust the influencer	
	IT7	I believe that the influencer is presenting product information	
	IT8	I believe that the influencer's product is shared after first-hand experience	

(continued)

Table 3. (*continued*)

Construct	Items		Sources
Purchase Intention	PI1	I am willing to try the products of that brand	Xie & Feng's (2022); Bansal (2000)
	PI2	I am willing to buy products of that brand when I need that type of product	
	PI3	I am willing to buy the product of that brand when I happen to see it	
	PI4	After watching the video, I have the desire to buy the brand's products	
	PI5	I am willing to buy the product	
	PI6	I would like to buy products recommended by this influencer in the future	

6   Result Analysis

SPSS AMOS 16.1 software package was use for results analysis. To save space, only reliability and validity and stratified regression analysis are reported as the main results in this section. It can be told from Table 4 that all the measurements have met the suggested criterion for reliability and validity.

The regression results in Table 5 suggest that general sponsorship disclosure has a significant negative impact on influencer trust, thus H1 is supported. However, the results of specific sponsorship disclosure on influencer trust are not significant ($p > 0.05$), thus H2 is not supported. Comparing the effect size of general and specific sponsorship disclosure, H3 is not supported since the estimates of general sponsorship disclosure are overwhelmingly larger than specific sponsorship disclosure. H4 is supported that influencer trust is positively related with purchase intention. As to the moderation effect, only the interaction term of interactivity with general sponsorship disclosure is significant thus only H5 is supported.

Table 4. Measurement statistics of constructs

Construct	Factor Loading	Composite Reliability	Cronbach's Alpha	AVE
Interactivity with influencers	0.756	0.835	0.834	0.803
	0.717			
	0.761			
	0.755			
Influencer Trust	0.698	0.910	0.909	0.935
	0.704			
	0.769			
	0.705			
	0.745			
	0.805			
	0.764			
	0.789			
Purchase Intention	0.752	0.909	0.908	0.916
	0.758			
	0.789			
	0.784			
	0.85			
	0.804			

Table 5. Regression results

Variables	Dependent variable			
	Model 1	Model 2	Model 3	Model 4
(Constant)	4.334***	4.739***	2.148***	2.283***
Experience	0.036	0.017	−0.031	−0.020
Gender	−0.120	−0.121	−0.099	−0.106
Age	0.141	0.062	0.053	0.059
Education	0.190**	0.200**	0.117**	0.103*
Occupation	−0.036	−0.019	−0.003	−0.011
General sponsorship disclosure		−0.876***	−0.585***	−0.656***
Specific sponsorship disclosure		0.148	−0.006	−0.007
Interactivity with influencer			0.559***	0.536***
General sponsorship disclosure *interactivity with influencer				−0.247**

(*continued*)

Table 5. (*continued*)

Variables	Dependent variable			
	Model 1	Model 2	Model 3	Model 4
Specific sponsorship disclosure *interactivity with influencer				−0.073
Influencer trust				0.897***
Adjusted R Square	0.023	0.270	0.613	0.622
R Square Change	0.038	0.248	0.337	0.011
F value	2.532*	18.296***	65.805***	54.763***

Note: (a) dependent variable is influencer trust; (b) *$p < 0.05$, **$p < 0.01$, ***$p < 0.001$.

7 Contribution and Implication

This paper can advance the theoretical understanding of sponsorship disclosure and provide a better understanding of various types of sponsorship disclosure in influencer marketing. As a distinguished feature of video sharing platforms, the impact of influencer-consumer interactivity is examined as well. The findings can also offer managerial implications for marketers to develop better influencer marketing strategies through appropriate sponsorship disclosure.

References

Ba, S., Pavlou, P.A.: Evidence of the effect of trust building technology in electronic markets: price premiums and buyer behavior. MIS Q. **26**(3), 243–268 (2002)

Benlian, A., Hess, T.: The signaling role of IT features in influencing trust and participation in online communities. Int. J. Electron. Commer. **15**(4), 7–56 (2011)

De Jans, S., Cauberghe, V., Hudders, L.: How an advertising disclosure alerts young adolescents to sponsored vlogs: the moderating role of a peer-based advertising literacy intervention through an informational vlog. J. Advertising **47**(4), 309–325 (2018)

Evans, N.J., Phua, J., Lim, J., Jun, H.: Disclosing Instagram influencer advertising: the effects of disclosure language on advertising recognition, attitudes, and behavioral intent. J. Interact. Advertising **17**(2), 138–149 (2017)

Friestad, M., Wright, P.: The persuasion knowledge model: how people cope with persuasion attempts. J. Consum. Res. **21**(1), 1–31 (1994)

Kim, D.Y., Kim, H.Y.: Influencer advertising on social media: the multiple inference model on influencer-product congruence and sponsorship disclosure. J. Bus. Res. **130**, 405–415 (2021)

Mavlanova, T., Benbunan-Fich, R., Lang, G.: The role of external and internal signals in E-commerce. Decis. Support Syst. **87**, 59–68 (2021)

McKnight, D.H., Choudhury, V., Kacmar, C.: The impact of initial consumer trust on intentions to transact with a web site: a trust building model. J. Strateg. Inf. Syst. **11**(3–4), 297–323 (2002)

Morgan, R.M., Hunt, S.D.: The commitment-trust theory of relationship marketing. J. Mark. **58**(3), 20–38 (1994)

Pfeuffer, A., Huh, J.: Effects of different sponsorship disclosure message types on consumers' trust and attitudes. Int. J. Advertising **40**(1), 49–80 (2021)

Zhu, Y.Q., Chen, H.G.: Service fairness and customer satisfaction in internet banking: exploring the mediating effects of trust and customer value. Internet Res. **22**(4), 482–498 (2012)

How Restaurant Attributes Affect Customer Satisfaction: A Study Based on Sentiment Analysis, Neural Network Modelling and Kano Model Classification

Huijin Lu[1], Huidan Tan[2], Chenwei Li[1], and Xiaobo Xu[1(✉)]

[1] Xi'an Jiaotong-Liverpool University, Suzhou 215000, China
Xiaobo.Xu@xjtlu.edu.cn
[2] Duke University, Durham, NC 27708, USA

Abstract. The study aims to understand how the various attributes of restaurant affect its customer satisfaction. Different with prior literature with heavy reliance on self-reported data, we investigated 17 representative restaurant attributes extracted from online reviews, modeled the relationship between restaurant attributes and customer satisfaction leveraging neural network, and classified the attributes into five categories based on kano model. The findings show that, among the 17 attributes, waiter's attitude and taste of food are most important for a high customer satisfaction. This study could help restaurant allocate its resources with greater efficiency and improve customer satisfaction.

Keywords: Restaurant Attributes · Customer Satisfaction · Sentiment Analysis · Neural Network Modelling · Kano Model Classification

1 Introduction

Customer satisfaction has long been recognized as an important indicator of restaurant profitability (Luo and Homburg 2007). If consumers have a positive attitude toward its service quality, business would retain more customers and make more profits (Han and Ryu 2009). Exploring the factors affecting customer satisfaction is of great importance for resources allocation optimization and customer satisfaction improvement for restaurant as well (Kurt et al. 2003). Thus, customer satisfaction in the catering industry has attracted a lot of attention both from researchers and practitioners.

Previous research in customer satisfaction largely relies on self-reported data, which is not only time-consuming and unstable (Groves 2006) but also become outdated quickly (Culotta and Cutler 2016). In contrast, online user-generated reviews offer a relatively more objective and unbiased way for restaurants to hear from customers (Schuckert et al. 2015) and to understand their satisfaction and dissatisfaction (Xu and Li 2016).

Some researchers have noticed the importance of online user-generated reviews for restaurants and tried to understand customer satisfaction utilizing online reviews (Nam and Lee 2011; Bufquin et al. 2017). However, most of them merely focused on the

Y. Tu and M. Chi (Eds.): WHICEB 2023, LNBIP 480, pp. 233–241, 2023.
https://doi.org/10.1007/978-3-031-32299-0_20

linear relationship between the attributes of restaurant and customer satisfaction with an assumed normal distribution of online ratings. This can only provide restricted insights that if certain attributes are fulfilled, customers will feel satisfied and vice versa. Indeed, it may not be the real case. For example, customers might be more tolerant to certation attributes of restaurant but quite sensitive and picky to some other one. A nonlinear relationship between the attributes of restaurant and customer satisfaction together with a positively skewed asymmetric bimodal distribution of customer satisfaction is more realistic (Hu et al. 2017).

Kano model is effective in capturing non-linear relationship. Accordingly, the relationship between the attributes of restaurant and customer satisfaction could be divided into five categories, including one-dimensional relationship, attractive relationship, must-be relationship, reverse relationship, and indifferent relationship (Kano et al. 1984). Each corresponding attribute has a different impact on customer satisfaction (Li et al. 2018). For example, poor performance of must-be attributes would definitely lead to low customer satisfaction. But increase in the performance of must-be attributes would not bring higher customer satisfaction because they usually take the must-be attributes for granted. Therefore, understanding the category of attributes can identify influencing factors of customer satisfaction in a wise way.

RQ: How the various attributes of restaurant affect its customer satisfaction?

The study aims to understand how the various attributes of restaurant affect its customer satisfaction. To address this research question, we propose an approach combining sentiment analysis, neural network modelling and kano model classification. First, sentiment analysis is used to extract customer sentiment toward the attributes in the online reviews. Second, neural network modelling is adopted to model the relationship between restaurant attributes and customer satisfaction. Last, a set of rules is designed to classify the attributes into the five categories of Kano model.

2 Literature Review

In this section, literature about sentiment analysis, neural network and Kano model are reviewed.

2.1 Sentiment Analysis

Sentiment analysis is effective in understanding how consumers think about a product or a service (Liu 2010). Three approaches are mainly used in sentiment analysis, namely lexicon method, machine learning method, and deep learning method.

Lexicon method utilizes a sentiment lexicon to decide the text sentiment (Devika, Sunitha and Ganesh 2016). Due to its high requirement in powerful linguistic resources, this method is not very friendly.

Machine learning method includes naive bayes classifier, support vector machine (SVM) and decision trees. Naive bayes classifier is a probabilistic classifier based on Bayes theorem. It is helpful to determine whether the text is negative or positive (Troussas et al. 2013). Decision trees are nonparametric method to predicting target variables by learning decision rules (Bhoi and Joshi 2018). SVM is a classifier based on a linear function. Compared with Naive Bayes and decision tree, SVM has a relatively higher accuracy of classification (Raghuvanshi and Patil 2016) but requires a large dataset (Fernández-Gavilanes et al. 2016).

Compared with supervised machine learning methods, deep learning method does not need to tune feature manually based on available linguistic resources and expert knowledge (Rojas-Barahona 2016). Typical deep learning models include convolutional neural networks (CNN), deep neural networks (DNN), and recurrent neural networks (RNN) (Schmidhuber 2015). Among them, RNN has distinct advantages due to its ability to handle sequences of arbitrary length (Wen et al. 2021). The introduction of long short term memory (LSTM) in RNN also help solve the problem of gradient vanishing and explosion (Zaremba and Sutskever 2014). Therefore, our study develops a LSTM classifier to obtain customers' sentiment toward each restaurant attribute and prepare for further relationship modeling.

2.2 Neural Network

Neural network refers to a model designed to stimulate the human brain. Back propagation (BP) neural network is a multi-level feed forward network based on error back propagation algorithm (Li et al. 2012). It uses mean square error and gradient descent to constantly modify the weight of neural network and to achieve minimum loss error.

Compared with multiple regression, neural network can fix the problem of high-level complexity in business world and handle much more variables (Garver 2002). It can also better fit the non-normal data and capture nonlinear or multi-collinearity relationship (Phillips et al. 2015). Thus, we adopt neural network for the relationship modeling between restaurant attributes and customer satisfaction.

2.3 Kano Model

The Kano model is a theory of product development and customer satisfaction which classifies customer preferences into five categories (Kano et al. 1984). These five relationships include one-dimension relationship, attractive relationship, must-be relationship, reverse relationship, and indifferent relationship. One-dimension relationship is a linear relationship depicting that customer satisfaction increases when the attributes are fulfilled and vice versa. In the attractive relationship, fulfillment in the attributes will result in satisfaction. However, they won't affect customers' dissatisfaction when they are not fulfilled. Customers usually take the attributes in the must-be relationship for granted. When these attributes are fully fulfilled, customers are neutral. But their absence would result in high dissatisfaction. In the reverse relationship, fulfillment of attributes makes customer rather unhappy. In the indifferent relationship, these attributes do not contribute to customers' satisfaction or dissatisfaction. Kano model is a comprehensive model to understand customer satisfaction. However, it has not be used well in the analysis of online reviews. Therefore, this study tries to deepen the understanding of customer satisfaction by analyzing online reviews based on Kano model.

3 Research Framework

This section describes the proposed framework which is consisted of sentiment analysis, neural network modelling and kano model classification as shown in Fig. 1.

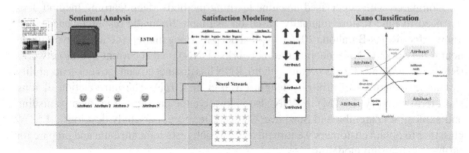

Fig. 1. Research Framework

Since online reviews are usually in an unstructured form, in the first stage, we need to use LSTM to convert the unstructured data into structured. The corresponding sentiment of each attribute will also be identified. In the second stage, a neural network method is used to capture the impact of customers' sentiment of each attribute on their satisfaction. Then, in the third stage, a set of rules are designed to classify the attributes to the five categories of kano model.

4 Methodology

4.1 Data Collection

Data for sentiment analysis was obtained from a typical online website of restaurant, Dazhongdianping, provided by AI Challenger 2018. The dataset contains 17 attributes after deleting "others" and "recommendations" (Table 1). Data for customer satisfaction prediction was crawled from Dazhongdianping by using Octopus. In total, 36851 reviews were obtained after some error deletion with both textual reviews and ratings.

4.2 Data Analysis

Based on LSTM sentiment analysis, first, data cleaning and tokenization were conducted to make the text pure and clean. Tencent word embedding provided by Tencent AI Lab is used to convert text data to numerical data. After the sentiment analysis, the sentiment could be extracted from each review, and the review attribute sentiment matrix. To better capture sentiment orientation, we only considered strong sentiment, e.g., positive or negative, thus the matrix was refined.

Then a three-layer neural network was created. The input layer is the review attribute sentiment matrix, the output layer is to predict customer satisfaction. Each neuron connects with another with the function $wx + b$, where w denotes the weight and b denotes

Table 1. Attribute list

Category	Attribute	Numbering
Location	Transportation	$f1$
	Distance from the business district	$f2$
	Easy to find	$f3$
Service	Wait time	$f4$
	Waiter's attitude	$f5$
	Parking convenience	$f6$
	Serving speed	$f7$
Price	Level	$f8$
	Cost effective	$f9$
	Discount	$f10$
Ambience	Decoration	$f11$
	Noise	$f12$
	Space	$f13$
	Cleanness	$f14$
Food	Portion	$f15$
	Taste	$f16$
	Look	$f17$

the bias. After several epochs' training, the weight for each neural on each layer could be obtained. *Wmpositive* denotes the effect of positive sentiment toward mth attribute on customer satisfaction while *Wmnegative* denotes the effect of negative sentiment toward mth attribute on customer satisfaction. Based on *Wmpositive* and *Wmnegative*, a set of rules is proposed to identify the relationship category of each attribute as shown below.

5 Results

It can be seen from the Fig. 2 that the taste of the food and waiter's attitude are mentioned most. Meanwhile, positive sentiments of the attributes are more frequently mentioned by customers than negative sentiments.

For neural network, the number of hidden layer neurons was chose based on $m = \sqrt{n} + a$, n denotes the number of input features, which is 34 (17 attributes and two sentiments 17×2). a is a number from 1 to 10.

The weights obtained from neural network modelling are presented in Table 2. From Fig. 3, it can be found find that food taste and waiter's attitude have higher impact on customer satisfaction.

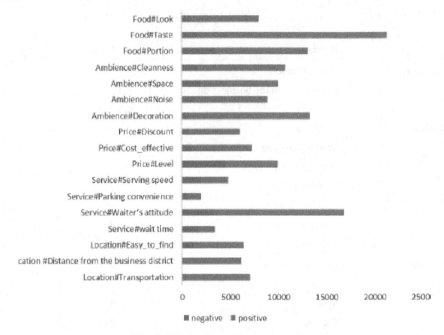

Fig. 2. The sentiment for each attribute

Table 2. Weights of attributes

Attribute	$w^{positive}$	$w^{negative}$	Attribute	$w^{positive}$	$w^{negative}$
$f1$	0.000275	0.002317	$f10$	0.040628	0.019104
$f2$	0.009862	0.010434	$f11$	0.025192	0.024845
$f3$	0.008136	0.008173	$f12$	0.049072	0.020961
$f4$	0.014292	0.03006	$f13$	0.005357	0.002675
$f5$	0.079686	0.25355	$f14$	0.003405	0.099681
$f6$	0.010376	0.001097	$f15$	0.025995	0.044811
$f7$	0.019885	0.055386	$f16$	0.232504	0.206922
$f8$	0.023946	0.039605	$f17$	0.033556	0.057646
$f9$	0.043296	0.059443			
Threshold $w^{positive}$ for indifference			Threshold $w^{negative}$ for indifference		
0.006255			0.009367		

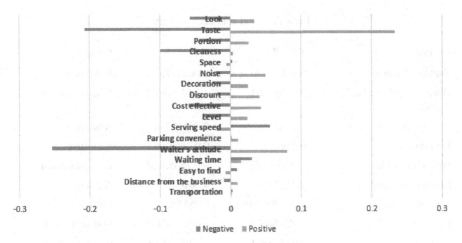

Fig. 3. Positive and negative sentiment weight toward each attribute

The results of Kano model classification are list in Table. Most of attributes belong to one-dimension relationship, such as "Distance from the business district", "Waiter's attitude", "Price level", etc. They all have a linear relationship with customer satisfaction that the increase in these attributes will largely improve customer satisfaction. But if the performance of these attributes is not good, customer satisfaction will decrease proportionally. Only "serving speed" is labelled as a must-be attribute. It means that when the restaurant could serve the food in a timely manner, customers would have any negative comments. But if not the case, it will make the customers very unhappy. Therefore, the restaurant should pay much attention to guarantee the quality of "serving speed". Attractive attributes include "waiting time" and "parking convenience". The absence of these attributes won't affect customer's dissatisfaction. But the fulfillment of them could largely enhance customer satisfaction. Therefore, the restaurant may try to make effort on these attractive attributes. Reverse attributes include "easy to find" and indifference attributes include "transportation" and "ambience". These three are not very related with customer satisfaction thus the restaurant may save effort on them (Table 3).

Table 3. Weights of each attribute

Attribute	$W^{positive}$	$W^{negative}$	Category
Transportation	0.00027496	0.00231703	Indifference
Distance from the business district	0.00986201	−0.01043371	One-dimension
Easy to find	−0.00813591	0.00817348	Reserve
Wait time	0.014292	0.03005956	Attractive
Waiter's attitude	0.07968552	−0.25355035	One-dimension
Parking convenience	0.01037645	0.00109737	Attractive
Serving speed	−0.01988516	0.05538633	Must-be
Level	0.02394627	−0.03960495	One-dimension
Cost effective	0.04329604	−0.05944266	One-dimension
Discount	0.04062787	−0.01910394	One-dimension
Decoration	0.02519204	−0.02484462	One-dimension
Noise	0.04907202	−0.02096099	One-dimension
Space	−0.00535662	0.00267455	Indifference
Cleanness	0.0034049	−0.09968126	One-dimension
Portion	0.025995	−0.04481082	One-dimension
Taste	0.23250425	−0.20692174	One-dimension
Look	0.03355601	−0.05764644	One-dimension

6 Conclusion

This study proposes a framework for understanding how restaurant attributes affect its customer satisfaction. A comprehensive investigation of sentiment analysis, customer satisfaction modeling and Kano model classification was conducted. This study could provide guidance for restaurants to best allocate its resources to achieve higher customer satisfaction. However, there are still some limitations. For instance, this study only focused on the positive or negative sentiment and ignored the valence of sentiment. Besides, the impact of demographic features on customer satisfaction was not considered, e.g., gender. Further study is highly encouraged.

References

Bhoi, A., Joshi, S.: Various approaches to aspect-based sentiment analysis. ArXiv (abs/1805.01984) (2018)

Bufquin, D., DiPietro, R., Partlow, C.: The influence of the DinEX service quality dimensions on casual-dining restaurant customers' satisfaction and behavioral intentions. J. Foodserv. Bus. Res. **20**(5), 542–556 (2017)

Culotta, A., Cutler, J.: Mining brand perceptions from twitter social networks. Mark. Sci. **35**(3), 343–362 (2016)

Devika, M.D., Sunitha, C., Ganesh, A.: Sentiment analysis: a comparative study on different approaches. Proc. Comput. Sci. **87**, 44–49 (2016)

Fernández-Gavilanes, M., Álvarez-López, T., Juncal-Martínez, J., Costa-Montenegro, E., González-Castaño, F.J.: Unsupervised method for sentiment analysis in online texts. Expert Syst. Appl. **58**, 57–75 (2016)

Garver, M.S.: Using data mining for customer satisfaction research. Mark. Res. **14**, 8–17 (2002)

Groves, R.M.: Nonresponse rates and nonresponse bias in household surveys. Public Opinion Q. **70**(5), 646–675 (2006)

Han, H., Ryu, K.: The roles of the physical environment, price perception, and customer satisfaction in determining customer loyalty in the restaurant industry. J. Hosp. Tour. Res. **33**(4), 487–510 (2009)

Kurt, M., Elmar, S., Kenneth, H.: Importance-performance analysis revisited: the role of the factor structure of customer satisfaction. Serv. Ind. J. **23**(2), 112–129 (2003)

Li, J., Cheng, J., Shi, J., Huang, F.: Brief introduction of Back Propagation (BP) neural network algorithm and its improvement. Adv. Intell. Soft Comput. **169**, 553–558 (2012)

Li, Y.L., Du, Y.F., Chin, K.S.: Determining the importance ratings of customer requirements in quality function deployment based on interval linguistic information. Int. J. Prod. Res. **56**(14), 4692–4708 (2018)

Nam, J.H., Lee, T.J.: Foreign travelers' satisfaction with traditional Korean restaurants. Int. J. Hosp. Manag. **30**(4), 982–989 (2011)

Phillips, P., Zigan, K., Santos Silva, M.M., Schegg, R.: The interactive effects of online reviews on the determinants of swiss hotel performance: a neural network analysis. Tour. Manag. **50**, 130–141 (2015)

Raghuvanshi, N., Patil, J.M.: A brief review on sentiment analysis. In: 2016 International Conference on Electrical, Electronics, and Optimization Techniques (ICEEOT), pp. 2827–2831 (2016)

Rojas-Barahona, L.M.: Deep learning for sentiment analysis. Lang. Linguist. Compass **10**(12), 701–719 (2016)

Schmidhuber, J.: Deep learning in neural networks: an overview. Neural Netw. **61**, 85–117 (2015)

Schuckert, M., Liu, X., Law, R.: Hospitality and tourism online reviews: recent trends and future directions. J. Travel Tour. Mark. **32**(5), 608–621 (2015)

Troussas, C., Virvous, M., Espinosa, K.J., Liaguno, K., Caro, J: Sentiment analysis of Facebook statuses using Naive Bayes classifier for language learning. In: 2013 Fourth International Conference on Information, Intelligence, Systems and Applications (IISA), pp. 1–6. IEEE (2013)

Wen, S., et al.: Memristive LSTM network for sentiment analysis. IEEE Trans. Syst. Man Cybern.: Syst. **51**, 1794–1804 (2021)

Xu, X., Li, Y.: The antecedents of customer satisfaction and dissatisfaction toward various types of hotels: a text mining approach. Int. J. Hosp. Manag. **55**, 57–69 (2016)

A Method for Recommending Resources Across Virtual Academic Communities Based on Knowledge Graph and Prompt Learning

Zhihao Chen, Jun Yin[✉], Shilun Ge, and Nianxin Wang

School of Economics and Management, Jiangsu University of Science and Technology, Zhenjiang 212003, China
bamhill@163.com

Abstract. In the era of big data, virtual academic communities are flourishing and resources are growing explosively. As a result, heterogeneous fragmentation of resources and massive disorder have created constraining problems, which exacerbate the "knowledge island" effect among academic communities and challenge researchers to acquire knowledge effectively. To solve these problems, we propose a method for recommending resources across virtual academic communities (MRRVAC) based on knowledge graph and prompt learning. Firstly, we use the knowledge graph to link resources in different communities, which enables resources to be transferred between communities. Secondly, prompt learning is used to acquire the potential knowledge of knowledge graph. The final recommendation list of academic resources is obtained by training the prompt template with the improved P-tuning method and using it to mine the injected knowledge in the model. Finally, data experiments were conducted on the datasets of two virtual academic communities, Zhihu and ScienceNet. The results show that the average improvement over the original method in HR and NDCG is 0.296% and 0.271%, which validates the effectiveness of the method.

Keywords: Virtual Academic Community · Knowledge Association · Knowledge Recommendation · Knowledge Graph · Prompted Learning

1 Introduction

With the advent of the Web 2.0 era, the development of Internet technology has led to significant changes in the way people exchange information [1]. According to the survey data of the Statista Research Department, as of April 2022, there are more than 4.7 billion social media researchers worldwide, accounting for 59% of the global population [2]. With the development of new knowledge exchange carriers, the academic communication mode has also changed, and social networks have become the main venue for scholars to communicate. Many scholars with the same interests gather here to share knowledge and communicate with each other, forming a new type of academic communication platform-virtual academic community (VAC), such as ScienceNet, Zhihu, Mendeley and Arxiv. Virtual academic communities can effectively improve scholars'

Y. Tu and M. Chi (Eds.): WHICEB 2023, LNBIP 480, pp. 242–252, 2023.
https://doi.org/10.1007/978-3-031-32299-0_21

academic exposure, promote academic innovation and accelerate the research process. However, with the rapid development of virtual academic communities, there are now more and more registered users in virtual academic communities and the problem of information overload is becoming more and more serious. Thus, how to provide effective resources services for researchers has become an urgent problem [3].

At present, the research on resource services of virtual academic communities is mainly conducted in two aspects: knowledge association and knowledge recommendation. In the aspect of knowledge association, most researchers take a single virtual academic community [4–7] as the research object, but the knowledge information of a single virtual academic community is often not perfect. Researchers need to spend a lot of time and effort to find the optimal solution of knowledge among multiple platforms, which will lead to much time and effort loss. In terms of knowledge recommendation, the current studies [3, 7–9] have the following two shortcomings: First, they do not establish effective knowledge associations and thus lack the effectiveness of knowledge recommendation. Most of the current studies have neglected to model the relationships among academic resources in virtual academic communities, which results in the models missing this part of the information in learning and their recommendation effects will be reduced. Second, the interpretation of knowledge recommendations needs to be improved. Deep learning methods have been widely used for knowledge recommendation tasks in virtual academic communities, but deep learning methods as a "black box" do not have any interpretability.

Based on the above background, we propose a **method** for **r**ecommending **r**esources across **v**irtual **a**cademic **c**ommunities (MRRVAC) based on knowledge graph and prompt learning and validate the effectiveness through real data experiments. We use knowledge graph to associate academic resources in different virtual academic communities and provide a good basis for subsequent knowledge recommendations. Knowledge graph provide an effective means to address the "knowledge silo" effect [10]. Further, we introduce prompt learning to mine the knowledge in knowledge graph and improve the interpretability of recommendations. Because Traditional fine-tuning models (like BERT, xlnet) use the training form of auto-regressiveand and auto-encoding during pretraining, which has a huge gap with the form of downstream tasks and cannot fully exploit the capability of the pre-training model itself. In contrast prompt learning transforms the data of downstream tasks into natural language form with specific templates to fully exploit the capability of the pre-trained model itself.

2 Related Work

Effective knowledge association is the key to realizing knowledge recommendation, and knowledge recommendation can facilitate researchers' knowledge acquisition. However, the current research on knowledge association and knowledge recommendation in virtual academic communities is still in the exploration stage, and the diversity of knowledge associations and the accuracy of recommendations are still inadequate. Table 1 summarizes the current research on knowledge association and knowledge recommendation in virtual academic communities.

Table 1. Summary of Related Work

Author (Chronological order)	KA	KR	SVAC	MVAC	Method
Zeng Ziming [9]		✓	✓		CF
Chen, Chien Chin [3]		✓	✓		MBFRM
Ahmed [11]	✓	✓	✓		KG&Matepath2vec
Zhang Lianfeng [5]	✓		✓		LDA&SECI
Xiong Huixiang [6]	✓			✓	KG
Xu, Yunhong [7]		✓	✓		Meta path
Tao Xing [4]	✓			✓	LDA&W2V-MMR
Lu Heng [12]	✓	✓		✓	KG (No Experiments)
Qian, Liangfeng [8]		✓	✓		Word2Vec
Zhao Haiyan [13]		✓	✓		GAT

Note: KA-Knowledge Association, KR-Knowledge Recommendation, SVAC-Single Virtual Academic Community, MVAC-Multiple Virtual Academic Community

To obtain richer and more comprehensive knowledge, researchers often go to browse multiple virtual academic communities, but the variability among different virtual academic communities poses a great burden to them. From the above table, we can see that the knowledge association and knowledge recommendation of virtual academic communities are still in the initial stage. From the research perspective, most of the existing studies can only take one of the aspects of knowledge association or knowledge recommendation into account, but only effective knowledge association can lay a good foundation for knowledge recommendation, while knowledge recommendation can help researchers bring convenience in knowledge acquisition. In terms of whether it is cross-community or not, most studies only focus on a single virtual academic community, ignoring the researchers' need to acquire more comprehensive knowledge. In terms of usage methods, more and more researchers use knowledge graph for virtual academic community knowledge associations, but they still focus on a single virtual academic community and do not exploit the ability of knowledge graph to handle heterogeneous data from multiple sources. In terms of knowledge recommendation, recommendation methods have also shifted from traditional collaborative filtering to deep learning, but these studies do not perform effective knowledge association before recommendation, so their recommendation effects and interpretability are also lacking. Therefore, we focus on knowledge association and knowledge recommendation across virtual academic communities and use knowledge graph to enhance knowledge association and recommendation across virtual academic communities. Based on this, we use prompt learning to compensate for the poor interpretability caused by the "black box" of deep learning in the past and bring convenience to researchers in virtual academic communities to meet their needs for comprehensive expertise.

3 Research Framework

Our proposed method uses more complex multivariate relationships for modeling, which effectively remedies problems such as the single traditional recommendation relationship. The specific steps of the method: firstly, we need to collect academic resources data from different academic community websites and perform knowledge complementation and knowledge disambiguation on them. Then the architecture of the knowledge graph is designed, and the processed data are imported into the knowledge graph and stored in the Neo4j database. The paths of the knowledge graph are extracted using a meta-path generator, and the path data are transformed and used for the training of the pre-trained model. Finally we extract the positive and negative example data from the knowledge graph and add prompt words and special words. These data are then used to train a prompt learning recommendation model using an improved P-tuning algorithm. When the model is trained, different recommendation lists can be generated for different researchers. Figure 1 illustrates the research framework.

3.1 Knowledge Association Architecture Design

Knowledge Graph Structure. The architecture of the knowledge graph is generally divided into two layers: the schema layer and the data layer. The schema layer is the core of the knowledge graph structure, built on top of the data layer, and usually adopts ontology management to implement the schema layer of the knowledge graph, through the definition of different entity classes and the definition of relationships between entities. The data layer is mainly composed of a series of data facts and the knowledge will be stored in facts, for example, by expressing the facts in the form of triples like (entity A, relation, entity B), (entity, attribute, attribute value). Since there is no knowledge mapping framework for cross-virtual academic communities, we adopt a bottom-up approach by collecting data first and then constructing the knowledge map. The structure of the knowledge graph defined is shown in Fig. 2.

Knowledge Processing and Storage. Since the data structures of different virtual academic communities are not identical and there are duplicate contents. Therefore, we have to perform preprocessing operations on the data to complete the missing keyword entities and to identify the same authors and articles in different communities and fuse them. For knowledge completion, to complete the missing keyword entities, we use the TextRank method to extract the keywords in articles as entities in the knowledge graph. For researchers or articles in different academic communities, they may be the same person or the same article, so knowledge disambiguation is needed. We use FastText to perform article content characterization and calculate similarity to disambiguate. We use the following rules to fuse researchers and academic resources. Firstly, we need to determine whether there are researchers or academic resources with the same name in different academic communities and if so, add them to the candidate set to be fused. Then, we fuse academic resources by performing a rapid vectorized representation of academic resources in the candidate set with FastText and calculating the similarity. If the similarity exceeds 90%, the academic resources are fused with their researchers.

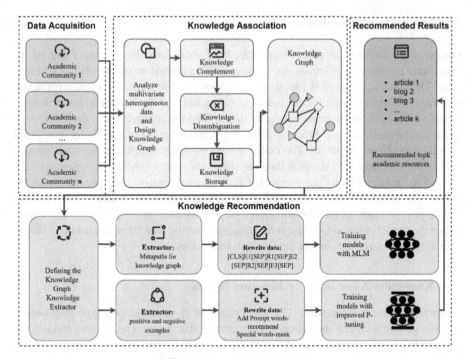

Fig. 1. Research Framework

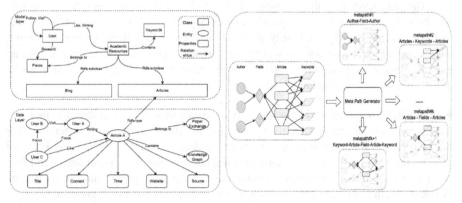

Fig. 2. Knowledge Graph Framework   **Fig. 3.** Multiple Meta Path Generator

Finally, we conduct the integration of researchers. We use FastText to represent the academic resources provided by researchers and calculate the similarity. If the similarity exceeds 90%, researchers will be fused.The above-processed data are imported into the Neo4j database as subgraph.

3.2 Knowledge Recommendation Architecture Design

Knowledge Extraction and Injection. To fully mine the knowledge graph, knowledge extraction paths need to be extracted from the knowledge graph and injected into the pre-trained model. Among the path of the traditional graph extraction models, DeepWalk [14], although powerful, is only applicable to homogeneous networks. There is only 1 type of all node in homogeneous networks, such as researcher-focused relationship networks and paper citation networks, and the information conveyed is limited. But there are numerous heterogeneous networks in real life, which contain many types of nodes, such as academic resource networks. Heterogeneous networks contain more semantic information than homogeneous networks. If we use methods like DeepWalk, then the type information of the nodes is ignored and a lot of semantic information is lost. To address this problem, we use a meta-path-based wandering strategy in Metapath2vec [15]. A meta-path is a predefined sequence of node types, such as ABA representation (Author (Author)-Blog (Blog)-Author (Author)). The definition of meta-paths allows us to obtain a sequence of nodes in a heterogeneous network. Figure 3 shows the schematic diagram of multipath generation.

We are inspired by the work of KG-BERT [16] to use BERT [17] to learn and represent knowledge graph. BERT is an advanced pre-trained contextual language representation model based on a multilayer bidirectional encoder whose encoder is based on a self-attentive mechanism. We use the pre-trained BERT model as the base model and perform knowledge injection operations on this model. We use a multivariate path generator to generate different meta-path templates, and then use the templates to extract the corresponding paths from the knowledge graph as training data and transform them into the following format "[CLS] Entity 1 [SEP] Relationship 1 [SEP] Entity 2 [SEP] Relationship 2 [SEP] Entity 3". The transformed data is fed into the BERT model, which takes a full word mask pattern. After multiple encoders, the output word vector is compared with the masked word vector to calculate the loss. It has been demonstrated that the NSP task is not conducive to the convergence of the overall model loss, so only the masked language modeling task is completed without the next sentence prediction task at the time of knowledge injection. The knowledge from the knowledge graph is injected into the pre-trained model by continuously training the model.

Knowledge Recommendation Based on Prompt Learning. Designing a reasonable prompt template is the key to effectively mining the implicit knowledge in the pre-trained model. However, the current manual design of prompt templates is problematic, and the models are sensitive to the prompt templates, and the results obtained from different templates vary greatly. Therefore, to avoid this failure to mine the knowledge in the pre-trained model due to template design errors, a P-tuning [18] approach is used to enable the model to learn the prompt templates automatically. p-tuning algorithm: using Prompt Encoder (usually Long Short Term Memory (LSTM)) to encode a set of vectors. A new prompt template is formed with the encoded vectors and some keywords, and the data is put into the template and fed into the model for training. The gradient information is passed backward through the model to allow the model to learn the values of these vectors automatically. We have improved P-tuning to obtain more robust templates. Specifically, we introduce a double-layer Transformer encoder and adversarial learning to replace the original LSTM, which still suffers from gradient vanishing and explosion problems when facing long sequences. In contrast, the Transformer encoder can better handle longer sequences with faster parallelism, and the adversarial learning can further improve the robustness of the model to different data. Finally, the training data is filled into the base template and the above-improved P-tuning algorithm is used to train the prompt learning template. We combine the trained template, the pre-training model with knowledge injection and the verbalizer, and use the test data to verify the effect of the model. The model outputs and ranks the researcher's interest level for each article and takes Top-K as the final recommendation list.

4 Data Experiment

4.1 Dataset and Knowledge Graph Construction

We crawled a total of 21326 ScienceNet blogs from December 2015 to June 2022 and 14635 Zhihu articles from September 2013 to June 2022. Academic blogs provide an open space for scholars to disseminate their work and discuss research issues, and its typical representative is ScienceNet. A typical example of a social Q&A community is Zhihu, a well-known and trusted Q&A community on the Chinese Internet.

By summarizing the knowledge fusion strategy, we have integrated 3 users and 5 articles. To verify the validity of the model, the like attribute in the article attribute is regarded as the user's favorite relationship for the article, and this is the target recommended to the user. 3135 users and their favorite relationships are reserved as a test set to verify the effectiveness of the model. Finally, the data is stored in Neo4j and there are 404,920 entities and 924,941 relationships.

4.2 Model Training and Testing Results

A meta-path generator was used to extract 1064747 paths from the knowledge graph and input them into the model in batches. The number of paths for each input model is 128, and the model learning rate is 5E-5. At the same time, to ensure the structure of the original knowledge in the model, only three rounds of training were carried out on the model. For template training, we use "Do you recommend [Y] to [X]? Answer [MASK]" and randomly insert 16 learnable vectors into the template. The training data of the template is mainly the knowledge in the knowledge graph. For example, if user A likes article B, it is considered that article B can be recommended to user A. To simulate the real situation, that is, users are not interested in most articles irrelevant to them, so a lot of users and articles with a distance greater than 3 hops in the knowledge graph are sampled as negative samples. Through the above method, a total of 409425 template training data were extracted. Each time, 512 pieces of data were extracted for model training, and the learning rate was set as 1E-5 for 30 rounds of training.

To verify the validity of the model, we compare the proposed model(MRRVAC) with a meta-path-based recommendation method (Matepath2RS), collaborative filtering (CF), Matepath2vec, Matepath2vec using BERT as a word embedding encoder (Matepath2vec-BERT), graph attention neural network (GAT) and the model without training templates using the improved P-tuning algorithm (MRRVAC(base)) are compared. All of these methods used for comparison were used in the virtual academic community resource recommendation study. In this paper, 3135 links that are not in the knowledge graph are used as test data, and hit rate (HR) and normalized discounted cumulative gain (NDCG) are used for evaluation. The HR mainly emphasizes the accuracy of recommendations, and the NDCG mainly emphasizes the sequential nature of the recommendation. The specific formula is as follows:

$$HR = \frac{\# \, hits}{\# \, users} \tag{1}$$

$$NDCG = \frac{DCG}{IDCG}, DCG = \sum_{i=1}^{n} \frac{2^{ree_i} - 1}{\log_2(i + 1)} \tag{2}$$

where # hits is the intersection of the results recommended by the model and the real preferred results of users in the test set, and # users is the preferred results of users in the test set. IDCG (Ideal Discounted Cumulative Gain) is the most desirable recommendation ranking result. We truncate the recommendation list into different lengths K, K ∈ [5, 10, 15, 20], as a way to verify the comprehensiveness of the results. The following table shows the experimental results for different models (Table 2).

Table 2. Comparison of Recommended Results

Model	HR@K (%)				NDCG@K (%)			
	5	10	15	20	5	10	15	20
Matepath2RS	0.114	0.153	0.212	0.250	0.101	0.143	0.193	0.232
CF	0.112	0.142	0.197	0.238	0.153	0.174	0.218	0.240
Matepath2vec	0.231	0.321	0.394	0.572	0.125	0.207	0.261	0.354
Matepath2vec-BERT	0.315	0.426	0.674	0.853	0.146	0.267	0.356	0.449
GAT	0.226	0.336	0.387	0.492	0.135	0.201	0.252	0.329
MRRVAC (base)	0.310	0.574	0.738	1.164	0.265	0.402	0.488	0.669
MRRVAC	**0.495**	**1.028**	**1.130**	**1.315**	**0.453**	**0.750**	**0.809**	**0.896**

As can be seen from the above table and figure, Matepath2RS requires the manual definition of meta-path, and how to define an effective meta-path requires a large amount of expert knowledge, which directly affects its recommendation effect. CF only considers which articles users like, and does not explore and mine the more complex relationships between users and articles, articles and articles, etc., which makes it difficult to reason and expand. The skip-gram of Matepath2vec needs to set the window size for graph embedding representation, which is effective for short paths (the general window size is 3), but for long paths, it cannot consider more complex context relations. When its encoder is changed to BERT, its graph representation ability is significantly enhanced compared with skip-gram. However, the model does not know that it is a recommendation task, and can only take into account the overall situation, such as predicting whether there is a friend relationship between two people. GAT trains the entire graph as an isomorphic network, which greatly loses heterogeneous information in the network, resulting in poor performance of the model. The unimproved P-tuning method is better than the five recommended methods in both Hit indexes and NDCG indexes. Our method was validated by an average improvement of 0.296% and 0.271% on two metrics.

Furthermore, an ablation experiment is conducted to verify the effectiveness of the proposed architecture design in this paper. The ablation experiment of improving the P-tuning template is carried out first, followed by the ablation experiment of knowledge injection and template training. The ablation results are shown in Table 3.

Table 3. Ablation Experiments

Model	HR@K (%)				NDCG@K (%)			
	5	10	15	20	5	10	15	20
MRRVAC	**0.495**	**1.028**	**1.130**	**1.315**	**0.453**	**0.750**	**0.809**	**0.896**
- w/o BERT-encoder	0.133	0.352	0.400	0.417	0.288	0.344	0.375	0.387
- w/o awp	0.237	0.342	0.470	0.605	0.226	0.300	0.376	0.447
- w/o both	0.310	0.574	0.738	1.164	0.265	0.402	0.488	0.669
- w/o knowledge	0.012	0.033	0.071	0.109	0.018	0.037	0.057	0.074
- w/o template train	0.009	0.034	0.066	0.080	0.015	0.031	0.052	0.062
- w/o both	0.006	0.033	0.056	0.076	0.009	0.024	0.040	0.052

From the ablation experiment, it can be seen that when only the LSTM module is replaced, the BERT-Encoder has a higher risk of overfitting. When adversarial weight perturbation is introduced, the LSTM module has more parameters than the BERT-Encoder, which leads to the underfitting phenomenon of LSTM. Therefore, by combining the advantages and disadvantages of both, the p-tuning can be improved significantly. At the same time, this also verifies the rationality of introducing the two improvement methods simultaneously.

It can be seen from the ablation experiment of knowledge injection and template training that the improvement effect is greater after template training. This may be because the original training data of the pre-training model may contain similar data, so the effect of knowledge injection is not as good as that of template training. When the two are combined, the effect is far better than that of single-use. Therefore, the method of knowledge injection and template training is proved to be reasonable.

5   Conclusion

The emergence of virtual academic communities has enabled researchers to communicate and learn across limitations, but the knowledge in a single virtual academic community often does not meet the needs of researchers. Moreover, we are currently in the era of information explosion, and it is important to consider how to obtain the required knowledge accurately and comprehensively and reduce the expenditure of unnecessary energy. Given the current problems in the study of cross-virtual academic communities, we propose a method for recommending cross-virtual academic communities based on knowledge graph and promptd learning. The method uses knowledge graph to correlate resources in different virtual academic communities and uses prompt learning to achieve recommendations that help researchers access information effectively. We conducted experiments on real data, and the results showed superiority over other recommendation methods for virtual academic communities, verifying the effectiveness of the model recommendation. And after the ablation experiment, we verify the rationality of the model structure.

However, there are some shortcomings in this paper. Since the researcher behavior information of each academic community is not available, we can only rely on the ontology information of the articles when making recommendations. Therefore, in future research, we will build an academic knowledge recommendation platform through which to obtain researcher behavior information, and recommend more accurate and effective academic resources for researchers.

Acknowledgment. This research was supported by Jiangsu Provincial Graduate Research Innovation Program: Research on the Composition, Evolution, and Performance Influencing Mechanism of "Task-based Work Embedding" of Employees in Digital Context (NO. KYCX22_3743), Jiangsu Higher Education Reform Research Project: Talent Training Mode Reform of Big Data and Credit Management from the Perspective of "Industry Embedment" (No. 2021JSJG227) and Research on Panoramic Decision Value Discovery Method based on Manufacturing Enterprise Information System Using Multi-source Data (NO. 71972090).

References

1. Xiaoli, W., Jing, Z., Shuqin, C.: The evolution and its internal knowledge flow in virtual academic community knowledge ecosystem. Inf. Stud.: Theory Appl. **45**(12), 156–163 (2022). (in Chinese)
2. Social, W.A., DataReportal, and Hootsuite: Number of internet and social media users worldwide as of July 2022 (in billions) (2022). https://www.statista.com/statistics/617136/digital-population-worldwide/
3. Chen, C.C., Shih, S.-Y., Lee, M.: Who should you follow? Combining learning to rank with social influence for informative friend recommendation. Decis. Support Syst. **90**, 33–45 (2016)
4. Xing, T., et al.: Automatic summarization of user-generated content in academic Q&A community based on Word2Vec and MMR. Data Anal. Knowl. Discov. **4**(04), 109–118 (2020). (in Chinese)
5. Lianfeng, Z., Hui, L., Yunhe, T.: Knowledge aggregation model based on virtual academic community. Inf. Sci. **37**(06), 55–60+74 (2019). (in Chinese)
6. Huixiang, X., Zirong, Y., Wuxuan, J.: Semantic correlation of multimodal data in the construction of cross-media knowledge graph. Inf. Stud.: Theory Appl. **42**(02), 13–18+24 (2019). (in Chinese)
7. Xu, Y., Zhou, D., Ma, J.: Scholar-friend recommendation in online academic communities: an approach based on heterogeneous network. Decis. Support Syst. **119**, 1–13 (2019)

8. Qian, L., Deng, S.: An empirical study on knowledge aggregation in academic virtual community based on deep learning. Data Inf. Manag. **5**(4), 372–388 (2021)
9. Ziming, Z., Hong, Z.: A study of reputation-based collaborative filtering recommendation techniques in knowledge network communities. Inf. Stud.: Theory Appl. **38**(05), 116–120 (2015). (in Chinese)
10. Yu, T., et al.: Knowledge graph for TCM health preservation: design, construction, and applications. Artif. Intell. Med. **77**, 48–52 (2017)
11. Ahmed, I., Kalhoro, Z.A.: Knowledge driven paper recommendation using heterogeneous network embedding method. J. Comput. Commun. **6**(12), 157 (2018)
12. Heng, L., et al.: Research on deep aggregation framework of academic resources in online community based on knowledge graph. Inf. Stud.: Theory Appl. **44**(01), 180–187 (2021). (in Chinese)
13. Haiyan, Z., et al.: Graph attention network based participant recommendation for issue resolution in open source community. Appl. Res. Comput. **39**(08), 2352–2356+2380 (2022)
14. Perozzi, B., Al-Rfou, R., Skiena, S.: Deepwalk: online learning of social representations. In: Proceedings of the 20th ACM SIGKDD International Conference on Knowledge Discovery and Data Mining (2014)
15. Dong, Y., Chawla, N.V., Swami, A.: metapath2vec: scalable representation learning for heterogeneous networks. In: Proceedings of the 23rd ACM SIGKDD International Conference on Knowledge Discovery and Data Mining (2017)
16. Yao, L., Mao, C., Luo, Y.: KG-BERT: BERT for knowledge graph completion. arXiv preprint arXiv:1909.03193 (2019)
17. Devlin, J., et al.: BERT: pre-training of deep bidirectional transformers for language understanding. arXiv preprint arXiv:1810.04805 (2018)
18. Liu, X., et al.: GPT understands, too. arXiv preprint arXiv:2103.10385 (2021)

How Industrial Supportive Policies Drive the Corporation Attention Shifting: A Case Study of BYD from New Energy Vehicles Industry

Yankun Pan, Meilian Ye, Zhen Zhu[✉], and Shiwei Yu

School of Economics and Management, China University of Geosciences (Wuhan),
Wuhan 430074, Hubei, China
zhuzhen@cug.edu.cn

Abstract. Policies in emerging economies, as environmental factors, have played an important role in promoting the disruptive technology industry development such as new energy vehicle. From Attention-based view, this paper explores how industrial supportive policies drive corporation attention from policy orientation to market orientation by strategy response in a case study of BYD. This paper establishes a three-dimensional framework of "motivate-regulate-shift" and identifies the two phases of China's NEV industrial supportive policy. Based on these, we open the black box of corporate attention shifting: Driven by the changing of policies, firms' regulation in every aspect from strategic direction and organizational restructuring to personnel allocation, resource acquisition and allocation promotes their attention focus to market orientation, which is an inside-out and gradually permeable shifting process. Further, all these strategic responses motivated by policies promote companies' ability to improve their innovation R&D and output results. The finding provides lessons for NEV corporations to become more policy sensitive and more innovative R&D emphasized in disruptive technologies industry.

Keywords: Attention-based view · Disruptive technologies industry · Market and policy orientation · BYD

1 Introduction

In an emerging economy such as China, the government guides economic activity by formulating industrial supportive plans and policies, including the provision of various scarce resources [1] to drive industry development, which motivate corporations to respond and make strategic regulations. Disruptive technologies are technologies that change existing economic sectors, production and consumption principles, causing a broader social transformation [2]. It has the following characteristics [3]: (1) intelligence (2) big data driven (3) facilitation of innovation collaboration within and outside the organization (4) high rate of technology diffusion and adoption. These characteristics

© The Author(s), under exclusive license to Springer Nature Switzerland AG 2023
Y. Tu and M. Chi (Eds.): WHICEB 2023, LNBIP 480, pp. 253–263, 2023.
https://doi.org/10.1007/978-3-031-32299-0_22

create technological barriers that lead to the inability to develop related industries only by corporations themselves, which requires government's coordination and policy drive [4].

The new energy vehicle (NEV) industry is an industry with disruptive technology because of its significant originality and non-linear stepwise growth in battery-motor-electric control, chip technologies and so on. At the same time, the successful nurture of the NEV industry will bring about changes in the vehicle industry and drive economic growth. In line with the two strategic transformations of the national digital economy and the dual carbon plan, new energy vehicles are developing rapidly with policy support. This is why we are focusing on the impact of supportive policies on NEV industry with disruptive technologies.

Existing researches have showed that industrial supportive policy has facilitated the development of new industries. For instance, the Chinese government launched relevant policy to help China's high-speed rail overcome barriers in market and technology [5], which enhance industrial deployment and heighten the industrial structure. However, industrial supportive policies are changed in terms of both aim and content as the industry continues to become more market-oriented, and responded by corporations accordingly. Previous studies have only examined the role of policy in motivating technological innovation and promoting strategic transformation of organizations, and little has been said about how policy change motivate the shifting of corporate attention. Exploring the impact of policy changes on corporations can not only help us understand explicitly the complete process of policy-oriented industrial development in emerging economies, but it also helps us understand the direction of attention and the transition path of innovation transformation in disruptive technology corporations. Based on these, it is significant to dynamically analyze the impact of policy on the attention shifting of firms from a theoretical perspective.

Grounded in Attention-based view, combined with the characteristics of policy drive in emerging markets, we use BYD compony as the research object, try to explore how industrial supportive policies drive corporations' attention from policy orientation to market orientation by strategy response. The findings from our research can be extended to other emerging economies around the world and provide lessons for disruptive technology companies, especially when policy guidance changes.

2 Literature Review

2.1 Attention Based View

Attention-based view(ABV) argues that firm behavior is the result of the situated distribution and allocation of managerial attention, embedded in the broader context of the organization [6]. It consists of three interrelated meta-theoretical principles: focus of attention, situated attention, and attention structures. Enterprise decisions are determined by focus of attention, which is a limited set of issues concerned by decision makers, and attention structures regulate these focuses, embedded in a broader external context, the situated attention. Therefore, ABV provides a behavioral basis to explain how a corporation responds to changes in the external environment by attention structures.

The attention structures include four "regulators": (1) the roles of the game, (2) Resources, (3) Structure positions, (4) Players. The roles of the game is considered to be "the formal and informal principles that guide decision makers in accomplishing the organization's mission and gaining rewards in the process [6]". Resources are "the human, physical, technological, and financial capital that a firm acquires at any given time to achieve its goals". Structural positions define the functions, direction and public relations of decision makers. And Players are all the people involved in the process of conducting strategic behavior. The four regulators interact to guide what, when and how an organization formulates and responds to its environment.

The ABV has applied in a wide range of domains, scholars have focused mostly on attention structures and its regulation. For example, Stevens [7] targeted at for-profit companies, with firm performance influencing the allocation of CEOs' attention structures(the roles of the game, resources, and players), explored how attention allocation affects conflicting organizational goals. Most studies on ABV have selectively focused on specific parts of the theory to the neglect of other parts [8], and few studies have used policy motivation as a situated attention.

2.2 Market and Policy Orientation

ABV emphasizes the impact of its focus, and previous research has argued that strategic orientation reflects a firm's focus of attention and influences the intensity of its allocation [9]. From the perspective of corporate action, strategic orientation includes both market orientation and policy orientation. Market orientation reflect the corporate's focus to market elements, it is closely associated with technology orientation, entrepreneurial orientation, consumer orientation... And policy orientation embodies the corporation's attention to government policy motivation in emerging economy. These two major strategy orientations can well explain the strategic response to policies change focused by NEV corporations based on this study.

Market Orientation. Market orientation refers to the generation, transmission, and response of the entire organization to market intelligence, customer needs, and competitive trends [10]. It guiding decision makers to focus on the market, including customers, competitors, and industry structure, to better guide corporations in their strategic decisions. Market orientation has played an important role in promoting corporation innovation, and Distanont [11] argued that innovation is an important source of competitive advantage for companies, market orientation has a significant positive influence on it. Thus, market orientation guides corporations to respond mainly by focusing on the current state of the market and focuses on innovation to improve performance.

Policy Orientation. Policy orientation is defined as the activities of corporations that regulate their operations by paying attention to the industrial supportive policies published by the government. This strategic orientation guides corporations to adapt to corresponding changes in the external environment [12], such as the behavioral principle of regulating their strategic activities to ensure their viability and performance in response to policy changes. In an emerging economy like China, national policy motivation is crucial for the development of industries. At different stages of the development of industries, policy instruments are flexibly changed, which affects corporations in different ways. Industrial policy plays an active role in the transformation of China's economy from high growth to high quality growth [13].

When the industry in its early stage, corporations usually focus on the drive of government policies to gain profits, which is manifested as policy orientation. When the industry market is large enough, corporations tend to focus their attention on market information, which is embodied in market orientation. Corporations will selectively focus their attention on relevant issues [6], so that the focus of attention will be concentrated on policy orientation or market orientation.

In many industries in China, including NEVs, two strategic orientation mechanisms complement each other and provide strategic guidance for corporations to adapt to the turbulence of the external environment and demand uncertainty in stages. Using BYD as a case study, this study takes industrial supportive policies as a motivation situation and examines how corporations regulate their attention structure, and thus realize the process of changing their attention focus from policy orientation to market orientation.

3 Case Study and Discussion

3.1 Case Selection and Data Collection

BYD Company Limited (BYD) is chosen as research case for the following reasons. Firstly, BYD's responsive behavior motivated by the policy is remarkable. From the 2019 China's Government Public Notice Document, it can be seen that BYD received close to 1/5 of the total subsidy amount, which was the most. BYD thus has a 30% Chinese market share in 2021. Secondly, BYD has completed its transformation to the NEV track by establishing advantages in core technologies through its independent innovation strategy. That's means its successful experience is a good reference for the study of the transformation process of NEV corporations from policy orientation to market orientation.

In this study, the data collection is divided into two parts: (1) BYD's corporate data: From BYD's official website, annual reports, industry development reports, and Internet news, and we continuously tracked the updates of secondary information. (2) Policy information: Through the database of "Political Eyesight", and used the China Government Website, Policy Research Reports, we obtain policy implementation.

Secondary data can provide a feasible and general research method for case studies. Firstly, we compared case information disclosed in industry research reports and literature to identify case study subjects. Secondly, by identifying and building a chain of evidence for the case data from these data, we triangulate the validity of the data.

3.2 BYD'S Background in NEV Industry

Following the ABV, the allocation of BYD's attention in recent years can be summarized into two stages: In the first stage, BYD leveraged the dividends of policies and focused mainly on gaining profits. Firstly, on technology R&D, the company absorbed and accumulated existing technologies in a low-cost manner. Secondly, in terms of supply chain and organizational structure, the company adopted a vertical integration model. Thirdly, in terms of products, the company relied on cost-effective fuel vehicles and NEVs to have a high share in the low-end market.

In the second stage, as the industry matured, policies began to motivate corporations to focus on the market, manifested mainly in the support for innovative R&D. For BYD, it is mainly demonstrated as follows: firstly, the company received funds from the market and invested them in the R&D of disruptive technologies, such as blade battery and e3.0. Secondly, it opened up the supply chain and adjusted the organizational structure to support innovative R&D. Third, BYD focused on NEV only and entered the mid-to-high end market through disruptive technologies.

3.3 Case Discussion

We will discuss how BYD's attention structure is regulated to reflect the shifting of attentional focus in response to the policy change.

Situated Attention. As an external environment, policies are constantly changed Macroscopically to reflect new trends in industry development [14], thus influencing corporations to make strategic responses. We will research how the drive for industry support policies and their changes have influenced a shift in attention from policy to market orientation for NEV corporations.

In the first stage, the NEV subsidy policy and the initial version of the "double-points" (双积分) policy are launched as industrial supportive policies. Subsidy policy provides funds for business operations. The "double-points" includes positive and negative ones, positive-points can bring additional trading profits, while negative-points can lead to higher prices or even forced discontinuation of the relevant models. The effects of the two policies are as follows: (1) Motivating corporations to carry out business activities and survival with sufficient financial support. (2) Promoting the healthy development of corporations and the electrification of the industry by regulation of "double-points". These encourages BYD to make policy orientation to adapt the characteristics of the industry and achieve economic goals by the subsidy.

In the second stage, the domestic market is maturing as NEV corporations respond the policies positively in the first stage. The country's subsidy reduction policy, "double-points" revision policy and chip development policy are the change of the industrial supportive policies, which manifested in (1) Staged reduction of subsidy funds. (2) Regulate the points supply and demand balance by lowing the number of points per vehicle. (3) Encouraging chip R&D and relevant corporations to go public. These changes aimed at motivating corporations to turn their attention to the market and improve disruptive technologies standards. Driven by these policies, BYD regulate its attention structure, increase its sensitivity to the market, including consumers, collaborators, inter-organizations… And enhance the profitability of the company's innovation.

Attention Structure Regulation. *The Roles of The Game.* The Roles of The Game embodies a set of norms, values and beliefs shared by the organization, providing a logic of action that guides the organization's strategic interests and decision making.

Policy orientation identification: The "double-points" policy pushes traditional car corporations to change their strategic direction, at this time BYD, as a major holder in positive-points, already has a very obvious advantage in low-end market share. Therefore, by complying with the "double-points" policy, BYD develops both fuel and new energy vehicles. These can maintain its advantage and achieve company's economic goals, performing as policy orientation.

Market orientation identification: The intensified competition in the NEV industry led to an oversupply of positive-points, the government thus lowered the number of points per vehicle, BYD thus becomes less profitable. BYD's strategy of shifting focus to the market and concentrating on the NEV business only is in line with the current market development trend. Firstly, this strategy action release production capacity for NEV development and promote brand image upgrading by entering the mid-to-high end market. Meanwhile, the discontinuation of fuel car production also marks the roles of BYD's game formally regulated to completion.

Structure Positions. This regulator provides decision makers with identities that govern how they think and act in the organization [6]. At the same time the business will develop specialized subsidiaries that give the business entrepreneur greater flexibility to act.

Policy orientation identification: In the early stage of industry development, the subsidy policy encouraged corporations to enter the industry vigorously and reduced technology licensing. BYD combined the subsidy funds with its vertical integration model to accumulate the core technology of NEV at a lower cost. This allowed the company to gain profits just by conforming to the policy.

Market orientation identification: As the disruptive technology industry maturing, the government began to increase the technology threshold to promote high-quality development, launched policy to encourage semiconductor company to go public to raise funds. Grounded in this motivation, on the one hand, BYD opened up its supply chain and increased its subsidiaries (see Fig. 1.) to release the market potential of the businesses, the semiconductor subsidiary introduced diversified strategic investors and aimed at going public, which has seized the market opportunity brought by the disruptive technology industry upstream of NEV. On the other hand, BYD adjusted TMT appointments at semiconductor subsidiary, this enhanced the flexibility and innovation of the subsidiary.

Players. Not only do Players include decision-makers, but they also include other actors within and outside the corporation: departmental management, workers, active board members and so on [6].

Policy orientation identification: The initial subsidy policy led to the "rough" development of the industry, which was manifested in companies' focus on profitability. And BYD conformed the policy, aimed to maintain market share by selling more at lower margins and paying more attention to the training of non-R&D employees.

Market orientation identification: Firstly, influenced by the subsidy reduction policy, BYD's market orientation emphasized on innovation ability step-by-step. The company enhanced its market competitiveness fundamentally by improving their talent training system, especially the increase of the R&D talents (see Fig. 2). Secondly, motivated by the chip policy, BYD paid attention to the technology executives in this field, and implemented equity incentives for Players in semiconductor subsidiary, which released strategic-level importance signals in semiconductor innovation development.

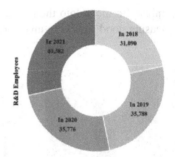

Fig. 1. BYD New subsidiary corporations   **Fig. 2.** BYD R&D employees

Resources. The reallocation of Resources can shape the organization's consideration of additional programs [6], allowing decision makers to focus more on goals other than economic ones, facilitating a switch in focus of attention.

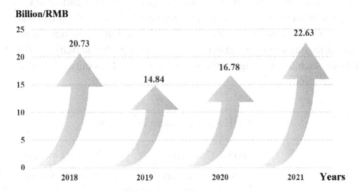

Fig. 3. Government funding for BYD

Policy orientation identification: Corporations prioritized the allocation of subsidy funds to their daily operations. Under the orientation of this industrial supportive policies, BYD successfully increased market share in low-end market, and the company achieved profitability mainly by cost-effective products rather than disruptive and innovative products. As a result, the company's R&D investment and internal R&D intangible assets are also maintained at a relatively low proportion.

Market orientation identification: As a situated attention, when the subsidy policy reduced (see Fig. 3), BYD was motivated to produce a three-fold Resource regulation. Firstly, in terms of Resource sources, the company shifted from relying on government subsidies to investors in the market for equity financing. Secondly, in terms of Resource allocation, the BYD's vertical integration model advantage has formally shifted to market orientation that enhances innovation capabilities. These manifested in the increase of R&D investment (see Fig. 4) and intangible assets for internal R&D (see Fig. 5). Further, the market opening and cooperation of technology, such as the blade battery and e3.0, has helped BYD's open supply chain ecological layout. The diversified products enabled the company to move into the mid-to-high-end market, increasing market penetration and releasing good signals to investors in the capital market.

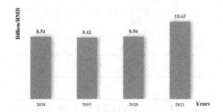

Fig. 4. BYD R&D investment   **Fig. 5.** BYD Internal R&D intangible assets

In summary (see Table 1), industrial supportive policies as situated attention in changing to motivate BYD to regulate its four aspects of attention structure. Grounded in the attention structure, the attention focus of policy orientation is manifested in the focus on policy dividends to achieve economic goals and low-end market share at low cost. The attention focus market orientation reflects the focus on consumers, collaborators, and interorganizational in the market. To achieve long-term development of NEV products, technologies and penetration into the mid-to-high-end markets, BYD conducts strategy actions such as opening up the supply chain and encouraging the development of disruptive technologies.

Table 1. Case discussion summary

		Policy Orientation	Market Orientation
Situated Attention		• Support new energy vehicle corporations' survival by subsidies • Promote electrification of the industry by "double-points"	• Stimulate innovation and Cooperation by subsidy rollback • Regulate the points market balance by lowing the number of points per vehicle • Encourage chip R&D
Regulators	The Roles of game	• Low-end market • NEV and Fuel Vehicle Business	• Development of NEV only • Mid-to-high end market
	Players	• Emphasize non-R&D employees	• Cultivating R&D employees • Incentivize R&D executives

(continued)

Table 1. (*continued*)

		Policy Orientation	Market Orientation
Structure Positions		• Vertical integration model	• Open Supply Chain • New chairman of subsidiary • Subsidiary gone public
Resources		• Subsidy bonuses • Profitability	• Equity financing • Technology openness • Diversified product ecology
Outcome		• Increased market share in low-end market • Lower cost for technology accumulation and per vehicle	• Open supply chain ecological layout • Strategy to focus on NEV business • Mid-to-high-end market penetration by disruptive technologies

4 Results and Conclusions

The NEV industry is booming around the world, and more corporations are entering the stage of high-quality development and taking the initiative in the market. Thus our conclusions are instructive. It includes the following two aspects:

On the one hand, we establish a framework that summarized in three dimensions of "motivate-regulate-shift" (see Fig. 6): (1) Policy changes serve as a situated attention to motivate strategic actions. (2) The strategic action of the company is reflected in the four regulators. (3) The regulate of the attention structure reflects the change of the corporate attention focus shift from policy orientation to market orientation. Moreover, through the description of the case and the framework, two phases of China's NEV industrial supportive policy are identified, with the former phase aiming to guide the convergence of resources for industrial development and the latter phase aiming at the marketisation of industry when the industry has reached a certain scale.

On the other hand, we open the black box of corporate attention shifting. Firstly, driven by the changing of policies, firms' regulation in every aspect from strategic direction and organizational restructuring to personnel allocation, resource acquisition and allocation promotes their attention focus to market orientation, which is an inside-out and gradually permeable shifting process. Secondly, as disruptive technology companies, all these strategic responses motivated by policies promote companies' ability to improve their innovation R&D and output results, which in turn enable them to develop a competitive advantage at the technology level.

The contributions of this study can be summarized as follows: Firstly, from the theoretical application perspective, we extend the research and application of Situated attention based on ABV. We analyze the industrial supportive policy and its change as an element of Situated attention. This provides an empirical case study for the ABV in the context of policy situated attention. Meanwhile, we demonstrate the relationship

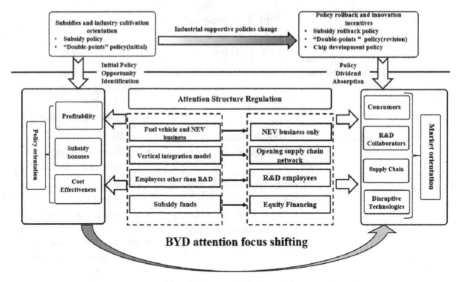

Fig. 6. Research framework

and the process of action between the three metatheories of ABV, further enriching the application of the theory. These are conducive to provide new ideas for subsequent researches about this theory, especially the policy element in emerging markets.

In addition, from a view of practical, we explore a case study about how BYD complete the shifting from policy to market orientation through a series of strategic actions driven by industrial supportive policies. This finding provides lessons for NEV corporations to become more policy sensitive and more innovative R&D emphasized in the disruptive technologies industry.

Acknowledgement. This research was supported by the National Natural Science Foundation of China under Grant 72293572.

References

1. Sheng, S., Zhou, K.Z., Li, J.J.: The effects of business and political ties on firm performance: evidence from China. J. Mark. **75**(1), 1–15 (2011)
2. Bongomin, O., Gilibrays Ocen, G., Oyondi Nganyi, E., Musinguzi, A., Omara, T.: Exponential disruptive technologies and the required skills of industry 4.0. J. Eng. **2020**, 1–17 (2020). https://doi.org/10.1155/2020/4280156
3. Bailey, D., Faraj, S., Hinds, P., von Krogh, G., Leonardi, P.: Special issue of organization science: emerging technologies and organizing. Organ. Sci. **30**(3), 642–646 (2019). https://doi.org/10.1287/orsc.2019.1299
4. He, J.: The role of government in catching up and surpassing emerging technology industries: a new perspective on industrial policy research. Soc. Sci. China (11), 105–124+206–207 2022. (in Chinese)

5. Wong, Z., Chen, A., Shen, C., Wu, D.: Fiscal policy and the development of green transportation infrastructure: the case of China's high-speed railways. Econ. Chang. Restruct. **55**(4), 2179–2213 (2022)
6. Ocasio, W.: Towards an attention-based view of the firm. Strateg. Manag. J. **18**, 187–206 (1997)
7. Stevens, R., Moray, N., Bruneel, J., Clarysse, B.: Attention allocation to multiple goals: the case of for-profit social enterprises: attention allocation to multiple goals. Strateg. Manag. J. **36**(7), 1006–1016 (2015)
8. Brielmaier, C., Friesl, M.: The attention-based view: review and conceptual extension towards situated attention. Int. J. Manag. Rev. **25**(1), 99–129 (2022). https://doi.org/10.1111/ijmr.12306
9. Chen, X., Chen, A.X., Zhou, K.Z.: Strategic orientation, foreign parent control, and differentiation capability building of international joint ventures in an emerging market. J. Int. Mark. **22**(3), 30–49 (2014)
10. Ho, K.L.P., Nguyen, C.N., Adhikari, R., Miles, M.P., Bonney, L.: Exploring market orientation, innovation, and financial performance in agricultural value chains in emerging economies. J. Innov. Knowl. **3**(3), 154–163 (2018)
11. Distanont, A., Khongmalai, O.: The role of innovation in creating a competitive advantage. Kasetsart J. Soc. Sci. **41**(1), 15–21 (2020)
12. Hakala, H.: Strategic orientations in management literature: three approaches to understanding the interaction between market, technology, entrepreneurial and learning orientations: orientations in management literature. Int. J. Manag. Rev. **13**(2), 199–217 (2011)
13. Yu, L.C., Zhang, W.G., Bi, Q.: Industrial policy and enterprises' transition from real economy to virtual economy: market orientation or policy arbitrage? Nankai Bus. Rev. **24**(04), 128–142 (2021). (in Chinese)
14. Nadkarni, S., Barr, P.S.: Environmental context, managerial cognition, and strategic action: an integrated view. Strateg. Manag. J. **29**(13), 1395–1427 (2008)

Optimal Platform Intrusion and Supplier Selection Strategy Oriented by Fresh Agriculture Product Supply Chains of Different Power-Structure

Zhenhai Tan, Chunnian Liu, and Lan Yi[✉]

Nanchang University, 999 Xuefu Avenue, Nanchang, China
tzh20230119@163.com

Abstract. In light of the growing prevalence of online channels, e-commerce platforms have increasingly collaborated with suppliers or rural cooperatives to open self-operated stores, with the aim of maximizing profits. However, given the regional variation in supply chain dynamics, suppliers and rural cooperatives may not always occupy the same position in the supply chain, leading to simultaneous challenges of channel conflicts and power imbalances. About the channel intrusions by e-commerce platforms, this study introduces one fresh-product supply chain of one producer, one provider and one B2C e-commerce platform and studies the optimal strategy for enterprises in the fresh-product pricing and channel selection with a theoretical model construction. Results from the study show that e-commerce platforms in any model will support the weaker side in the supply chain for much more profits. At the same time, rural cooperatives and suppliers will actively cooperate with e-commerce platforms' opening self-run stores. The theoretical value of this study lies in its insights into the optimal strategies for supply chain enterprises in the face of e-commerce platform intrusion and power-structure competition. The practical value of the research lies in its provision of guidance for e-commerce platforms to support the weaker party in the supply chain and to actively cooperate with rural cooperatives in launching self-run stores. However, further research is needed to explore optimal strategies for enterprises under different power structures and information asymmetry.

Keywords: Power Structure · Fresh-keeping Effort · Channel Conflict

1 Introduction

Due to the perishable products, the demand and price fluctuation and the increasing awareness of food safety, fresh-product supply chains show more complicated comparing with traditional supply chains. In B2C, preservation efforts play a vital role for the consumers' option to purchase, triggering their willingness and thus growing the profitability. Herein, self-run stores by e-commerce platforms were gradually started up to cater for the changing ideas on consumption [1]. For instance, Luochuan Apple initially

© The Author(s), under exclusive license to Springer Nature Switzerland AG 2023
Y. Tu and M. Chi (Eds.): WHICEB 2023, LNBIP 480, pp. 264–277, 2023.
https://doi.org/10.1007/978-3-031-32299-0_23

opened its official flag store on Jingdong platform in 2015[1] followed by Jingdong's intrusion with its self-run stores in 2021[2]. To platforms, such intrusion by self-run stores would bring some advantages and disadvantages. On the one hand, it would be easier to gain more consumers' trust and more profits for platforms [2]. And their reputation would be maintained properly. On the other hand, self-run stores introduced would cause channel conflicts [3] and resistances among suppliers.

Rural cooperatives [4] are of regional monopoly and more control of supply chains than any single agriculture products suppliers. As a result, rural cooperatives have greater power than suppliers in the supply chain. However, if the supplier monopolizes the sales channel, the power of the supplier in the supply chain will exceed that of the rural cooperative. The relationship between e-commerce platforms and rural cooperatives is complex. On the one hand, e-commerce platforms need to partner with rural cooperatives to open their own stores to boost profits. On the other hand, they are concerned about suppliers' dissatisfaction. Rural cooperatives cooperate with e-commerce platforms to push agricultural products to a wider market for higher profits. Therefore, the relationship between e-commerce platforms and rural cooperatives is based on cooperation. Moreover, e-commerce platforms occupy relatively large channel advantages in the supply chain. Therefore, there exists three power balance models between rural cooperatives and suppliers: Nash game (NE), Stackelberg game (FL) and Stackelberg game (SL). The power of e-commerce platforms in the supply chain is always the largest.

Based on the above analysis, target questions to be solved are as follows: Should e-commerce platforms intrude the market by opening self-run stores? And if yes, who should be selected as the supplier of those stores? Facing the channel intrusion by e-commerce platforms, how would rural cooperatives and suppliers under different power structures formulate optimal strategies or refuse to cooperate with e-commerce platforms' self-run stores? The paper offers a new perspective on the impact of changes in power structure on decision-making within the supply chain when e-commerce platforms dominate, as well as how e-commerce platforms can alter the power structure to optimize channel intrusion strategies.

The following are the latest related literature review in Section Two, the question description and utility function composition in Section Three, three theoretical models under different power structures in Section Four, and the summary and remark in Section Five. And the appendix covers all verification related and optimal solutions.

2   Literature Review

2.1   Agriculture Product Supply Chain

The Chinese government at all levels has attached great importance to the supply chain of agricultural products in e-commerce. Research on e-commerce and supply chain

---

[1] https://shop.m.jd.com/?shopId=171136&gx=RnE2y2MNbmXZydTACj6h2HDKjFNp8Rw&
ad_od=share&utm_source=androidapp&utm_medium=appshare&utm_campaign=t_3351
39774&utm_term=QQfriends.

[2] https://shop.m.jd.com/?shopId=1000372103&gx=RnE2y2MNbmXZydTACj6h2HDKjFN
p8Rw&ad_od=share&utm_source=androidapp&utm_medium=appshare&utm_campaign=
t_335139774&utm_term=QQfriends.

optimization mainly focuses on the intermediary and information sharing functions of e-commerce. Zeng et al. believes that rural e-commerce can alleviate the negative effects of information asymmetry caused by physical distance and improve the selling prices of small farmers [5]. GuoHua et al. compared traditional and modern agricultural supply chains using an evolutionary game model and found that e-commerce can solve the problem of information asymmetry [6]. In addition, a considerable number of scholars have studied the pricing decisions of the agricultural supply chain from the perspective of e-commerce pricing strategy. Ma et al. discussed the pricing strategy and coordination mechanism of the three-tier cold chain supply chain under the supervision of quota and trade [7]. Wang and Zhao explored cold chain investment and optimal pricing decisions by establishing an optimization model of the fresh supply chain [8]. Chen et al. constructed four dynamic pricing models based on different price adjustment frequencies and analyzed the influence of menu costs on dynamic pricing decisions [9]. Ye et al. analyzed the effects of the uncertainty of the yield and demand of fresh agricultural products and the degree of risk aversion of farmers on the optimal production and pricing decisions of contract agricultural supply chain members [10].

However, most of the literature focuses on the information-mediating role of e-commerce and the pricing strategy of the agricultural product supply chain. Few studies have considered the channel conflicts of e-commerce platforms and the influence of power structures on the supply chain.

2.2 Power Structure

Power in the supply chain is often modeled through the sequence of actions of the parties, assuming that the first mover has more power than the late mover or even the third party. Yang et al. [11] and Hu et al. [12] believed that different supply chain power structures led to significant differences in the operational decisions made by participants. Li and Mizuno studied dynamic pricing and inventory management in dual-channel supply chains under different power structures [13]. Moreover, with the continuous development of e-commerce and the channel subsidence of e-commerce platforms, the traditional secondary power structure is faced with more complex channel conflicts. Zhi et al. examined how power structures affect the financing decisions of cash-strapped downstream retailers who can raise money from third-party logistics providers or suppliers [14]. Liu et al. discussed the influence of power structure in a three-tier supply chain using a collector-led Stackelberg game, a retailer-led Stackelberg game, and a manufacturer-led Stackelberg game [15].

However, most studies on power structure focus more on the second-level supply chain and the influence of supply chain rights on profits and less on the cross-impact of the third-level supply chain, channel intrusion, and e-commerce.

2.3 E-Commerce Platform Settlement

Channel conflict is a critical aspect of supply chain management that plays a significant role in enterprise strategy and profit. The influence of different channel structures on the performance of the supply chain has been empirically and theoretically tested in previous studies (Jena and Mina) [16]. Most researchers believe that manufacturers' direct channel intrusion poses a threat to downstream retailers and leads to serious channel conflicts (Alaei et al.) [17]. Therefore, many scholars have designed various coordination contracts to improve the performance of supply chains and alleviate channel conflicts (Chen et al.) [18]. Additionally, some scholars have explored the channel strategies of different industries from various perspectives, such as retailers, upstream enterprises, and other factors. For example, Chen and Wang believe that there are two channels in the smartphone supply chain, namely free channels and bundled channels. The results show that the power structure significantly affects the channel preferences of enterprises and the entire supply chain [19]. He considered selling products through different channels at different times to alleviate channel conflicts [20].

Most studies consider the influence of channel conflict from the perspective of supply chain participants and other factors, and few studies discuss the influence of power structure on channel conflict. Therefore, this paper discusses the optimal strategy of other members with weak power in the supply chain when the e-commerce platform with a strong position conducts channel intrusion from the perspective of power structure.

3 Problem Description and Model

Here is to consider a fresh product supply chain of one producer, one provider and one B2C e-commerce platform. On the B2C platform, there is a self-run store and a third-party non-self-run store. They sell respective fresh products with different preservation levels to the same group of consumers, with "t" for self-run and "s" for third-party non-self-run respectively. Three models are considered: NE, where the power is balanced between rural cooperatives and suppliers; SL, where suppliers dominate and rural cooperatives introduce self-run stores; and FL, where rural cooperatives dominate and suppliers introduce self-run stores. The e-commerce platform is the leader in all models, with different followers. Table 1 lists symbols used in the models:

3.1 Demand Function

In practice, consumers may value the products of third-party seller differently [18]. The product valuation is denoted by $\theta\phi$, in which ϕ is the consumers' initial evaluation products and is uniformly distributed above [0, 1). Therefore, the consumers' utility function in purchasing fresh products under only third-party stores is defined as:

$$u_s = \theta\phi - p_s + b\tau_s \tag{1}$$

Hereby, non-self-run stores' demand function for fresh products can be easily deduced as:

$$D_s = 1 - \frac{(p_s - b\tau_s)}{\theta} \tag{2}$$

Therefore, self-run stores' demand function for fresh products can be easily deduced as:

$$\begin{cases} u_t = \phi - p_t + b\tau_t \\ u_s = \theta\phi - p_s + b\tau_s \end{cases} \tag{3}$$

Table 1. Model Symbols and Definition

Symbols	Variable description
p_i	$i = s$ Retail price of fresh products in third-party non-self-run stores $i = t$ Retail price of fresh products in self-run stores
f	Share or commission by self-run suppliers of e-commerce platforms
w_i	$i = s$ Wholesale price in third-party non-self-run stores (Unit cost of third-party non-self-run stores) $i = t$ Wholesale price of fresh products in self-run stores (Unit cost of self-run stores)
τ_i	$i = s$ Suppliers' fresh-keeping effort level $i = t$ E-commerce platforms' fresh-keeping effort level
ϕ	Consumers' willingness-to-pay for fresh products'
θ	Consumers' acceptance level to non-self-run stores
h_i	$i = s$ Suppliers' fresh-keeping cost $i = t$ E-commerce platforms' fresh-keeping cost
b	Consumers' sensitiveness to fresh-keeping effort
T	Annual service charge
D	Product demand
$\prod$	Profit

Due to the requirements $D_t \geqslant 0$ and $D_s \geqslant 0$ of the model B, $p_s \geqslant 0$ must exist, and the endogenous variables in models DS and DF should also be greater than 0. However, due to space limitations, this paper does not provide a detailed discussion of the variables. It is assumed that all variables are greater than zero, including the demand function.

Preservation efforts involve a cost problem, but we have observed that most e-commerce platforms invest less in cold chain infrastructure. In order to better reflect the reality of e-commerce, we did not choose preservation efforts as endogenous variables. Instead, we focused on the commission fee, which can be adjusted by larger suppliers or rural cooperatives through negotiations with the local e-commerce platform.

Notably, u_t and u_s respectively represent the fresh-product purchase utility from self-run and third-party stores. Thus, $u_t(\phi) = u_s(\phi)$ is the assumption, in which ϕ_0 is the indifference point between "t" and "s".

Hence, the product demand of both types of stores is described as:

$$
\begin{cases}
D_T = 1 - \dfrac{p_t - p_s + b(\tau_s - \tau_t)}{1 - \theta} \\[4mm]
D_S = \dfrac{p_t - p_s + b(\tau_s - \tau_t)}{1 - \theta} - \dfrac{(p_s - b\tau_s)}{\theta}
\end{cases}
\tag{4}
$$

Next, another assumption that $h_s = \frac{k\tau_s^2}{2}$ stands for the supplier fresh-keeping cost [9], and $h_t = \frac{k\tau_t^2}{2}$ is the e-commerce platform fresh-keeping cost.

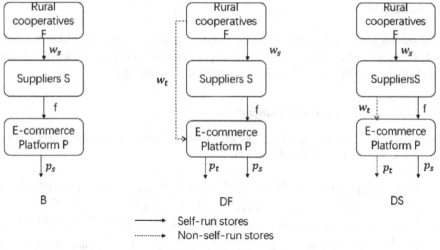

Fig. 1. Model B, DF and DS

3.2 Basic Model, DF Model and DS Model

This section introduces three models: the basic model without self-run stores (B) for power structures NE, FL, and SL, extended by introducing self-run stores for each of them in model DF; and model DS, where suppliers also introduce self-run stores under power structures NE, FL, and SL. Detailed calculation results are in Appendix 1. Table 2 and Fig. 1 lists calculation formula used in the models:

Table 2. Model and calculation formula.

Model	Calculation formula
B	$\Pi_F^B = w_s D_S$ $\Pi_S^B = (p_s - w_s - f)D_S - \frac{k\tau_s^2}{2} - T$ $\Pi_P^B = fD_S + T$
DF	$\Pi_F^{DF} = w_t D_T + w_s D_S$ $\Pi_S^{DF} = (p_s - w_s - f)D_S - \frac{k\tau_s^2}{2} - T$ $\Pi_P^{DF} = (p_t - w_t)D_T + fD_S - \frac{k\tau_t^2}{2} + T$
DS	$\Pi_F^{DS} = w_s(D_T + D_S)$ $\Pi_S^{DS} = (w_t - w_s)D_T + (p_s - w_s - f)D_S - \frac{k\tau_s^2}{2} - T$ $\Pi_P^{DS} = (p_t - w_t)D_T + fD_S - \frac{k\tau_t^2}{2} + T$

4 Analysis

This section observes two circumstances: under the same model and under the same power-structure. We further consider the impact of introducing the model of self-run stores on the optimal decision-making of supply chain participants.

4.1 Main Conclusion-Profit Comparison

Proposition 1. Comparison of the optimal profit of rural cooperatives under three power-structure models of B, DF and DS.

(a) Under the model B, $\Pi_F^{B-FL} > \Pi_F^{B-NE} > \Pi_F^{B-SL}$; under model DF, $\Pi_F^{DF-FL} > \Pi_F^{DF-NE} > \Pi_F^{DF-SL}$; under model DS, $\Pi_F^{DF-FL} > \Pi_F^{DF-NE} > \Pi_F^{DF-SL}$.

(b) Under the same power-structure, the NE model gets $\Pi_f^{DF-NE} > \Pi_f^{DS-NE} = \Pi_f^{B-NE}$; under the power of SL, $\Pi_f^{DF-SL} > \Pi_f^{DS-SL} = \Pi_f^{B-SL}$; under the power of FL, $\Pi_f^{DF-FL} > \Pi_f^{DS-FL} = \Pi_f^{B-FL}$.

Proposition 1(a) shows that the rural-cooperative-dominated supply chain (FL) achieves profit maximization, followed by power equilibrium (NE), and the supplier-dominated supply chain (FL) receives the smallest profits. This indicates the competitiveness of rural cooperatives from being the leader of the Stackelberg game to the participant of the Nash-equilibrium, and to the followers of the Stackelberg game. Proposition 1(b) indicates that the profit of rural cooperatives from their self-run stores (DF) is greater than the profit of suppliers from their self-run stores (DS) under any power structure. Therefore, rural cooperatives are more likely to introduce e-commerce platforms to conduct supply directly.

Proposition 2. Three power structure models of B, DF and DS, the optimal profit comparison of suppliers.

(a) Under the model B, $\Pi_s^{B-SL} > \Pi_s^{B-NE} > \Pi_s^{B-FL}$; under model DF, $\Pi_s^{DF-SL} > \Pi_s^{DF-NE} > \Pi_s^{DF-FL}$; under model DS, $\Pi_s^{DS-SL} > \Pi_s^{DS-NE} > \Pi_s^{DS-FL}$.

(b) Under the same power-structure, under the NE model, if $\theta_1 < \theta < \theta_2, \Pi_s^{DS-NE} > \Pi_s^{B-NE} > \Pi_s^{DF-NE}$, other $\Pi_s^{DS-NE} > \Pi_s^{DF-NE} > \Pi_s^{B-NE}$; under the power of SL, if $\theta_1 < \theta < \theta_2$, $\Pi_s^{DS-SL} > \Pi_s^{B-SL} > \Pi_s^{DF-SL}$, other, $\Pi_s^{DS-SL} > \Pi_s^{DF-SL} > \Pi_s^{B-SL}$; under the power of FL, if $\theta_1 < \theta < \theta_2$ $\Pi_s^{DS-FL} > \Pi_s^{B-FL} > \Pi_s^{DF-FL}$, other, $\Pi_s^{DS-FL} > \Pi_s^{DF-FL} > \Pi_s^{B-FL}.\theta_1 = \frac{-b^2\tau_t^2 - 2b\tau_s + 1}{2} - \frac{(b\tau_t+1)(b^2\tau_t^2+4b\tau_s-2b\tau_t+1)^{1/2}}{2}$ $\theta_2 = \frac{-b^2\tau_t^2-2b\tau_s+1}{2} + \frac{(b\tau_t+1)(b^2\tau_t^2+4b\tau_s-2b\tau_t+1)^{1/2}}{2}$.

Proposition 2(a) states that profits are highest in supplier-dominated supply chains, followed by power equilibrium and lowest in rural cooperatives. Proposition 2(b) shows that suppliers tend to introduce e-commerce platforms and generate larger profits. When consumer acceptance of non-self-run stores is moderate, the basic model generates more profit than self-run stores of rural cooperatives. Self-run stores generate more profit when consumer acceptance is either high or low.

Management inspiration: suppliers should invest certain resources to increase competition with rural cooperatives for the maintenance of power-structure advantages, and at the same time actively cooperate with e-commerce platforms to open self-run stores.

Proposition 3. Three power structure models of B, DF and DS; the optimal profit comparison of e-commerce platforms.

(a) Under the model B, $\Pi_P^{B-NE} > \Pi_P^{B-FL} = \Pi_P^{B-SL}$; under model DF, $\Pi_P^{DF-NE} > \Pi_P^{DF-FL} = \Pi_P^{DF-SL}$; under model DS, $\Pi_P^{DS-NE} > \Pi_P^{DS-FL} = \Pi_P^{DS-SL}$.

(b) Under the same power-structure, under the NE model, if $\theta_1 < \theta < \theta_2$, $\Pi_P^{DF-NE} > \Pi_P^{DS-NE} > \Pi_P^{B-NE}$, other $\Pi_P^{DS-NE} > \Pi_P^{DF-NE} > \Pi_P^{B-NE}$; under the power of SL, if $\theta_1 < \theta < \theta_2$, $\Pi_P^{DF-SL} > \Pi_P^{DS-SL} > \Pi_P^{B-SL}$, other, $\Pi_P^{DS-SL} > \Pi_P^{DF-SL} > \Pi_P^{B-SL}$; under the power of FL, if $\theta_1 < \theta < \theta_2$ $\Pi_P^{DF-FL} > \Pi_P^{DS-FL} > \Pi_P^{B-FL}$, other, $\Pi_P^{DS-FL} > \Pi_P^{DF-FL} > \Pi_P^{B-FL}$. $\theta_1 = \frac{-b^2\tau_t^2 - 2b\tau_s + 1}{2} - \frac{(b\tau_t+1)(b^2\tau_t^2 + 4b\tau_s - 2b\tau_t + 1)^{1/2}}{2}$ $\theta_2 = \frac{-b^2\tau_t^2 - 2b\tau_s + 1}{2} + \frac{(b\tau_t+1)(b^2\tau_t^2 + 4b\tau_s - 2b\tau_t + 1)^{1/2}}{2}$.

Proposition 3(a) shows that the optimal profit for e-commerce platforms is highest in power equilibrium, and the same for supplier-dominated supply chains and rural-cooperatives-dominant structures. Proposition 3(b) indicates that e-commerce platforms generate more profit with self-run stores under all three power structures. Rural cooperatives generate more profit with self-run stores when consumer acceptance of non-self-run stores is moderate, while suppliers generate more profit when it's either too high or too low. Introducing a self-run store leads to higher profits for e-commerce platforms regardless of power structure.

Management inspiration: E-commerce platforms can improve their management strategies by promoting fair distribution of profits throughout the supply chain. To achieve this, they can prioritize support for vulnerable parties and selectively source products from suppliers or rural cooperatives that align with consumers' preferences for non-self-run stores. These measures can optimize profitability and foster a sustainable business ecosystem.

4.2 Optimal Decision

The following propositions discover the changes of the non-self-run sellers' wholesale prices under three power structures and in three models.

Proposition 1. Wholesale price comparison of third-party sellers in three power structures and three models:

(a) Under the same model, the B model gets $w_s^{B-FL} > w_s^{B-NE} > w_s^{B-SL}$; the DF model demonstrates $w_s^{DF-FL} > w_s^{DF-NE} > w_s^{DF-SL}$; the DS model obtains $w_s^{DS-FL} > w_s^{DS-NE} > w_s^{DS-SL}$.

(b) Under the same power structure, the NE power shows $w_s^{DF-NE} > w_s^{DS-NE} = w_s^{B-NE}$; the SL power drives $w_s^{DF-SL} > w_s^{DS-SL} = w_s^{B-SL}$; the FL power obtains $w_s^{DF-FL} = w_s^{DS-FL} = w_s^{B-FL}$.

Proposition 1(a) states that as rural cooperatives gain power in any model, the whole-sale price for third-party stores increases due to improved bargaining power. This leads to higher profits with constant sales prices. Proposition 1(b) shows that in power equilibrium and supplier-led supply chains, introducing self-run stores raises the wholesale price for non-self-run stores of rural cooperatives, but not for suppliers' non-self-run sellers.

Proposition 2. Comparison of self-run stores' wholesale prices in three power structures and two models (DF and DS).

(a) Under the same model, the B model gets $w_t^{DF-FL} = w_t^{DF-NE} = w_t^{DF-SL}$; the DS model obtains $w_t^{DS-FL} = w_t^{DS-SL} > w_t^{DS-NE}$.
(b) Under the same power structure, the NE power shows $w_t^{DS-NE} > w_t^{DF-NE}$; the SL power drives $w_t^{DS-SL} > w_t^{DF-SL}$; the FL power obtains $w_t^{DS-FL} > w_t^{DF-FL}$.

Proposition 2 (a) indicates that in the model DF, after the introduction of rural cooperatives into a self-operated store, the wholesale price of the self-operated store has not changed. Proposition 2(b) under any power structures, the suppliers' wholesale price by the introduction of self-run stores (DS) would be higher than the rural cooperatives' wholesale price by introducing their self-run stores (DF). This is because compared with rural cooperatives, suppliers have stronger bargaining power in dealing with e-commerce platforms, suppliers will obtain higher self-run store profits under any power structures.

Proposition 3. Comparison of third-party non-self-run stores' sales price in three power structures and three models.

(a) Under the same model, the B model gets $p_s^{B-FL} = p_s^{B-SL} > p_s^{B-NE}$; the DF model demonstrates $p_s^{DF-FL} = p_s^{DF-SL} > p_s^{DF-NE}$; the DS model obtains $p_s^{DS-FL} = p_s^{DS-SL} > p_s^{DS-NE}$.
(b) Under the same power structure, the NE power shows $p_s^{DS-NE} = p_s^{B-NE} > p_s^{DF-NE}$; the SL power drives $p_s^{DS-SL} = p_s^{B-SL} > p_s^{DF-SL}$; the FL power obtains, $p_s^{DS-FL} = p_s^{B-FL} > p_s^{DF-FL}$.

Proposition 3(a) shows that in any model, the selling price of the other-run store will only fall under the equilibrium of power. When the rural cooperatives led the supply chain (FL), the wholesale prices of other camps rose and the profit of supplier units decreased, resulting in increased sales prices. When rural cooperatives and suppliers, when the power balance (NE), the decline in the wholesale price of third-party seller has led to a relatively increased profit of the unit. Proposition 3(b) shows that in the case of arbitrary power structure, in the case of supplier-dominated supply chain (SL), the sales price of third-party seller decreases, and the sales prices of third-party seller remain unchanged in other cases.

Proposition 4. Comparison of self-run stores' sales prices in three power structures and two models (DF and DS).

(a) Under the same model, the B model gets, $p_t^{DF-FL} = p_t^{DF-NE} = p_t^{DF-SL}$; the DS model obtains, $p_t^{DS-FL} = p_t^{DS-SL} > p_t^{DS-NE}$.

(b) Under the same power structure, the NE power shows $p_t^{DS-NE} > p_t^{DF-NE}$; the SL power drives $p_t^{DS-SL} > p_t^{DF-SL}$; the FL power obtains, $p_t^{DS-FL} > p_t^{DF-FL}$.

Proposition 4(a) states that introducing self-employed stores in rural cooperatives (DF) does not change the sales price of self-operated stores, and rural cooperatives' bargaining power on e-commerce platforms remains unaffected. Proposition 4(b) shows that sales prices are higher when suppliers introduce self-run stores (DS) than when rural cooperatives introduce them (DF), as suppliers have stronger bargaining power with e-commerce platforms, leading to higher prices for self-run stores.

Management inspiration: Starting from the interplay between competition and cooperation in the supply chain, it is possible to delve into the management implications of this dynamic. It is undeniable that competition is an integral part of the supply chain; however, excessive competition can destabilize the entire chain, causing disruptions and imbalances. Consequently, e-commerce platforms must strike a balance between competition and cooperation to ensure the sustainability and smooth functioning of the supply chain. This insight also highlights the need for managers to consider the interplay between competition and cooperation in the supply chain and leverage effective collaborative mechanisms to optimize and coordinate the chain.

5 Conclusion

Faced with the e-commerce platforms' support on rural cooperatives, suppliers or distributors open self-run stores on the e-platforms to attract more consumers' purchase. Transactions on some e-commerce platforms such as Pinduoduo and Taobao rely heavily on the O2O retail model, including self-run and third-party stores. Such platforms can benefit from both self-run and non-self-run stores.

Rural cooperatives can benefit from power-structure competition with suppliers, as greater supplier power results in higher profits for the cooperatives. Therefore, it is an optimal choice for rural cooperatives to actively introduce self-run stores, regardless of the power structure. However, it is important to note that if the bargaining power of rural cooperatives is inferior to that of e-commerce platforms, their overall unit profits may decrease when introducing self-run stores. To address this issue, effective management strategies can be employed by rural cooperatives to navigate the competitive e-commerce market and retain competitiveness.

For suppliers, they would proactively introduce self-run stores under informal power structures and with the acceptance of casual consumers. Moreover, their sale prices would remain constant regardless of the power structure under which they introduce self-run stores. At this point, suppliers will actively establish self-run stores to counter rural cooperatives' self-run stores and also to increase their competitive edge against rural cooperatives. From a management perspective, the introduction of self-run stores by suppliers requires careful consideration of various factors, such as market demand, consumer behavior, and supply chain management.

To increase profits, e-commerce platforms must prioritize supporting the weaker party in the supply chain in any business model. However, channel conflicts can arise, and e-commerce platforms may take advantage of their stronger position to open self-run stores, which can negatively impact suppliers' profits. When consumer preferences towards non-self-run stores become too extreme, e-commerce platforms are more likely to introduce suppliers' self-run stores. From a management perspective, e-commerce platforms must strike a balance between maximizing profits and maintaining positive relationships with their suppliers.

Above researches provides some vital reference for e-commerce platforms to support the weak party in supply chains and theoretical supports for them to actively cooperate with rural cooperatives to start up self-run stores. However, this paper does not only consider the optimal channel tactics for supply enterprises' power-structure competition under different channels and the optimal strategy of multi and double channels for enterprises under different power structures. What's more, contents of such research are based on the information symmetry which, still, requires further study on whether it will affect the optimal strategy for enterprises in the supply chain.

Acknowledgement. The paper is the research result of the key research base project of Jiang xi philosophy and social sciences (farmers' digital literacy, e-commerce adoption and rural revitalization performance promotion path: empirical research based on threshold heterogeneity and spatial differential spillover, No: 22SKJD05). This research was supported by the National Natural Science Foundation of China under Grant 72064027.

Appendix 1

Model	Result
B-NE	$p_s^{B-NE} = \frac{(6\tau_s+\theta)}{6} \quad w_s^{B-NE} = \frac{(5b\tau_s+5\theta)}{6} \quad f^{B-NE} = \frac{(b\tau_s+\theta)}{2}$ $\Pi_F^{B-NE} = \frac{(b\tau_s+\theta)^2}{36\theta}$ $\Pi_S^{B-NE} = \frac{(b^2-18k\theta)\tau_s^2+2\tau_s b\theta+\theta^2}{36\theta} - T$ $\Pi_P^{B-NE} = \frac{(b\tau_s+\theta)^2}{12\theta} + T$
B-SL	$p_s^{B-SL} = \frac{7(b\tau_s+\theta)}{8} \quad w_s^{B-SL} = \frac{(b\tau_s+\theta)}{8} \quad f^{B-SL} = \frac{(b\tau_s+\theta)}{2}$ $\Pi_F^{B-SL} = \frac{(b\tau_s+\theta)^2}{64\theta}$ $\Pi_S^{B-SL} = \frac{(b^2-16k\theta)\tau_s^2+2b\tau_s\theta+\theta}{32\theta} - T$ $\Pi_P^{B-SL} = \frac{(b\tau_s+\theta)^2}{16\theta} + T$

(*continued*)

(*continued*)

Model	Result
B-FL	$p_s^{B-FL} = \frac{7(b\tau_s+\theta)}{8}$ $w_s^{B-FL} = \frac{(b\tau_s+\theta)}{4}$ $f^{B-FL} = \frac{(b\tau_s+\theta)}{2}$ $\Pi_F^{B-FL} = \frac{(b\tau_s+\theta)^2}{32\theta}$ $\Pi_S^{B-FL} = \frac{(b^2-32k\theta)\tau_s^2+2b\tau_s\theta+\theta}{64\theta} - T$ $\Pi_P^{B-FL} = \frac{(b\tau_s+\theta)^2}{16\theta} + T$
DF-NE	$p_s^{DF-NE} = \frac{(-\tau_t\theta+10\tau_s)b+9\theta}{12}$ $p_t^{DF-NE} = \frac{3(\tau_t b+1)}{4}$ $w_t^{DF-NE} = \frac{(b\tau_t+1)}{4}$ $w_s^{DF-NE} = \frac{(\tau_t\theta+2\tau_s)b+3\theta}{12}$ $f^{DF-NE} = \frac{(b\tau_s+\theta)}{2}$ $\Pi_F^{DF-NE} = \frac{(5\tau_t^2 b^2+18\tau_s b+9)\theta^2+[-9+(8\tau_t\tau_s-9\tau_t^2)b^2-18\tau_t b]\theta-4\tau_s^2 b^2}{144\theta(\theta-1)}$ $\Pi_S^{DF-NE} = \frac{(-\tau_t^2 b^2-18k\tau_s^2)\theta^2+(2\tau_s\tau_t b^2+18k\tau_s)\theta-\tau_s^2 b^2}{36\theta(\theta-1)} - T$ $\Pi_P^{DF-NE} = \frac{[3+(b^2-12k)\tau_t^2+6\tau_t b]\theta^2+[-3+(4\tau_s\tau_t-3\tau_t^2)b^2-6\tau_t b+12k\tau_t^2]\theta-2\tau_s^2 b^2}{24\theta(\theta-1)} + T$
DF-SL	$p_s^{DF-SL} = \frac{(-\tau_t\theta+7\tau_s)b+6\theta}{8}$ $p_t^{DF-SL} = \frac{3(\tau_t b+1)}{4}$ $w_t^{DF-SL} = \frac{(b\tau_t+1)}{4}$ $w_s^{DF-SL} = \frac{(\tau_t\theta+\tau_s)b+2\theta}{8}$ $f^{DF-SL} = \frac{(b\tau_s+\theta)}{2}$ $\Pi_F^{DF-SL} = \frac{(3\tau_t^2 b^2+8\tau_t b+9)\theta^2+[-4+2b^2\tau_t(\tau_s-2\tau_t)-8b\tau_t]\theta-\tau_s^2 b^2}{64\theta(\theta-1)}$ $\Pi_S^{DF-SL} = \frac{(-\tau_t^2 b^2-18k\tau_s^2)\theta^2+(2\tau_s\tau_t b^2+16k\tau_s^2)\theta-\tau_s^2 b^2}{32\theta(\theta-1)} - T$ $\Pi_P^{DF-SL} = \frac{[(b^2-8k)\tau_t^2+4\tau_t b+2]\theta^2+[2b^2\tau_t(\tau_s-\tau_t)-4b\tau_t+8k\tau_t^2-2]\theta-\tau_s^2 b^2}{24\theta(\theta-1)} + T$
DF-FL	$p_s^{DF-FL} = \frac{(-\tau_t\theta+7\tau_s)b+6\theta}{8}$ $p_t^{DF-FL} = \frac{3(\tau_t b+1)}{4}$ $w_t^{DF-FL} = \frac{(b\tau_t+1)}{4}$ $w_s^{DF-FL} = \frac{(b\tau_s+\theta)}{4}$ $f^{DF-FL} = \frac{(b\tau_s+\theta)}{2}$ $\Pi_F^{DF-FL} = \frac{(\tau_t^2 b^2+4b\tau_t+2)\theta^2+[-2+2\tau_t b^2(\tau_s-\tau_t)-4b\tau_t]\theta-\tau_s^2 b^2}{32\theta(\theta-1)}$ $\Pi_S^{DF-FL} = \frac{(-\tau_t^2 b^2-32k\tau_s^2)\theta^2+(2\tau_s\tau_t b^2+32k\tau_s^2)\theta-\tau_s^2 b^2}{64\theta(\theta-1)} - T$ $\Pi_P^{DF-FL} = \frac{[(b^2-8k)\tau_t^2+4b\tau_t+2]\theta^2+[(-2b^2+8k)\tau_t^2+(2b^2\tau_s-4b)\tau_t-2]\theta-\tau_s^2 b^2}{16\theta(\theta-1)} + T$
DS-NE	$p_s^{DS-NE} = \frac{5(b\tau_s+\theta)}{12}$ $p_t^{DS-NE} = \frac{9b\tau_t+b\tau_s+\theta+9}{4}$ $w_s^{DS-NE} = \frac{b\tau_s+\theta}{6}$ $w_t^{DS-NE} = \frac{\tau_s b+\theta+3\tau_t b+3}{12}$ $f^{DS-NE} = \frac{b\tau_s+\theta}{2}$ $\Pi_F^{DS-NE} = \frac{(\tau_s b+\theta)^2}{36\theta}$ $\Pi_S^{DS-NE} = \frac{M1}{144\theta(\theta-1)} - T$ $\Pi_P^{DS-NE} = \frac{M2}{24\theta(\theta-1)} + T$

(*continued*)

(continued)

Model	Result
DS-SL	$p_s^{DS-SL} = \frac{7(b\tau_s+\theta)}{8} p_t^{DS-SL} = \frac{6b\tau_t+b\tau_s+\theta+6}{8} w_s^{DS-SL} = \frac{b\tau_s+\theta}{8}$ $w_t^{DF-SL} = \frac{2b\tau_t+b\tau_s+\theta+2}{8} f^{DF-SL} = \frac{b\tau_s+\theta}{2}$ $\Pi_F^{DS-SL} = \frac{(b\tau_s+\theta)^2}{64\theta}$ $\Pi_S^{DS-SL} = \frac{M3}{32\theta(\theta-1)} - T$ $\Pi_P^{DS-SL} = \frac{M4}{16\theta(\theta-1)} + T$
DS-FL	$p_s^{DS-FL} = \frac{7(b\tau_s+\theta)}{8} p_t^{DS-FL} = \frac{6b\tau_t+b\tau_s+\theta+6}{8} w_s^{DS-FL} = \frac{b\tau_s+\theta}{4}$ $w_t^{DS-FL} = \frac{6b\tau_t+b\tau_s+\theta+6}{8} f^{DS-FL} = \frac{b\tau_s+\theta}{2}$ $\Pi_F^{DS-FL} = \frac{(b\tau_s+\theta)^2}{32\theta}$ $\Pi_S^{DS-FL} = \frac{M5}{64\theta(\theta-1)} - T$ $\Pi_P^{DS-FL} = \frac{M6}{16\theta(\theta-1)} + T$

Notes:

$$M1 = -5\theta^3 + [(-10\tau_s + 18\tau_t)b - 72k\tau_s^2 + 14]\theta^2$$
$$+ [-5(\tau_s-3\tau_t)(\tau_s-\tfrac{3\tau_t}{5})b^2 + (10\tau_s^2-18\tau_t)b + 72k\tau_s^2-9]\theta - 4\tau_s^2b^2$$
$$M2 = -\theta^3 + (-12k\tau_t^2 - 2b\tau_s + 6b\tau_t + 4)\theta^2$$
$$+ [(-\tau_s^2 + 6\tau_s\tau_t - 3\tau_t^2)b^2 + (2\tau_s - 6\tau_t)b + 12k\tau_t^2 - 3]\theta - 2\tau_s^2b^2$$
$$M3 = -\theta^3 + [(-2\tau_s + 4\tau_t)b + 16k\tau_s^2 + 3]\theta^2$$
$$+ [(-\tau_s^2 + 4\tau_s\tau_t - 2\tau_t^2)b^2 + (2\tau_s - 4\tau_t)b + 16k\tau_s^2 - 5]\theta - \tau_s^2b^2$$
$$M4 = -\theta^3 + [(-2\tau_s + 4\tau_t)b - 8k\tau_t^2 + 3]\theta^2$$
$$+ [(-\tau_s^2 + 4\tau_s\tau_t - 2\tau_t^2)b^2 + (2\tau_s - 4\tau_t)b + 8k\tau_t^2 - 2]\theta - \tau_s^2b^2$$
$$M5 = -3\theta^3 + [(-6\tau_s + 8\tau_t)b - 32k\tau_s^2 + 7]\theta^2$$
$$+ [(-3\tau_s^2 + 8\tau_s\tau_t - 4\tau_t^2)b^2 + (6\tau_s - 8\tau_t)b + 32k\tau_s^2 - 4]\theta - \tau_s^2b^2$$
$$M6 = -\theta^3 + [(-2\tau_s + 4\tau_t)b - 8k\tau_t^2 + 3]\theta^2$$
$$+ [(-\tau_s^2 + 4\tau_s\tau_t - 2\tau_t^2)b^2 + (2\tau_s - 4\tau_t)b + 8k\tau_t^2 - 2]\theta - \tau_s^2b^2$$

References

1. He, Y., Xu, Q., Shao, Z.: "Ship-from-store" strategy in platform retailing. Transp. Res. Part E Logistics Transp. Rev. **145**, 102153 (2021)
2. Qin, L., Qu, Q., Zhang, L., Wu, H. Platform trust in C2C e-commerce platform: the sellers' cultural perspective. Inf. Technol. Manage., 1-11 (2021)

3. Wang, C., Peng, Z., Yu, H., Geng, S.: Could the e-commerce platform's big data analytics ease the channel conflict from manufacturer encroachment? an analysis based on information sharing and risk preference. IEEE Access **9**, 83552–83568 (2021)
4. Micu, M.M., Dumitru, E.A., Vintu, C.R., Tudor, V.C., Fintineru, G.: Models underlying the success development of family farms in Romania. Sustainability **14**(4), 2443 (2022)
5. Zeng, Y., Jia, F., Wan, L., Guo, H.: E-commerce in agri-food sector: a systematic literature review. Int. Food Agribusiness Manage. Rev. **20**(4), 439–460 (2017)
6. Luo, M., Zhou, G., Wei, W.: Study of the game model of E-commerce information sharing in an agricultural product supply chain based on fuzzy big data and LSGDM. Technol. Forecast. Soc. Chang. **172**, 121017 (2021)
7. Ma, X., Wang, J., Bai, Q., Wang, S.: Optimization of a three-echelon cold chain considering freshness-keeping efforts under cap-and-trade regulation in Industry 4.0. Int. J. Prod. Econ. **220**, 107457 (2020)
8. Wang, M., Zhao, L.: Cold chain investment and pricing decisions in a fresh food supply chain. Int. Trans. Oper. Res. (2018)
9. Chen, J., Dong, M., Rong, Y., Yang, L.: Dynamic pricing for deteriorating products with menu cost. Omega **75**, 13–26 (2018)
10. Ye, F., Lin, Q., Li, Y.: Coordination for contract farming supply chain with stochastic yield and demand under CVaR criterion. Oper. Res. **20**(1), 369–397 (2017). https://doi.org/10.1007/s12 351-017-0328-3
11. Yang, F., Wang, M., Ang, S.: Optimal remanufacturing decisions in supply chains considering consumers' anticipated regret and power structures. Transp. Res. Part E Logistics Transp. Rev. **148**, 102267 (2021)
12. Hu, S., Fu, K., Wu, T.: The role of consumer behavior and power structures in coping with shoddy goods. Transp. Res. Part E Logistics Transp. Rev. **155**, 102482 (2021)
13. Li, M., Mizuno, S.: Dynamic pricing and inventory management of a dual-channel supply chain under different power structures. Eur. J. Oper. Res. **303**(1), 273–285 (2022)
14. Zhi, B., Wang, X., Xu, F.: The effects of in-transit inventory financing on the capital-constrained supply chain. Eur. J. Oper. Res. **296**(1), 131–145 (2022)
15. Liu, W., Qin, D., Shen, N., Chang, X.: Optimal pricing for a multi-echelon closed loop supply chain with different power structures and product dual differences. J. Cleaner Prod. **257**, 120281 (2020)
16. Jena, S.K., Meena, P.: Shopping in the omnichannel supply chain under price competition and product return. J. Retail. Consum. Serv. **65**, 102848 (2022)
17. Alaei, A.M., Taleizadeh, A.A., Rabbani, M.: Marketplace, reseller, or web-store channel: the impact of return policy and cross-channel spillover from marketplace to web-store. J. Retail. Consum. Serv. **65**, 102271 (2020)
18. Chen, Z.S., Wu, S., Govindan, K., Wang, X.J., Chin, K.S., Boros, E.: Optimal pricing decision in a multi-channel supply chain with a revenue-sharing contract. Ann. Oper. Res. **318**, 67–102 (2022). https://doi.org/10.1007/s10479-022-04748-7
19. Chen, X., Wang, X.: Free or bundled: channel selection decisions under different power structures. Omega **53**, 11–20 (2015)
20. He, P., He, Y., Zhou, L.: Channel strategies for dual-channel firms to counter strategic consumers. J. Retail. Consum. Serv. **70**, 103180 (2023)

Investment Risk Analysis and Countermeasure in Five Central Asian Countries for Chinese Investors

Lili Ta[✉]

School of Law, Nanjing University of Finance and Economics, Nanjing 210023, China
talili@nufe.edu.cn

Abstract. With rapid progress of the "Belt and Road" initiative, China has become a capital exporter. More and more Chinese investors are increasing their overseas investment. Thus, investment risk assessment is very important. Central Asia is a key hub connecting the Europe and China. Cooperation between Chinese and Central Asian countries have bilaterally promoted rapid economic development. For Central Asian countries, there are many investment risk points. But in a comprehensive way, the main influencing factors include economic condition, debt ability, social environment, legal system and political factor. In order to improve the investment efficiency, this paper uses analytic hierarchy process to study the investment risks of the five Central Asian countries, and puts forward some countermeasures. Generally speaking, Central Asian countries are generally suitable for overseas investment. Kazakhstan and Uzbekistan have lower risk level. Tajikistan and Turkmenistan have moderate risk level since infrastructure construction in the two countries is imperfect. The investment risk of Kirghiz Tanzania is slightly higher. In order to reduce investment risks, China should promote RMB internationalization so as to facilitate overseas trade and investment. Strengthening policy communication can consolidate and expand the positive role of multilateral trade agreements. In addition, learning from advanced international experience, China can build a financial insurance system to reduce investment risk.

Keywords: Investment Risk · Central Asia · Analytic Hierarchy Process

1 Introduction

In January 2023, China signed Belt and Road Initiative (BRI) cooperation agreements with all five Central Asian countries after China signed a memorandum of understanding with Turkmenistan days ago, and China's BRI cooperation circle is still expanding [1]. Adjoining China, Central Asian countries are on prior situation of this project. In the process of Chinese global overseas investment, countries in Central Asia have gradually become the focus in the world [2]. Central Asia is a very unique region, which is a key hub connecting the Europe and China. It contains 5 countries, including Kazakhstan, Turkmenistan, Uzbekistan, Kirghiz Tanzania and Tajikistan, with a population of more than 74 million. The Eurasian Development Bank pointed out in the latest regional research report that the total GDP of the five countries was 347 billion US dollars in 2021. Central Asian countries have gradually become the key area of cross-border investment for Chinese enterprises. The initiative of "one belt and one road" has provided great opportunities for Chinese enterprises to carry out foreign trade and overseas investment in Central Asian countries.

The PRC built its first links to the Central Asian economies' decades ago and the BRI is a new, more advanced phase of the cooperation. The data collected and made available by the China Global Investment Tracker of the American Enterprise Institute and the Heritage Foundation suggests that Chinese companies invested almost USD 50 billion in four Central Asian countries in 2005–2020: USD 35.58 billion in Kazakhstan, 4.73 billion in Kyrgyzstan, 2.15 billion in Tajikistan, and 5.79 billion in Uzbekistan. According to another source12 China invested more than USD 70 billion in Kazakhstan; about 80% of its investment in the region. After the epidemic era, Central Asia needs more help from China. Therefore, Chinese enterprises should seize the opportunity to increase investment in Central Asia, rapidly expand overseas markets, and take a long-term path of peaceful development with friends [3]. International macro political and economic situation are grim and complicated. Enormous risks, such as poor political stability and immaturity should not be overlooked in Central Asian countries. It is necessary and urgent to accurately identify and quantify the investment risks in Central Asian countries.

2 Research Status of Investment Risk

In addition to debt trap, there are other risks linked to Chinese investment and construction projects in Central Asia. Information about large Chinese projects is either completely closed or lacks the specifics of project lending, the participation of the parties in its implementation and further operation, the payback, and economic and political significance. Supporting the established resource economics in the countries of the region (one could describe it as "predatory aid") threatens the possibility of more sustainable production in Central Asia. There is a high probability of financing economically damaging and environmentally dirty projects in the region. A "race to the bottom" that further lowers the social-environmental demands from all investors in the region. The rapidly growing presence of China in Central Asia is creating concern and contributing to growth in anti-Chinese sentiment among the population.

Many research methods were performed on risk assessment of foreign investment. Framework and index selection of quantitative analysis are developing continuously. At present, U.S. National Risk International Guidelines Index is the most widely used among them. First-level index system is political risk, financial risk and economic risk. S&P, Moody's and Fitch regularly issue authoritative reports on sovereign credit rating, accounting for about 90% of the world's sovereign credit rating market [4]. In recent years, Economist Information Agency, Transparency International and World Bank have also carried out quantitative risk assessment with different methods and emphasis. But index system is built around economic risk, political risk, social risk and other first-level indicators. Among them, economic risk reflects the macro level of a country's economic development. Political risk is usually regarded as willingness of government to repay debts. It mostly uses indicators such as social stability, speech freedom, governance efficiency and government corruption. Social risks mostly reflect the ability of Foreign Direct Investment to operate independently. Degree of social flexibility, perfection of the legal system, religious issues, racial issues, openness and cultural acceptance are all considered to risks.

Undoubtedly, risk control is beneficial to overseas investment. Some researchers believed that we should pay attention to whole process of source and flow of funds in order to reduce risks in all aspects. Project declaration, approval, contract signing, legal protection and supervision of overseas direct investment involve both sides of the investment [5]. It is recognized that docking of relevant laws and regulations and keeping perfect data for reference are necessary means of risk reduction. Normative management could reduce risk levels. Firstly, it designs the overall risk management strategy according to the main purpose and mode of investment; secondly, it standardizes the pre-investigation, pays attention to the social and cultural environment; thirdly, it uses financial instruments to intervene in the diversification of investment risks. Risk of overseas direct investment is concentrated in the financial field, and a complete and standardized risk early warning system is the necessary basis for risk diversification. Disperse political risks, first, we should strictly monitor the implementation of laws and regulations; second, we should build up the system. Special databases for foreign investment can reduce the risks brought by information asymmetry. Third, we should focus on standardizing the compatibility of specific standards.

In recent years, many researchers investigated outward foreign investment risk. Zhang Xiaotong et al. (2020) believed that continuous rise of political risks will cause investment fluctuations of Chinese companies in countries along the belt and route. When geopolitical risks are high, it will even slow down the pace of Chinese companies "going out" [6]. Gao Bo et al. (2020) conducted international study on the effects of the host country's internal conflict risk of the Belt and Road Initiative on bank liquidity creation, and found that the host country's internal conflict risk negatively affects bank liquidity creation [7]. In concert with the Belt and Road Initiative, China is identifying and deploying bilateral and multilateral diplomatic mechanisms aimed at security coordination with countries in Central Asia and Middle East. Hoh A. (2019) provided an overview of Belt and Road Initiative developments in the two regions and examines some of the diplomatic mechanisms that China is using to coordinate security and reduce risks [8]. Panibratov A et al. (2022) systematically classified and further scrutinized the Belt and Road Initiative literature within the management and economics field in order to navigate further academic inquiry into the Belt and Road Initiative phenomenon [9]. Hong Zhao et al. (2022) found that Chinese banking has two-way risk contagion with banks in East Asia and Association of Southeast Asian Nations, South Asia, West Asia, and Central Asia [10].

3   Analysis of Investment Risk in Central Asia

The analytic hierarchy model is shown in Fig. 1. As can be seen from this diagram, the model is composed by goal layer, criterion layer and alternative layer [11]. Each evaluation factor should be applicable to the alternatives, but the effects and importance are different.

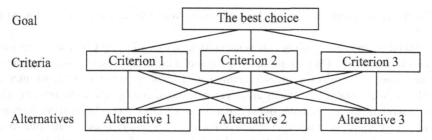

Goal

Criteria

Alternatives

Fig. 1. Analytic hierarchy process model.

3.1 Setting Criteria to Countries

The feasibility analysis refers to the reasonable application of analytic hierarchy process (AHP) to analyze the investment risks of Central Asian countries. The structural model consists of target layer, criterion layer and selection scheme. Evaluation factors at the criteria level should be applicable to the alternatives, but they have different impact and importance [12]. The key to building the structural model is to determine the evaluation criteria and set the criteria layer. In order to comprehensively quantify the risk of investment in Central Asia, five factors are included in risk rating analysis, those are economic condition, debt ability, social environment, legal system, and political Factor.

As a standard to measure the level of economic growth and fluctuation of a country, economic condition is basis to determine whether a region or country has superior investment and financing environment. Better economic conditions always bring higher investment reward and investment security level. GDP gross, per capita GDP and Gini coefficient are used to measure scale and degree of development of a country's economy. Stability of economic growth is measured fluctuation coefficient of GDP growth published by the World Bank. Across Central Asian states, only Kazakhstan is expected to see its economy grow from 3% in 2022 to 3.5% in 2023 and 4% in 2024. Inflation, however, is hitting its record high of 19.6% in the past 14 years. Uzbekistan's economic growth is set to decline from 5.7% in 2022 to 4.9% in 2023, Tajikistan – from 7% in 2022 to 5% in 2023, and Kyrgyzstan – from 5.5% in 2022 to 3.5% in 2023. The report, however, does not indicate any data for Turkmenistan. Trade openness is the ratio of a country's total import and export to GDP [13].

Debt ability refers to a country's total dynamic debt level of the public and private sectors and the external debt capacity that economic conditions can bear. For the host countries participating in international trade, debt crisis breaks will affect the direct and financial investment and other types of investment security of the investing countries. Proportion of foreign debt to GDP and short-term foreign debt to total foreign debt can be used to measure the scale of a country's foreign debt and the risk of a short-term debt crisis. Proportion of fiscal balance to GDP measures a country's financial strength [14]. Its share of GDP is mainly used to measure the terms of trade transactions [15]. Up to 2020, Kyrgyzstan and Tajikistan are especially reliant on external debt; such obligations which make up 77% and 86% of their total debt, respectively. The situation is different in countries rich in natural resources. Loans from China account for 16–17% of the GDP of Turkmenistan and Uzbekistan. In comparison, Kazakhstan's figure is the lowest at 6.5%.

Social environment mainly covers social risk factors affecting Chinese enterprises' overseas investment. On premise that a good social order can ensure orderly operation of investment enterprises. Factors affecting social stability mainly come from internal conflicts. Social stability includes eight sub-indicators, among which the level of education work measures the basic quality of a country's labor force. Internal conflicts are mainly manifested in extreme conflicts of society, race and religion. Crime rate measures the degree of internal conflicts and social security of a country. Environmental policies, capital and personnel mobility restrictions, labor market regulation and commercial regulation reflect the business environment in which a country allows domestic and foreign investment enterprises to operate [16]. According to the evaluation criteria established by international financial organizations, the higher the education level of labor force, the lower the degree of internal conflict; the better the social security and business environment, the smaller investment risk of foreign enterprises.

Legal system examines the stability and efficiency of a government, as well as the legal environment and external conflicts. Lower legal risk is one of the prerequisites for foreign enterprises to invest safely. Corruption control reflects the government's awareness and control degree of public power. The effectiveness of the government reflects the public's views on the quality of public services. Quality of regulation reflects the government ability to formulate and implement sound policies and regulations. Legal rules reflect the degree of trust and compliance of agents with social rules, especially the quality of contract enforcement, property rights, police and courts. Democracy and accountability reflect the extent to which citizens of a country can participate in the choice of their government, as well as the views of freedom of expression, freedom of association and free media. The higher the stability and governance quality of a government, the better the legal environment and the smaller the external conflicts, the lower the risk of foreign enterprises.

Political factor is mainly used to measure the important factors affecting the investment risk of Chinese enterprises in the host country, such as investment policy, investment smoothness and investment dependence. It is generally believed that a better bilateral relationship is an important buffer to reduce the risk of Chinese enterprises' overseas investment. Investment dependence measures the proportion of bilateral investment between China and a country in its investment. There are many political risks in the investment, such as the widespread ethnic and religious conflicts, the international risk and the instability of internal political situation. The degree of investment hindrance and bilateral political links refer to the results of Delphi method used in the report of National Risk Rating of Overseas Investment in China, International Investment Research Department, Institute of World Economy and Politics, Chinese Academy of Social Sciences. Lower investment hindrance and better bilateral political relations help to reduce risk of Chinese enterprises investing in host country.

In analytic hierarchy process model, as shown in Fig. 2, the goal layer is investment risk rank of Central Asian countries. Criterion layer contains economic condition, debt ability, social environment, legal system, and political factor [17]. Alternatives are five countries in Central Asia. Risk identification and quantization can provide reference for overseas investment of Chinese enterprises, and improve the success rate of foreign investment. Data indicators selected in the whole evaluation system come from the open data information of authoritative institutions at home and abroad, such as the Economist, the global economy, the official websites of the United Nations and China Customs. Other annual reports are issued by above mentioned institutions, such as the Statistical Bulletin on China's Foreign Direct Investment, the Human Development Report of the United Nations Development Programme.

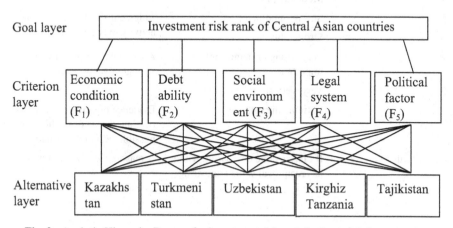

Fig. 2. Analytic Hierarchy Process for investment risk rank in Central Asian countries.

The hierarchy has been constructed. It can be analyzed through a series of pairwise comparisons that derive numerical scales of estimation for the nodes. The criteria are pair-wise compared against the goal for importance. The alternatives are pair-wise compared against each of the criteria for preference. The comparisons are processed mathematically, and priorities are derived for each node. An important task is to determine the weight of each criterion in investment risk rank of Central Asian countries. Another important task is to determine the weight of each alternative with regard to each of the criteria. In the analytic hierarchy process, a meaningful and objective numerical value should be put on each of the five criteria.

3.2 Constructing Judgment Matrix and Assigning Value

To make comparisons, we need a scale of numbers that indicates how many times importance of one element over another element with respect to each criterion. Table 1 exhibits the nine scales. After one by one pair comparison, judgment matrices form. All the criteria are the same importance to each other with respect to investment risk rank of Central Asian countries. Criterion layer judgment matrices of alternatives are shown respectively in Table 2, Table 3, Table 4, Table 5 and Table 6, which includes economic condition (F_1), debt ability (F_2), social environment (F_3), legal system (F_4), and political Factor (F_5).

Hierarchical single ranking is the criterion of evaluating the relative weight of each factor according to the relative weight of the criterion layer. According to matrix theory,

Table 1. Fundamental scale of absolute numbers

Intensity of Importance	Definition	Explanation
1	Equal Importance	Two activities contribute equally to the objective
2	Weak or slight	
3	Moderate importance	Judgment slightly favors one activity over another
4	Moderate plus	
5	Strong importance	Judgment strongly favors one activity over another
6	Strong plus	
7	Very strong or demonstrated importance	An activity is favored very strongly over another
8	Very, very strong	
9	Extreme importance	Evidence favoring one activity over another is of the highest possible order of affirmation
Reciprocals of above	If i has a value comparing with j, j has reciprocal value comparing with i	A reasonable assumption

the characteristic vector of the judgment matrix is obtained through mathematical calculation. The feature vector represents the influence degree of some elements (or all) in this layer on the elements in upper layer, that is, the weight value. In this way, the results of the single ranking of this layer form. Therefore, the matrix feature vector determination is very critical in hierarchical single ranking.

In the layers ranking, the consistency should be checked in judgment matrix. From the human understanding law, a correct importance ranking of judgment matrix must be logical. Such as, if A is important than B, B is important than C, logically, A should be more important than C. In order to ensure the conclusion of the analytic hierarchy process is basically reasonable, it is necessary to test the consistency of the judgment matrix. Only passing the test, the judgment matrix is logically reasonable. After that, the results can be continuously analyzed. The consistency check can be carried out according to three steps.

The first step is to calculate the maximum eigen-value of the judgment matrix, and then get the consistency index CI (consistency index)

$$CI = \frac{\lambda_{max} - n}{n - 1} \tag{1}$$

If CI = 0, judgment matrix has complete consistency, and the test is over. If CI $\neq$ 0, the random consistency ratio (CR = CI/RI) should be calculated. The second step is to determine the average consistency random index (RI). For order 5 matrix, RI = 1.1185. The third step is to calculate the consistency ratio CR = CI/RI. If CR < 0.1, the consistency of judgment matrix and single ranking results are acceptable.

Single ranking and consistency test were carried on the criteria layer and 5 alternatives which include Kazakhstan, Turkmenistan, Uzbekistan, Kirghiz Tanzania, and Tajikistan. The results are shown in Table 2, Table 3, Table 4, Table 5 and Table 6. The evaluation results show that they all pass the consistency test.

Table 2. Judgment matrix and hierarchical single ranking of economic condition (F_1) in criterion layer

Weight ratio to F_1	Kazakhstan	Turkmenistan	Uzbekistan	Kirghiz Tanzania	Tajikistan	Ranking result
Kazakhstan	1	1	1	1	1/2	0.1682
Turkmenistan	1	1	1	1/2	1/2	0.1460
Uzbekistan	1	1	1	1	1/2	0.1682
Kirghiz Tanzania	1	2	1	1	1	0.2257
Tajikistan	2	2	2	1	1	0.2920
$\lambda_{max} = 5.0776$		CI = 0.0194			CR = 0.0173 < 0.1	

Table 3. Judgment matrix and hierarchical single ranking of debt ability (F_2) in criterion layer

Weight ratio to F_2	Kazakhstan	Turkmenistan	Uzbekistan	Kirghiz Tanzania	Tajikistan	Ranking result
Kazakhstan	1	1/2	1/9	2	2	0.0952
Turkmenistan	2	1	1/3	3	4	0.1923
Uzbekistan	9	3	1	9	9	0.6010
Kirghiz Tanzania	1/2	1/3	1/9	1	1	0.0574
Tajikistan	1/2	1/4	1/9	1	1	0.0542
$\lambda_{max} = 5.0555$		CI = 0.0139			CR = 0.0124 < 0.1	

3.3 Hierarchical Total Ranking and Conclusion

Total ranking is relative weight of each element in every judgment matrix, which aims at goal layer. The weight is calculated by the top-down layer by layer synthesis. Calculating total ranking of certain layer, it must be used that total ranking of the higher layer and single ranking of this layer. Yet the single ranking of second layer to first layer is total ranking of the second layer. In this way, the total ranking is obtained from the highest to the lowest one. Consistency test should also be carried out.

Table 4. Judgment matrix and hierarchical single ranking of social environment (F_3) in criterion layer

Weight ratio to F_3	Kazakhstan	Turkmenistan	Uzbekistan	Kirghiz Tanzania	Tajikistan	Ranking result
Kazakhstan	1	1	2	2	2	0.2985
Turkmenistan	1	1	1	1	1	0.1983
Uzbekistan	1/2	1	1	1	1	0.1688
Kirghiz Tanzania	1/2	1	1	1	1	0.1688
Tajikistan	1/2	1	1	1	1	0.1688
$\lambda_{max} = 5.0586$		CI = 0.0146		CR = 0.0131 < 0.1		

Table 5. Judgment matrix and hierarchical single ranking of legal system (F_4) in criterion layer

Weight ratio to F_4	Kazakhstan	Turkmenistan	Uzbekistan	Kirghiz Tanzania	Tajikistan	Ranking result
Kazakhstan	1	2	2	2	2	0.3333
Turkmenistan	1/2	1	1	1	1	0.1667
Uzbekistan	1/2	1	1	1	1	0.1667
Kirghiz Tanzania	1/2	1	1	1	1	0.1667
Tajikistan	1/2	1	1	1	1	0.1667
$\lambda_{max} = 5$		CI = 0		CR = 0 < 0.1		

Table 6. Judgment matrix and hierarchical single ranking of political Factor (F_5) in criterion layer

Weight ratio to F_5	Kazakhstan	Turkmenistan	Uzbekistan	Kirghiz Tanzania	Tajikistan	Ranking result
Kazakhstan	1	9	8	7	5	0.6307
Turkmenistan	1/9	1	1	1	1/2	0.0744
Uzbekistan	1/8	1	1	1	1/2	0.0761
Kirghiz Tanzania	1/7	1	1	1	1	0.0910
Tajikistan	1/5	2	2	1	1	0.1279
$\lambda_{max} = 5.0497$		CI = 0.0124		CR = 0.0111 < 0.1		

$$CI = (0.0194\ 0.0139\ 0.0146\ 00.0124) \begin{pmatrix} 0.2 \\ 0.2 \\ 0.2 \\ 0.2 \\ 0.2 \end{pmatrix} = 0.0121 \qquad (2)$$

$$CR = 0.0121/1.1185 = 0.0108 < 0.1 \qquad (3)$$

Table 7 gives the results of the hierarchical total ranking. It can be seen that the comprehensive evaluation of Kazakhstan is the best, the value is 0.3647, Turkmenistan is slightly lower, Kirghiz Tanzania and Tajikistan are ranking in middle. Uzbekistan is the lowest one. Two conclusions can be drawn. First, Central Asian countries are generally suitable for overseas investment. This is due to the complementary effect of industrial structure between the host country and China, and governance level is in a relatively superior position. Secondly, different countries have different risk levels. Among them, Kazakhstan has the lowest risk, regardless of economic condition, social environment, legal system, and political factor. Uzbekistan also has lower risk. Uzbekistan has very high degree of enthusiasm in attracting Chinese investment. Tajikistan and Turkmenistan have moderate risk, and infrastructure constructions in the two countries are imperfect. They have attracted lots of Chinese investment. Kirghiz Tanzania has slightly higher investment risk. In recent years, growth rate of Chinese investment in Kirghiz Tanzania is lower than that in other countries.

Table 7. Hierarchical total ranking of investment risk

Criteria	F_1	F_2	F_3	F_4	F_5	Evaluation of total ranking
Weight	0.2	0.2	0.2	0.2	0.2	
Kazakhstan	0.1682	0.0952	0.2985	0.3333	0.6307	0.3052
Turkmenistan	0.1460	0.1923	0.1983	0.1667	0.0744	0.1555
Uzbekistan	0.1682	0.6010	0.1688	0.1667	0.0761	0.2362
Kirghiz Tanzania	0.2257	0.0574	0.1688	0.1667	0.0910	0.1419
Tajikistan	0.2920	0.0542	0.1688	0.1667	0.1279	0.1619

4 Countermeasure to Investment Risk

RMB internationalization should be promoted in order to facilitate financial overseas trade and investment. With increasing recognition of belt and road initiative, China formally accessed to Special Drawing Right basket of currencies. RMB begins to multi-lateralize and internationalize, and gradually expands to Central Asia. Wide RMB currency shows not only improvement recognition of China's comprehensive national power, but also conducive to bilateral cooperation so as to reduce settlement and investment risks [18]. Currently, RMB is mainly used for loan, liquidation, settlement and other services of infrastructure construction projects. RMB internationalization is mainly manifested in four aspects: China is trying to establish an RMB clearing system; RMB has gradually realized its settlement function in international investment; it supports establishment of multilateral financial institutions such as Asian Investment Bank and Silk Road Fund; functions become increasingly prominent. Relevant institutions around the world begin to explore the feasibility of RMB for petroleum and iron ore, laying foundation for RMB settlement of commodity transactions [19]. Therefore, RMB internationalization can effectively reduce settlement risk of investment, and effectively promote development of common financial markets.

To avoid investment risk, communication should be strengthened, multilateral trade agreements should be consolidated and expanded. Central Asian countries have a certain economic base and solid political foundation. From perspective of comparative advantage, China and Central Asian countries are mostly similar in geographical location [20]. The industrial structure also shows relatively broad basis for industrial complementary cooperation, and strong demand for economic and trade cooperation with China. Based on international experience, China can actively sign bilateral or multilateral investment agreements with Central Asian countries. A stable political foundation and strong economic capacity will provide the basis for Central Asian countries to abide by and implement the signed agreements, which can significantly and effectively reduce the political and economic risks that Chinese enterprises may face in overseas investment. At present, China's trade with Central Asia has shown a more obvious linkage effect. Our government should further deepen its economic and trade cooperation with Central Asian countries. China should use the advantages of oversea culture by organizing cultural activities and setting up cultural exchange organizations, and establish a peaceful and friendly international image [21].

Learning from advanced international experience, we should improve our overseas investment and financing insurance system. An important function of financial products is to transfer and disperse risks. At present, China Export Credit Insurance Company has designed a guarantee system for overseas investment risk and carried out relevant business. However, nowadays the unilateral model is not distinguished for specific national condition. Absent investment protection agreements, it is difficult for China's export credit insurance companies to obtain subrogation rights. It increases the operating costs and risks of insurance companies. China's insurance industry needs to be improved in terms of the scale and types of overseas investment products. Improving the overseas investment insurance system will effectively improve the risk control system of Chinese enterprises' overseas investment. One hand, investment insurance systems under a bilateral model have been further established with Central Asian countries that have signed trade protection agreements with China. On the other hand, for countries that have not signed a trade protection agreement, they should focus on early warning of risks in investment cooperation and work to urge both parties to sign a trade protection agreement [22].

References

1. Westland, J.C.: Introduction to the special issue: electronic commerce in China's Belt and Road initiative. Electron. Commer. Res. **19**(4), 747–748 (2019). https://doi.org/10.1007/s10 660-019-09384-1
2. Saud, S., Chen, S., Haseeb, A.: The role of financial development and globalization in the environment: accounting ecological footprint indicators for selected one-belt-one-road initiative countries. J. Clean. Prod. **250**, 119518 (2020)
3. Molling, G., Zanela Klein, A.: Value proposition of IoT-based products and services: a framework proposal. Electron. Mark. **32**, 899–926 (2022)
4. Ai, J., Zhang, H.: Impact of the "Belt and Road" initiative on the development level of e-commerce. In 18 provinces and cities along China ——based on PSM-DID method. In: 19th Wuhan International Conference on E-Business, pp. 81–92. University of Calgary Press, Calgary (2020)
5. Li, J., Yao, Y., Xu, Y., Li, J., Wei, L., Zhu, X.: Consumer's risk perception on the Belt and Road countries: evidence from the cross-border e-commerce. Electron. Commer. Res. **19**(4), 823–840 (2019). https://doi.org/10.1007/s10660-019-09342-x
6. Zhang, X., Xu, Z.: BRI projects' geopolitical risks: concepts and theorization. Glob. Rev. **12**(03), 80–96+156 (2020). (in Chinese)
7. Gao, B., Li, J., et al.: Internal conflict and bank liquidity creation: evidence from the belt and road initiative. Res. Int. Bus. Finance **53**, 101227 (2020)
8. Hoh, A.: China's belt and road initiative in Central Asia and the Middle East. Dig. Middle East Stud. **28**(2), 241–276 (2019)
9. Panibratov, A., et al.: The belt and road initiative: a systematic literature review and future research agenda. Eurasian Geogr. Econ. **63**(1), 82–115 (2022)
10. Zhao, H., Li, J., Lei, Y., Zhou, M.: Risk spillover of banking across regions: evidence from the belt and road countries. Emerg. Mark. Rev. **52**, 100919 (2022)
11. Liu, X., Chen, Z.: Service quality evaluation and service improvement using online reviews: a framework combining deep learning with a hierarchical service quality model. Electron. Commer. Res. Appl. **54**, 101174 (2022)
12. Ta, L.: Coexistence mode of electronic and traditional paper bills of lading to regulate goods delivery without bill of lading in China. In: 16th Wuhan International Conference on E-Business, pp. 328–337. University of Calgary Press, Calgary (2017)
13. Zhu, H., Zhang, Q., Zhang, S.: Spatial and temporal characteristics of socio-economic development in central Asia based on a series of nighttime light images from 1992 to 2017. J. Geoinform. Sci. **22**(7), 1449–1462 (2020). (in Chinese)
14. Wei, S., Yin, J., Chen, W.: How big data analytics use improves supply chain performance: considering the role of supply chain and information system strategies. Int. J. Logist. Manag. **33**(2), 620–643 (2022)
15. Zhang, S., Zheng, H.: Local government debt risk assessment and early warning system based on machine learning. In: 21st Wuhan International Conference on E-business, pp. 673–683. University of Calgary Press, Calgary (2022)
16. Wang, W., Qu, W., Wang, X.: Enterprise technology innovation and customer concentration under the uncertainty of market environment. In: 20th Wuhan International Conference on E-business, pp. 194–205. University of Calgary Press, Calgary (2021)
17. Ta, L.: Investment risk analysis of Southeast Asian countries along the "Belt and Road" and countermeasure by analytic hierarchy process. In: 19th Wuhan International Conference on E-business, pp. 526–538. University of Calgary Press, Calgary (2020)
18. Alt, R.: Electronic markets on business model development. Electron. Mark. **30**(3), 405–411 (2020). https://doi.org/10.1007/s12525-020-00438-z

19. Mi, C., Wang, Y., Xiao, L.: Prediction on transaction amounts of China's CBEC with improved GM (1, 1) models based on the principle of new information priority. Electron. Commer. Res. **21**(1), 125–146 (2020). https://doi.org/10.1007/s10660-020-09434-z
20. Wei, S., Sheng, S.: Does geographic distance to customers improve or inhibit supplier innovation? A moderated inverted-U relationship. Ind. Mark. Manag. **108**, 134–148 (2023)
21. Qing, W., Muhammad, S., Zhou, D.: Transnational entrepreneurship education system based on cross-border e-commerce in the context of Belt and Road. In: 19th Wuhan International Conference on E-business, pp. 519–525. University of Calgary Press, Calgary (2020)
22. Ni, L., Shuai, S., Li, W.: Research on the competitiveness and trade potential of China-India pharmaceutical trade under the one belt and one road initiative. In: 20th Wuhan International Conference on E-business, pp. 406–415. University of Calgary Press, Calgary (2021)

How Knowledge Characteristics and Platform Characteristics Drive Users' Purchase Intention of Online Paid Health Knowledge?

Yuanlu Li, Jiaxin Xue, and Zhaohua Deng[⊠]

Huazhong University of Science and Technology, Wuhan 430074, China
zh-deng@hust.edu.cn

Abstract. In the knowledge economy era, access to health knowledge via online health platforms has become increasingly popular. This paper aims to explore the impact of relevant characteristics on users' intention of paying for health knowledge. Based on the perceived value theory and S-O-R model, we propose the research model consisting of knowledge characteristics and platform characteristics as stimuli, perceived value as organism, and purchase intention as response. A total of 432 valid questionnaires is collected, and analyzed using SmartPLS3.0 software. Our results show that regarding knowledge characteristics, knowledge rarity has no significant influence on perceived value, and knowledge personalization positively affects utilitarian value and hedonic value; regarding platform characteristics, both platform information quality and platform service quality positively influence utilitarian value and hedonic value; both utilitarian value and hedonic value have positive effects on purchase intention. And the partial mediation role of perceived value is tested. Research findings and implications are discussed as well.

Keywords: Health Knowledge Payment · Purchase Intention · Perceived Value Theory · S-O-R Model · Online Health Platform

1 Introduction

In the era of knowledge economy, knowledge payment market in China has gradually formed and grown in a few years. According to the iiMedie Report [1], knowledge payment is a means of accessing high-quality information services, where the provider transforms personal knowledge or skills into knowledge products and the consumer purchase knowledge. The report shows that the user scale of knowledge payment is expected to exceed 640 million in 2025, with the expected market size of 280.88 billion RMB. Meanwhile, with the development of mobile Internet, knowledge payment gradually develops from terminal systematization to mobile fragmentation.

With online knowledge payment rapidly rising, consumers' purchase behavior is concerned by massive scholars. Numerous research in antecedent factors of purchase behavior is conducted in different contexts, such as paid Q&A [2], online course [3], online health consultation [4], social networking communities [5]. From the perspective of knowledge characteristics, extant results demonstrated that price, perceived value, knowledge rareness positively influence purchase intention [3, 6]. Regarding knowledge platform characteristics, previous research proposed platform interactivity, information quality and service quality [6, 7]. As to knowledge contributor characteristics, extant research proposed contributor reputation, professionalism and charism [2, 3, 6].

Correspondingly, with the enhancement of Chinese residents' health awareness and literacy, more and more Internet users are taking the initiative to purchase needed health knowledge through various online health platforms (OHPs) such as Good Doctor (online health consultation), Keep (fitness courses), DingXiangMom (knowledge of pregnancy and childbirth). Health knowledge payment has become an important channel for many online users to alleviate health anxiety and build disease prevention and health promotion capacity. Most research focused on the context of online health consultation. Li et al. [4] found physicians' knowledge contribution and reputation positively affect patient consultation. In order to find more generally applicable factors affecting purchase intention of online health knowledge including articles, consultation services, fitness courses and others, this study attempts to explore:

1. What are the main factors of knowledge itself that affect users' purchase intention of online health knowledge?
2. What are the main factors of the platform that affect users' purchase intention of online health knowledge?
3. How do knowledge characteristics and platform characteristics drive users' purchase intention of online paid health knowledge?

To sum up, aiming to understand OHP users' intention to pay for health knowledge more intuitively as a whole, we establish a research model of factors affecting users' purchase intention. Based on perceived value theory and S-O-R model, we extract two antecedent dimensions (knowledge characteristics, platform characteristics) from existing research. We propose that knowledge characteristics (rarity, personalization), and platform characteristics (information quality and service quality of OHP) as stimuli, perceived value as organism, and purchase intention as response. This study helps to further understand knowledge payment behavior of OHP users and can enrich the research on online paid health knowledge in China to a certain extent.

2 Theoretic Background

2.1 S-O-R Model

The S-O-R model is a general model to describe human behavior. The stimuli act on the individual's organism, thus leading to the individual's response. Stimuli (S) are the factors that affect the individual's cognition or emotion, which includes both internal psychological and physiological factors and external environmental factors. Organism (O) refers to the individual's emotional or cognitive state after being stimulated, which is an internal change between stimuli and final response. Response (R) refers to the individual's final response under the influence of various stimuli, including psychological and behavioral reaction results. S-O-R model is widely used to explain online consumer behavior, including online knowledge payment [6]. Therefore, this paper explores health knowledge payment in OHPs based on the S-O-R framework, where the stimuli cover two aspects: knowledge characteristics and platform characteristics, with perceived value as the organism and purchase intention as the response.

2.2 Perceived Value Theory

Perceived value has its roots in consumer behavior science and plays a critical role in explaining consumer behavior. It is the result of weighing the benefits against the costs paid for the entire process of purchasing, using or enjoying a product or service. It is often divided into utilitarian value and hedonic value. Utilitarian value represents the consumer's overall assessment of functional benefits and costs, such as convenience, time costs [8]. Hedonic value refers to the consumer's overall assessment of experiential benefits and costs, emphasizing the pleasure, satisfaction or even relief obtained from the consumer behavior [9].

Perceived value is the internal psychological (cognitive and emotional) process of consumers when making consumption behaviors. Many studies based on the S-O-R framework regard perceived value as the organism [6] and study its mediating role between stimuli and response. Perceived value is closely associated with consumer intentions, and both utilitarian value and hedonic value positively affect future intentions [8]. Consequently, this study combines the perceived value theory with the S-O-R model, takes the perceived value as the organism (O), and purchase intention as the response (R) to explore the factors affecting OHP users' intention to pay for health knowledge.

3 Conceptual Framework and Hypotheses

Based on the S-O-R model and perceived value, we discuss the factors influencing users' intention to pay for health knowledge in OHPs. We propose knowledge characteristics (rarity, personalization) and platform characteristics (information quality, service quality), functioning as external stimuli, positively impact users' perceived value as the organism (utilitarian value, hedonic value), and thus purchase intention. The research model is shown in Fig. 1.

3.1 Stimuli (S) and Perceived Value (O)

In this paper, the model stimuli are mined from the perspective of knowledge characteristics and platform characteristics, while the perceived value is functioned as the model organism. The common dimensional division of perceived value is adopted with reference to [8, 9], where utilitarian value represents OHP users' perception of the functional benefits and costs of paying for health knowledge, including cost effectiveness, convenience, and time costs; hedonic value represents consumers' perceived emotional benefits and costs of paying for health knowledge in the OHPs, emphasizing the pleasure and satisfaction, even relief, derived from user's behavior.

Knowledge Characteristics

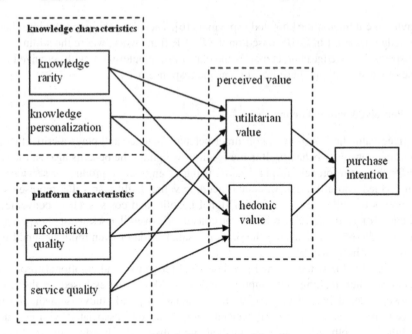

Fig. 1. Research model

Knowledge Rarity. Rarity is derived from the concept of strategic management. According to the VRIO model, resources and capabilities that affect enterprise competitiveness mainly include four aspects: Value, Rarity, Inimitability, Organization. Rarity refers to some strategic resources that only a handful of enterprises control and possess. In the context of knowledge payment, it is defined as the perceived rarity degree of paid knowledge or the difference with other knowledge products. The opinion that rarity will increase the perceived value of commodities was proposed in the commodity theory. Wu and Lee [10] found that in the context of online retail, product rarity will affect consumers' perceived value of products and thus increase purchase intention. Therefore, the following hypotheses are proposed in this study:

H1a: Knowledge rarity positively affects the utilitarian value of online paid health knowledge.
H2a: Knowledge rarity positively affects the hedonic value of online paid health knowledge.

Knowledge Personalization. Personalization is generally defined as the ability to provide users with services that meet their needs based on information such as user preference and behavior [11]. In the context of knowledge payment, the degree of knowledge personalization reflects the extent to which the paid health knowledge provided in the OHPs can meet the knowledge needs of users. Wang et al. [12] found that personalization is positively correlated with perceived value in their research on the continuous use behavior of mobile government service. Referring to existing studies, this study believes that the higher the degree of knowledge personalization, the higher the perceived value of users to health knowledge products will be. Therefore, the following assumptions are made in this paper:

H2a: Knowledge personalization positively affects the utilitarian value of online paid health knowledge.
H2b: Knowledge personalization positively affects the hedonic value of online paid health knowledge.

Knowledge Platform Characteristics

Platform Information Quality. It reflects the authenticity, accuracy, immediacy, and comprehensibility of the information for paid knowledge published by the platform [7]. Many studies have shown that platform information quality has positive impacts on online users' perceived benefits, satisfaction, and perceived value [13, 14]. It positively affects the perceived value of knowledge payment users [6]. In this study, platform information quality refers to the quality level of descriptive information about paid health knowledge in OHPs. Description information is one of the most important channels for potential buyers to measure the value of knowledge, and plays an important role in the process of convincing users to purchase. Therefore, this study makes the following hypotheses:

H3a: Platform information quality positively affects the utilitarian value of online paid health knowledge.
H3b: Platform information quality positively affects the hedonic value of online paid health knowledge.

Platform Service Quality. Platform service quality reflects the service level of the platform, including service personalization, specialization, reliability, and timeliness. CHEN et al. [15] pointed out that airline service quality positively affects passengers' perceived value and thus enhances repurchase intention; Pearson et al. [13] proposed that service quality positively affects consumers' perceived value of e-services. And it has been found that platform service quality has a positive impact on the perceived value of knowledge payment users [7]. In the current study, platform service quality emphasizes the level of service related to paid health knowledge provided by OHPs. Therefore, this paper makes the following hypotheses:

H4a: Platform service quality positively affects the utilitarian value of online paid health knowledge.
H4b: Platform service quality positively affects the hedonic value of online paid health knowledge.

3.2 Perceived Value (O) and Purchase Intention (R)

Perceived value in this study represents the OHP users' overall assessment of the utility of paid health knowledge (products or services), and is the result of weighing the benefits gained against the costs paid for the entire product use or service enjoyment process. Existing research in many fields has shown that perceived value is closely related to consumer intentions, and both utilitarian and hedonic values are positively associated with the future intentions of online shopping users [8]. In the context of knowledge payment, previous research found that perceived value positively affects users' purchase intention [6, 7]. Therefore, this paper makes the following hypotheses:

H5a: Utilitarian value positively affects purchase intention.
H5b: Hedonic value positively affects purchase intention.

4   Research Methodology

4.1   Sample and Data Collection

An online questionnaire consisted of two main parts was developed to test the model. One of parts covered screening questions, knowledge payment experience and demographic information. In this part, participants were asked whether they experienced or exposed to any OHPs and paid health knowledge such as health courses, health consultation. The other part consisted of the measurement items for each model construct.

The survey was conducted online during May 2022 with the help of Credamo.com. Users of OHPs who had experience in paying for health knowledge or had contacted paid health knowledge were selected as valid survey subjects. After eliminating invalid questionnaires that did not pass the screening questions, had too short a response time or almost unchanging answers, a total of 432 valid questionnaires was obtained.

4.2   Instrument

The measured items for constructs were adapted from previous studies and contextualized for online paid health knowledge setting. The measures for knowledge rarity were adapted from Pérez-Nordtvedt et al. [16] and knowledge personalization were adapted from Zhou et al. (2022) [6]. The measured items for platform information quality were adapted from Lee et al. [17], and platform service quality were adapted from Fang et al. [18]. The measures for utilitarian value were adapted from Overby and Lee [8], and hedonic value were adapted from Hsu and Lin [9]. The measures for purchase intention were adapted from Kim et al. [5]. All items were measured using 7-point Likert scale ranging from 1 (strongly disagree) to 7 (strongly agree).

5   Data Analysis and Results

There are two widely used structural equation modeling methods: covariance-based SEM and variance-based SEM. Drawing on Zhou et al. (2022) [6], when the test result of Kolmogorov-Smirnov test indicates that the data in our study are not normally distributed, the variance-based approach of partial least squares SEM is more suitable, because it does not make restrictive assumptions on the distribution of the data and is robust to non-normal distribution. In the current study, we adopted PLS-SEM to assess the measurement model and structural model using SmartPLS 3.0 software.

Table 1. Results of reliability and validity

Construct	Item	Loading	Cronbach's α	CR	AVE
Knowledge rarity (KR)	KR1	0.915	0.891	0.931	0.818
	KR2	0.891			
	KR3	0.907			
Knowledge personalization (KP)	KP1	0.837	0.701	0.832	0.624
	KP2	0.782			
	KP3	0.747			
Platform information quality (PIQ)	PIQ1	0.764	0.707	0.82	0.534
	PIQ2	0.777			
	PIQ3	0.719			
	PIQ4	0.656			
Platform service quality (PSQ)	PSQ1	0.719	0.766	0.850	0.586
	PSQ2	0.767			
	PSQ3	0.779			
	PSQ4	0.795			
Utilitarian Value (UV)	UV1	0.798	0.800	0.869	0.625
	UV2	0.808			
	UV3	0.749			
	UV4	0.806			
Hedonic value (HV)	HV1	0.685	0.705	0.836	0.631
	HV2	0.842			
	HV3	0.846			
Purchase intention (PI)	PI1	0.847	0.761	0.862	0.676
	PI2	0.804			
	PI3	0.815			

Note: CR = composite reliability, AVE = average variance extracted.

5.1 Measurement Model

We employed Cronbach's alpha and composite reliability (CR) to assess internal reliability of the constructs. The results in Table 1 show that the values of Cronbach's alpha are above 0.7 and the values of CR of each construct exceed 0.8, indicating that each construct has good reliability performance. As shown in Table 1, each latent variable includes three or more measured items, the factor loadings of all items are higher than 0.65, and the AVE values of each construct are higher than 0.5, suggesting good convergent validity. Results in Table 2 show that the square root of AVE for each construct is higher than the correlations across constructs, suggesting great discriminant validity.

In addition, all the VIF values are less than 2 (lower than the threshold value of 5), indicating that there is no serious multicollinearity problem in the model.

Table 2. Results of discriminant validity analysis

Construct	PI	UV	PIQ	PSQ	HV	KP	KR
PI	**0.822**						
UV	0.683	**0.791**					
PIQ	0.647	0.668	**0.731**				
PSQ	0.657	0.645	0.604	**0.766**			
HV	0.699	0.643	0.581	0.587	**0.795**		
KP	0.386	0.414	0.441	0.373	0.397	**0.790**	
KR	0.145	0.136	0.145	0.203	0.195	0.180	**0.904**

5.2 Common Method Bias (CMB)

Since our data was self-reported, CMB was investigated. We firstly adopted Harman's single factor test. The first factor explained 35.128% of the total variance, less than 40%. A marker variable technique was then used to test CMB [19]. The result showed insignificant effects of life satisfaction as a marker variable on purchase intention (p = 0.161 > 0.05). And no obvious difference was observed in the R^2 value before and after adding the marker variable. In conclusion, there was no serious CMB in this study.

5.3 Structural Model

SmartPLS 3.0 was used to examine the structural model. We adopted a bootstrapping procedure with 5000 samples to verify the significance of the path coefficients. The results show that the estimated value of SRMR was 0.068, less than the critical value of 0.08, suggesting a good model fitting effect.

Results shown in Fig. 2 indicate that all proposed hypotheses are supported, except hypothesis H1. The variance interpretation rates R2 of utilitarian value, hedonic value and purchase intention are 54.6%, 44.1% and 58.6% respectively, indicating that this research model has good explanatory power. Specifically, the effects of knowledge rarity on utilitarian value (p = 0.580) and hedonic value (p = 0.054) were not significant, suggesting that H1a and H1b are not valid. Knowledge personalization positively affects utilitarian value (β = 0.102, p = 0.030) and hedonic value (β = 0.122, p = 0.010), indicating that H2a and H2b are supported. Platform information quality has significantly positive impacts on utilitarian value (β = 0.404, p = 0.000) and hedonic value (β = 0.314, p = 0.000), which supports H3a and H3b. Platform service quality is positively associated with utilitarian value (β = 0.366, p = 0.000) and hedonic value (β = 0.340, p = 0.000), which supports H4a and H4b. In support of H5a and H5b, both utilitarian value (β = 0.398, p = 0.000) and hedonic value (β = 0.443, p = 0.000) have significantly positive effects on purchase intention.

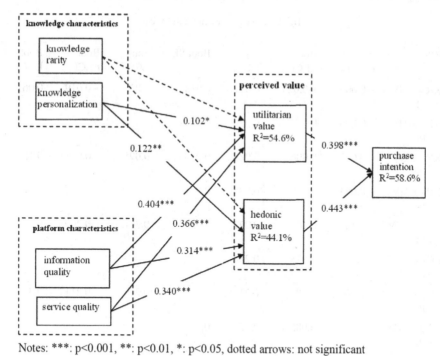

Notes: ***: p<0.001, **: p<0.01, *: p<0.05, dotted arrows: not significant

Fig. 2. Research model results

5.4 Mediation Test

We adopted the bootstrapping approach to test the mediating effect of perceived value. The criterion for judgement is that the mediating effect is significant when 0 is not within the 95% confidence interval. The results shown in Table 3 support that perceived value (utilitarian value, hedonic value) partially mediates the relationship between stimuli (except knowledge rarity) and purchase intention.

6 Discussion

6.1 Findings

This paper reveals the following findings: (1) Knowledge rarity has no significant impact on perceived value, which is not consistent with previous research on knowledge payment [6]. This may be due to the fact that more and more health practitioners offer professional health knowledge products or services, especially during the epidemic period, and the role of knowledge rarity is mitigated. (2) Knowledge personalization positively affects utilitarian value and hedonic value, which is still not consistent with Zhou et al. (2022) [6], reflecting its crucial impacts on the current OHP users' purchase intention. According to the iiMedia Report [1], most of popular fields and hot contents are highly standardized and easy to reproduce. There is no exception in the paid field of health knowledge,

Table 3. Results of mediation test

Path	Indirect Effect	Boot LLCI	Boot ULCI	Boot SE	Total Effect	Boot LLCI	Boot ULCI
KR -> UV -> PI	−0.006	−0.029	0.017	0.012	0.02	−0.019	0.061
KR -> HV -> PI	0.026	0	0.056	0.014			
KP -> UV -> PI	0.041	0.006	0.081	0.019	0.095	0.033	0.157
KP -> HV -> PI	0.054	0.015	0.095	0.021			
PIQ -> UV -> PI	0.161	0.101	0.227	0.032	0.3	0.209	0.39
PIQ -> HV -> PI	0.139	0.078	0.204	0.032			
PSQ -> UV -> PI	0.146	0.09	0.21	0.031	0.296	0.211	0.38
PSQ -> HV -> PI	0.151	0.085	0.229	0.037			

thus making knowledge personalization matters. (3) Platform information quality has positive impacts on utilitarian value and hedonic value, which further confirms Zhou et al. (2019) [7]. (4) Platform service quality has a positive effect on utilitarian value and hedonic value, which further confirms conclusions obtained by previous research [7]. (5) Both utilitarian value and hedonic value positively affect the OHP users' intention to purchase health knowledge, which further supports previous findings [6, 7]. The partial mediation role of perceived value is also supported.

6.2 Implications

We have several theoretical implications. First, this study extends the application of the S-O-R model and the perceived value theory to the online paid health knowledge context. We propose a comprehensive theoretical framework to find more generally applicable factors that affect purchase intention of health knowledge including articles, consultation services, fitness courses and others. Besides, we propose the antecedents of OHP users' purchase intention regarding knowledge characteristics and platform characteristics, testing several predictors relatively novel to the existing research. Considering the freshness of the online health knowledge payment industry, there is still a lack of research associated with it, most of which focus on the online health consultation context [4, 20]. Based on the S-O-R model and the perceived value theory, we propose more generally applicable factors from the perspective of knowledge characteristics and platform characteristics affecting OHP uses' perceived value of health knowledge, thus purchase intention. This paper demonstrates that the framework of S-O-R model and the mediation mechanism of perceived value can be applied to guide future research on health knowledge payment. But this article is merely a small step forward, much more efforts need to be put into further development in this area.

We also have some practical implications. Firstly, it can be seen that more and more professional health knowledge is provided in OHPs due to the rapid development of online health knowledge payment industry. Knowledge rarity is not the key factor affecting OHP users' purchase behavior. Besides, health knowledge contents emerge one after another, but there is a serious problem of content homogeneity. Health knowledge products are generally homogenized with high repetition rate, thus making OHP users tend to favor more personalized health knowledge. Apart from that, users pay much attention to platform information quality and platform service quality as well. Therefore, on the one hand, OHPs need to face the dilemma of content homogeneity. Through the screening and auditing mechanism, knowledge content duplication can be reduced. At the same time, users' preferences and needs for health knowledge can be obtained through reasonable user data analysis, so as to provide users with relatively personalized knowledge products and services. On the other hand, it is of critical importance to improve the production process of knowledge products, ensuring that the description information of knowledge products provided by the platform is accurate and clear, and easy for users to understand. Emphasizing the active operation of knowledge payment service system for better service quality and respond efficiency is necessary as well.

There are certain limitations in the current study: (1) This study measures health knowledge payment behavior of users through purchase intention, but there may be some discrepancies between actual purchase behavior and intention. Future studies may consider the combination with actual payment data of OHP users. (2) The research samples come from Chinese markets, so the findings are relatively more applicable to the health knowledge payment field in China. In the future, consideration can be given to obtaining data from multiple countries to conduct more in-depth research and obtain more generalized findings.

Acknowledgements. This research was supported by the National Natural Science Foundation of China under Grant 71971092.

References

1. iiMedia Report. https://www.iimedia.cn/c400/86348.html. Accessed 15 January 2023
2. Zhao, Y., Zhao, Y., Yuan, X., Zhou, R.: How knowledge contributor characteristics and reputation affect user payment decision in paid Q&A? An empirical analysis from the perspective of trust theory. Electron. Commer. Res. Appl. **31**, 1–11 (2018)
3. Zhang, M., Zhang, Y., Zhao, L., Li, X.: What drives online course sales? Signaling effects of user-generated information in the paid knowledge market. J. Bus. Res. **118**, 389–397 (2020)
4. Li, J., Tang, J., Jiang, L., Yen, D.C., Liu, X.: Economic success of physicians in the online consultation market: a signaling theory perspective. Int. J. Electron. Commer. **23**(2), 244–271 (2019)
5. Kim, H.-W., Gupta, S., Koh, J.: Investigating the intention to purchase digital items in social networking communities: a customer value perspective. Inf. Manag. **48**(6), 228–234 (2011)

6. Zhou, S., Li, T., Yang, S., Chen, Y.: What drives consumers' purchase intention of online paid knowledge? A stimulus-organism-response perspective. Electron. Commer. Res. Appl. **52**, 101126 (2022)
7. Zhou, T., Tan, Q., Deng, S.: Research on users' willingness to pay for knowledge based on the IS success model. J. Mod. Inf. **39**(08), 59–65 (2019). (in Chinese)
8. Overby, J.W., Lee, E.-J.: The effects of utilitarian and hedonic online shopping value on consumer preference and intentions. J. Bus. Res. **59**(10), 1160–1166 (2006)
9. Hsu, C.-L., Lin, J.C.-C.: Effect of perceived value and social influences on mobile app stickiness and in-app purchase intention. Technol. Forecast. Soc. Change **108**, 42–53 (2016)
10. Wu, L., Lee, C.: Limited edition for me and best seller for you: the impact of scarcity versus popularity cues on self versus other-purchase behavior. J. Retail. **92**(4), 486–499 (2016)
11. Arora, N., et al.: Putting one-to-one marketing to work: personalization, customization, and choice. Mark. Lett. **19**(3), 305–321 (2008)
12. Wang, C., Teo, T.S.H., Liu, L.: Perceived value and continuance intention in mobile government service in China. Telemat. Inform. **48**, 101348 (2020)
13. Pearson, A., Tadisina, S., Griffin, C.: The role of e-service quality and information quality in creating perceived value: antecedents to web site loyalty. Inf. Syst. Manag. **29**(3), 201–215 (2012)
14. Zheng, Y., Zhao, K., Stylianou, A.: The impacts of information quality and system quality on users' continuance intention in information-exchange virtual communities: An empirical investigation. Decis. Support Syst. **56**, 513–524 (2013)
15. Chen, L., Li, Y.-Q., Liu, C.-H.: How airline service quality determines the quantity of repurchase intention - mediate and moderate effects of brand quality and perceived value. J. Air Transp. Manag. **75**, 185–197 (2019)
16. Pérez-Nordtvedt, L., Kedia, B.L., Datta, D.K., Rasheed, A.A.: Effectiveness and efficiency of cross-border knowledge transfer: an empirical examination. J. Manag. Stud. **45**(4), 714–744 (2008)
17. Lee, S.W., Sung, H.J., Jeon, H.M.: Determinants of continuous intention on food delivery apps: extending UTAUT2 with information quality. Sustainability **11**(11), 3141 (2019)
18. Fang, Y., Chiu, C., Wang, E.T.G.: Understanding customers' satisfaction and repurchase intentions: an integration of IS success model, trust, and justice. Internet Res. **21**(4), 479–503 (2011)
19. Tehseen, S., Ramayah, T., Sajilan, S.: Testing and controlling for common method variance: a review of available methods. J. Manag. Sci. **4**(2), 142–168 (2017)
20. Cao, X., Liu, Y., Zhu, Z., Hu, J., Chen, X.: Online selection of a physician by patients: empirical study from elaboration likelihood perspective. Comput. Hum. Behav. **73**, 403–412 (2017)

An Empirical Study on the Impact of Government Microblogs on Online Engagements During the Covid-19 Outbreak

Anqi Nie[✉], Hao Jiang, Jiayi Xu, and Jing Fan[✉]

Beijing Foreign Studies University, No. 2, North Road, West 3rd Ring, Beijing, China
{202220216107,fanjing}@bfsu.edu.cn

Abstract. While government microblogs show increasing significance as a bridge connecting the government and the people, its role has become more prominent during the covid-19 outbreak, when the government released all kinds of official information in a timely manner and obtained public participation and feedback. Two important aspects to measure online participation are likes and comments, and the content topic of posts is an important influencing factor in online engagement studies. However, except for a few case studies, few researches have been conducted to provide an objective insight into the content topics of government blogs based on amass data in the context of the epidemic, and subsequently studies the impact of content topics on engagements. This paper analyzes the overall release pattern of government microblogs during pandemic in China by extracting 9 topics through LDA model based-on datasets from Sina Weibo. With a 5W-framework, we empirically confirm the relationship between content topics and public engagement with negative binomial analysis beyond the limitations of previous studies focusing only on some local factors. The results show that in general government releases focus mainly on the topics of epidemic science and uplifting spirits. However, information about police and public interaction and important instructions receives more discussion and likes, while news about treatment progress and praise of uplifting spirits receive little attention. Contributions to the literature and practice are discussed.

Keywords: Government Microblogs · Covid-19 Outbreak · Public Engagement · LDA Topic Model · Negative Binomial Regression

1 Introduction

In recent years, the growth of online social media has been ubiquitous, attracting a large number of users to participate in it. Government microblogs, as an application of social media by government agencies, have grown rapidly since they first appeared in 2009. As shown by People's Daily Online, as of December 31, 2020, the number of certified government accounts on Sina Weibo reached 177,437. As public departments continue to promote the development of new media in government affairs, the government social media is taking a more prominent role in especially situations of emergency. The covid-19 outbreak in late 2019 was a public health emergency. With it ravaging the world in the era of data explosion, the public demand for trustworthy information continues to increase. And government microblogs serve exactly as a key channel for government information dissemination and are a crucial role in maintaining social stability. In emergencies as such, the untimely or inappropriate disclosure of government information can make the public prone to irrational behavior, resulting in even secondary damage on social order [1]. Therefore, whether government release matches public's needs matter a lot. And researchers have found that online participation towards government release help mitigate public losses. [2] In face of danger, anxiety naturally appeared and the public always turn to the government first for help. [3] And today, apart from people telling you directly what they need, the need can be demonstrated exactly by the data shown on government social media. So, engagement is not only a variable worth studying for better social welfare, but also one that can measure the extent of people's information needs on certain topics in a crisis.

Existing literature about the microblogs' content factors that influence participation has focused, from the micro level, on social psychology theories to ex-plain individual participation decisions, and from the macro level, on datasets to verify the impacts of influential features of the publisher and of the posted con-tent on engagements. However, governmental release-related studies often only focus on the influence of limited features, such as microblog account characteristics, without a comprehensive and systematic framework. On top of the independent variables discussed, scholars emphasized that the context-related factors should also be considered [4] Zhang made some improvements on 5W framework and provides a solution to this problem in studies about government release [5].

As we dig deeper into related research in the context of crisis. Related studies have mostly found the effects of different content topics on online engagement at the descriptive level through case studies. Another thing is that clustering algorithm and other scientific way of extracting content feature have been widely used in studies of public opinion. But no study has yet applied these methods to extract topic features of government microblogs in epidemic scenarios, which means that studies about government release content during covid-19 outbreak do not receive enough attention and are limited to case studies and subjective pre-defined topic classification.

Therefore, this study uses the LDA topic modeling approach to form an objective categorization of governmental microblogs topics based on a large number of epidemic-related posts from Sina Weibo during the epidemic, and further through negative binomial regression, to answer the important questions of whether and how governmental release topics influence online engagement and of what does the government focus on during the epidemic.

2 Literature Review and Research Hypothesis

2.1 Online Engagement

Vivek et al. define online engagement as the intensity of an individual's involvement in an event or connection to products or activities initiated by a client or organization [8]. Engagement is highly context-dependent [6]. The intensity of engagement behavior changes from contexts, which actually confirms the necessity to distinguish between research of government posts in general or in emergency situations, because the two contexts are essentially different not only in release topics, but the logic of engagement behavior may be different. The online engagement is roughly divided into two categories: the autonomous posting of relevant content, and the reaction to certain posts such as comments or likes. Engagement is studied in both business and government scenarios, the number of likes and comments are frequently used as mutually alternative measurements of online engagement [6]. This study will also use the two variables as dependent variables to explore the factors influencing engagement during pandemic.

A bunch of researches empirically proves that marketing or government post topics have different impacts on people's engagement [4, 6], providing insights for similar studies in the covid-19 epidemic scenario. Given the official and authoritative nature of government social media, which differs itself from ordinary media, a 5W framework was further applied to consider the impact of government microblogs on participation from three aspects [5]: subject characteristics, technical characteristics and content themes, and this also provides a basic framework for subsequent studies (Fig. 1).

Fig. 1. 5W framework

2.2 Content Topic and Its Influence on Engagement

Content Topic is an underestimated topic in public management related research, especially when in the context of crisis scenarios. From the perspective of research methods, scholars at home and abroad study public opinion governance under emergencies with sophisticated clustering method. Lyu et al. used text mining analysis based on the tweet data and found that real-time information release could reduce the negative public sentiment [7]. However, when it comes to government release, the research methods are limited. A considerable number of studies have studied the differences in information release content by case studies [8] and questionnaires [9]. It is reasonable to assume that there may be significant differences in people's attention to different release topics during covid-19 epidemic, studies are needed to break away from traditional case studies to analyze the topic of information releases based on amass data and to empirically demonstrate whether such characteristics have an impact on engagements. This type of study will be very helpful for us to better understand the pattern and problems of government communication under the epidemic scenario.

2.3 Research Hypotheses

ELM Model and 5W Model. ELM model is a framework about explaining the changing behavior or attitude based on a sum of related theory about the changes of cognition and attitude, and is widely used in areas like information dissemination, commercial adds and so on. [10] Sussman et al. make the point based on ELM that the quality and source of information can respectively influence the central and peripheral route of information adoption action and later on researchers share a mutual understanding on that point. [11] When it comes to studies about online posts, characteristics about the source such as number of fans and contents characteristics such as emotions cannot be neglected. However, the rapidly developing government social media has some of its own characteristics: compared with the fair attention to technical characteristics focusing on work or post itself from the perspective of communication studies for better dissemination [5], and existed fair attention to the account characteristics related to the publisher itself, either of these attentions can fully reflect the uniqueness of the research on government releases. Government media is rather official and authoritative, and is a typical source dominated perspective when it comes to information dissemination [12]. While the special characteristics of the source matters, government media has always had greater room for progress than other social media in terms of content release [13]. So Zhang developed a model based on 5W where we focus on the publisher's influence-who, the specific content topic-says what and technical features of posts - in which channel, to study how the government release influence public engagement, and in this paper we further extend this framework to the pandemic context.

Cognition-Behavior Model. People are anxious about useful release during pandemic, especially those from the government [14] Some studies on public opinions found that people are in need for information more about the epi-science, the report of infected cases [15]. Yet do they really get what they want from the government posts? Engagement, to some extent can show us whether the content posted is needed. According to Cognition-behavior model, people, in awareness of the severity of situation, would feel anxious and desperate for guidance to ease the anxiety. When they get to know more about the situation as the covid is spreading, they feel more anxiety and more anxious to get rid of the attitude or state of bad emotion, and that can get them more participated into the gov-people channel provided by government social media, which can usually be shown in the number of likes and comments.

Based on the 9 topics we found later in this paper, we made the hypothesis 1: There is a significant difference in people's engagement between different topics of governmental releases during the covid-19 outbreak.

For publisher features, in addition, information disclosure by central and local governments had different effects on the public's response [16], with local releases stimulating public demand for up-to-date information and anxiety about potential risks, while central releases reduced such concern. Previous view of studying government as a whole has certain shortcomings. We believe that the level can also act as a marginal signal in ELM model, with central level representing a more credible information source and thus promote public participation. What's more, according to the information demand bias theory, relevant information released by the central government highlights the severity of the crisis and prompts the public to pay more attention to the sudden crisis, thus more anxiety and more actions. Then we make the hypothesis H2: Central government accounts can get more public engagement than local accounts.

As for control variables, we consider the influence of microblogs as a composite index for the publisher characteristics, which will affect engagement. Activeness measures whether a publisher is active in posting, which is usually linked to higher opinion status and stronger appeal to the public [17]. Integration refers to the comprehensive ability to utilize and integrate trending topics, which is key to a higher opinion status and thus can attract the target audience. The number of following accounts and followers measure the scope of knowledge networks and direct influence of bloggers, which are generally considered to have an impact on engagement. Technical features include, the length of the tweet, which generally indicates more information and promote engagement, whether a post contains hashtags, videos, links, etc. And they will serve as control variables for our model. Variables are listed as below (Table 1).

Table 1. Variables and measurement

Type	Variables	Measurement
DV	Likes	Number of likes on a post
	Comments	Number of comments on a post
Core IV	Content topic	Dummy variable, 9 topics extracted through LDA
CV (Publisher features)	Influence	Influence score in the 2020 Annual Government Microblog Influence Report
	Activeness	Total number of related posts posted in 2020 (Jan. And Feb.), ln
	Integration	Total number of hashtags used in 2020 (Jan. And Feb.), ln
	Subscribe	Number of followers, ln
	Follow	Number of following accounts, ln
	Level	Dummy variable, 1 if central, 0 if not
CV (Technical posts features)	Len	Number of total characters in a post, ln
	Hashtag	Dummy variable, 1 if at least 1 hashtag appears in a post, 0 if not
	Video	Dummy variable, 1 if at least 1 video appears in a post, 0 if not
	URL	Dummy variable, 1 if at least 1 link appears in a post, 0 if not
	@	Dummy variable, 1 if function of "at" is used in a post, 0 if not

3   Data Collection and Processing

3.1   Collecting Data

During Jan. And Feb. 2020, the number of government disclosure experienced the whole purposeful and timely process from the initial response to crisis to the high-frequency disclosure stage. [18] Samples from this period can be representative. And the 2020 Annual Government Microblog Influence Report contains the ranking of influential government accounts, by the People's Daily Online Public Opinion Data Center, Sina Data Center, and Sina Weibo, from both the central and local levels, and all industries. Through random sampling, we found that the accounts with communication ability score below 60, interaction ability below 70, and comprehensive influence score less than 70 points, has hardly received any likes and comments, and is not suitable for research. We further eliminated accounts with missing data or without reading rights or cancelled, and 95 government with a total of 112695 posts and related data were obtained.

3.2   Processing Data

Based on the Continuously updated Sina Weibo Public Opinion Datasets, which was updated in March 2021, with "epidemic prevention", "#Wuhan cheer", and other manually added keywords, posts related to the covid-19 epidemic were selected by regular expression matching. After excluding the account "National Museum" with only 13 related posts. A total of 52,943 records are obtained.

Then, we removed meaningless symbols such as emoticons, links from posts. Ultra-short posts with less than 4 words were also deleted. Jieba was used with added dictionaries to supplement the epidemic-related words to improve the separation accuracy. Finally, we kept the nouns, verbs and adjectives with relatively more information to extract the content topics.

4   Empirical Analysis and Results

4.1   Extraction of Topics

The LDA method shows a high performance among various kinds of topic modeling methods [19]. Through LDA, we got a document-topic and a topic-keyword matrix. 9 topics were obtained by analyzing logical connections between keywords (Fig. 2). Based on LDA model, we get machine labeled variable of content topic. To test the effectiveness of this method, 966 sample were randomly selected and manually categorized as sample 1. Each post was categorized by five participants, and was confirmed if three or more people categorized the post as the same [6]. Kappa value of a consistency test was 0.881, which means the machine labeled results were reliable. Those 9 specific content topic variables are Epi-Science (ES), Guides to Action (GTA), Work Resumption (WR), Progress in Treatment (PIT), Uplifting Spirits (US), Important Instructions (II), Police and Public (PAP), Medical Resources (MR), and Case Notification (CN). What's more, we notice that governments microblogs on epidemic science (about the science and suggestions on how to get through), uplifting spirits (which is about inspirational messages such as inspiring stories), and infected case notifications take the biggest release proportion.

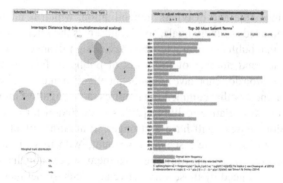

Fig. 2. Visualized distance between topics

4.2 Negative Binomial Regression

Table 2. Descriptive statistics - comments

Topics	0	1	2	3	4	5	6	7	8
Ave	42.31	68.59	60.07	40.10	50.48	85.64	84.73	56.23	51.14
Median	5	6	6	5	6	6	6	6	6
Std	232.56	580.19	481.47	205.64	333.84	869.12	950.25	296.33	289.70

Table 3. Descriptive statistics - likes

Topics	0	1	2	3	4	5	6	7	8
Ave	238.99	814.24	368.84	249.10	349.98	666.90	802.92	513.31	305.38
Median	17	20	19	20	19	20	19	20	21
Std	1819.04	17684.9	3209.54	2000.03	3657.56	9187.56	13251.7	5365.60	2253.56

Among the 20588 labeled posts, one post issued the first Wuhan Lockdown notice, receiving millions of likes. It's removed from the regression sample to avoid the extreme value. The final input was 20587 records.

There is over-dispersion in DV, and the value of the Chi-square Value/df in Poisson regression is more than 3, the negative binomial regression model is appropriate. A descriptive analysis is conducted as shown in Tables 2 and 3. Models 1, 3, 5, and 7 gradually add publisher characteristic variables, technical characteristic variables, level and topic variables, with likes as the dependent variable. Models 2,4,6,8 were treated similarly with comments as the dependent variable. The variables vif in the models are all less than 2 with no covariance problem. The model fit was measured by the AIC and BIC. Models 7 and 8 fits best with the data.

We noticed the mean, extreme value and variance of the likes and comments in theme 3-treatment progress are significantly lower, and it is more about the long-term trends and progress in medicine and of others' rehabilitation, which is far from the current urgent information needs of individuals, so it's chosen as the reference group.

Results show that publisher characteristics have a significant effect on engagements (Table 4). Influence and number of followers of publisher features positively affect engagement. Integration does not have a significant effect on likes but does on comments, which can be explained by that commenting requires more cognitive input and expresses more complex attitudes relative to liking [20], so integration for contents containing various information sources will have a stronger stimulating effect on commenting. Unlike the results in the business scenario, accounts with more followers and more active accounts receive significantly fewer engagement. we explain that by homogeneity in the amass posts produced by those very active accounts, sometimes they even share a common template. Although a higher number of followers may represent a broader source of knowledge and thus satisfy the needs of the public, yet may also represent more homogeneous content from one account to another. Higher activeness may also be associated with lower quality and homogeneity, which negatively affect engagement [12]. And this can be explored in future research. On the structural content factor, longer posts receive significantly more likes, which is consistent with the findings related to information richness. Other characteristics do not have a significant effect in the crisis politics scenario. Posts with videos receive significantly fewer comments and have no significant effect on likes.

According to Models 7 and 8, the conclusions are roughly similar for the likes and comments. All other things being equal, themes "police and people interaction" and "important instructions" got the most public attention whether it's in terms of likes and comments. That's in line with the cognitive-behavior model where people are anxious for guidance that could help them out of the anxiety. Important instruction is about a serious guidance, spirit or method against the epidemic brought out by the government or the CPC, which is official and trustworthy from the macro level to guide you through. And the police enforcement during epidemic is about all the details of stories between the police and people, from which one can tell what kind of behavior is appropriate during the special period through examples and debates. This conclusion is also consistent with the recent trend of "turn to police in case of trouble" among Internet users. In any case, the public not only gave great recognition to the public security enforcement work during the epidemic released by government microblogs, but also contributed a considerable degree of discussion, making it a rather important category of topics.

What's more there's slight difference on the results of guidance to act, which receives significantly more comments but not likes, and of the case notification, which receives significantly more likes but not comments. Though likes and comments are frequently used as mutually alternative measurements of online engagement [6], when we further understand engagements in three dimensions-the cognitive state, emotional state, and behavioral state exhibited during the participation process, we know there are differences. While cognitive state refers to the level of effort expended in understanding cognition, commenting behavior generally requires more cognitive input than liking and is a comprehensive communication behavior that needs time and strong cognitive skills, whereas liking is considered a "one-click action". In terms of emotional complexity, liking tends to express positive mind states, while comments tend to be more complex in

Table 4. Regression result

Variables	Model 1	Model 2	Model 3	Model 4	Model 5	Model 6	Model 7	Model 8
Influence	0.15***	0.09***	0.17***	0.11***	0.17***	0.11***	0.15***	0.10***
Activeness	−1.49***	−1.24***	−1.24***	−1.09***	−1.30***	−1.10***	−1.14***	−1.03***
Integration	0.51***	0.41***	0.20	0.18*	0.23*	0.19**	0.19	0.17*
Subscribe	−0.30**	−0.36**	−0.19*	−0.30***	−0.20*	−0.30***	−0.20**	−0.30**
Follow	0.58***	0.29***	0.45***	0.19***	0.46***	0.20***	0.49***	0.21***
Len			0.56***	0.42***	0.57***	0.42***	0.55***	0.42***
Hashtag			0.28	0.12	0.26	0.12	0.29*	0.13
Video			−0.27	−0.45***	−0.27	−0.50***	−0.24	−0.45***
URL			0.48	−0.14	0.41	−0.17	0.39	−0.20
@			−0.05	0.02	−0.10	−0.00	−0.13	−0.03
Level					0.33*	0.21*	0.32*	0.21*
0							0.14	0.1
1							0.55	0.32*
2							0.38	0.25
4							0.11	0.13
5							0.46*	0.42**
6							0.78**	0.54**
7							0.35	0.19
8							0.36*	0.33
AIC	262302.38	196617.59	258776.76	194245.14	258337.03	194068.92	257367.48	193589.27
BIC	262349.98	196665.19	258864.02	194332.40	258432.22	194164.10	257546.13	193747.92

* $p < 0.05$; ** $p < 0.01$; *** $p < 0.001$.

expressing emotions. For case notification, it is always about the numbers but not often about specific travelling routes and there seems not many disputes or much difficulty in understand, but is needed as well. And for guidance to act, it's more about local instructions on what to do from especially communities, we could see there's much discussion over it, showing people's great care for such information but the positive attitude is not so obvious, which might indicate some problem in community management during epidemic.

However, there's no evidence that news on rehabilitation of work, uplifting spirits, medical resources are really more attractive for the public compared with the base line. And that might show the public is more in need of detailed and specified guidance information in front of danger rather than just encouraging words and information that's not so related to their current lives. As for epi-science, peoples not engaged enough might also have something to do with the quality of contents. We can see epi-science content between different accounts either contrast with each other or actually are talking the same thing. Yet there's a big proportion of post on uplifting spirits and epi-science. Future research is also expected to explain the phenomenon thus come out with better suggestion.

By changing the reference group in Table 5, we further confirm the conclusion above.

And for hypothesis about the account levels, according to Models 5–8, compared to local accounts, central account posts receive 38% more likes and 23% more comments. Hypothesis 2 was proved. And that further confirms government accounts from central level do enjoy more reputation among people and are preferred as first choice when there's need for information during Covid-19 period.

Table 5. Regression result-shifting control group

Control topic	Likes	Comments
#0	#6 > #5 > #0	#6 > #5 > #0
#1		#1 > #3
#3	#6 > #5 > #3	#6 > #5 > #8 > #1 > #3
#4	#6 > #5 > #4	#6 > #5 > #4
#5	#5 > #0 > #4 > #3	#5 > #4 > #0 > #3
#6	#6 > #0 > #4 > #3	#6 > #0 > #3
#8		#8 > #3

5 Discussion

5.1 Conclusion and Implications

Through this study we answer what are contents that government microblogs focus on during the covid-19 epidemic and how the posts topic of government release influence online engagements? We have 3 key findings to fulfil the research gap and offer suggestions on government microblogs during Covid-19 outbreak.

First, based on a large dataset from weibo, we extract 9 content topics that government work on. In particular, epidemic science and uplifting spirits occupy a fairly high proportion of releases.

Then, during the covid-19 outbreak, releases on "police and people interaction" and "important instructions" attracts most of the public's attention and reflection, indicating these two releases are most relevant to their needs, this helps to maintain social security through debates over cases and concerns of instructions. In contrast, "epidemic science," "uplifting spirits," and "treatment progress" are less attractive. The findings may suggest that the public is less concerned about encouraging words or things not directly with what to do in lives, but more interested in detailed guidance during crisis.

However, in general, the government releases on the topics of "epidemic science" and "uplifting spirits" are much more frequent, which might indicate a large amount of homogeneity. So, policy publishers need to pay further attention to this phenomenon in order to make better use of public resources. On the one hand, operations of government releases should consider to reduce the number of releases on these two topics and instead to improve the quality of content. On the other hand, the important role of "police and public interaction" and "important instructions" should be more affirmed and noted, so as to mobilize people's participation.

In the end the study further expands the application of the Lasswell model in the context of information release during crisis. And the discovery of public engagement significantly more on central accounts further complements the theory of Information Demand Preference.

6   Limitations and Future Work

Though we offered reasonable explanation, we measure engagement with only the number of likes and comments in this study. While commenting is a complex behavior with high cognitive requirements, further mining of comment content such as sentiments is also an important dimension to measure user engagement for more connotations of engagement behavior. What's more, based on the data set from Weibo, we can further study the macro characteristics of related government releases on social media platform by making comparisons between accounts of different levels and from different sectors and to further study the quality problem such as homogeneity.

Acknowledgement. This research was supported by The Ministry of Education Humanities and Social Sciences Fund Project "Research on the mechanism and strategy of online medical precision service based on intelligent methods" (22YJA630018).

References

1. An, L., Wu, Y.: Maturity diagnosis model of public opinion guidance capability of government microblogging in the context of public emergencies. Inf. Stud. Theory Appl. **45**(5), 133–141 (2022). in Chinese

2. Chatfield, A.T., Scholl, H.J., Brajawidagda, U.: Tsunami early warnings via Twitter in government: net-savvy citizen's co-production of time-critical public information services. Gov. Inf. Q. **30**(4), 377–386 (2013)

3. Palen, L., Starbird, K., Vieweg, S.: Twitter-based information distribution during 2009 Red River Valley flood threat. Bull. Assoc. Inf. Sci. Technol. **36**(5), 13–17 (2010)

4. Feng, X., Hui, K., Deng, X., Jiang, G.: Understanding how the semantic features of contents influence the diffusion of government microblogs: moderating role of content topics. Inf. Manage. **58**(8), 103547.1-103547.15 (2021). in Chinese

5. Zhang, J., Fang, H., Wang, W.: Research on the status quo and influential factors of the communication effect of China's government affairs on bilibili. e-government **234**(06), 49–62 (2022). in Chinese

6. Yang, M., Ren, Y., Adomavicius, G.: Understanding user-generated content and customer engagement on Facebook business pages. Inf. Syst. Res. **30**(3), 839–855 (2019)

7. Lyu, J., Luli, G.: Understanding the public discussion about the centers for disease control and prevention during the COVID-19 pandemic using Twitter data: text mining analysis study. J. Med. Internet Res. **23**(2), e25108 (2021)

8. Chen, S., Huang, C., Chen, Q., Yang, L., Xu, X.: Information-releasing strategy of local government microblog group during public emergency ———A case study of tianjin port explosion. J. Inf. **35**(12), 28–33 (2016). in Chinese

9. Zhu, Y., Wang, R.: Reasons to E-participation in public health emergency in China: A perspective of civic voluntarism model and social value exchange. J. Inf. **39**(6), 164–171 (2020). in Chinese

10. Petty, R.E., Cacippo, J.T.: Source factors and the elaboration likelihood model of persuasion. Adv. Consum. Res. **11**(1), 668–672 (1984)

11. Li, C.Y.: Persuasive messages on information system acceptance a theoretical extension of elaboration likelihood-model and social influence theory. Comput. Hum. Behav. **29**(1), 264–275 (2013)

12. Fan, Y., Guo, Y.: From limited to effective: analysis of the role of factors in reconstructing the influence of political communication. Acad. Res. **5**, 63–67 (2018). in Chinese

13. Zhang, A.: Characteristics of information dissemination and governance strategies for major public health emergencies. Exploration **04**, 169–181 (2020). in Chinese

14. Tang, L., Zou, W.: Health Information consumption under COVID-19 lockdown: An interview study of residents of Hubei Province, China. Health Commun. **36**(3), 74–80 (2021)

15. Yang, K., Yang, C., Zhu, Q.: Research on public information demand and crisis management of public health emergency based on social media. Inf. Stud. Theory Appl. **44**(3), 59–68 (2021). in Chinese

16. Preece, J., Shneiderman, B.: The reader-to-leader framework: motivating technology-mediated social participation. AIS Trans. Hum. Comput. Int. **1**(1), 13–32 (2009)

17. Zhao, A., Cao, G.: Positive study on evaluation and comparison of government affairs microblog influence: Based on factor analysis and cluster analysis. J. Inf. **33**(3), 6 (2014). in Chinese

18. Cao, S., Yue, W.: Topic mining and evolution analysis of public opinion on microblog of public health emergencies. J. Inf. Resour. Manage. **10**(6), 10 (2020). in Chinese

19. Chiru, C., Rebedea, T., Ciotec, S.: Comparison between LSA-LDA-lexical chains. WEBIST (2014)

20. Brodie, R.J., Hollebeek, L.D., Juric, B., Ilic, A.: Customer engagement: conceptual domain, fundamental propositions, and implications for research. J. Serv. Res. **17**(3), 1–20 (2011)

The Concept and Connotation of Enterprise Digital Transformation

Jiangping Wan[⊠], Siting Lin[⊠], and Qingchen Wu

School of Business Administration, South China University of Technology, Guangzhou 510640, China
csjpwan@scut.edu.cn, 202220131906@mail.scut.edu.cn

Abstract. In the era of digital economy, the digital transformation of enterprises is a key strategic choice for the survival and development of enterprises. This paper gives the definition of enterprise digital transformation based on the subject, technology, scope and expected results through literature induction and comparison. This paper expounds the research status of digital transformation in the view of technological innovation and application, process, results and industrial application. The future development direction is also predicted. Digital transformation is defined as the application of digital technology by enterprises (subject) to build a digital world with full perception, full link, full scene and full intelligence (the technologies involved), and then optimize and reconstruct the business of the physical world, innovate and reshape the traditional management model, business model (scope), and finally achieve business success (expected results). Enterprise digital transformation is an inevitable product driven by internal and external factors. Relevant research on technological innovation and application mainly focuses on the cross-system transformation of enterprises. Process research focuses on transformation process and realization path, etc. Results research focuses on the impact of digital transformation on production efficiency and organizational performance, as well as possible data security problems. The industrial application perspective mainly provides practical cases and data.

Keywords: Enterprise digital transformation · Digital technology · Transformation process · Organizational performance · Industrial application

1 Introduction

In the era of digital economy, the development of emerging digital technologies, such as 5G network, artificial intelligence, block chain, edge computing, cloud computing, big data, has brought disruptive effects on the production mode and organizational form of enterprises [1], and enterprises have embarked on the path of digital transformation. The '2022 Accenture Digital Transformation Index for Chinese Enterprises' shows that Chinese enterprises' willingness to invest in digitalization continues to increase, and 59% of enterprises said they will increase digital investment in the next 1–2 years [2]. However, digital transformation has high cost, long cycle, great difficulty and high

© The Author(s), under exclusive license to Springer Nature Switzerland AG 2023
Y. Tu and M. Chi (Eds.): WHICEB 2023, LNBIP 480, pp. 315–324, 2023.
https://doi.org/10.1007/978-3-031-32299-0_27

uncertainty [3]. There are only a few leading enterprises in China's digital field, and the digital transformation of enterprises is full of challenges.

This paper systematically summarizes the concept and connotation of digital transformation, and gives the definition of this paper based on the subject, technology, scope and expected results in order to make up for the lack of relevant theoretical research, and also explores the internal and external factors that promote the digital transformation of enterprises, expounds the research status of digital transformation from the perspective of technological innovation and application, process, results, and industrial application [4]. This paper predicts the development direction of future research, and is committed to promoting the theoretical research of digital transformation and providing inspiration for the practice of digital transformation. The research model is shown in Fig. 1.

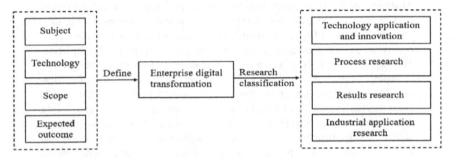

Fig. 1. Research model

2 Definition of Concept and Connotation of Enterprise Digital Transformation

Today, the concept of digital transformation has not been unified [5]. Generally speaking, it can be divided into two perspectives: technology application and enterprise transformation. Technology application focuses on the supporting role of digital technology and the transformation caused by technology upgrading, while the perspective of enterprise transformation focuses on the transformation of enterprise organization and business model caused by digital transformation (Table 1).

The definition of enterprise digital transformation in relevant research includes four basic attributes: subject, scope, technology involved in transformation and expected results. In this paper, digital transformation is defined as the application of digital technology by enterprises (subject) to build a digital world with full perception, full link, full scene and full intelligence (the technologies involved), and then optimize and reconstruct the business of the physical world, innovate and reshape the traditional management model, business model (scope), and finally achieve business success (expected results). The fully-perceptive, fully-linked, fully-scenario, and fully-intelligent digital world refers to a highly interconnected and highly intelligent fully digital world. It integrates emerging technologies such as artificial intelligence, the Internet of Things, big data, and cloud computing with traditional industries to create a more intelligent,

Table 1. Definition of digital transformation in relevant research

Focused perspective	Related research	Definition of digital transformation
Technology application	Valdez-de-Leo	Technological progress is a key driver of digital transformation. Digital transformation is the use of technologies such as analytics, mobility, social media and intelligent embedded devices to improve the performance or scale of enterprises [6]
	Reddy	Digital transformation is to use computer and Internet technology to create more efficient economic value, fundamentally improve the performance of enterprises or expand the scope of influence [7]
	Li	Digital transformation is precipitated by a transformational information technology, which can cause planned digital impact on a normal operating system [8]
Enterprises reform	Karimi	In the process of digital transformation, the company uses new digital technologies to achieve major business improvements and organizational changes, create new business models, rethink investment strategies, and then participate in a broader ecosystem, and learn from interactions with customers, suppliers, and partners to maintain competitiveness [9]
	LiBozhou	Digital transformation has changed the fundamental transformation of business model and management mode and reshaped the way of value growth [10]
	XiaoJinghua	Digital transformation is to upgrade the business through the new generation of digital technology, so that the digital technology and the real economy can be deeply integrated, so as to improve production efficiency and carry out management innovation [4]
	QiYudong	From the industrial level, digital transformation is defined as the process of improving the quantity and efficiency of production [11]

efficient, convenient, and comfortable digital life. "Fully-perceptive" means that various sensors and devices are used to perceive and collect data from the physical world, enabling the digital world to sense various data from the real world. "Fully-linked" refers to the connection between devices and the connection between devices and cloud services through various network technologies, enabling information sharing and collaborative work. "Fully-scenario" means that the digital world deeply integrates with the real world, providing users with a more intelligent and closer-to-life scenario experience. "Fully-intelligent" means that through deep learning, natural language processing, machine vision, and other artificial intelligence technologies, the digital world will become more intelligent, better understand user needs, and provide more personalized services. Digital transformation can help companies improve business efficiency, reduce costs, enhance market competitiveness, and create more business opportunities, thereby achieving business success. The connotation of digital transformation includes digitalization and transformation. Digitization usually includes three processes: forming data assets, accumulating data assets, and using data assets. The 2022 Accenture points out that the three core digital capabilities of enterprises are as follows: main business growth, business innovation and intelligent operation. Achieve main business growth through digital channels, marketing, product and service innovation. Digital business model and digital venture capital and incubation realize business innovation. Intelligent production and manufacturing and intelligent support and control to realize smart operation [2]. Informatization is the premise, digitalization is the core, and intelligence is the goal for the digital transformation of enterprises. The essence is that organizations apply Internet thinking to innovate and realize sustainable evolution.

Digital transformation is an inevitable choice for enterprises to maintain competitiveness in the digital world. Cao Peng, chairman of the Technical Committee of JD Group, believes that we can form a more advanced industrial competitiveness only by integrating technology into the whole process of the industrial chain on a large scale and systematically. It is a more efficient method to promote the application of artificial intelligence and other technologies around the whole process of the supply chain in practice [2]. Fu Heping, vice president of TCL Technology Group, pointed out that the expectation of changing the business logic with the help of IT system will often fall through when there is no change in the business. The digitalization movement should be in line with the pace of business transformation, slightly ahead of half a step or one step [2].

3 Motivation of Enterprise Digital Transformation

3.1 External Factors

The digital transformation and upgrading of enterprises is imminent. First of all, driven by the fourth industrial revolution, the digital economy has become the driving force of economic growth, and data has become a new resource enabling economic growth in the view of external factors. Secondly, new breakthroughs in the development of emerging industries and great changes in global production methods, enterprises around the world are undergoing digital transformation under the trend of technological innovation. Developed countries and other developing countries are facing the challenges of "two-way extrusion" [13], However, in recent years, China's technological and human costs have been rising, and the demographic dividend has disappeared. It still needs further research that how enterprises can successfully transform without incurring excessive costs. In recent years, the volatility of the global economy will increase due to multiple factors on the supply side and the demand side.

3.2 Internal Factors

In the past, it was limited due to high trial and error costs and slow development in the process of breakthrough innovation of key processes and products, the innovation ability of enterprises. Enterprises can build a fully perceptive, fully connected and fully intelligent digital world, and realize the digital simulation of the whole business with the in-depth application of digital technology. The scale cost and time cost of the digital world tend to be zero, and the value realization of enterprises presents the characteristics of increasing returns to scale [4], which helps enterprises to find the key nodes of innovation, break through the technical bottleneck, improve the efficiency of enterprise updating and iteration, and accelerate the pace of innovation, so as to enable enterprises to move to a new level.

In our understanding, the digital transformation of enterprises is an inevitable choice to seek high-quality development, improve competitiveness, and achieve business success with combining effect of internal and external factors.

4   Classification of Enterprise Digital Transformation Research

The research can be summarized into the following: technological innovation and application, the process, results and industrial application of digital transformation [4].

4.1 Technological Innovation and Application

The digital transformation of enterprises cannot be separated from the application of digital technology. The information technologies that represented by the Internet can reduce the search costs of organizations and produce more effective decisions [14]. Since then, the innovation and upgrading of technology, such as artificial intelligence, cloud computing, big data and other more extensive computing resources and computing models [5], has changed the original attribute of resources from scarcity, monopoly and static to relatively abundant, shared and dynamic, and have also made qualitative changes in the information structure, from the original untimely, discontinuous, refined and incomplete to timely, continuous, refined and complete [4]. For example, Newell and Marabelli believed that the ability of enterprises to implement algorithmic decision-making might depend on the ability of enterprises to analyze big data collected by individuals using social media on mobile phones [15].

4.2 Research on the Process of Digital Transformation

ZengDelin et al. combed the process of enterprise digital transformation from the three levels of individual, organization and industry [5]. The existing literature mainly focuses on the change of the role of executives in the process of digital transformation and the impact of digital transformation on employee employment [16]. The digital transformation of enterprises is a top-down driven transformation. Enterprise executives should have "digital mindset" [12] and "digital leadership" [3] in order to meet the challenges of digital transformation. Most employees are worried that the application of emerging technologies such as artificial intelligence may ban their original work and threaten their future survival and development, which will cause resistance to enterprise change.

Besson and Rowe believed that information technology will have a disruptive impact on organizational resources and organizational structure [17], changing the deep structure of the organization. Karimi et al. pointed out that digital transformation will reshape the dynamic capabilities of enterprises [9]. The view of enterprise dynamic capability is used to explain the viability of enterprises in the environment. With the accumulation of time, organizations can rely on digital technology to achieve a leap in organizational performance and improve dynamic capabilities. The process of enterprise digital transformation is the process of adjusting and iterating the development strategy of the organization.

First of all, enterprises often take measures to strengthen cross-border cooperation and use the new business model for collaborative development in order to obtain broader resources in terms of business model due to the change of resource attributes and information structure under the digital system [18]. Under the new business model of sharing economy, enterprises can use the digital platform to achieve efficient use of resources and value sharing. Secondly, the rise of the value chain is also the research focus of digital transformation. The popularity of mobile devices and the development of digital technology enable users to receive market information from multiple channels, talk directly with enterprises, and participate in the production of enterprises [11]. User value dominance has become the core concept of enterprise value creation, forcing enterprises to participate in the reconstruction of value chain.

4.3 Research on the Results of Digital Transformation

The results of the change may not only have a positive impact on enterprises, such as the improvement of production efficiency and organizational performance, but also may lead to adverse results, which may pose a threat to enterprises [12].

The application of artificial intelligence, machine learning and other technologies can help enterprises solve many problems and improve efficiency. In repetitive and high-frequency business scenarios, enterprises can use intelligent means to promote artificial intelligence to achieve efficient decision-making, analysis and action [16]. By injecting agility into business operations, a rapid feedback loop is formed between the business department and the information technology department, enabling enterprises to move from the original 'after-the-fact system, reporting system' to a real real-time operating model [5]. It can be seen that digital transformation can improve the efficiency of production and operation of enterprises. In addition, HeFan et al. believed that in the digital transformation of entity enterprises, digital technology has the characteristics of connection, openness and sharing, which can reduce the cost of information search, as well as the cost of bargaining and supervision of transactions. In the stage of "digital technology + industry", the information service architecture of "cloud + network + terminal" can stimulate the vitality of data and information elements and promote enterprise innovation [19]. The goal of improving organizational performance is achieved through cost reduction, efficiency improvement and innovation path.

4.4 Industrial Application of Digital Transformation

Industry application mainly focuses on the research of industry survey, industrial policy and management strategy, and provides practical cases and data of enterprise digital transformation [4], summarizes the success factors in typical transformation cases, and draws lessons from failure practices. For example, Furr et al. studied 50 digital transformation cases and found that in the process of digital transformation, the success rate of projects headed by insiders is about 80% [21]. It is concluded that the best way for enterprises to digitally transform is to be led by insiders and hire external experts to join the team. In addition, Furr also points out that digital transformation does not necessarily subvert existing value propositions, and the best results come from adaptation rather than reengineering. Lin Yan et al. analyzed the transformation cases of four enterprises, and summarized the different influencing factors in the breeding and implementation stages of digital transformation of manufacturing enterprises with grounded theory [22], which has certain practical significance.

5 Discussion and Inspiration

5.1 Technological Innovation and Application

The research on digital infrastructure management and digital platform construction should be strengthened in technology [5]. Digital technology has the power of subversion [16]. This subversion is dynamic. The digital technology introduced will not necessarily completely replace the existing mature technology. The traditional theory also fails to make a reasonable explanation for the practical application of digital technology in enterprise activities [1]. Future research needs to enrich the research on the motivation of the organization to use progressiveness, upgrade and update digital technology. Digital technology may also cause data security problems [20]. The security and privacy of digital technology is also a topic worthy of attention. Digital platform in digital technology is an important category [12]. The enterprise business includes R&D, marketing, service and other links. These links are interlinked. The enterprise needs to build a unified digital battle force and create a strong digital platform. Therefore, attention should be paid to the management of digital infrastructure and the construction of digital platform.

5.2 Process

It is necessary to further explore the specific mechanism driving digital transformation. The timing of digital transformation is very important for enterprises [3]. If the transformation is too early, the mismatch of digital capabilities may lead to supply chain friction and increase the cost of digital transformation. If the transformation is too late, enterprises cannot meet the changing needs of users, and may gradually lose competitiveness and development opportunities. Today, there are few studies on the starting time of digital transformation of enterprises, which need to be further studied. Secondly, digital technology innovation can promote the innovation of business models of enterprises and bring disruptive effects to enterprises themselves and market structures [9], but the existing research has not incorporated this disruptive process into the theoretical model [5], and future research can further explore how to incorporate the disruptive characteristics of the digital transformation process into the theoretical model. In addition, an important reason for the high failure rate of enterprise digital transformation is the disconnection between the strategic positioning and implementation of digital transformation [23]. The strategic positioning and implementation need to be dynamically adjusted according to the implementation results. How can enterprises adjust? What is the adjustment logic for the adjustment process? All these problems need to be deepened.

5.3 Result

It needs to pay more attention to the impact of digital transformation on enterprise performance and how enterprises respond to the market structural challenges brought by transformation. There are few literatures on whether transformation can improve enterprise performance, and the research conclusions vary greatly. For example, HeFan et al. [19] believe that enterprise digital transformation can reduce costs, accelerate innovation, and improve enterprise performance. Some studies have also shown that digital transformation can promote the development of business models, and also increase management costs and labor costs. The impact of the two on performance can offset each other. Overall, enterprise performance has not significantly improved [24]. Consumers are becoming active participants in the interaction between the company and its stakeholders [11]. The change in the role of consumers in value co-creation may bring new challenges to the digital transformation of enterprises. How do consumers participate in value creation? What are the challenges? These are all worthy of in-depth discussion [5].

5.4 Industrial Application

The academic research methods are basically industry research and case studies. However, the successful path and mode of enterprise digital transformation through research and analysis, or the conclusions drawn from typical case studies, may not be the basis for the successful transformation of other enterprises [3]. The theoretical research is relatively backward. Most enterprises are "crossing the river by feeling the stones". The digital transformation of the industry needs the guidance of relevant theories. Therefore, academia should actively respond to social needs, strengthen cooperation with industry, and make more valuable and meaningful contributions to the practice of enterprise digital transformation. Secondly, the digital community has become an inevitable result of enterprise development [10]. In the era of digital economy, no enterprise has all the technologies, resources and capabilities to maintain leadership in all fields. It can develop and grow only in the process of continuous cohesion and display of new ideas [11]. Innovation should not only be built behind closed doors within the organization, but also require the concerted efforts of the whole ecosystem. The connectivity provided by digital technology enables consumers, suppliers and other stakeholders to participate in the process of enterprise value creation and improve the ability of innovation. It still need to be further explored such as how enterprises can better build an innovation ecosystem led by themselves [5].

6   Conclusions

This paper considers that the research on technology innovation and application mainly focuses on the cross-system transformation of enterprises, and the research on digital infrastructure management and digital platform construction should be strengthened in the future. The research focuses on the transformation process and realization path of enterprises in different management fields, the resources and capabilities required for transformation, and the management measures to promote transformation in the view of process. It is necessary to further explore the specific mechanism driving digital transformation in the future. The digital transformation of enterprises may bring positive results, improve the production efficiency and organizational performance of enterprises, and also pose a threat to data security. Future research needs to focus on the impact of digital transformation on enterprise performance, and how enterprises respond to the market structural challenges. It mainly focuses on the research of industry survey, industrial policy and management strategy, and provides practical cases and data of enterprise digital transformation in industrial application. The relevant theories of enterprise digital transformation lag behind the practice. The academic community should strengthen cooperation with the industry and feed back or inspire the industry through the research results.

Acknowledgement. This research was supported by Guangzhou key industrial technology project modern industrial technology under Grant 201802010035.

References

1. Nambisan, S., Lyytinen, K., Majchrzak, A., et al.: Digital innovation management: reinventing innovation management research in a digital world. MIS Q. **41**(1), 223–238 (2017)
2. Acccenture: Accenture digital transformation index for Chinese enterprises. https://www.acc enture.cn/cn-zh/insights/strategy/china-digital-transformation-index-2022 (2022). Accessed 02 Jan 2023
3. Yao, X., Qi, H., Liu, L., et al.: Enterprise digital transformation: re-understanding and re-starting. J. Xi'an Jiaotong Univ. (Soc. Sci. Ed.) **42**(3), 1–9 (2022). (in Chinese)
4. Xiao, J.: Cross-system digital transformation and adaptive changes of management. Reform **33**(4), 37–49 (2020). (in Chinese)
5. Zeng, D., Cia, J., Ouyang, T.: A research on digital transformation: integration framework and prospects. Foreign Economies Manage. **43**(5), 63–76 (2021). (in Chinese)
6. de Leon Omar, V.: A digital maturity model for telecommunications service providers. Technol. Innov. Manage. Rev. **6**(8) (2016)
7. Srinivas, K., Reddy, W.R.: Digital transformation and value creation: sea change ahead. GfK Mark. Intell. Rev. **9**(1), 10–17 (2017)
8. Li, L., Su, F., Zhang, W., et al.: Digital transformation by SME entrepreneurs: a capability perspective. Inf. Syst. J. **28**(6), 1129–1157 (2018)

9. Karimi, J., et al.: The role of dynamic capabilities in responding to digital disruption: a factor-based study of the newspaper industry. J. Mark. Manage. **32**(1), 39–81 (2015)

10. Li, B., Yin, S.: Research on ecological partner selection of ICT enterprises under the background of digital transformation: based on prospect theory and field theory. Manage. Rev. **32**(5), 165–179 (2020)

11. Qi, Y., Xiao, X.: Enterprise management reform in the digital economy era. J. Manage. World **36**(06), 135–152+250 (2020). (in Chinese)

12. Vial, G.: Understanding digital transformation: a review and a research agenda. J. Strat. Inf. Syst. **28**(2), 118–144 (2019)

13. Wang, Y., Lin, H.: Effects of global value chain embeddedness on industrial transformation and upgrading: an empirical study on China's industrial panel data. J. Int. Trade **41**(11), 51–61 (2015). (in Chinese)

14. Andal-Ancion, A., Cartwright, P.A., Yip, G.S.: The digital transformation of traditional businesses. MIT Sloan Manage. Rev. **44**(4), 34–41 (2003)

15. Newell, S., Marabelli, M.: Strategic opportunities (and challenges) of algorithmic decision-making: a call for action on the long-term societal effects of 'datification.' J. Strat. Inf. Syst. **24**(1), 3–14 (2015)

16. Balsmeier, Benjamin, et al: Is this time different? How digitalization influences job creation and destruction. Research Policy 48(8), 103765–103765 (2019)

17. Besson, P., Rowe, F.: Strategizing information systems-enabled organizational transformation: A transdisciplinary review and new directions. J. Strateg. Inf. Syst. **21**(2), 103–124 (2012)

18. Chen, J., Huang, S., Liu, Y.: From enabling to enabling - enterprise operation management in the digital environment. Manage. World **36**(2), 117–128 (2020). (in Chinese)

19. He, F., Liu, H.: The performance improvement effect of digital transformation enterprises from the digital economy perspective. Reform **32**(4), 137–148 (2019). (in Chinese)

20. Ragesh, G.K., Baskaran, K.: Cryptographically enforced data access control in personal health record systems. Procedia Technol. **25**(Complete), 473–480 (2016)

21. Harvard Business Review. https://hbr.org/2019/08/dont-put-a-digital-expert-in-charge-of-your-digital-transformation. Accessed 02 Jan 2023

22. Lin, Y., Zhang, X.: Influencing factors at different stages of manufacturing enterprises' digital transformation—multiple case studies based on grounded theory. Forum Sci. Technol. China **38**(6), 123–132, 142 (2022). (in Chinese)

23. Correani, A., de Massis, A., Frattini, F., et al.: Implementing a digital strategy: learning from the experience of three digital transformation projects. Calif. Manage. Rev. **62**(4), 37–56 (2020)

24. Yudong, Q., Chengwei, C.: Research on the multiple impacts of digitalization on the performance of manufacturing enterprises and their mechanisms. Stud. Explor. **42**(7), 108–119 (2020). (in Chinese)

Research Hotspots and Frontier Analysis
of Digital Marketing in China

Jiangping Wan[✉], Qingchen Wu, and Qianling Feng

School of Business Administration, South China University of Technology, Guangzhou 510640,
China
csjpwan@scut.edu.cn

Abstract. Digital marketing is the main marketing method and development trend
of enterprises in the era of digital economy. The study of digital marketing is of
great significance to the practice of digital economy in China. This paper takes
the digital marketing papers published by CNKI database from 2012 to 2022 as
the research object, analyzes the authors, publishing institutions and keywords,
shows the temporal and spatial distribution characteristics and research hotspots
of digital marketing research in China, and tracks the most cutting-edge research
issues by the CiteSpace tool to draw a visual knowledge graph. The development
momentum of digital marketing in China is good, but it needs to be strengthened
the cooperative relationship between authors and institutions. The research hot
topic is mainly the strategy research in different fields, which needs to be further
deepened. The focus of future research is mainly on community, intelligence,
diversification and virtual reality.

Keywords: Digital Marketing · Knowledge Graph · Bibliometrics

1 Introduction

Digital marketing used to be distributed through traditional media such as website advertising, e-mail, and search engines. Nowadays, digital marketing is represented by new
media such as social media, short video and live broadcast. About the connotation of
digital marketing, there are the following categories: MBA Library summarizes digital
marketing as: a marketing method that uses the fastest speed and the lowest cost to meet
the needs of customers most accurately. Yao Xi and others believe that the essence of digital marketing is marketing based on virtual practice, and it acts on the virtual experience
of consumers [1]. Li Xiaoxia said that digital marketing not only represents a change in
technical means, but also includes a deeper change in marketing concepts. It is a combination of target marketing, direct marketing, decentralized marketing, customer-oriented
marketing, two-way interactive marketing, remote or global marketing, virtual marketing, online trading, customer participatory marketing [2]. Although there is no unified
expression, this paper summarizes digital marketing as a marketing driven by digital
means, integrating emerging marketing concepts, and constantly updating iteration.

© The Author(s), under exclusive license to Springer Nature Switzerland AG 2023
Y. Tu and M. Chi (Eds.): WHICEB 2023, LNBIP 480, pp. 325–337, 2023.
https://doi.org/10.1007/978-3-031-32299-0_28

The key element of digital marketing is to provide marketing services to customers. The service areas include marketing strategy formulation, creative content production, digital advertising, digital technology support, digital public relations strategy and social media marketing [3]. Philip Kotler, the father of modern marketing, mentioned in an interview that marketing 1.0 is product-centered marketing in the industrial era. Marketing 2.0 is consumer-oriented marketing. Marketing 3.0 is cooperative, cultural and spiritual marketing, and value-driven marketing. Marketing 4.0 is to help customers achieve self-worth. Marketing 4.0 is a change of thinking based on values, connection, big data, community and new generation of analytical technology [4]. China's theoretical research on marketing mainly stays in the marketing 1.0 to 3.0, and lacks literature analysis on the marketing 4.0.

In this paper, digital marketing is defined as: under the background of digital economy, traditional marketing integrates network marketing, social media marketing and big data marketing.

Today, Chinese literature focuses on analyzing the marketing strategy of a certain industry, and there is little literature analyzing the research hotspots and trends in digital marketing. This paper uses CiteSpace software to analyze the time series distribution of digital marketing research, the authors and institutions and keywords, and provides a positive reference for further research on the development of data marketing.

2 Data Sources and Research Methods

The data of the article is derived from the CNKI database. The theme is set to "digital marketing", the time range is set to 2012–2022, and the journal type is selected as core journal + CSSCI + CSCD. We exclude the literature that does not belong to this field, 664 related literatures were obtained. We use CiteSpace to visualize the research literature of digital marketing: co-occurrence network map is used for the analysis of authors and institutions, and co-occurrence map, clustering map and burst map are used for keyword analysis to show the current situation, hot spots and trends of the research field. The research framework is shown in Fig. 1.

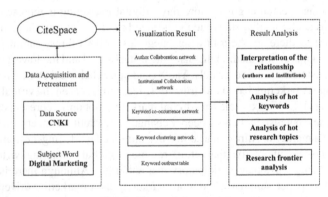

Fig. 1. Research framework

3 Statistical Analysis of Literature

3.1 Literature Growth Trend Analysis

We use the bibliometric function of CNKI to analyze the trend of digital marketing publications (Fig. 2). It can be seen that 2012–2017 is a period of growth and development, of which 2016 reached its peak, with a total of 105 articles published. At this stage, the country promotes the development of Internet innovation, and small and medium-sized enterprises relying on digital marketing have risen one after another, ushering in the upsurge of digital marketing research. Digital marketing research entered the precipitation stage from 2017 to 2019. 2020–2022 is a period of fluctuating development, and digital marketing research continues to develop with the emergence of new formats and new models. In the past three years, the average annual number of publications was about 60. In 2023, the number of digital marketing publications is predicted to be 66, and future research on digital marketing will continue to deepen.

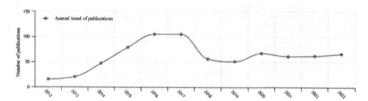

Fig. 2. Trend of digital marketing publications from 2012 to 2022

3.2 Analysis of Author Collaboration Network

The author cooperation network map is generated to visually display the research authors and their relationships through co-occurrence analysis (Fig. 3). It can be seen that.

Fig. 3. Author co-occurrence map (This paper analyzes the Chinese literature; the graphic language is Chinese. The following illustration is no longer repeated.)

the research field has not yet formed a leader. The author has published up to five articles, and the remaining authors are one to four articles (Table 1). Wang Yonggui and Zou Peng and the other 8 researchers formed the research team. Hu Jinsong and Ma Deqing, Yao Xi and Qin Xuebing, Hu Zhenyu and Xing Liang, Yang Xianshun and Chen Zihao and other researchers have two-two cooperation, and the rest of the authors are studied separately, showing a scattered distribution. The relevant scientific research cooperation team needs to be formed.

Table 1. Authors with high number of articles

Name	Quantity
Yao Xi	5
Hu Jingsong	4
Ma Deqing	4
Yang Xianshun	3
Feng Yanfang	3
Cai Liyuan	3
Hu Zhenyu	3

3.3 Institutional Cooperation Network Analysis

A network map of research institutions' cooperation is generated to visually display research institutions and their relationships through co-occurrence analysis (Fig. 4). It can be seen that Wuhan University has the largest number of papers, 31, followed by.

Fig. 4. Institutional cooperation co-occurrence map

Communication University of China, 16, Jinan University and Peking University, 10, and the remaining institutions have less than seven papers (Table 2). Communication University of China, Qingdao Agricultural University and Shandong Press and Publication Radio and Television Bureau have formed a cooperative team, and Wuhan Business College have a cooperative relationship. Except for the small research groups formed around universities, the remaining institutions are independent research. There are many research institutions with different nature, including undergraduate colleges, vocational and technical colleges and some enterprises.

Table 2. Institutions with high number of publications

Institution	Quantity
Wuhan University	31
Communication University of China	16
Jinan University	10
Peking University	10

4 Research Hotspots Analysis

4.1 Keyword Co-occurrence Map Analysis

The keyword co-occurrence map (Fig. 5) is generated, and the keyword distribution table is further sorted out to reflect the research hotspots in this field through co-occurrence analysis (Table 3). It can be seen that the keyword with the highest frequency is the Internet, 189 times; followed by big data, 114 times; the third is digital marketing, 59 times; marketing strategy, precision marketing, network marketing, marketing mode,

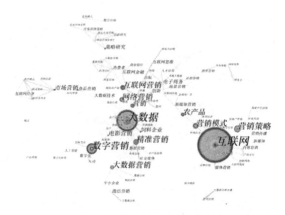

Fig. 5. Keywords co-occurrence map.

Internet marketing, big data marketing, agricultural products in 23–40 times; other keywords are below 20 times. The Internet, big data, and digital marketing nodes are more connected, indicating that these three keywords are strongly related to other keywords. Table 3 shows the keywords with high frequency and high between centrality.

Table 3. Keywords with high frequency and high centrality

Keywords	Frequency	Centrality
Internet	189	0.43
Big data	114	0.38
Digital Marketing	59	0.26
Internet Marketing	28	0.14
Marketing strategy	40	0.12

4.2 Keyword Clustering Map Analysis

Keyword clustering analysis is based on keyword co-occurrence analysis, which simplifies the keyword co-occurrence network relationship into a relatively small number of clusters by clustering statistics [5]. This paper analyzes the research hotspots of digital marketing through keyword clustering analysis to explore the research hotspots of digital marketing.

Run CiteSpace, set the node type as the keyword, and select the LLR algorithm based on the keyword knowledge network map to obtain the keyword clustering network map shown in Fig. 6. The figure shows 10 clusters of "digital marketing", "innovation network", "agricultural product marketing", "Internet marketing", "precision marketing", "network marketing", "big data marketing", "marketing strategy", "cross-border marketing" and "Internet finance", reflecting the research hotspots of digital marketing in China.

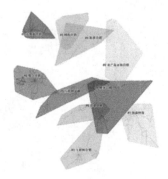

Fig. 6. Keyword clustering graph

The keyword co-occurrence network clustering table is obtained in "Cluster Explorer" based on the keyword clustering knowledge graph, (Table 4).

Table 4. Keyword clustering table

No	Size	Tag words (select the first 5)
0	42	Digital marketing; chaos; artificial intelligence; interactive orientation; performance evaluation
1	39	Innovation network; internet; network research; 4P theory; marketing model innovation
2	31	Marketing of agricultural products; big data; integration mode; integrated publishing; hashmap
3	28	Internet marketing; management; multi-source big data; tea; remote service
4	21	Precision marketing; e-commerce platform; social media; property rights; search engine
5	19	Network marketing; food marketing; innovative research; food industry; media marketing
6	18	Big data marketing; logistics management; network bookstore; online monitoring; audience psychological analysis
7	18	Marketing strategy; weChat marketing; small and medium-sized enterprises; big data analysis; smart tourism
8	16	Cross-border marketing; viral marketing; internet thinking; co-creation experience; community marketing
9	15	Internet finance; new media; online banking; industrialization; financial services innovation

Through the analysis of the keywords in each cluster, it is found that the research contents of each cluster intersect with each other. Therefore, China's digital marketing research can be summarized into six thematic areas: "e-commerce and digital intelligence", "marketing strategy and model innovation", "enterprise management and talent training", "agricultural products and food industry", "Internet finance" and "community marketing". The details are as follows:

E-commerce and Digital Intelligence

This topic includes keywords such as "e-commerce platform", "artificial intelligence", "big data analysis" and "precision marketing". E-commerce is a series of commercial activities based on Internet communication technology. In the context of the rapid development of e-commerce, digital marketing uses artificial intelligence, big data, cloud computing and other technologies to accurately market users. Digital marketing helps e-commerce enterprises realize the integrated development of products, prices, promotion and channels in the view of 4P theory, [6]. Yao Kai further improves the theoretical framework of personalized recommendation field and helps e-commerce enterprises improve income and consumer satisfaction by analyzing the influence of recommendation effect based on multi-source big data on consumer shopping behavior [7].

Marketing Strategy and Model Innovation

The theme includes keywords such as "marketing model innovation", "marketing strategy" and "cross-border marketing". The digital marketing model is different from the traditional marketing model, and many scholars are also committed to analyzing the innovation of marketing strategies and models. Yao Xi and others believe that it is mainly the change of consumption trend and marketing trend, and then put forward that the incentive of user participation constitutes the core mechanism of digital marketing communication effect [8].

Enterprise Management and Personnel Training

This topic contains keywords such as "performance evaluation", "management", "small and medium-sized enterprises" and "Internet thinking". Enterprise development needs to combine enterprise management with digital marketing in order to be compatible with the times. It mainly refers to the use of digital technology to optimize management work, so as to achieve cost control, improve operational efficiency and information accuracy. China promulgated the *"China Digital Marketing Talent Ability Evaluation Standard"* in January 2021. Deng Sha et al. built a new digital marketing talent training model in the view of talent training objectives, curriculum system, teacher training, internal and external practice, curriculum ideology and politics [9].

Agricultural Products and Food Industry

This field includes keywords such as"agricultural product marketing", "tea" and "food marketing". China's agricultural products online sales still face many problems, such as food storage, quality and brand uneven and so on. Some scholars take characteristic agricultural products in different regions as examples to study digital marketing strategies. Some scholars have paid attention to the marketing strategy of domestic emerging food brands.

Internet Finance

This topic includes keywords such as "Internet finance", "online banking" and "financial service innovation". In the new economic era, digital technology and finance are integrated with each other, and Internet financial marketing has undergone major changes. The new financial organization forms represented by online banking and third-party payment platforms continue to promote financial marketing innovation. Many scholars explore the development and innovation path of Internet financial marketing from the perspective of commercial banks. Therefore, Internet finance has become one of the hot topics in digital marketing research.

Community Marketing

The theme includes keywords such as "community marketing", "social media" and "WeChat marketing". Different media produces different marketing methods. Community marketing is a realization mode of online purchase and offline delivery activities by means of public social media platforms such as WeChat, Weibo and TikTok, so that users can generate community awareness. However, there are still some problems such as irregular management and serious loss of users. Therefore, some scholars combine with digital technology to propose the path of community marketing to solve the dilemma and the future development trend.

5 Research Frontier Analysis

Further study the changes in digital marketing hotspots is figured out through keyword burst diagrams (Table 5). The three periods of China's digital marketing development from 2012 to 2022 are summarized according to the chronological order.

5.1 Early Research Frontiers

The starting time of early emergence is 2012–2014, and the duration of emergence is 2–4 years. The research frontier of digital marketing in this stage mainly focused on "brand value", "mode", "all media", "interactive marketing", "publishing", "WeChat marketing" and so on. In 2012, the advantages of WeChat's high permeability were gradually reflected, and the social platform dividends enjoyed by Weibo in previous years were divided with the vigorous development of new media. The integration between social media and online shopping was more in-depth. O2O reached the golden age., China's O2O market size was 56.23 billion yuan in 2011, and about 90 billion yuan in 2012, an increase of nearly 70% according to the monitoring data of China Electronic Commerce Research Center. The issuance of 4G licenses had a certain impact on the development of all media until the end of 2013. The research of digital marketing paid more attention to interactive marketing and the marketing trend in the era of big data, and social media marketing, book publishing, traditional marketing model transformation and so on.

5.2 Early Research Frontiers

The starting time of early emergence is 2012–2014, and the duration of emergence is 2–4 years. The research frontier of digital marketing mainly focused on "brand value", "mode", "all media", "interactive marketing", "publishing", "WeChat marketing" and so on. In 2012, with the vigorous development of new media, the advantages of WeChat's high permeability were gradually reflected, and the social platform dividends enjoyed by Weibo in previous years were divided. The integration between social media and online shopping is more in-depth. At this time reached the golden age of O2O. According to the monitoring data of China Electronic Commerce Research Center, China's O2O market size was 56.23 billion yuan in 2011, and about 90 billion yuan in 2012, an increase of nearly 70%. The research of digital marketing paid more attention to interactive marketing and the marketing trend in the era of big data, and social media marketing, book publishing, traditional marketing model transformation and so on are the focus of scholars.

Table 5. Burst keywords

Keywords	Year	Strength	Begin	End	2012--2022
Brand value	2012	1.3376	2012	2015	
The model	2012	1.3376	2012	2015	
All media	2012	1.2624	2012	2013	
Digital Marketing	2012	2.6695	2012	2013	
Interactive Marketing	2012	1.4731	2013	2014	
Big data	2012	8.2513	2014	2015	
Publishing	2012	1.4694	2014	2016	
WeChat marketing	2012	2.209	2014	2016	
Internet thinking	2012	1.5527	2014	2016	
Big data marketing	2012	2.8854	2014	2015	
E-commerce	2012	1.4609	**2015**	2018	
Talent training	2012	1.7468	**2015**	2016	
Innovation	2012	1.3068	**2016**	2019	
Marketing strategy	2012	1.7201	**2016**	2017	
Scene marketing	2012	1.8024	**2017**	2019	
Marketing communication	2012	1.6597	**2018**	2020	
Film marketing	2012	1.9542	**2018**	2019	
Marketing	2012	2.7486	**2018**	2022	
Artificial intelligence	2012	2.0392	**2019**	2022	
Corporate Marketing	2012	1.6823	**2020**	2022	
Food marketing	2012	2.9851	**2020**	2022	

5.3 Mid-term Research Frontiers

The starting time of the mid-term frontier emergence is 2015–2018, and the continuous emergence time is 2–4 years. The research frontier of digital marketing mainly focused on "e-commerce", "talent training", "innovation", "scene marketing", "film marketing" and so on. 2015 officially entered the Internet + era, while the entertainment industry marketing began to blossom. In 2016, scene marketing flourished, short video and live broadcast platforms emerged, and expanded rapidly in 2017. Cross-border marketing has become a hot topic of marketing in 2018.

5.4 Latest Research Frontiers

The starting time of the latest frontier emergence is 2019–2020, and the continuous emergence time is 3–4 years. The research frontier of digital marketing i mainly focused on "artificial intelligence", "enterprise marketing", "food marketing" and so on. In 2019, China entered the 5G era, and technologies such as artificial intelligence, big data, and cloud computing continued to develop. However, it coincided with the winter of capital, and the development of digital marketing entered a stage of stagnation. The research on digital marketing of agricultural products and food has reached a certain climax, and there is still a certain heat on the theme of short videos and social media. The theme of enterprise marketing research shows a warming trend.

6 Discussion and Suggestions

The conclusions are as follows: First, the number of publications has transitioned from high-speed growth to fluctuating development, and the research heat of this topic still exists in the view of the time series distribution of the number of publications; secondly, digital marketing research mainly focused on the colleges of journalism and communication and management in colleges and universities and related marketing institutions On the whole, the researchers are scattered, which is not conducive to the exchange and sharing of knowledge and information; third, the hot areas of digital marketing research include "e-commerce and digital intelligence", "marketing strategy and model innovation", "enterprise management and talent training", "agricultural products and food industry", "Internet finance" and "community marketing". The latest research in the field of digital marketing is related to topics such as "artificial intelligence", "enterprise marketing", "food marketing" and so on. This paper put forward the following suggestions:

6.1 Focus Hotspots: Research on Private Domain Traffic and Social E-commerce Marketing

The community economy has re-entered people's vision in the post-epidemic period. Different from the public domain traffic that has been divided up by dividends, the space for private domain traffic to be developed is very large. Private domain traffic has the characteristics of decentralization, which can break the barriers of time and space to directly reach users, such as self-media fans, user groups, WeChat friends and so on. In recent years, the number of research literature on private domain marketing in core journals has continued to rise. Private domain marketing is also a new means for enterprises to realize digital marketing. However, the current research on private domain marketing in China is mostly theoretical research, and the depth and breadth of research need to be strengthened. Therefore, Chinese researchers need to pay attention to the field of social e-commerce and actively explore the standardization of private domain marketing.

6.2 Focus on the Frontier: Strengthen the Synergy Between Emerging Technologies Such as Artificial Intelligence and Digital Marketing

AI and digital marketing is in various industries. Therefore, when conducting empirical research on digital marketing, researchers will fully consider new models such as marketing automation and marketing cloud generated by emerging technologies enabling digital marketing. However, the user coverage and browsing volume are severely diluted due to the decentralization of users and the fragmentation of the Internet, and the media value is not well realized; and the increased budget problems after the adoption of emerging technologies. The above problems still need to be further explored by Chinese researchers in future.

6.3 Grasping the Trend: Promoting the Multi-field Organic Combination of Digital Marketing in Various Industries

This study finds that agricultural product marketing and food industry marketing are hot topics in the field of digital marketing in China. Smart tourism has also attracted the attention of domestic scholars. Some scholars have proposed that cross-border marketing combining rural tourism and cultural and creative specialties can help solve some existing problems of e-commerce sales of agricultural products, thus promoting rural revitalization [10]. It is a good performance that the organic combination of China's cultural and creative industries with the clothing industry, catering industry and other fields. In our understanding, researchers can expand marketing IP crossover research and further enrich IP marketing research content in future research,.

6.4 Follow the Trend: Explore the Marketing Scenario and Implementation of Metaverse Application

The metaverse usually refers to creating an interactive environment for the interaction of virtual or augmented reality. The development of the cosmos has attracted the attention of a large number of domestic researchers. Users will conduct business activities in future simulated reality scenarios. Today, a new digital marketing method can be created by live video, simulation scene and so on. However, most of the applied research is still in imagination due to the short research time, metaverse + marketing is still based on basic theoretical research. How to integrate virtual reality and marketing, and put it into practice and provide better marketing services for the whole society in the future.

References

1. Li, X.: Digital marketing empowers China's foreign trade enterprises. Marketing Management Review **19**(05), 110–111 (2021). https://doi.org/10.19932/j.cnki.22-1256/F.2021.05.110. (in Chinese)
2. Yao, X., Qin, X.: Technology and survival: the essence of digital marketing. Journalism Res. **33**(06), 58–63+33 (2013). (in Chinese)
3. Hu, Z.: Research on the causes and governance of domestic digital marketing ethical Chaos—based on the interview of digital marketing practitioners. Contemp. Commun. **34**(05), 80–84 (2018). (in Chinese)
4. Wang, S.: Marketing 4.0: from traditional to digital, the "change" and "unchanged" of marketing—Interview with Philip Kotler, the "father of modern marketing." Tsinghua Business Review **8**(03), 60–64 (2017). (in Chinese)
5. Zhong, W., Li, J., Yang, X.: Research on co-word analysis method (3)—The principle and characteristics of co-word clustering analysis method. J. Intell. **27**(07), 118–120 (2008). (in Chinese)
6. Peng, X.: Research on digital marketing strategy of fast fashion clothing brand based on big data. J. Commercial Econ. **39**(14), 81–83 (2020). (in Chinese)
7. Yao, K., Tu, P., Chen, Y., Su, M.: Research on the effect of personalized recommendation system based on multi-source big data. J. Manage. Sci. **31**(05), 3–15 (2018). (in Chinese)
8. Yao, X., Han, W.: Incentive for participation: the core mechanism of digital marketing communication effect. Journalism Res. **35**(03), 134–140+145 (2015). (in Chinese)

9. Deng, S., Feng, Z.: Research on the training mode of digital marketing talents in higher vocational new business under the background of integration of industry and education. China Manage. Informatization **25**(21), 152–155 (2022). (in Chinese)
10. Suqing, J.: "Agricultural tourism + cultural and creative cooperation" promotes rural revitalization: a case study of Xuelingwei village Zhirong county. Rural Econ. Sci. Technol. **33**(20), 175–177 (2022). (in Chinese)

Study on Spatio-Temporal Topic-Sentiment Synergy Model and Visualization of Online Public Opinion on Public Health Emergency

Yuhan Lu and Ziming Zeng$^{(\boxtimes)}$

Wuhan University, Wuchang District, Wuhan 430072, Hubei, China
zmzeng1977@aliyun.com

Abstract. Public health emergencies can generate online public opinion on social media platforms such as Weibo. Existing studies show that both temporal and spatial factors have an impact on public opinion, topic and sentiment mining of public health emergency microblogs can realize the monitoring, prediction and guidance of public opinion considering the temporal and spatial factors. Taking the outbreak period of the Delta variant in three different regions of China in 2021 as the research object, this paper constructed a model based on the Latent Dirichlet Allocation (LDA) model, improved SnowNLP lib and sentiment map. Data processing, topic mining and sentiment calculation were carried out to realize the synergistic analysis of topic and sentiment. Results illustrate that this model can reveal the law of online public opinion evolution and sentimental intensity, that online public opinion is influenced by spatial and temporal factors, especially that small cities with smaller volume and attention need to be focused on the observation and guidance of public opinion.

Keywords: Topic Mining · Sentiment Analysis · Online Public Opinion · Spatio-temporal Public Opinion

1 Introduction

In 2021, the Delta variant was rampant in the world, and occasional outbreaks in China were promptly contained. During the epidemic, Weibo, short videos and other social media are important platforms for the generation and dissemination of public opinion and public sentiment due to their fast propagation, timely control and guidance of such platforms can avoid the consequences of public unrest and the loss of government credibility.

Some studies have shown that there is a correlation between the differences and evolution trend of public opinion and geographical distribution [1]. However, most of the current studies on public health emergencies focus on the evolution trend of topics and sentiment over time, and lack of studies considering spatial factors.

Therefore, this paper will take microblogs posted by users during the epidemic as the research object, and use a topic mining model, quantitative sentiment analysis, sentiment map and other research methods to try to address the following questions: ① How to build a topic-sentiment synergy model based on topic mining and sentiment cognition theory, combining temporal and spatial factors? ② How to carry out visual analysis of topics and sentiments for public health emergencies in different times and spaces? ③ Based on the spatio-temporal visual analysis of public health emergencies, how to provide suggestions and decision-making basis for public opinion guidance concerning geographical and temporal factors?

To solve the above problems, this paper first proposes an analysis scheme combining qualitative research and quantitative analysis. Secondly, a synergistic model of topic and sentiment is constructed, and graph visualization technology is utilized. Finally, the validity of the model is verified by specific events. In this paper, public health emergencies in Shijiazhuang, Ruili and Nanjing are taken as research objects. Through topic mining, quantitative sentiment analysis and map visualization, the spatio-temporal online public opinion topics and evolution characteristics of sentiments are revealed. This study can provide a theoretical and practical basis for online public opinion feedback, preplanning proposal, grasping the trend of public opinion, and governing online public opinion.

2   Literature Review

2.1   The Influence of Spatial Factor on Public Opinion

The propagation of public opinion is strongly correlated with time, so the analysis methods referring to the temporal factor are mainly used to reveal the law of public opinion, such as combining the life cycle theory [2], referring to the change of discussion heat of hot events [3], introducing the topic model with time parameters [4], and manually dividing the period [5].

In specific events with prominent geographical factors, the spatial factor will be included in the study as an independent variable affecting people's psychology, perceptions, and thoughts. For example, the H7N9 epidemic was used as a research object to conclude that there is consistency in the geographic spread of online public opinion and epidemics, with some deviations in local areas [6]. In public health emergencies, there is an influence of geographic marginal interaction effects considering the spread of diseases among groups [7]. The research shows that public opinion is influenced by both geographical location and social space. Geographical factors such as climate and inter-provincial influence the behavior, mentality and attention of local residents through social-ecological mechanisms. The degree of discussion and attention of public opinion is regulated by the political, economic and cultural systems that make up social space [8]. The small-scale epidemics at different times in China were strongly related to geographical factors, so it is necessary to consider the analysis of public opinion in terms of spatial parameters.

2.2   Literature Review of Topic Mining on Weibo Public Opinion

Weibo has become one of the most influential platforms due to its monopoly in the field of short-text social networking, which is prone to public opinion crises. Public opinion research on such short-text social platforms has been conducted on a certain scale both at home and abroad, with foreign research mainly focusing on Twitter, a website similar to Weibo, covering multiple disciplines of humanities and social sciences.

The evolution of Weibo public opinion topics is mainly studied by monitoring time series, and studies that incorporate spatial factors are gradually being emphasized. For example, some studies point out that the study of public opinion in spatial dimension is an effective supplement to the vacancies in social psychology research, and has practical significance in public opinion governance in corresponding regions [8]. Using spatio-temporal big data and IoT modeling reveals the interaction effect of marginal behavior of contagion [7].

Public opinion on Weibo can reflect people's views and attitudes toward events to a certain extent. Researching online public opinion is helpful for the government and decision-making departments to quickly grasp the trend of public opinion, timely curb the spread of rumors, and make agile responses to possible development trends of public opinion.

2.3 Weibo Sentiment Analysis and Sentiment Map

Sentiment analysis is the process of identifying the subjective sentiments, opinions, and attitudes of users from textual data [9]. There are two main approaches for sentiment analysis, which are unsupervised sentiment lexicon-based and supervised machine learning based.

Sentiment analysis of short texts has been fully studied, such as combining semantic rules to expand Weibo phrases, emoticons and emoji characters into the sentiment lexicon to improve the accuracy of sentiment analysis [10]. Taking time series as variables to analyze the public opinion evolution trend by calculating the score change of Weibo comments based on sentiment lexicon [11]. The recursive neural network was used to avoid relying on manual annotation corpus sets, and sentiment polarity transfer model was introduced for sentiment analysis of Weibo [12].

Sentiment map is an effective way to analyze the distribution of group sentiment and the evolution of communication, with the addition of sentiment calculation to obtain the distribution map of dynamic changes of sentiment [13], and the main application fields of sentiment map include social media [14], comment analysis [15], and online public opinion [16].

Therefore, considering the temporal and spatial factors, this paper selected the cities that had a small-scale outbreak of the epidemic in 2021 as the research objects, extracted Weibo texts, and used the SnowNLP lib to score the sentiment, mined the distribution and heat of topics using the LDA topic model, analyzed the changing trends of online public opinion over time and space, and proposed a public opinion analysis framework under similar events.

3   Study Design

This paper selects public health emergencies with different locations and certain time intervals as research cases, and takes the short text data published by Weibo users as the research content. The overall research framework is shown in Fig. 1, which consists of three major parts: corpus collection, topic analysis model construction, and sentiment analysis. In the first part, get the microblogs on the timeline by a crawler, select the corpus containing the specific region, and process the noisy raw data. In the second part, the improved LDA topic model is used for topic mining and topic heat analysis. In the third part, the sentiment evolution of emergencies under different times and space is analyzed by SnowNLP lib, and the sentiment intensity under different periods is visualized using sentiment map.

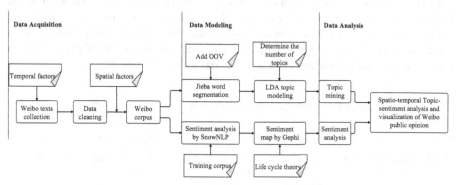

Fig. 1. Study framework of Weibo public opinion analysis

4 Empirical Study

4.1 Data Collection and Pre-processing

The research objects of this paper are the cities with epidemic outbreaks in 2021. Considering the development time and trend of the epidemic in each control group, cities with similar periods were selected for the study. Excluding cities with less than 50 confirmed cases in total, three cities, Shijiazhuang, Ruili and Nanjing, were selected as the study samples for Weibo public opinion in a comprehensive consideration.

According to the daily release of epidemic information, we selected the period from the first confirmed case to one week after the zero-COVID of each city, i.e. from January 2 to February 12 for Shijiazhuang, from March 30 to April 29 for Ruili, and from July 20 to August 20 for Nanjing, and crawled the raw text of microblogs with the keyword "COVID-19". The number of microblogs collected from January 2 to February 12, March 30 to April 29, and July 20 to August 20 were about 200,000, 64,000, and 166,000 respectively, and 140,000, 51,000, and 130,000 microblogs remained after removing duplicate items. After keyword filtering by city name, 19,063, 6,042, and 20,463 microblogs remained respectively.

This paper refers to the Chinese and English words approved by CIPG on COVID-19, and includes the OOV into the sentiment lexicon, and the accuracy of word segmentation is significantly improved. Jieba lib is utilized to segment texts to obtain the final corpus.

4.2 Spatio-Temporal Topic Analysis of Public Opinion on Public Health Emergencies

The topic coherence scores under different numbers of topics in the three periods were calculated separately, and the number with the highest score was selected as the number of topics in that period. The experiments show that the highest topic coherence scores are obtained when the number of topics in Shijiazhuang, Ruili and Nanjing is 4, 3 and 6. The words with the highest probability are selected as the feature words that summarize the topics, and some words with no practical meaning are screened out, such as the conjunctions, "province", "city", etc. It can effectively reduce the influence of irrelevant feature words on the topic performance and enhance the generalization degree of each topic. The eight feature words with the highest probability in each topic under different times and spaces after screening are selected and shown in Table 1.

Table 1. Spatio-temporal public opinion topic mining results

City	Topic	Feature words	Topic summary
Shijiazhuang	Topic 1-1	Housing estate, Nangong, risk, adjustment, Xingtai, Shijiazhuang, Gaocheng, Hebei	Shijiazhuang adjustment risk regions
	Topic 1-2	Community, people, epidemic, street, prevention and control, masks, health, high risk	Epidemic prevention and control in Shijiazhuang
	Topic 1-3	Epidemic, Shijiazhuang, COVID-19, pneumonia, prevention and control, news, confirmed, new	Notification of the epidemic in Shijiazhuang
	Topic 1-4	Disease, diagnosis, year, detection, Gaocheng, quarantine, track, go out	Tracing the source of the epidemic in Shijiazhuang
Ruili	Topic 2-1	Case, confirmed, infected, asymptomatic, new, COVID-19, epidemic, pneumonia	Notification of the epidemic in Ruili
	Topic 2-2	Epidemic, Ruili, Yunnan, COVID-19, surveillance, nucleic acid, prevention and control, region	Epidemic prevention and control in Ruili
	Topic 2-3	Prevention and control, personnel, pneumonia, vaccination, vaccines, housing estate, work, protection	Prevention and control work and promotion of vaccination in Ruili

(continued)

Table 1. (*continued*)

City	Topic	Feature words	Topic summary
Nanjing	Topic 3-1	Epidemic, prevention and control, personnel, testing, COVID-19, nucleic acid, health, vaccination	Epidemic prevention and control in Nanjing
	Topic 3-2	Case, confirmed, local, infected, new, asymptomatic, pneumonia, COVID-19	Notification of the epidemic in Nanjing
	Topic 3-3	Detection, Nanjing, epidemic, airport, nucleic acid, prevention and control, Lukou, international	Prevention and control work in high-risk areas of Nanjing
	Topic 3-4	Street, community, natural village, region, risk, Nanjing, Jiangning District, region	Nanjing adjustment risk regions
	Topic 3-5	Epidemic, pneumonia, COVID-19, press conference, case, situation, video, Weibo	Public opinion of the epidemic in Nanjing
	Topic 3-6	Airport, positive, case, nucleic acid, work, quarantine, flight, round trip	Tracing the source of the epidemic in Nanjing

The number of Weibo public opinion topics in Shijiazhuang, Ruili and Nanjing were 4, 3 and 6 respectively. During the outbreak of the epidemic in three different cities, Weibo public opinion topics are focused on epidemic notification and epidemic prevention and control (Topic 1-3, Topic 1-2, Topic 2-1, Topic 2-2, Topic 3-2, Topic 3-1), which are closely related to people's daily lives and policies, and then reflected in Weibo public opinion. Among them, Nanjing had the highest topic heat, while Ruili had the lowest. The comparison of the topic heat of epidemic notification and epidemic prevention and control in the three cities is shown in Fig. 2.

In addition to the regular topics of epidemic notification and epidemic prevention and control, the other two topics of Shijiazhuang Weibo opinion are the adjustment risk regions (Topic 1-1) and the source traceability of epidemic (Topic 1-4), the timing of the outbreak in Shijiazhuang is close to the Spring Festival, so the heat of topic 1-4 was the highest. The Weibo opinion of Ruili also focused on prevention and control work and vaccination promotion (Topic 2-3). Due to the existence of smuggling, Chinese border cities are under great pressure for epidemic prevention, so it's significant to increase vaccination rates, and this topic is slightly more popular than the other two topics. There are more Weibo opinion topics in Nanjing, which are risk regions adjustment (Topic 3-4), prevention, control and traceability of high-risk areas (Topic 3-3 and Topic 3-6), and public opinion (Topic 3-5), topic 3-5 and topic 3-6 are the hottest, nearly twice as hot as other topics. The opinion topics showed that the epidemic in Nanjing was highly

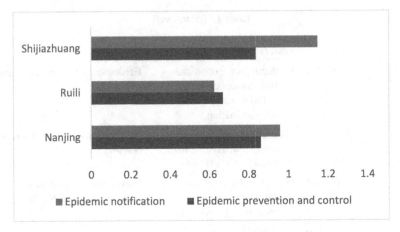

Fig. 2. Comparison of topic heat in different regions

popular on social platforms such as Weibo and short videos, and the epidemic was spread from Lukou Airport, the popularity of public opinion center and topic was consistent with the transmission path.

In terms of the scale of the outbreak, more than 800 cases were confirmed in Shijiazhuang with a permanent population of 11.2 million, with an epidemic life cycle of about 40 days, more than 100 cases were confirmed in Ruili with a permanent population of 230 thousand, with an epidemic life cycle of about 30 days, and more than 200 cases were confirmed in Nanjing with a permanent population of 9.42 million, with an epidemic life cycle of about 30 days. In terms of topic heat, Shijiazhuang and Nanjing had comparable discussion heat, and Ruili was about one-third of that in the two cities. In terms of geographical location, Shijiazhuang and Nanjing are provincial capitals, Nanjing is an important city for exchange and trade in the Yangtze River Delta, and Ruili is adjacent to the border. In summary, Weibo public opinion can cover the whole geographic region, the popularity of public opinion is positively correlated with the population of the region, the number and heat of public opinion topics are greatly influenced by space. Border cities have further advancement in prevention work due to their special geographical locations.

4.3 Spatio-Temporal Sentiment Evolution Analysis of Public Opinion on Public Health Emergencies

Since the built-in corpus of SnowNLP comes from e-commerce reviews, the accuracy of public opinion sentiment judgment is not high. Therefore, it is comprehensively considered to introduce Hownet sentiment lexicon to rebuild the corpus. A sample of 200 Weibo texts was randomly selected, the sentiment score and sentiment polarity were calculated using SnowNLP and Hownet sentiment lexicon respectively, in which the sentiment polarity calculated using the sentiment lexicon was -1 for negative, 0 for neutral, and 1 for positive. The sentiment polarity was compared with the sentiment score calculated by SnowNLP, the sentiment score of 0–0.3 was selected as negative,

0.3–0.5 as neutral, and 0.5–1 as positive. The starting date in the corpus was marked as the first day, and the sentiment score of each day within the three cycles was calculated respectively, the sentiment trends in the three cities were analyzed as shown in Fig. 3.

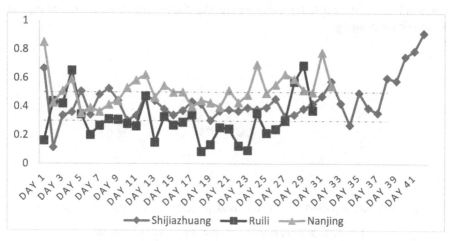

Fig. 3. Sentiment trends by city during the epidemic cycle

In the cycle of the epidemic spread, the sentiment during the transmission and outbreak periods is negative, while the positive sentiment will gradually rebound during the receding period. Combined with the analysis results of public opinion topic mining, all three cities have different degrees of restrictions and source tracing during the transmission and outbreak periods, and netizens' concerns about being infected, resulting in more negative sentiment. When the epidemic is controlled, daily life and economy gradually rebound, online public topics turn to hope and thanks, and the sentiment tends to be calm and the positive sentiment is on the rise.

In terms of overall trends, the sentiment scores of Nanjing and Shijiazhuang were higher than those of Ruili, while the scores of Shijiazhuang are slightly lower than Nanjing. The sentiment of Nanjing shifted from neutral to positive in the late period, while the sentiment scores of Shijiazhuang did not fluctuate much. The sentiment scores of Ruili were much lower, with significant negative sentiment during the transmission and outbreak periods. Analyzed from a temporal perspective, the outbreak in Shijiazhuang was close to the Spring Festival, and the negative sentiment of netizens was reflected in the consumption of holidays and the reduced possibility of reunion, while China had extensive experience in dealing with the Delta variant at the time of the outbreak in Nanjing, and quickly traced the source to Lukou Airport, so the sentiment of netizens in Nanjing was relatively positive. Analyzed from the spatial perspective, all three cities are transportation hubs with developed transportation and frequent exchanges with outside, Shijiazhuang is located around Beijing, and Ruili is located at the border, which bears great pressure of prevention. According to the analysis of opinion topics, Ruili has fewer public opinion topics, and all of them are focused on prevention and governance, which are reflected in public opinion sentiment mostly favoring negative sentiment.

The corpus within different cities was divided into periods of epidemic transmission, outbreak and receding, and the sentiment map within each phase was formed using Gephi software with users as nodes. Among them, red indicates positive sentiment, green indicates neutral sentiment, and purple indicates negative sentiment, which are shown in Fig. 4a, 4b, and 4c for Shijiazhuang, Fig. 5a, 5b, and 5c for Ruili, and Fig. 6a, 6b, and 6c for Nanjing.

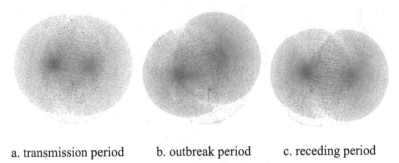

a. transmission period   b. outbreak period   c. receding period

Fig. 4. Sentiment map of different periods in Shijiazhuang

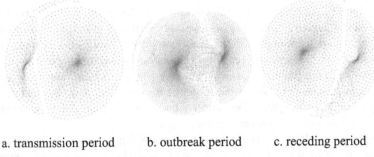

a. transmission period   b. outbreak period   c. receding period

Fig. 5. Sentiment map of different periods in Ruili

The evolution process of sentiment map is similar to the above analysis results. Taking the transmission period as the initial state, Weibo sentiment showed a trend of decreasing positive sentiment in the outbreak period and rebounded in the receding period. The density of online sentiment during the outbreak period was higher than that during the transmission and receding periods, when people paid the highest attention to the epidemic and had most willing to voice their opinions on social media, consistent with the epidemic life cycle. Negative sentiment generally decreased in the receding period and was slightly lower than the initial level during the transmission period.

Shijiazhuang and Nanjing have the same trend of sentiment map evolution, with roughly equal numbers of positive and negative sentiment, and sentiment scores showed a trend of decreasing first and then rising with the epidemic cycle. The overall positive sentiment in Nanjing was slightly higher than that in Shijiazhuang. Ruili had the lowest

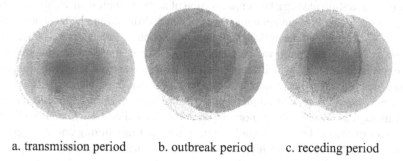

a. transmission period   b. outbreak period   c. receding period

Fig. 6. Sentiment map of different periods in Nanjing

sentiment density, which was consistent with the number of Weibo posts collected, and the negative sentiment accounted for a large proportion in each period. At the same time, the topic of "Ruili as a small border town has taken on an overload of prevention pressure" was widely discussed on Weibo, causing a higher-than-average discussion among Ruili netizens and more negative sentiment was generated around the topic.

5 Discussion

This paper takes the epidemic period of Delta variant in 2021 as the research object, comprehensively considers the outbreak scale, longitude and latitude differences, and combines the dual influence of geographical location and social space. Firstly, several cities with similar outbreak duration and infection scale are selected. Considering that in social space, democratization, economic and agricultural development, education level, etc., have a certain impact on the spread and trend of public opinion, such as netizens in culturally open cities pay more attention to public opinion, in physical space, climate, topography and population distribution all have an impact on the development of public opinion. Therefore, three cities with different geographical location, economic level and political culture are comprehensively selected as the research objects, namely Shijiazhuang, Ruili and Nanjing. In terms of population composition, Weibo users aged between 20–30 account for 80%, and according to the age structure data of the census, the percentage of this age group is the highest in Nanjing and the lowest in Ruili. Shijiazhuang has a relatively high proportion of middle-aged people aged between 30 and 50, and Ruili has the largest number of teenagers aged between 0 and 20, which will also influence the heat and trend of public opinion. It can be found that the heat and number of Weibo opinion topics were the highest in Nanjing, and the lowest in Ruili. Online public opinions was concentrated on epidemic notification, epidemic prevention and control, epidemic tracing, etc. Therefore, as regards guiding online public opinion, the geographical location, economy, culture and local customs of the region should be taken into account, so as to detect the areas with less public opinion as early as possible, and give timely guidance and solution to the topics with high public opinion heat.

During the epidemic period, positive sentiment showed a trend of decreasing first and then rising, with Shijiazhuang and Nanjing having neutral to positive sentiment the whole time, and Ruili having a higher proportion of negative sentiment. Public sentiment can reflect the local efforts in epidemic control, which differs from the level of supplies, economic conditions and the optimism of the public about the epidemic response. Since the outbreak in Shijiazhuang was near the Spring Festival, the negative sentiment was more than that of Nanjing, which was also affected by the controls. Due to the long-term pressure of border control, the source tracing and control of the epidemic in Ruili cannot be as timely as in cities with ample economy, and the sentiment expressed on social platforms such as Weibo will be more negative than inland cities, while also reflecting the severity of the epidemic to some extent. In terms of monitoring and management, it is suggested that cities with high sentiment scores and stable trends can appropriately reduce manual intervention, while cities with large sentiment fluctuations and a high proportion of negative sentiment should achieve timely warnings and appropriate guidance, and establish initiatives to deal with negative sentiment as soon as possible.

In order to conduct a more fine-grained and diversified study of Weibo public opinion under public health emergencies, this paper constructs a spatio-temporal topic-sentiment synergy model based on Weibo big data using the LDA topic mining model and the SnowNLP lib that combines Hownet sentiment lexicon, visualizes sentiment map using Gephi, analyzes online public opinion topics and sentiment evolution trends in three cities with epidemic outbreaks at different time, and obtains a spatio-temporal topic-word table, sentiment trends and sentiment evolution map. At the theoretical level, this paper verifies the feasibility of exploring the evolutionary analysis of public opinion topics and sentiments from the spatio-temporal perspective, and verifies the influence characteristics of regional differences on the development of public opinion. At the practical level, this paper analyzes the evolution trends of key topics of public opinion and the tendency of sentiment evolution in different periods and geographical areas, combined with specific cases and visualization studies, which can provide targeted basis and decision reference for government departments in monitoring public opinion, predicting public opinion and guiding the trend of public opinion in public health emergencies.

There are also some limitations in this paper. The object of the study is Weibo, a text-based social media, which lacks the comparison of public topics and sentiments on other platforms. The evolution of other new mass media such as short video platforms can be contrasted with the subsequent research.

6 Conclusion

This paper takes the online public opinion of public health emergencies as the research object, collects Weibo corpus with epidemic outbreaks, combines spatio-temporal evolution and constructs a synergistic topic-sentiment model to study the evolution of public opinion, and reveals the trend of public opinion and sentiment through quantitative analysis and data visualization. The results of this study confirm the validity of the framework proposed in this paper, and it can provide references for the analysis and visualization of spatio-temporal topic-sentiment for similar events.

The next research direction is to carry out research on online public opinion of public health emergencies, such as public opinion risk perception, intelligent risk warning, dynamic emergency decision-making, etc.

References

1. Howe, P.D., Mildenberger, M., et al.: Geographic variation in U.S. climate change opinion at state and local scales. SSRN Electron. J. (2014). https://doi.org/10.2139/ssrn.2515649
2. Wang, D., Zhang, H., et al.: Sentiment analysis and ideological guidance of key nodes in micro-blog public opinion. Lib. Inform. Serv. **63**(04), 15–22 (2019). In Chinese
3. Zhao, C., Wu, Y., Wang, J.: Twitter text topic mining and sentiment analysis under the belt and road initiative. Lib. Inform. Serv. **63**(19), 119–127 (2019). https://doi.org/10.13266/j.issn. 0252-3116.2019.19.012
4. Cao, L., Tang, X.: Trends of BBS topics based on dynamic topic model. J. Manage. Sci. China **17**(11), 109–121 (2014). In Chinese
5. Lin, L., Ma, X.: The theme discovery and evolution analysis of domestic library and information science research based on LDA. Inform. Sci. **37**(12), 87–92 (2019). In Chinese
6. Li, J., Chen, S., et al.: On the Spatiotemporal relationships between epidemic spread and internet public opinion using big data. Geom. World **27**(03), 31–34+41 (2020). (In Chinese)
7. Pfeiffer, D.U., Stevens, K.B.: Spatial and temporal epidemiological analysis in the Big Data era. Prev. Vet. Med. **122**(s1–2), 213–220 (2015)
8. Lai, K., Fu, H., et al.: Geographical public opinion: a new approach of public opinion research in big data era. Inform. Stud. Theory Appl. **43**(08), 64–69 (2020). In Chinese
9. Mikolov, T., Sutskever, I., et al.: Distributed representations of words and phrases and their compositionality (2013)
10. Wan, Y., Du, Z.: Fine-grained sentiment analysis of microblog comments based on fusion of sentiment lexicon and semantic rules. Inform. Res. **2020**(11), 34–41 (2020). (In Chinese)
11. Kong, J., Teng, G., et al.: Impact of party's responses on netizens' emotions in public opinion. Lib. Inform. Serv. **64**(18), 89–96 (2020). In Chinese
12. Liang, J., Chai, Y., et al.: Deep learning for Chinese micro-blog sentiment analysis. J. Chin. Inform. Process. **28**(05), 155–161 (2014). In Chinese
13. Dai, X., Zhang, L., et al.: Research on emotional mapping of social networks. Manage. Rev. **28**(08), 79–86 (2016). In Chinese
14. Li, J.: The study of emotional map of university public opinion users in social media: a case of "anti-academic misconduct" in Sina Weibo. Inform. Sci. **38**(07), 100–104 (2020). In Chinese
15. You, L., Lang, Y.: Construction and query application of emotion knowledge graph based on semantic analysis of product reviews. Inform. Stud. Theory Appl. **41**(08), 132–136+131 (2018). (In Chinese)
16. Li, J.: A Study on the emotional map of public opinion evolution in social net-work emergencies– a case study of "pickled cabbage soil pit in weibo." Public Commun. Sci. Technol. **14**(16), 130–134 (2022). In Chinese
17. Blei, D.M., Ng, A.Y., Jordan, M.I.: Latent dirichlet allocation. Ann. Appl. Statist. (2001)

The Impact of Blockchain on the Credit Risk of Supply Chain Finance: A Tripartite Evolutionary Game Analysis

Zhichao Liu, Lubin Wang$^{(\boxtimes)}$, and Jiayi Gu

School of Information, Central University of Finance and Economics, Beijing 102206, China
13910888789@163.com

Abstract. In light of the reality that supply chain finance is plagued by credit risk, this study constructs a tripartite evolutionary game model involving financial institution, small and medium-sized enterprise (SME), and core enterprise to analyze the credit risk in the case of accounts receivable factoring. The micro-mechanism of how blockchain mitigates the credit risk of supply chain finance is analyzed by comparing the changes in the system's evolutionary stability strategy before and after the introduction of blockchain. Numerical simulation is also conducted to verify the system's evolutionary stability strategy. The results reveal that whether the traditional supply chain finance business produces credit risk depends on the amount of accounts receivable, the income obtained by SME and core enterprise when maintaining the stability of the supply chain, and the default income and default cost of both. After the introduction of blockchain, a strict regulatory environment increases the default cost of enterprises in the supply chain. Therefore, the system strictly converges to the Pareto-optimal solution of financial institution accepting financing applications, core enterprise repayment, and SME compliance. In addition, the decrease in the amount of accounts receivable held by a single SME can accelerate the convergence of the tripartite evolutionary game to equilibrium after the introduction of blockchain. Thus, blockchain can effectively mitigate the credit risk that financial institutions face while conducting supply chain finance business. Our research provides theoretical support for optimizing credit risk management in supply chain finance using blockchain.

Keywords: Blockchain · Supply chain finance · Accounts receivable · Credit risk · Tripartite evolutionary game

1 Introduction

The supply chain finance model integrates the capital flow, information flow, and logistics of supply chain, thereby providing a viable solution to the small and medium-sized enterprises (SMEs) financing problem in China. However, in the process of developing supply chain finance, credit risk issues frequently arise as a result of information asymmetries in the supply chain and the absence of repayment willingness or ability among debt repayment subjects [1]. For example, in February 2020, Hang Qian Communication Company fraudulently obtained a bank loan by allegedly forging contracts

© The Author(s), under exclusive license to Springer Nature Switzerland AG 2023
Y. Tu and M. Chi (Eds.): WHICEB 2023, LNBIP 480, pp. 350–361, 2023.
https://doi.org/10.1007/978-3-031-32299-0_30

and fictitiously pledging accounts receivable with affiliated companies, involving a total amount of RMB 220 million. Moreover, due to the relevance of the supply chain, the credit risk will be transmitted in the supply chain, resulting in systemic risks [2].

The new generation of information technology especially blockchain has developed rapidly in recent years. The consensus mechanism, non-tampering, traceability, and other characteristics of blockchain technology have created a strict regulatory environment within the chain [3, 4]. In addition, blockchain also increased the level of trust between supply chain financial system businesses organizations [5] and provided a viable solution to credit risk issues experienced during the development of the supply chain finance business. For example, after Baowu Group introduced blockchain technology in accounts receivable financing, it greatly alleviated the information asymmetry between the group's core enterprises and SMEs, guaranteed the authenticity of transaction information, and reduced the possibility of credit risk.

Existing research on the impact of Blockchain technology on the credit risk of supply chain finance is predominantly qualitative. Through theoretical analysis of the types and influencing factors of supply chain financial credit risk, combined with the coupling mechanism of blockchain and supply chain finance, it is concluded that blockchain can reduce the credit risk of supply chain finance [6–9]. And case studies demonstrate the benefits of blockchain technology in the field of credit risk management for supply chain finance [10]. Although the academic community has extensively acknowledged the importance of Blockchain technology in reducing the credit risk of supply chain finance, the micro-mechanism has yet to be thoroughly investigated. However, the mechanism research and quantitative analysis of blockchain to prevent the credit risk of supply chain finance are not sufficient.

The decision-making of each participant in the supply chain financial system is dynamic. All parties must make repeated decisions based on the existing and historical conditions to get a long-term stable outcome. In addition, there is incomplete information throughout the supply chain finance process since each participant cannot comprehend all market information. In the situation of incomplete information, the parties to a game make decisions with limited rationality, and the optimal strategy of all parties can only be attained by repeated play [11]. The evolutionary game is a dynamic game process to attain system equilibrium based on the limited rationality of the group, which provides a strong quantitative method for the micro-level research of the influence of blockchain on the credit risk of supply chain finance. However, the majority of recent studies examine the strategy selection of supply chain financial actors based on a static game [12], ignoring the dynamic behavior decision-making process of participants. Some scholars also assume that there is no default risk in the core enterprise, construct a dynamic evolutionary game between SME and financial institution, and classify the behavioral strategies of the participants [13, 14]. However, this ignores the crucial characteristics of self-compensation of supply chain finance. Under the premise that the blockchain guarantees the real trade background, the initial repayment source and credit risk are still borne by the core enterprise.

Therefore, In order to quantitatively and mechanistically analyze the issue of blockchain affecting credit risk in supply chain finance from a microscopic perspective. This paper takes the factoring financing of accounts receivable in supply chain finance as the research object, constructs a credit risk evolutionary game model among a financial institution, SME and core enterprise. The impact factors of blockchain on preventing credit risk in supply chain finance are analyzed by comparing the changes in stabilization strategies of the tripartite evolutionary game in supply chain finance before and after the introduction of blockchain. This study assigns values according to different conditions in the model analysis and tests the system equilibrium strategy through numerical simulation by referencing current research on simulation and data acquisition [13, 15]. The influencing factors that accelerate the formation of Pareto-optimal solutions for supply chain finance participants after the introduction of blockchain are further discussed. The following are the major contributions of this paper: Firstly, this work develops a credit evolutionary game model of a financial institution, SME, and core enterprise, and incorporates the repayment risk of the core enterprise into the model, so making the analysis more reasonable and compensating for deficiencies in prior studies. Secondly, this paper not only identifies the decisive factors by which blockchain affects the credit risk of supply chain finance, but also verifies the impact of the amount of accounts receivable on the supply chain financial system after the introduction of blockchain, which enriches the mechanism analysis and quantitative research of blockchain in the credit risk of supply chain finance.

The rest of this study is organized as follows. Section 2 provides a detailed description of the research problems, and makes assumptions and construction of the credit evolutionary game model. Section 3 analyzes the strategic stability of the system equilibrium point before and after the introduction of blockchain. Numerical simulation is used to validate the system equilibrium strategy before and after the introduction of blockchain, as well as the factors that accelerate the system's convergence to the equilibrium point after the introduction of blockchain in Sect. 4. Section 5 concludes the study and provides some directions for future research.

2   Model Assumptions and Construction

2.1   Problem Description

The advantage of supply chain finance over conventional financing is that it converts the uncontrollable risk of a single enterprise into the controllable risk of multiple enterprises in the supply chain. However, in the practice of supply chain finance business, there are often credit risk issues such as overdue repayment of core enterprise and default of SME. Credit risk refers to the debtor's default behavior due to insufficient repayment ability or lack of willingness to repay [16]. Even if the core enterprise has sufficient solvency, they may also refuse to repay due to the quality of SME's good or speculative interests. The SME may engage in opportunistic behavior and refuse to repay the loan to the financial institution when the financial institution recovers the loan. Due to information asymmetry, it is difficult for financial institution to detect the changes in the credit level of credit providers, and it is simple to treat high-risk projects as low-risk projects, hence increasing the credit risk associated with approving such financing applications.

The deployment of blockchain in the field of supply chain finance has effectively addressed the issue of information asymmetry. Due to the non-tamperable characteristics of the blockchain, once a credit risk issue such as default occurs, the default record will be broadcasted and shared in real-time throughout the network, and it will also exist forever in the defaulting enterprise's credit record. This solves the problem of tampering and denying the default history after the default of the enterprise in the traditional situation, which causes irreparable damage to the reputation system of the defaulting enterprise and makes it difficult for it to continue production and operations in the industry and financing business with financial institutions. In addition, the use of blockchain technology improves the trust transfer mechanism in the supply chain finance business. The accounts receivable can be split and circulated throughout the supply chain [17], reducing the amount of accounts receivable held by a single SME. When the recourse mechanism is triggered, the debt repayment amount and repayment pressure of SMEs will be significantly reduced.

2.2 Model Assumptions

To construct the tripartite game model among a financial institution, SME, and core enterprise under the factoring financing mode of accounts receivable, and to analyze the game strategy and game equilibrium point of each participant, the following assumptions are made:

Assumption 1: Financial institution, SME, and core enterprise are all participants of bounded rationality. They continually adjust their strategy based on information in the game, and eventually evolve to a stable point over time.

Assumption 2: The strategy space of the financial institution is (acceptance, non-acceptance), and it chooses acceptance with the probability of x ($0 < x < 1$); The strategy space of SME is (default, non-default), the probability of choosing no default is y ($0 < y < 1$); the core enterprise's strategy space is (repayment, non-repayment), the probability of choosing repayment is z ($0 < z < 1$).

Assumption 3: After receiving the receivables for the amount R, the financial institution must conduct due diligence on the relevant enterprises and debts, and it needs to pay the due diligence cost C_b. When accepting loan applications from financing enterprise, they need to issue loans with a limit of kR to financing enterprises based on the credit rate k. When a loan application is denied, the funds are available for other loan businesses. The loan interest rate is set to r_{b1}, whereas the deposit interest rate drawn by the financial institution during this period is set to r_{b2}.

Assumption 4: If a SME is able to obtain loans from a financial institution using accounts receivable, the funds might be invested in reproduction. The rate of return for reproduction is r_s, while the production cost is C_s. The breach of contract of SME is reflected in two aspects. One is that the delivery of non-contracted goods to the core enterprises due to operational problems. The second is that if the core enterprise fails to return at the account's maturity, the financial institution will exercise its recourse right against the SME of the financier. If the SME refuses to repay, the default income is R_s and the default cost is n. If SME can deliver goods with high quality and quantity as agreed and make up the loan repayment when the core enterprise extends the repayment period, the cooperation relationship between supply chain enterprises will be more stable in the long run, bringing potential benefits such as lower transaction costs and more stable production. Set this income as S, and the closer the cooperation relationship, the more stable the supply chain, and the greater the value of S [18].

Assumption 5: The core enterprise is solvent enough. If they timely reimburse the financial institution when the receivables are due, the enterprise can likewise obtain the benefit S of maintaining the supply chain's stability. If the core enterprise chooses to extend the repayment period and reinvested the capital in the expanded production, the yield rate is set to r_c, and the production cost is C_c. When the core enterprise fails to repay, its reputation will decline, which will have a certain impact on its production, operations, and market transactions, as well as the financial institution's credit limit. The default cost is set to m. In addition, if the SME chooses to default, the core enterprise will incur a loss of cost A.

Assumption 6: Following the introduction of blockchain to the supply chain finance model, the financial institution may efficiently obtain the credit records and trading contracts of relevant enterprises through blockchain. The due diligence cost at this time is assumed to be C_{bl}, which tends to be infinitesimal. The financing efficiency of SME is improved, and blockchain-generated incentive is set to U. The core enterprise is improved due to the increase in the revenue of the suppliers on the chain, and the incentive generated by the blockchain is set to V. Due to the non-tamperable characteristics of the blockchain, if SME and core enterprise want to default after the introduction of the blockchain, they will be required to pay much higher than the traditional cost of masking. In addition, as a result of the consensus mechanism in the alliance chain, once one-party defaults, the message will be broadcast, which will have a huge impact on the reputation of the defaulting enterprise, and the credit record will be permanent. After the introduction of the blockchain, the default costs of SME and core enterprise are N and M, respectively, and N and M tend to be infinite.

2.3 Model Construction

According to the above assumptions and parameter settings, the construction of payoff matrix of the Mixed Strategy Game of financial institution, SME, and core enterprise is shown in Table 1.

Table 1. Payoff matrix of financial institution, core enterprise, and SME before the introduction of blockchain

SME		CE			
		Repayment		Non-Repayment	
		Non-Default	Default	Non-Default	Default
FI	Acceptance	$(1-k)R-C_b-$ kRr_{b2} $kR(1+r_s)-C_s+S$ S	$(1-k)R-C_b-$ kRr_{b2} $kR(1+r_s)-$ $C_s+R_s-n;$ $S-A$	$(1-k)R-C_b-$ kRr_{b2} $kR(1+r_s)-C_s+$ $S-R$ $R(1+r_c)-C_c-m$	$-kR(1+r_{b2})-C_b$ $kR(1+r_s)-C_s+$ R_s-n $R(1+r_c)-C_c-$ $m-A$
	Non-Acceptance	$kR(r_{b1}-r_{b2})-C_b$ $R-C_s+S$ S	$kR(r_{b1}-r_{b2})-$ C_b $R-C_s+R_s-n$ $S-A$	$kR(r_{b1}-r_{b2})-C_b$ $S-R$ $R(1+r_c)-C_c-m$	$kR(r_{b1}-r_{b2})-C_b$ R_s-R-n $R(1+r_c)-C_c-$ $m-A$

3 Model Analysis

3.1 Stability Analysis of System Equilibrium Point Strategy Before the Introduction of Blockchain

Replication Dynamic Equations of Different Game Subjects. The replication dynamic equations of financial institution, SME and core enterprise are:

$$F(x) = x(1 - x)\left[(y + z - yz)R - (1 + r_{b1})kR\right] \tag{1}$$

$$F(y) = y(1 - y)\left[(S - R_s + n) - x(1 - z)R\right] \tag{2}$$

$$F(z) = z(1 - z)\left[S - R(1 + r_c) + C_c + m\right] \tag{3}$$

Stability Analysis of System Equilibrium Point. Let $F(x) = 0$, $F(y) = 0$, $F(z) = 0$, and the equilibrium points of the whole system can be obtained, which are $E1$ (0,0,0), $E2$ (1,0,0), $E3$ (0,1,0), $E4$ (0,0,1), $E5$ (1,1,0), $E6$ (1,0,1), $E7$ (0,1,1), $E8$ (1,1,1), $E9$ (($S - R_s + n$) / R, $k + kr_{b1}$,0). To analyze the evolutionarily stable strategy of the system, the Jacobian matrix needs to be constructed.

According to Lyapunov's first law, when all eigenvalues of the Jacobian matrix are negative, the equilibrium point is the evolutionary stable strategy (ESS) of the system, otherwise, it is the unstable point (UP) of the system. Based on this, we analyzed the stability of each equilibrium point of the receivables factoring financing model before the application of blockchain, as shown in Table 2.

Table 2. Stability analysis of system equilibrium point before the introduction of blockchain

Point of equilibrium	Eigenvalues of the Jacobian matrix $\lambda_1\lambda_2\lambda_3$	Sign	Stability conclusion	Case
$E_1(0, 0, 0)$	$-Rk(1 + rb1), S - Rs + n, Cc - R(1 + rc) + S + m$	$-,*,*$	ESS	1
$E_2(1, 0, 0)$	$Rk(1 + rb1), S - Rs - R + n, Cc - R(1 + rc) + S + m$	$+,*,*$	UP	\
$E_3(0, 1, 0)$	$Rs - S - n, R - Rk(1 + rb1), Cc - R(1 + rc) + S + m$	$*, + , *$	UP	\
$E_4(0, 0, 1)$	$R - Rk(1 + rb1), S - Rs + n, R(1 + rc) - Cc - S - m$	$+,*,*$	UP	\
$E_5(1, 1, 0)$	$Rk(1 + rb1) - R, R + Rs - S - n, Cc - R(1 + rc) + S + m$	$-,*,*$	ESS	2
$E_6(1, 0, 1)$	$Rk(1 + rb1) - R, S - Rs + n, R(1 + rc) - Cc - S - m$	$-,*,*$	ESS	3
$E_7(0, 1, 1)$	$Rs - S - n, R - Rk(1 + rb1), R(1 + rc) - Cc - S - m$	$*, + , *$	UP	\
$E_8(1, 1, 1)$	$Rs - S - n, Rk(1 + rb1) - R, R(1 + rc) - Cc - S - m$	$*,-,*$	ESS	4
$E_9(x^*, y^*, 0)$	$\sqrt{(k(1 + rb1)(k(1 + rb1) - 1)(S - Rs + n)(R + Rs - S - n))},$ $-\sqrt{(k(1 + rb1)(k(1 + rb1) - 1)(S - Rs + n)(R + Rs - S - n))},$ $Cc - R(1 + rc) + S + m$	$+$ $,-,*$	UP	\

Combined with the details in Table 3, the following four possible cases are discussed:

Case 1: When $S < R_s - n$ and $S < R(1 + r_c) - C_c - m$, the eigenvalues corresponding to $E1$ (0,0,0) are all negative, and there is only one equilibrium point of $E1$(0,0,0), that is, the evolution strategy of the system is (no acceptance, default, no repayment), which is the most unsatisfactory situation.

Case 2: When $S > R + R_s - n$ and $S < R(1 + r_c) - C_c - m$, the eigenvalues corresponding to $E5$(1,1,0) are negative, and the system has only one equilibrium point $E5$ (1,1,0), that is, the evolution strategy of the system is (acceptance, no default, no repayment).

Case 3: When $S < R(1 + r_c) - C_c - m$, the eigenvalues corresponding to $E6$(1,0,1) are all negative, and there is only one equilibrium point of $E6$ (1,0,1) in the system, that is, the evolution strategy of the system is (acceptance, default, repayment).

Case 4: When $S > R_s - n$ and $S > R(1 + r_c) - C_c - m$, the eigenvalues corresponding to $E8$ (1,1,1) are all negative, and there is only one equilibrium point of $E8$ (1,1,1) in the system, that is, the evolution strategy of the system is (acceptance, no default, repayment).

3.2 Stability Analysis of System Equilibrium Point Strategy After the Introduction of Blockchain

According to the assumptions in Sect. 2, after the introduction of blockchain, the cost of information acquisition by financial institution due diligence is C_{b1}. When the financial institution accepts a financing application. The SME and core enterprise can receive additional benefits of U and V, but their default costs change to N and M. Same to the above analysis, the stability of the equilibrium point of the system after the introduction of blockchain is shown in Table 3. It can be seen that the factors that affect the equilibrium result after the introduction of blockchain are the default costs M and N formed by the strict regulatory environment. The fact that the use of blockchain for supply chain finance

Table 3. Stability analysis of system equilibrium point after the introduction of blockchain

Point of equilibrium	Eigenvalues of the Jacobian matrix $\lambda_1\lambda_2\lambda_3$	Sign	Stability conclusion
$E_1(0, 0, 0)$	$-Rk(1 + rb1), S - Rs + N, Cc - R(1 + rc) + S + M$	$-, +, +$	UP
$E_2(1, 0, 0)$	$Rk(1 + rb1), S - Rs - R + N, Cc - R(1 + rc) + S + M$	$+, +, +$	UP
$E_3(0, 1, 0)$	$Rs - S - N, R - Rk(1 + rb1), Cc - R(1 + rc) + S + M$	$+, +, +$	UP
$E_4(0, 0, 1)$	$R - Rk(1 + rb1), S - Rs + N, R(1 + rc) - Cc - S - M$	$+, +, -$	UP
$E_5(1, 1, 0)$	$Rk(1 + rb1) - R, R + Rs - S - N, Cc - R(1 + rc) + S + M$	$-, -, +$	UP
$E_6(1, 0, 1)$	$Rk(1 + rb1) - R, S - Rs + N, R(1 + rc) - Cc - S - M$	$-, +, -$	UP
$E_7(0, 1, 1)$	$Rs - S - N, R - Rk(1 + rb1), R(1 + rc) - Cc - S - M$	$-, +, -$	UP
$E_8(1, 1, 1)$	$Rs - S - N, Rk(1 + rb1) - R, R(1 + rc) - Cc - S - M$	$-, -, -$	ESS
$E_9(x^*, y^*, 0)$	$\sqrt{(k(1 + rb1)(k(1 + rb1) - 1)(S - Rs + N)(R + Rs - S - N))},$ $-\sqrt{(k(1 + rb1)(k(1 + rb1) - 1)(S - Rs + N)(R + Rs - S - N))},$ $Cc - R(1 + rc) + S + M$	$+, -, +$	UP

decreases the due diligence cost of financial institutions and provides incentives for SME and core enterprise does not impact the system's choice of a stable strategy. Since the values of M and N tend to infinity, according to the Lyapunov first law, only the Jacobian matrix with the stable point $E8$ (1,1,1) has negative eigenvalues, and the system has a unique evolutionary stable point.

4 Simulation Analysis

4.1 Simulation Analysis of System Evolutionary Stable Strategy Before the Introduction of Blockchain

To verify the effectiveness of evolutionary stability analysis and more intuitively reflect the evolution process of strategic choices of financial institution, SME and core enterprise, we use MATLAB2016a for numerical simulation to simulate the dynamic evolution process of five stable strategies before and after the introduction of blockchain in Sect. 3. Referring to the simulation process and data of the existing research [13, 15], we assign the initial parameters in the paper and set the basic array: $R = 100, k = 80\%$, $C_b = 5, r_{b1} = 4\%, r_{b2} = 2\%, r_s = 20\%, C_s = 10, R_s = 30, r_c = 50\%, C_c = 10, A = 20$.

Since the stable points of the first four cases before the introduction of blockchain technology are determined by the relative size of the amount of accounts receivable, the supply chain's stable income, default income, and the corresponding penalty. Therefore, we set the arrays in four cases as array 1: $n = 10, m = 30, S = 15$; array 2: $n = 10, m = 10$, $S = 125$; array 3: $n = 10, m = 130, S = 15$; array 4: $n = 10, m = 30, S = 125$. In addition, we combined the basic array with the array in four cases, starting from different initial strategy combinations respectively, and evolving 50 times over time. Last, the trajectory of the system in the four cases before the introduction of the blockchain is shown in Fig. 1.

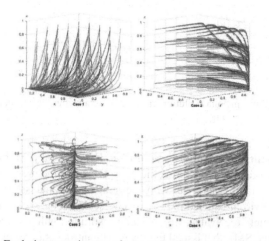

Fig. 1. Evolutionary trajectory of system equilibrium point in four cases

4.2 Simulation Analysis of System Evolutionary Stable Strategy After the Introduction of Blockchain

Simulation Verification of System Evolutionary Stable Strategy. Due to information asymmetries in the supply chain finance business before the introduction of blockchain, the financial institution's default cost was relatively low. After the introduction of blockchain technology, the immutability based on the timestamp causes the enterprise's dishonesty record to be broadcast in the alliance chain and to exist permanently in the system. It is difficult for enterprises to apply for financing from any financial institution after default, and the default cost of enterprises tends to be infinite. Therefore, we set array 5: $S = 15, N = 1000, M = 3000, C_{bl} = 0.1, U = 30, V = 20$. And we combined the basic array and array 5, respectively, starting from different initial strategy combinations respectively, and evolving 50 times over time. The trajectory is shown in Fig. 2. The strategy selections of SME, core enterprise, and financial institution will eventually converge to 1 regardless of the magnitude of the enterprise's default income and the income of the stable supply chain.

By comparing the evolution results of the system equilibrium points before and after the introduction of blockchain, we find that the strict regulatory environment and enormous default costs brought by the application of blockchain technology to the supply chain finance business can effectively regulate the cooperation behavior of supply chain enterprises. Whether or not the collaboration of enterprises in the supply chain is stable, and regardless of whether or not they can obtain excess default income, the final strategy selections of SME and core enterprise is (non-default, repayment). To maximize benefits, financial institutions will also take financing applications at this time.

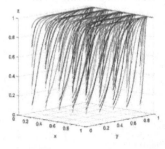

Fig. 2. System equilibrium point evolution trajectory diagram after the introduction of blockchain

Impact of Accounts Receivable Amount on Evolutionary Stable Strategy. We assumed that the core enterprise has sufficient solvency in the previous analysis. However, there are often large enterprises with operating operational issues due to the impact of the economic environment and industry cycle factors. If the core enterprise is unable to repay the accounts receivable, the financial institution will enforce its the right of recourse against the SME that issued the loans. The introduction of blockchain enables SME to split accounts receivable, increases the liquidity of accounts receivable, and reduced the amount of accounts receivable held by a single SME in the supply chain.

This section simulates the strategy evolution of SME under different accounts receivable amounts. Therefore, we set the initial strategy of the model as 0.2, 0.2 and 0.2, and the amount of accounts receivable is 200,100, and 50 respectively. The impact of different amounts of accounts receivable on the evolutionary stability strategy of SME is shown in Fig. 3.

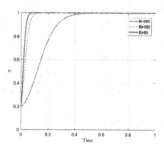

Fig. 3. The influence of the amount of accounts receivable on SME's strategy choice

The simulation results indicate that the decrease of accounts receivable can greatly expedite the convergence of SME strategies to compliance. This suggests that a reduction in the amount of accounts receivable held by a single SME increases the likelihood of contract compliance. If the core enterprise fails to repay the loan due to insufficient solvency, a financial institution in the blockchain environment can recover the loan from SME in the supply chain more quickly by exercising the right of recourse, thereby decreasing the credit risk they face when making loans.

5 Conclusions and Suggestions

This study develops a tripartite evolutionary game model of a financial institution, SME, and a core enterprise in light of the credit risk issues, such as default and overdue non-repayment, that frequently occur during the course of supply chain finance business development. The following are the key findings.

First, whether the tripartite game in the traditional supply chain finance business can converge to the Pareto-optimal solution of financial institution accepting financing applications, SME compliance and core enterprise repayment depends on the amount of accounts receivable, the default income and cost of SME and core enterprise, and the benefits obtained when maintaining the stability of the supply chain. Under the situation that the default cost of the traditional model is low, supply chain businesses are more likely to default. Therefore, we encourage that the development of traditional supply chain finance business should be oriented towards enterprises with stable supply chain cooperation relationships and appropriate control of the amount of accounts receivable, thus reducing the credit risk faced by financial institutions.

Second, the introduction of blockchain has brought significant impacts on the supply chain finance business. Due to the characteristics of consensus mechanism and non-tampering, a strict regulatory environment has been formed, which increases the default cost of supply chain enterprises and minimizes the credit risk a financial institution faces while conducting supply chain finance business. We suggest that financial institutions should actively adopt blockchain to layout supply chain finance business and attract more enterprises to the chain, so as to maximize the advantages of blockchain.

Finally, the blockchain environment improves the trust transfer mechanism of supply chain finance, allowing accounts receivable to be split and transferred within the alliance chain, thus reducing the amount of accounts receivable held by a single SME in the supply chain. If the core enterprise declares bankruptcy and is unable to repay the account at maturity, financial institutions can recover the loan from the SMEs that apply for financing in the supply chain by exercising the right of recourse more quickly. Therefore, we encourage financial institutions to set reasonable incentives to facilitate the flow of notes held by SMEs in the alliance chain to further reduce the credit risk they face.

Acknowledgement. This work is supported by the Emerging Interdisciplinary Project of CUFE.

References

1. Li, J., Zhang, J.: Credit risk identification and early warning model of supply chain finance. Econ. Manage. **41**(08), 178–196 (2019). (In Chinese)
2. Xie, X., Yang, Y., Zhang, F., et al.: Contagion effect of related credit risk in supply chain under multiple relationships. China Manage. Sci. **29**(09), 77–89 (2021). (In Chinese)
3. Ehrenberg, A.J., King, J.L.: Blockchain in context. Inf. Syst. Front. **22**(1), 29–35 (2020)
4. Hofmann, E., Strewe, U.M., Bosia, N.: Discussion—how does the full potential of blockchain technology in supply chain finance look like? In: Supply Chain Finance and Blockchain Technology. SF, pp. 77–87. Springer, Cham (2018). https://doi.org/10.1007/978-3-319-623 71-9_6
5. Song, X., Mao, J.: Inter-organizational trust building process based on blockchain: a case study of digital supply chain finance. China Indust. Econ. **2022**(11), 174–192 (2022). (In Chinese)
6. Li, J., Zhu, S., Zhang, W., Yu, L.: Blockchain-driven supply chain finance solution for small and medium enterprises. Front. Eng. Manage. **7**(4), 500–511 (2020). https://doi.org/10.1007/s42524-020-0124-2
7. Zhang, T.L., Li, J.J., Jiang, X.: Analysis of supply chain finance based on blockchain. Procedia Comput. Sci. **187**, 1–6 (2021)
8. Fu, H., Zhang, F., Su, Z., et al.: Application of blockchain technology in supply chain financial risk management. Finan. Sci. **2021**(02), 152–160 (2021). (In Chinese)
9. Bal, M., Pawlicka, K.: Supply chain finance and challenges of modern supply chains. LogForum **17**(1) (2021)
10. Rijanto, A.: Blockchain technology adoption in supply chain finance. J. Theor. Appl. Electron. Commer. Res. **16**(7), 3078–3098 (2021)
11. Shen, L., Wang, Y.: Research on collaboration mechanism in public service outsourcing: an evolutionary game analysis. Manage. Rev. **29**(03), 219–230 (2017). (In Chinese)
12. Luo, Y., Tang, Y.: Comparative research on the game behavior of the participants in the traditional supply chain finance and the supply chain finance on the blockchain. Discrete Dynamics in Nature and Society (2022)
13. Sun, R., He, D., Su, H.: Evolutionary game analysis of blockchain technology preventing supply chain financial risks. J. Theor. Appl. Electron. Commer. Res. **16**(7), 2824–2842 (2021)

14. Xie, W.: Study on enterprise financial risk prevention and early warning system based on blockchain technology. Mobile Inform. Syst. (2022)
15. Wang, X., Gu, C., He, Q., et al.: Tripartite evolutionary game dynamics of supply chain financial credit market. Oper. Manage. **31**(01), 30–37 (2022). (In Chinese)
16. Witzany, J.: Credit Risk Management. Springer, Cham (2017)
17. Du, M., Chen, Q., Xiao, J., et al.: Supply chain finance innovation using blockchain. IEEE Trans. Eng. Manage. **67**(4), 1045–1058 (2020)
18. Cao, W., Ma, C.: Analysis of accounts receivable financing game based on supply chain finance. Bus. Res. **2013**(03), 168–173 (2013). (In Chinese)

Author Index

Printed in the United States
Baker & Taylor Publisher Services